Chapters 1-10

College
Accounting

17TH EDITION

James A. Heintz, DBA, CPA,
Professor of Accounting
University of Kansas
Lawrence, Kansas

Robert W. Parry, Jr., PhD
Professor of Accounting
Indiana University
Bloomington, Indiana

SOUTH-WESTERN
THOMSON LEARNING

Australia · Canada · Mexico · Singapore · Spain · United Kingdom · United States

College Accounting, 17e, Chapters 1–10 by James A. Heintz and Robert W. Parry

Acquisitions Editor:	Scott Person
Senior Developmental Editor:	Sara Wilson
Marketing Manager:	Larry Qualls
Production Editor:	Marci Dechter
Production House:	Navta Associates, Inc.
Manufacturing Coordinator:	Doug Wilke
Internal Design:	Ann Small/A Small Design Studio
Cover Design:	Craig Ramsdell/Ramsdell Design
Cover Photography:	© PhotoDisc, Inc.
Editorial Assistant:	Sara Froelicher
Printer:	Quebecor World

Printed in the United States of America
1 2 3 4 5 04 03 02 01

For more information contact South-Western, 5101 Madison Road, Cincinnati, Ohio, 45227 or find us on the Internet at http://www.swcollege.com
For permission to use material from this text or product, contact us by
• **telephone: 1-800-730-2214**
• **fax: 1-800-730-2215**
• **web: http://www.thomsonrights.com**

Library of Congress Cataloging-in-Publication Data
Heintz, James A.
   College Accounting. Chapters 1–10 / James A. Heintz, Robert W. Parry, Jr. — 17th ed.
     p. cm.
   Includes index.
   ISBN 0-324-10097-3 (alk paper)
   1. Accounting.   I. Parry, Robert W.   II. Title.

HF5635 .C227 2002
657'.044—dc21   00-049286

Student Edition, Chapters 1–29	ISBN:	0-324-06369-5
Student Edition, Chapters 1–16	ISBN:	0-324-10098-1
Student Edition, Chapters 1–10	ISBN:	0-324-10097-3

Chapters 1-10

College
Accounting

17TH EDITION

James A. Heintz, DBA, CPA,
Professor of Accounting
University of Kansas
Lawrence, Kansas

Robert W. Parry, Jr., PhD
Professor of Accounting
Indiana University
Bloomington, Indiana

SOUTH-WESTERN
TM
THOMSON LEARNING

Australia · Canada · Mexico · Singapore · Spain · United Kingdom · United States

College Accounting, 17e, Chapters 1–10 by James A. Heintz and Robert W. Parry

Acquisitions Editor:	Scott Person
Senior Developmental Editor:	Sara Wilson
Marketing Manager:	Larry Qualls
Production Editor:	Marci Dechter
Production House:	Navta Associates, Inc.
Manufacturing Coordinator:	Doug Wilke
Internal Design:	Ann Small/A Small Design Studio
Cover Design:	Craig Ramsdell/Ramsdell Design
Cover Photography:	© PhotoDisc, Inc.
Editorial Assistant:	Sara Froelicher
Printer:	Quebecor World

Printed in the United States of America
1 2 3 4 5 04 03 02 01

For more information contact South-Western, 5101 Madison Road, Cincinnati, Ohio, 45227 or find us on the Internet at http://www.swcollege.com
For permission to use material from this text or product, contact us by
• **telephone: 1-800-730-2214**
• **fax: 1-800-730-2215**
• **web: http://www.thomsonrights.com**

Library of Congress Cataloging-in-Publication Data
Heintz, James A.
   College Accounting. Chapters 1–10 / James A. Heintz, Robert W. Parry, Jr. — 17th ed.
      p. cm.
   Includes index.
   ISBN 0-324-10097-3 (alk paper)
   1. Accounting.   I. Parry, Robert W.   II. Title.

HF5635 .C227 2002
657'.044—dc21   00-049286

Student Edition, Chapters 1–29	ISBN: 0-324-06369-5
Student Edition, Chapters 1–16	ISBN: 0-324-10098-1
Student Edition, Chapters 1–10	ISBN: 0-324-10097-3

Photo Credits: Pages xxxiii, 1 (bottom), 15 (bottom), 47 (bottom), 87 (bottom), 133 (bottom), 175 (bottom) © Eric Crichton/CORBIS; Pages 1 (top), 15 (top), 47 (top), 87 (top), 133 (top) Photo by Erik Snowbeck/Digital Imaging Group; Page 5 Photo courtesy of Rob Parry; Pages 17, 175 (top), © SuperStock; Page 59 © Susan Van Etten/PhotoEdit; Page 91 Sears Roebuck and Co.; Page 135 Photo by Cary Benbow; Page 185 © Davidson Chigmaroff/SuperStock; Pages 219, 221 (bottom), 257 (bottom), 293 (bottom), 325 (bottom) Andrew J.G. Bell, Eye Ubiquitous/CORBIS; Pages 221 (top), 257 (top), 293 (top) Photography by Ryan Hulvat; Pages 232, 260, 269 © PhotoDisc, Inc.; Page 307 ADP, Inc.; Page 325 (top) © Spencer Grant/PhotoEdit; Page 329 © Jacques M. Chenet/CORBIS

Chapters 1-10

College
Accounting

17TH EDITION

James A. Heintz, DBA, CPA,
Professor of Accounting
University of Kansas
Lawrence, Kansas

Robert W. Parry, Jr., PhD
Professor of Accounting
Indiana University
Bloomington, Indiana

SOUTH-WESTERN
™
THOMSON LEARNING

Australia · Canada · Mexico · Singapore · Spain · United Kingdom · United States

College Accounting, 17e, Chapters 1–10 by James A. Heintz and Robert W. Parry

Acquisitions Editor:	Scott Person
Senior Developmental Editor:	Sara Wilson
Marketing Manager:	Larry Qualls
Production Editor:	Marci Dechter
Production House:	Navta Associates, Inc.
Manufacturing Coordinator:	Doug Wilke
Internal Design:	Ann Small/A Small Design Studio
Cover Design:	Craig Ramsdell/Ramsdell Design
Cover Photography:	© PhotoDisc, Inc.
Editorial Assistant:	Sara Froelicher
Printer:	Quebecor World

Printed in the United States of America
1 2 3 4 5 04 03 02 01

For more information contact South-Western, 5101 Madison Road, Cincinnati, Ohio, 45227 or find us on the Internet at http://www.swcollege.com
For permission to use material from this text or product, contact us by
• **telephone: 1-800-730-2214**
• **fax: 1-800-730-2215**
• **web: http://www.thomsonrights.com**

Library of Congress Cataloging-in-Publication Data
Heintz, James A.
   College Accounting. Chapters 1–10 / James A. Heintz, Robert W. Parry, Jr. — 17th ed.
     p. cm.
   Includes index.
   ISBN 0-324-10097-3 (alk paper)
   1. Accounting.   I. Parry, Robert W.   II. Title.

HF5635 .C227 2002
657'.044—dc21   00-049286

Student Edition, Chapters 1–29	ISBN:	0-324-06369-5
Student Edition, Chapters 1–16	ISBN:	0-324-10098-1
Student Edition, Chapters 1–10	ISBN:	0-324-10097-3

Photo Credits: Pages xxxiii, 1 (bottom), 15 (bottom), 47 (bottom), 87 (bottom), 133 (bottom), 175 (bottom) © Eric Crichton/CORBIS; Pages 1 (top), 15 (top), 47 (top), 87 (top), 133 (top) Photo by Erik Snowbeck/Digital Imaging Group; Page 5 Photo courtesy of Rob Parry; Pages 17, 175 (top), © SuperStock; Page 59 © Susan Van Etten/PhotoEdit; Page 91 Sears Roebuck and Co.; Page 135 Photo by Cary Benbow; Page 185 © Davidson Chigmaroff/SuperStock; Pages 219, 221 (bottom), 257 (bottom), 293 (bottom), 325 (bottom) Andrew J.G. Bell, Eye Ubiquitous/CORBIS; Pages 221 (top), 257 (top), 293 (top) Photography by Ryan Hulvat; Pages 232, 260, 269 © PhotoDisc, Inc.; Page 307 ADP, Inc.; Page 325 (top) © Spencer Grant/PhotoEdit; Page 329 © Jacques M. Chenet/CORBIS

SIMPLY BETTER THAN EVER!

HOW CAN YOU IMPROVE ON THE BEST COLLEGE ACCOUNTING TEXT?

That's simple; start with the best text available and enhance it to make it even better. This is precisely what we've done with *College Accounting, 17e*. We've kept intact everything that has made *College Accounting* so successful, then added new features, supplements and technology that make it simply better than ever. ■ Our main objective has and always will be to make accounting understandable to virtually every student and to do so without sacrificing crucial substance and technical correctness. ■ Our step-by-step, straightforward approach helps build practical accounting skills that are needed when entering the world of work. The text presents basic topics first and builds to more advanced coverage so that learners are never overwhelmed. Likewise, the narrative approach covers a simpler example of a service business first before moving on to a merchandising business and then to a manufacturing environment. ■ In the end, *College Accounting, 17e* combines an easily readable style that prepares students for good jobs by building practical accounting skills with an unparalleled learning package that makes the most of class preparation. ■ We're confident that this updated new edition represents a text that achieves our goals – even further improving a text with a longstanding reputation for fundamental excellence.

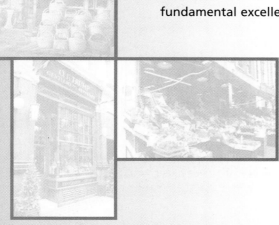

SIMPLY A BETTER APPROACH.

Heintz&Parry has proven that students excel when they're not rushed into financial statements or overloaded with theory. This text presents concepts simply and ensures the best, most accurate coverage, which allows students to build on their foundation of knowledge one topic at a time.

SIMPLY BETTER IMPROVEMENTS.

The 17th edition incorporates numerous improvements prompted by both instructors' feedback and our own commitment to meet the evolving needs of an ever-changing learning environment. Newly revised and expanded *Computers and Accounting* coverage as well as expanded technology choices encourage students to understand how the computerized environment enhances the world of accounting. A restructuring of coverage provides increased flexibility that allows subject matter to be taught with or without special journals. We also have added new "Challenge Problems" to provide students an opportunity to apply their understanding of basic concepts to new situations.

SIMPLY BETTER PEDAGOGY.

College Accounting, 17e employs time-tested, classroom-proven educational techniques. Repetition of key topics, a continuing topic example, and relevant demonstration problems are some of the methods used to ensure — and enhance — student progress.

SIMPLY A BETTER AND EXPANDED PACKAGE.

An enhanced instructor's resource manual, teaching transparencies as well as solution transparencies, and completely revised PowerPoint® slides are just a few of the features that constitute the extensive supplement package. See complete descriptions of these and other ancillary products below under "For the Instructor."

SIMPLY BETTER TECHNOLOGY.

Our WebTutor™, Personal WebTutor™ and Personal Trainer™ offer high-impact technology tools that are proven to enhance personal learning styles.

SIMPLY BETTER SERVICE.

You have our commitment to always provide you with the best of everything accompanying our products. From your ITP sales representative, to the Academic Resource Center staff, to the authors themselves, our professional resource and support team is committed to helping you.

Take a closer look at *College Accounting, 17e* and see for yourself why it's simply the best.

WHAT MAKES OUR APPROACH BETTER THAN OTHERS?

A steady flow of feedback provides us excellent opportunities to continually enhance our newest edition with user requests and suggestions. Skill development and mastery are encouraged and assisted by a number of features.

College Accounting, 17e, doesn't rush students into financial statements or overwhelm them with theory. The text presents simple concepts first and builds to more advanced content. In each chapter students focus on only one major topic or procedure, ensuring that they master each new concept before moving on.

- **Real-world skills** are developed to help students get jobs after graduation.

- **Careful development of topics** prevents "information overload."

- **Repetition of key topics** throughout helps students master important concepts and procedures.

- **Narrative approach** covers the simpler example of a service business first before moving on to merchandising.

- **Demonstration problems** can be used as study aids or in-class examples.

- **Comprehensive problems** provide important opportunities to review skills.

- **Three versions** of the text (10, 16, or 29 chapters) create a custom fit for your course.

WHAT'S NEW WITH THIS EDITION?

Completely Revised and Expanded!
Computers and Accounting, written by Gary Schneider of the University of San Diego, puts computers in the context of their importance to accounting in the real world. This coverage, which appears in Chapters 6 and 9:

- Describes how the computer is used in bookkeeping

- Explains the computer's use in payroll accounting

- Tells how the computer helps process cash receipt, cash payment, sales, and purchase transactions through a special journal environment

- Explores the computer's company-wide influence in corporate and manufacturing environments.

Challenge Problems
Perhaps the most important measure of student understanding is the ability to apply newly learned concepts to new and unfamiliar situations. At the end of each chapter, the Challenge Problem tests the ability of more advanced or ambitious students to apply concepts to transactions, events, or economic conditions one step beyond what is laid out in the text.

Comprehensive Problems
The text includes three comprehensive problems that can be used as a mini-practice set. Two will be multi-period transactions.

WHY IS OUR PEDAGOGY SIMPLY THE BEST?

This text facilitates student learning by employing a classroom-proven pedagogy.

✓ **A narrative approach** uses a continuing example to help students understand topics.

✓ **Repetition of key topics** benefits students by repeated exposure to important concepts and techniques.

✓ **Learning Objectives** preview the skills that will be studied and mastered in that chapter.

✓ **Chapter openers** present the topic in context and pose a question that is answered at the end of the chapter.

✓ **Learning Keys** emphasize important new points and help students gain a clearer understanding of the key coverage in each chapter.

✓ **Margin Notes** enrich student understanding of concepts and terms beyond what is contained in the text narrative.

✓ **A Broader View** provides students with interesting examples of actual events or situations that tie to accounting.

✓ **Profiles in Accounting** feature real people successfully working and using their College Accounting skills.

✓ **Arrow pointers** and **text pointers** emphasize the sources and calculations of numbers.

✓ **Key steps** demonstrate steps to accomplish specific objectives – such as how to prepare a bank reconciliation or work sheet.

✓ **Accounting forms** are presented on rulings to emphasize structure and help students quickly learn how to prepare these documents.

✓ The **statement of cash flows coverage** reflects its importance today.

✓ The most current **payroll information** is presented in two chapters (Chapters 8 and 9).

✓ The **combination journal** is featured in Chapter 10.

✓ **Depreciation methods** are introduced in Chapter 5 with some detailing in that chapter's appendix.

✓ **Text & Supplements double and triple verified** to guarantee an accurate and error free text and package.

Color-coding enhances understanding by highlighting accounts in a consistent color scheme. Assets are shown in blue, liabilities in yellow, ownership equity in purple, revenues in green, expenses in light red, and drawing accounts in mauve. All journals are on blue rulings to differentiate those chronological records from ledgers and other processing documents, which are shown in yellow. Financial statements are white. Source documents vary in color, in the same manner as real-life documents.

Some additional specific examples include:
- Transactions reflected in the accounting equation *(Page 18)*
- The interaction of the key financial statements *(Page 29)*
- Owner's equity umbrella *(Page 50)*
- Source documents *(Page 90)*
- General Journal and General Ledger relationship *(Page 99)*
- Work sheet development *(Page 144G)*
- Linkages between the work sheet and the financial statements *(Pages 177and 178)*
- Tax forms *(Pages 264-266 and 303-309)*

Chapter-ending activities reinforce learning.

Key Points provide an effective review of important information covered in each chapter.

Reflection: Answering the Opening Question provides the answer to the question posed in the opening scenario.

Key Terms are defined at the end of each chapter, and the page of their first appearance is listed.

The Demonstration Problem brings together key concepts and principles. Students can work through the problems and solutions independently to gain confidence before working the homework assignments. The problems are also effective for in-class examples.

Review Questions for each chapter help students understand and assimilate the important points covered and determine where additional review is required.

Managing Your Writing, introduced in a Chapter 1 module and written by Ken Davis of Indiana University – Purdue University, guides students through an easy-to-follow, 12-step process for honing writing skills. An assignment at the end of each chapter allows students to apply critical thinking and writing skills to issues raised by material in that chapter.

Ethics Cases, written by Kim Belden of Daytona Beach Community College, help students think through what they would do in various situations. Case problems for individual and group use allow students to weigh the merits of various ethical considerations related to accounting.

Web Work assignments, identified by an icon, begin in Chapter 7. Web Work assignments expose students to the business applications of the Internet by directing them to Internet sites, where they obtain information to complete an assignment.

A & B Exercises and Problems, keyed to chapter learning objectives, provide a range of instructional choices. One set can be used in class and the other for assignments. Alternatively, both sets can be used for practice for students needing extra assistance.

Challenge Problems encourage the student to go beyond the text and to apply recently learned accounting concepts and techniques in new and different ways.

Mastery Problems challenge students to apply the essential elements introduced in the chapter.

Selected assignments may be solved using the **General Ledger software**. These are designated by icons shown here.

Comprehensive Problems - Comprehensive review problems are built directly into the text, providing an opportunity to review topics from multiple chapters. The Peachtree®, QuickBooks® or General Ledger workbooks contain guidance for solving the first problems.

Self-Study Test Questions, consisting of multiple choice and true/false items at the end of each chapter, allow students to assess their understanding of chapter material to determine if further study is required before proceeding to the next chapter. Answers to the questions are provided at the end of the text.

Enhanced Technology

WebTutor™ An interactive study guide, WebTutor uses the Internet to provide interactive reinforcement that helps students grasp complex concepts. WebTutor also offers the following benefits:

■ Customizable support so you can develop and teach your way - online.

■ Powerful communication tools like e-mail, discussion forums, and chat rooms for greater interaction and involvement.

■ Real-world, Web-savvy links for timely content.

Personal WebTutor™ Personal WebTutor is a content-rich, easy-to-use Web-based learning tool that reviews critical text material chapter-by-chapter. Concepts are reinforced through extensive exercises, problems, cases, flashcards, self-tests, and other online resources.

Personal Trainer Personal Trainer is a compelling, Internet-based learning support tool designed to help students get the most out of crucial end-of-chapter exercises. Students get specific hints about the accuracy of their work so they can pinpoint key concepts they may not fully understand. This allows them to concentrate more on mastering those concepts than on organizing their homework answers. Students can email their answers to their instructor, providing an easy way to monitor homework progress.

QuickBooks® Supplement This edition has now added a QuickBooks workbook and electronic files for those schools wishing to use that software. As with the Peachtree® workbook, students may solve key selected assignments in a commercial, accounting environment.

WHAT MAKES OUR SERVICE EVEN BETTER?

The entire Heintz&Parry team is ready to help instructors. Your South-Western Representative is always available to provide individualized assistance. The Heintz&Parry Web site at **http://heintz.swcollege.com** gives you access to supplement downloads, a help line, teaching ideas, hot links, and more.

An enhanced Web site is a rich resource

The Heintz&Parry Web site (**http://heintz.swcollege.com**) provides easy access assistance to both students and instructors. This central site will be updated should any of the original addresses listed in the text become unavailable. Links for Web Work assignments provide a helpful way to connect with assignment resources.

On-line quizzes – Students at adopting schools may access chapter-by-chapter quizzes (at the Heintz&Parry homepage) that reinforce key concepts within the 17th edition. Now students can get valuable feedback the night before that big exam.

Crossword puzzles provide additional activities for students.

The new **PowerPoint® presentation slides** are also available at the site.

■ Call the Academic Resource Center for desk copies and product information:
Career College Customers: 800-477-3692
Community College or University Customers: 800-423-0563

■ Call the Preferred Accounting Customer Hotline for special requests: 800-342-8798

■ E-mail the authors and Ken Davis through the hot link at http://heintz.swcollege.com

DEDICATION

We are grateful to our wives, *Celia Heintz and Jane Parry,* and our children, *Andrea Heintz, John Heintz, Jessica Jane Parry, and Mitch Parry,* for their love, support, and assistance during the creation of this seventeenth edition. We especially appreciate Jessie Parry's willingness to let us use her name throughout the first six chapters.

ACKNOWLEDGMENTS

We thank the following individuals for their helpful contributions in assisting us in the revision of *College Accounting.*

Anthony I. Abongwa	*Monroe College*
William C. K. Alberts	*National Business College*
Jim Benedum	*Milwaukee Area Technical College*
Richard H. Berken	*Southeastern University*
Mary Dianne Bridges	*South Plains College*
James Carriger	*Ventura College*
Janet Caruso	*Briarcliffe College*
Michael Casey	*Coconino Community College*
Richard Dugger	*Kilgore College*
Gregory P. Iwaniuk	*Lake Michigan College*
Libby Killian	*National Business College*
Barbara J. Kronk	*Florida Metropolitan University*
Donna M. Larner	*Davenport College*
Marvin Mai	*Empire College*
Cheryl A. Miner	*Institute of Career Education*
Lee Moore	*South Plains College*
Linda Moore	*National Business College*
Karen S. Mozingo	*Pitt Community College*
Phillip D. Reffitt	*Florida Metropolitan University*
Wayne Smith	*Indiana Business College*
Ronald Strittmater	*North Hennepin Community College*
Thomas H. Tolan	*Plaza Business College*
Ruth Turner	*National Business College*
Donna Ulmer	*St. Louis Community College*
V. Anne R. Wessely	*St. Louis Community College*
Andrew R. Williams	*Edmonds Community College*

Special thanks to Jane Parry and Andrea Heintz for assistance in the development of this text.

Through 16 editions, *College Accounting* has helped millions of students understand and employ basic accounting skills. But we know we can't rest on past success. The business world continues to change. And so do we. To prepare today's generation for a lifetime of accounting skills, the solution is simple. Depend on the text that's simply better than ever.

College Accounting, 17e. From the leader in college accounting, you wouldn't expect anything less.

– Jim Heintz
– Rob Parry

Supplements for Students	ISBN	Author, Affiliation, Description
Accounting Workbook for Peachtree® 8.0		Warren Allen, Mary Allen, James Heintz, Robert Parry
with CD, Ch. 2-29	0324073623	Available for use with selected problems (marked by an icon in the main text). A student
without CD, Ch. 2-29	032407364X	instruction book accompanies the software. The data files and a student version of the
with CD, Ch. 2-16	032412452X	software are included on the CD. This product assists students in learning how to use real-world
without CD, Ch. 2-16	0324124546	accounting software. Can be used as a stand-alone ancillary, also.
Accounting Workbook for QuickBooks® 2000		Warren Allen, Mary Allen, James Heintz, Robert Parry
with CD, Ch. 2-29	0324123930	Available for use with selected problems (marked by an icon in the main text). A student
with CD, Ch. 2-16	0324123965	instruction book accompanies the software. The data files and a student version of the software are included on the CD. This product assists students in learning how to use real-world accounting software. Can be used as a stand-alone ancillary, also.
General Ledger Software and Problem Booklet		Warren Allen, Mary Allen, James Heintz, Robert Parry
	0324101503	Available for use with selected problems found in the main text (identified by icons). As students use the opening balances, chart of accounts, and set-up functions to complete problems, they gain valuable, hands-on experience with full-functioning general ledger software.
Practice Sets		
Star ExpressCleaning Service	053888620X	Janet Caruso, Briarcliffe College
		This practice set is a sole-proprietorship service business simulation for use after text Ch. 10. It reviews the accounting cycle, the combination journal, and accounting for cash.
Ed's Electronics	0324112580	Toni Hartley, Laurel Business Institute
		This practice set contains information about a sole-proprietorship merchandising business. It emphasizes payroll and the use of special journals and subsidiary ledgers. It is appropriate for use after text Ch. 16.
Sun Coast Surf Products, Inc.	0538886315	Kim Belden, Daytona Beach Community College
		This practice set gives students hands-on experience with a small departmentalized wholesaler operating as a corporation. Includes preparation of financial statements and ratio analysis. For use after Ch. 27.
SG with Working Papers		James Heintz and Robert Parry
Ch. 1-10	0324073798	A study guide and the working papers for the text assignments are provided together in one
Ch. 1-16	0324073801	convenient resource. Students are able to reinforce their learning experience with chapter out-
Ch.17-29	032407381X	lines that are linked to learning objectives and a set "C" of assignments consisting of review questions, exercises, and problems. The working papers are tailored to the text's end-of-chapter assignments. (The text solutions manual contains the solutions to the working papers. The solutions to the study guide assignments are available separately.)
On the Internet		
WebTutor™ on WebCT	0324118570	
WebTutor™ on Blackboard	0324118589	
Personal WebTutor™ Access Certificate	0324118597	

Supplements for Instructors	ISBN	Author, Affiliation, Description
Solutions Manual to Accompany the Accounting Workbooks for Peachtree® 8.0 and for QuickBooks® 2000		James Heintz and Robert Parry
		For those adopting the Peachtree® or the QuickBooks® workbooks but not the HP text.
Chapters 2–16	0324073658	
Chapters 17–29	0324134967	
General Ledger Inspector Disk		Warren Allen, Mary Allen, James Heintz, Robert Parry
	0324112629	This disk contains the electronic solutions to the General Ledger Problem Booklet.

Supplements for Instructors	ISBN	Author, Affiliation, Description
Practice Set Solutions		
Star Express Cleaning Service Practice Set Key with Inspector Disk	0538886234	Janet Caruso, Briarcliffe College Printed and electronic solution to Star Express Cleaning Service practice set.
Ed's Electronics Practice Set Key with Inspector Disk	0324112610	Toni Hartley, Laurel Business Institute Printed and electronic solution to Ed's Electronics practice set.
Sun Coast Surf Products, Inc. Practice Set Key with Inspector Disk	053888634X	Kim Belden, Daytona Beach Community College Printed and electronic solution to Sun Coast Surf Products practice set.
Achievement Tests		
version A, Ch. 1-16	0324073666	Ann Germain, Heald College
version A, Ch. 17-29	0324073682	Significantly revised, these tests, grouped in "A" and "B" sets, allow for maximum flexibility
version B, Ch. 1-16	0324073704	in assigning in-class and out-of-class work for students.
version B, Ch. 17-29	0324073720	
Achievement Test Keys		
version A, Ch. 1-16	0324073674	Ann Germain, Heald College
version A, Ch. 17-29	0324073690	Solutions for the Achievement tests.
version B, Ch. 1-16	0324073712	
version B, Ch. 17-29	0324073739	
Instructor Resource Guide		
Ch. 1-16	0324073747	William CK. Alberts, National Business College
Ch.17-29	0324073755	This guide contains a wealth of resources to help instructors create an exciting and productive classroom experience. Included are enhanced chapter outlines and teaching tips; references to exhibits, PowerPoint® slides, and teaching transparencies; suggested enrichments and activities; check figures for text assignments; pretests tied to learning objectives; and Ten Questions Your Students Will Always Ask, to help anticipate student learning needs.
PowerPoint® Presentation		
	0324073763	Donna Larner, Davenport College A completely new PowerPoint® presentation of text content using extremely engaging visuals that are paced well for student comprehension.
Solutions Manual		
Ch. 1-16	0324073771	James Heintz and Robert Parry
Ch.17-29	032407378X	The complete, carefully verified solutions for all text assignments. Accounting rulings are used where appropriate. (Note: These are also the solutions to the working papers.)
Study Guide Solutions		
Ch. 1-10	0324073828	James Heintz and Robert Parry
Ch. 1-16	0324073836	Solutions to all study guide set "C" assignments found in the study guide. This may be packaged
Ch.17-29	0324073844	with the study guide at the instructor's discretion.
Solutions Transparencies		
Ch. 1-16	0324073852	James Heintz and Robert Parry
Ch.17-29	0324073860	Contains solutions for Series A & B Exercises and Problems, Mastery Problems, and Comprehensive Problems. Where appropriate, solutions appear on accounting rulings.
Teaching Transparencies		
Ch. 1-16	0324073879	James Heintz and Robert Parry
Ch.17-29	0324073887	Colorful teaching transparencies of many of the text illustrations for use in classroom presentations.
Test Bank		
Ch. 1-16	0324073895	Fred McCracken, Indiana Business College; Lee Moore, South Plains College
Ch.17-29	0324073909	These test banks have been significantly revised and carefully verified.
Check Figures		
	0324101538	James Heintz and Robert Parry Selected check figures for Series A & B exercise and problems and Mastery Problems are available on separate printed sheets, packaged in sets of 25 copies. They are also available in the Instructor's Resource Guides and on the Instructor Resources part of the Web site.
Examview		
	0324073917	This new, easy to use electronic test bank contains the test items found in the two printed test banks.

Website – visit heintz.swcollege.com for many resources.

Accounting for a Service Business

Introduction to Accounting

So, you have decided to study accounting. Good decision. A solid foundation in accounting concepts and techniques will be helpful. This is true whether you take a professional position in accounting or business, or simply want to better understand your personal finances and dealings with businesses.

Throughout Chapters 2 through 6, we will introduce Jessie Jane's Campus Delivery service. By studying Jessie's business transactions and accounting techniques, you will learn about business and accounting. This is a major advantage of studying accounting. While studying accounting, you also learn a lot about business.

Knowledge of how accounting works will help you evaluate the financial health of businesses and other

organizations. It will also give you a solid approach to dealing with financial and business transactions in your personal life. How do you plan to use the accounting skills developed in this class?

Careful study of this chapter should enable you to:

LO1 Describe the purpose of accounting.

LO2 Describe the accounting process.

LO3 Define three types of business ownership structures.

LO4 Classify different types of businesses by activities.

LO5 Identify career opportunities in accounting.

Accounting is the language of business. You must learn this language to understand the impact of economic events on a specific company. Common, everyday terms have very precise meanings when used in accounting. For example, you have probably heard terms like asset, liability, revenue, expense, and net income. Take a moment to jot down how you would define each of these terms. After reading and studying Chapter 2, compare your definitions with those developed in this text. This comparison will show whether you can trust your current understanding of accounting terms. Whether you intend to pursue a career in accounting or simply wish to understand the impact of business transactions, you need a clear understanding of this language.

THE PURPOSE OF ACCOUNTING

LO1 Describe the purpose of accounting.

The purpose of accounting is to provide financial information about the current operations and financial condition of a business to individuals, agencies, and organizations. As shown in Figure 1-1, owners, managers, creditors, and government agencies all need accounting information. Other users of accounting information include customers, clients, labor unions, stock exchanges, and financial analysts.

USER	INFORMATION NEEDED	DECISIONS MADE BY USERS
Owners— Present and future	Company's profitability and current financial condition.	If business is good, owners may consider making additional investments for growth. If business is poor, they may want to talk to management to find out why and may consider closing the business.
Managers— May or may not own business	Detailed measures of business performance.	Managers need to make operating decisions. How much and what kinds of inventory should be carried? Is business strong enough to support higher wages for employees?
Creditors— Present and future	Company's profitability, debt outstanding, and assets that could be used to secure debt.	Should a loan be granted to this business? If so, what amount of debt can the business support and what interest rate should be charged?
Government Agencies— National, state, and local	Company's profitability, cash flows, and overall financial condition.	The IRS will decide how much income tax the business must pay. Local governments may be willing to adjust property taxes paid by the business to encourage it to stay in town.

FIGURE 1-1   **Users of Accounting Information**

THE ACCOUNTING PROCESS

LO2 **Describe the accounting process.**

Accounting is a system of gathering financial information about a business and reporting this information to users. The six major steps of the accounting process are analyzing, recording, classifying, summarizing, reporting, and interpreting (Figure 1-2). Computers are often used in the recording, classifying, summarizing, and reporting steps. Whether or not computers are used, the accounting concepts and techniques are the same. Information entered into the computer system must reflect a proper application of these concepts. Otherwise, the output will be meaningless.

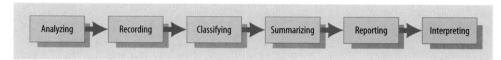

FIGURE 1-2   **The Accounting Process**

- **Analyzing** is looking at events that have taken place and thinking about how they affect the business.
- **Recording** is entering financial information about events into the accounting system. Although this can be done with paper and pencil, most businesses use computers to perform routine record-keeping operations.
- **Classifying** is sorting and grouping similar items together rather than merely keeping a simple, diary-like record of numerous events.
- **Summarizing** is bringing the various items of information together to determine a result.
- **Reporting** is telling the results. In accounting, it is common to use tables of numbers to report results.
- **Interpreting** is deciding the meaning and importance of the information in various reports. This may include percentage analyses and the use of ratios to help explain how pieces of information relate to one another.

Generally accepted accounting principles (GAAP) are followed during the accounting process. The Financial Accounting Standards Board develops these accounting rules, called GAAP, to provide procedures and guidelines to be followed in the accounting and reporting process. These rules provide some assurance that companies are reporting business activities in a similar manner. This allows users of financial statements to evaluate a company's financial performance and make comparisons with other companies.

THREE TYPES OF OWNERSHIP STRUCTURES

LO3 **Define three types of business ownership structures.**

One or more persons may own a business. Businesses are classified according to who owns them and the specific way they are organized. Three types of ownership structures are (1) sole proprietorship, (2) partnership, and (3) corporation (Figure 1-3). Accountants provide information to owners of all three types of ownership structures.

Sole Proprietorship

A **sole proprietorship** is owned by one person. The owner is often called a proprietor. The proprietor often manages the business. The owner assumes all risks
for the business, and personal assets can be taken to pay creditors. The advantage
of a sole proprietorship is that the owner can make all decisions.

TYPES OF OWNERSHIP STRUCTURES		
Sole Proprietorship	**Partnership**	**Corporation**
• One owner	• Two or more partners	• Stockholders
• Owner assumes all risk	• Partners share risks	• Stockholders have limited risk
• Owner makes all decisions	• Partners may disagree on how to run business	• Stockholders may have little influence on business decisions

FIGURE 1-3   Types of Ownership Structures—Advantages and Disadvantages

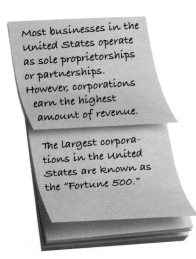

Most businesses in the United States operate as sole proprietorships or partnerships. However, corporations earn the highest amount of revenue.

The largest corporations in the United States are known as the "Fortune 500."

Partnership

A **partnership** is owned by more than one person. One or more partners may
manage the business. Like proprietors, partners assume the risks for the business,
and their assets may be taken to pay creditors. An advantage of a partnership is
that owners share risks and decision making. A disadvantage is that partners may
disagree about the best way to run the business.

Corporation

A **corporation** is owned by stockholders (or shareholders). Corporations may
have many owners, and they usually employ professional managers. The owners'
risk is usually limited to their initial investment, and they often have very little
influence on the business decisions.

TYPES OF BUSINESSES

LO4 Classify different types of businesses by activities.

Businesses are classified according to the type of service or product provided.
Some businesses provide a service. Others sell a product. A business that provides
a service is called a **service business**. A business that buys a product from
another business to sell to customers is called a **merchandising business**. A business that makes a product to sell is called a **manufacturing business**. You will
learn about all three types of businesses in this book. Figure 1-4 lists examples of
types of businesses organized by activity.

SERVICE	MERCHANDISING	MANUFACTURING
Travel Agency	Department Store	Automobile Manufacturer
Computer Consultant	Pharmacy	Furniture Maker
Physician	Jewelry Store	Toy Factory

FIGURE 1-4   Types and Examples of Businesses Organized by Activities

A BROADER VIEW

All Kinds of Businesses Need Accounting Systems

Even small businesses like the one that took the Parry family on a two-day, whitewater rafting trip down the Colorado River need good accounting systems. Proper records must be maintained for the cost of the rafts, food served, tour guides' salaries (second and third from left), and office expenses. Without this information, the company would not know how much to charge and whether a profit is made on these trips.

CAREER OPPORTUNITIES IN ACCOUNTING

LO5 Identify career opportunities in accounting.

Accounting offers many career opportunities. The positions described below require varying amounts of education, experience, and technological skill.

Accounting Clerks

> **ACCOUNTING CLERK**
> Travel agency is looking for an accounting clerk to handle bookkeeping tasks. 1–3 years experience with an automated accounting system required.

Businesses with large quantities of accounting tasks to perform daily often employ **accounting clerks** to record, sort, and file accounting information. Often accounting clerks will specialize in cash, payroll, accounts receivable, accounts payable, inventory, or purchases. As a result, they are involved with only a small portion of the total accounting responsibilities for the firm. Accounting clerks usually have at least one year of accounting education.

Bookkeepers and Para-Accountants

> **BOOKKEEPING/ACCOUNTING**
> Service company has an opening for a full charge bookkeeper/accountant. Previous accounting experience with an associate degree preferred. Salary commensurate with experience. Excellent knowledge of LOTUS 1-2-3® or Excel® required.

Bookkeepers generally supervise the work of accounting clerks, help with daily accounting work, and summarize accounting information. In small-to-medium-sized businesses, the bookkeeper may also help managers and owners interpret the accounting information. Bookkeepers usually have one to two years of accounting education and experience as an accounting clerk.

Para-accountants provide many accounting, auditing, or tax services under the direct supervision of an accountant. A typical para-accountant has a two-year degree or significant accounting and bookkeeping experience.

Accountants

The difference between accountants and bookkeepers is not always clear, particularly in smaller companies where bookkeepers also help interpret the accounting information. In large companies, the distinction is clearer. Bookkeepers focus on the processing of accounting data. **Accountants** design the accounting information system and focus on analyzing and interpreting information. They also look for important trends in the data and study the impact of alternative decisions.

Most accountants enter the field with a college degree in accounting. Accountants are employed in public accounting, private (managerial) accounting, and in governmental and not-for-profit accounting (Figure 1-5).

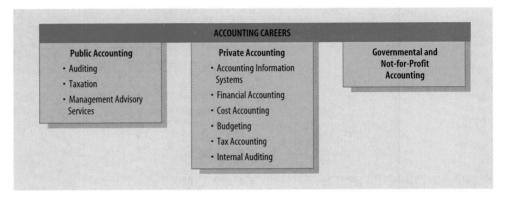

FIGURE 1-5   **Accounting Careers**

Public Accounting. Public accountants offer services in much the same way as doctors and lawyers. The public accountant can achieve professional recognition as a **Certified Public Accountant** (CPA). This is done by meeting certain educational and experience requirements as determined by each state, and passing a uniform examination prepared by the American Institute of Certified Public Accountants.

Many CPAs work alone, while others work for local, regional, or national accounting firms that vary in scope and size. The largest public accounting firms in the United States are known as the "Big Five." They are Arthur Andersen & Co., Deloitte and Touche, Ernst & Young, KPMG Peat Marwick, and PricewaterhouseCoopers.

Services offered by public accountants are listed below.

■   **Auditing.** Auditing involves the application of standard review and testing procedures to be certain that proper accounting policies and practices have been followed. The purpose of the audit is to provide an independent opinion that the financial information about a business is fairly presented in a manner consistent with generally accepted accounting principles.

■   **Taxation.** Tax specialists advise on tax planning, prepare tax returns, and represent clients before governmental agencies such as the Internal Revenue Service.

■   **Management Advisory Services.** Given the financial training and business experience of public accountants, many businesses seek their advice on a wide variety of managerial issues. Often, accounting firms are involved in designing computerized accounting systems.

Private (Managerial) Accounting. Many accountants are employees of private business firms. The **controller** oversees the entire accounting process and is the principal accounting officer of the company. Private or managerial accountants perform a wide variety of services for the business. These services are listed below.

- **Accounting Information Systems.** Accountants in this area design and implement manual and computerized accounting systems.
- **Financial Accounting.** Based on the accounting data prepared by the bookkeepers and accounting clerks, accountants prepare various reports and financial statements and help in analyzing operating, investing, and financing decisions.
- **Cost Accounting.** The cost of producing specific products or providing services must be measured. Further analysis is also done to determine whether the products and services are produced in the most cost-effective manner.
- **Budgeting.** In the budgeting process, accountants help managers develop a financial plan.
- **Tax Accounting.** Instead of hiring a public accountant, a company may have its own accountants. They focus on tax planning, preparation of tax returns, and dealing with the Internal Revenue Service and other governmental agencies.
- **Internal Auditing.** Internal auditors review the operating and accounting control procedures adopted by management to make sure the controls are adequate and are being followed. They also monitor the accuracy and timeliness of the reports provided to management and to external parties.

A managerial accountant can achieve professional status as a **Certified Management Accountant** (CMA). This is done by passing a uniform examination offered by the Institute of Management Accountants. An internal auditor can achieve professional recognition as a **Certified Internal Auditor** (CIA) by passing the uniform examination offered by the Institute of Internal Auditors.

Governmental and Not-for-Profit Accounting. Thousands of governmental and not-for-profit organizations (states, cities, schools, churches, and hospitals) gather and report financial information. These organizations employ a large number of accountants. Since these entities are not profit-oriented, the rules are somewhat different for governmental and not-for-profit organizations. However, many accounting procedures are similar to those found in profit-seeking enterprises.

Job Opportunities

Job growth in some areas will be much greater than in others. Newspaper advertisements often indicate that accountants and accounting clerks are expected to have computer skills. Computer skills definitely increase the opportunities available to you in your career. Almost every business needs accountants, accounting clerks, and bookkeepers. Figure 1-6 shows the expected growth for different types of businesses. Notice that growth will be greatest in the service businesses. Chapters 2 through 10 introduce accounting skills that you will need to work in a service business. Chapter 11 begins the discussion of merchandising businesses. Accounting for manufacturing businesses is addressed in the last chapters of the book.

Figure 1-7 shows the expected demand for accounting skills. Although a small drop in demand is expected for bookkeeping, accounting, and auditing clerks, these types of positions will offer the highest number of job opportunities over the next several years. The next highest demand is for accountants and auditors and this demand is expected to increase over the next several years.

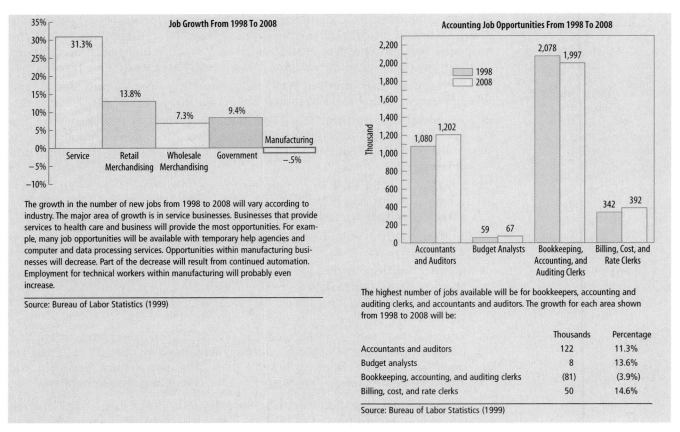

The growth in the number of new jobs from 1998 to 2008 will vary according to industry. The major area of growth is in service businesses. Businesses that provide services to health care and business will provide the most opportunities. For example, many job opportunities will be available with temporary help agencies and computer and data processing services. Opportunities within manufacturing businesses will decrease. Part of the decrease will result from continued automation. Employment for technical workers within manufacturing will probably even increase.

Source: Bureau of Labor Statistics (1999)

The highest number of jobs available will be for bookkeepers, accounting and auditing clerks, and accountants and auditors. The growth for each area shown from 1998 to 2008 will be:

	Thousands	Percentage
Accountants and auditors	122	11.3%
Budget analysts	8	13.6%
Bookkeeping, accounting, and auditing clerks	(81)	(3.9%)
Billing, cost, and rate clerks	50	14.6%

Source: Bureau of Labor Statistics (1999)

FIGURE 1-6   **Expected Growth**

FIGURE 1-7   **Expected Demand**

Regardless of the type of career you desire, writing skills are important in business and your personal life. Becoming a good writer requires practice and a strategy for the process used to prepare memos, letters, and other documents. On pages 9 and 10, Ken Davis offers an excellent approach to managing your writing. Take a moment to read Ken's tips. Then, practice his approach by completing the writing assignments as you finish each chapter.

Managing Your Writing

—Ken Davis

Here's a secret: the business writing that you and I do—the writing that gets the world's work done—requires no special gift. It can be managed, like any other business process.

Managing writing is largely a matter of managing time. Writing is a process, and like any process it can be done efficiently or inefficiently. Unfortunately, most of us are pretty inefficient writers. That's because we try to get each word, each sentence, right the first time. Given a letter to write, we begin with the first sentence. We think about that sentence, write it, revise it, even check its spelling, before going on to the second sentence. In an hour of writing, we might spend 45 or 50 minutes doing this kind of detailed drafting. We spend only a few minutes on overall planning at the beginning and only a few minutes on overall revising at the end.

That approach to writing is like building a house by starting with the front door: planning, building, finishing—even washing the windows—before doing anything with the rest of the house. No wonder most of us have so much trouble writing.

Efficient, effective writers take better charge of their writing time. They *manage* their writing. Like building contractors, they spend time planning before they start construction. Once construction has started, they don't try to do all of the finishing touches as they go.

As the following illustration shows, many good writers break their writing process into three main stages: planning, drafting, and revising. They spend more time at the first and third stages than at the second. They also build in some "management" time at the beginning and the end, and some break time in the middle. To manage *your* writing time, try the following steps.

At the **MANAGING** stage (perhaps two or three minutes for a one-hour writing job), remind yourself that writing *can* be managed and that it's largely a matter of managing time. Plan your next hour.

At the **PLANNING** stage (perhaps 20 minutes out of the hour):

1. **Find the "we."** Define the community to which you and your reader belong. Then ask, "How are my reader and I alike and different?"—in knowledge, attitudes, and circumstances.

2. **Define your purpose.** Remember the advice a consultant once gave Stanley Tool executives: "You're not in the business of making drills: you're in the business of making holes." Too many of us lose sight of the difference between making drills and making holes when we write letters and memos. We focus on the piece of writing—the tool itself—not its purpose. The result: our writing often misses the chance to be as effective as it could be. When you're still at the planning stage, focus on the outcome you want, not on the means you will use to achieve it.

3. **Get your stuff together.** Learn from those times when you've turned a one-hour home-improvement project into a three- or four-hour job by having to make repeated trips to the hardware store for tools or parts. Before you start the drafting stage of writing, collect the information you need.

4. **Get your ducks in a row.** Decide on the main points you want to make. Then, make a list or rough outline placing your points in the most logical order.

At the **DRAFTING** stage (perhaps 5 minutes out of the hour):

5. **Do it wrong the first time.** Do a "quick and dirty" draft, without editing. Think of your draft as a "prototype," written not for the end user but for your own testing and improvement. Stopping to edit while you draft breaks your train of thought and keeps you from being a good writer. (Hint: if you are writing at a computer, try turning off the monitor during the drafting stage.)

At the **BREAK STAGE** (perhaps 5 minutes):

6. **Take a break and change hats.** Get away from your draft, even if for only a few minutes. Come back with a fresh perspective—the reader's perspective.

At the **REVISING STAGE** (perhaps 25 minutes):

7. **Signal your turns.** Just as if you were driving a car, you're leading your reader through new territory. Use "turn signals"—*and, in addition, but, however, or, therefore, because, for example*—to guide your reader from sentence to sentence.

8. **Say what you mean.** Put the point of your sentences in the subjects and verbs. For example, revise "There are drawbacks to using this accounting method" to "This accounting method has some drawbacks." You'll be saying what you mean, and you'll be a more effective communicator.

9. **Pay by the word.** Reading your memo requires work. If your sentences are wordy and you are slow to get to the point, the reader may decide that it is not worth the effort. Pretend you are paying the reader by the word to read your memo. Then, revise your memo to make it as short and to the point as possible.

10. **Translate into English.** Keep your words simple. (Lee Iacocca put both these tips in one "commandment of good management": "Say it in English and keep it short.") Remember that you write to express, not impress.

11. **Finish the job.** Check your spelling, punctuation, and mechanics.

Finally, at the **MANAGING STAGE** again (2 to 3 minutes):

12. **Evaluate your writing process.** Figure out how to improve it next time.

By following these 12 steps, you can take charge of your writing time. Begin today to *manage your writing.* As a United Technologies Corporation advertisement in *The Wall Street Journal* admonished, "If you want to manage somebody, manage yourself. Do that well and you'll be ready to stop managing and start leading."

Dr. Ken Davis is Professor of English and coordinator of the Applied Writing Group at Indiana University-Purdue University at Indianapolis. He is president of Komei, Inc., a global communication consulting company.

Learning Objectives	Key Points to Remember
1 **Describe the purpose of accounting.**	The purpose of accounting is to provide financial information about a business to individuals and organizations.
2 **Describe the accounting process.**	The six major steps of the accounting process are analyzing, recording, classifying, summarizing, reporting, and interpreting.
3 **Define three types of business ownership structures.**	Three types of business ownership structures are sole proprietorship, partnership, and corporation.
4 **Classify different types of businesses by activities.**	Different types of businesses classified by activities are a service business, a merchandising business, and a manufacturing business.
5 **Identify career opportunities in accounting.**	Career opportunities in accounting include work in public accounting, private accounting, and governmental and not-for-profit accounting.

Reflection: Answering the Opening Question

Of course, your answer to the opening question depends on your specific plans. In general, though, accounting skills are helpful in all kinds of business, nonprofit, and personal activities. As discussed in the chapter, accounting knowledge is important when working in all types of businesses: service, merchandising, and manufacturing. It is also helpful regardless of the ownership structure: sole proprietorship, partnership, or corporation.

KEY TERMS

accountant, (6)   Designs the accounting information system and focuses on analyzing and interpreting information.

accounting, (3)   A system of gathering financial information about a business and reporting this information to users.

accounting clerk, (5)   Records, sorts, and files accounting information.

accounting information systems, (7)   Accountants in this area design and implement manual and computerized accounting systems.

analyzing, (3)   Looking at events that have taken place and thinking about how they affect the business.

auditing, (6)   Reviewing and testing to be certain that proper accounting policies and practices have been followed.

bookkeeper, (5)   Generally supervises the work of accounting clerks, helps with daily accounting work, and summarizes accounting information.

budgeting, (7)   The process in which accountants help managers develop a financial plan.

Certified Internal Auditor, (7)   An internal auditor who has achieved professional recognition by passing the uniform examination offered by the Institute of Internal Auditors.

Certified Management Accountant, (7)   An accountant who has passed an examination offered by the Institute of Management Accountants.

Certified Public Accountant, (6)   A public accountant who has met certain educational and experience requirements and has passed an examination prepared by the American Institute of Certified Public Accountants.

classifying, (3)   Sorting and grouping similar items together rather than merely keeping a simple, diary-like record of numerous events.

controller, (7)   The accountant who oversees the entire accounting process and is the principal accounting officer of a company.

corporation, (4)   A type of ownership structure in which stockholders own the business. The owners' risk is usually limited to their initial investment, and they usually have very little influence on the business decisions.

cost accounting, (7)   Determining the cost of producing specific products or providing services and analyzing for cost effectiveness.

financial accounting, (7)   Includes preparing various reports and financial statements and analyzing operating, investing, and financing decisions.

generally accepted accounting principles (GAAP), (3)   Procedures and guidelines developed by the Financial Accounting Standards Board to be followed in the accounting and reporting process.

internal auditing, (7)   Reviewing the operating and accounting control procedures adopted by management to make sure the controls are adequate and being followed; assuring that accurate and timely information is provided.

interpreting, (3)   Deciding the meaning and importance of the information in various reports.

management advisory services, (6)   Providing advice to businesses on a wide variety of managerial issues.

manufacturing business, (4)   A business that makes a product to sell.

merchandising business, (4)   A business that buys products to sell.

para-accountant, (5)   A paraprofessional who provides many accounting, auditing, or tax services under the direct supervision of an accountant.

partnership, (4)   A type of ownership structure in which more than one person owns the business.

recording, (3)   Entering financial information about events affecting the company into the accounting system.

reporting, (3)   Telling the results of the financial information.

service business, (4)   A business that provides a service.

sole proprietorship, (4)   A type of ownership structure in which one person owns the business.

summarizing, (3)   Bringing the various items of information together to determine a result.

tax accounting, (7)   Focusing on tax planning, preparing tax returns, and dealing with the Internal Revenue Service and other governmental agencies.

taxation, (6)   See tax accounting.

REVIEW QUESTIONS

1. What is the purpose of accounting?

2. Identify four user groups normally interested in financial information about a business.

3. Identify the six major steps of the accounting process and explain each step.

4. Identify the three types of ownership structures and discuss the advantages and disadvantages of each.

5. Identify three types of businesses according to activities.

6. What are the main functions of an accounting clerk?

7. Name and describe three areas of specialization for a public accountant.

8. Name and describe six areas of specialization for a managerial accountant.

MANAGING YOUR WRITING

1. Prepare a one-page memo to your instructor that explains what you hope to learn in this course and how this knowledge will be useful to you.

2. If you started a business, what would it be? Prepare a one-page memo that describes the type of business you would enjoy the most. Would it be a service, merchandising, or manufacturing business? Explain what form of ownership you would prefer and why.

SERIES A EXERCISES

EXERCISE 1-1A   **(LO1)**   **PURPOSE OF ACCOUNTING** Match the following users with the information needed.

1. Owners
2. Managers
3. Creditors
4. Government agencies

a. Whether the firm can pay its bills on time

b. Detailed, up-to-date information to measure business performance (and plan for future operations)

c. To determine taxes to be paid and whether other regulations are met

d. The firm's current financial condition

EXERCISE 1-2A   **(LO2)**   **ACCOUNTING PROCESS** List the six major steps of the accounting process in order (1–6) and define each.

_____   Recording

_____   Summarizing

_____   Reporting

_____   Analyzing

_____   Interpreting

_____   Classifying

SERIES B EXERCISES

EXERCISE 1-1B (LO1) **PURPOSE OF ACCOUNTING** Describe the kind of information needed by the users listed.

Owners (present and future)

Managers

Creditors (present and future)

Government agencies

EXERCISE 1-2B (LO2) **ACCOUNTING PROCESS** Match the following steps of the accounting process with their definitions.

Analyzing	a.	Telling the results
Recording	b.	Looking at events that have taken place and thinking about how they affect the business
Classifying	c.	Deciding the importance of the various reports
Summarizing	d.	Bringing together information to explain a result
Reporting	e.	Sorting and grouping like items together
Interpreting	f.	Entering financial information into the accounting system

Analyzing Transactions:
The Accounting Equation

Have you ever heard the expression "garbage in, garbage out"? Computer users commonly use it to mean that if input to the computer system is not correctly entered, the output from the system will be worthless. The same expression applies in accounting. In this chapter Jessica Jane enters into many transactions while running her delivery business. For example, she purchases a motor scooter to make deliveries. To understand the impact of this event, Jessie needs to know how to properly measure the cost of the asset, estimate its useful life, and keep records of whether she paid cash or promised to make payments in the future. If Jessie does not understand the economic events affecting her delivery business and their impact on the accounting equation, the events will

not be correctly entered into the accounting system. This will make the outputs from the system (the financial statements) worthless. What kinds of questions do you think Jessie should ask herself to improve her understanding of an event and its impact on the business?

LO1 Define the accounting elements.

LO2 Construct the accounting equation.

LO3 Analyze business transactions.

LO4 Show the effects of business transactions on the accounting equation.

LO5 Prepare and describe the purposes of a simple income statement, statement of owner's equity, and balance sheet.

LO6 Define the three basic phases of the accounting process.

The entire accounting process is based on one simple equation, called the accounting equation. In this chapter, you will learn how to use this equation to analyze business transactions. You also will learn how to prepare financial statements that report the effect of these transactions on the financial condition of a business.

THE ACCOUNTING ELEMENTS

LO1 Define the accounting elements.

Before the accounting process can begin, the entity to be accounted for must be defined. A **business entity** is an individual, association, or organization that engages in economic activities and controls specific economic resources. This definition allows the personal and business finances of an owner to be accounted for separately.

Three basic accounting elements exist for every business entity: assets, liabilities, and owner's equity. These elements are defined below.

LEARNING KEY: Pay close attention to the definitions for the basic accounting elements. A clear understanding of these definitions will help you analyze even the most complex business transactions.

Assets

Assets are items that are owned by a business and will provide future benefits. Examples of assets include cash, merchandise, furniture, fixtures, machinery, buildings, and land. Businesses may also have an asset called **accounts receivable**. This asset represents the amount of money owed to the business by its customers as a result of making sales "on account," or "on credit." Making sales on account simply means that the customers have promised to pay sometime in the future.

Liabilities

Liabilities represent something owed to another business entity. The amount owed represents a probable future outflow of assets as a result of a past event or transaction. Liabilities are debts or obligations of the business that can be paid with cash, goods, or services.

The most common liabilities are accounts payable and notes payable. An **account payable** is an unwritten promise to pay a supplier for assets purchased or services received. Acquiring assets or services by promising to make payments in the future is referred to as making a purchase "on account," or "on credit." Formal written promises to pay suppliers or lenders specified sums of money at definite future times are known as **notes payable**.

Owner's Equity

Owner's equity is the amount by which the business assets exceed the business liabilities. Other terms used for owner's equity include **net worth** and **capital**. If there are no business liabilities, the owner's equity is equal to the total assets.

The owner of a business may have business assets and liabilities as well as nonbusiness assets and liabilities. For example, the business owner probably owns a home, clothing, and a car, and perhaps owes the dentist for dental service. These are personal, nonbusiness assets and liabilities. According to the **business entity concept**, nonbusiness assets and liabilities are not included in the business entity's accounting records.

If the owner invests money or other assets in the business, the item invested is reclassified from a nonbusiness asset to a business asset. If the owner withdraws money or other assets from the business for personal use, the item withdrawn is reclassified from a business asset to a nonbusiness asset. These distinctions are important and allow the owner to make decisions based on the financial condition and results of the business apart from nonbusiness activities.

LEARNING KEY: The business entity's assets and liabilities are separate from the owner's nonbusiness assets and liabilities.

A BROADER VIEW

Assets and the Cost of Products We Buy

Next time you buy something, think of all the assets that a company needs to produce that product. If the product comes from a "capital-intensive" industry, one that requires heavy investments in assets, the company must price the product high enough to cover the cost of using the assets and replacing them when they wear out. For example, General Motors recently reported that the cost of property, plant, and equipment used for operating purposes came to over $100 billion.

THE ACCOUNTING EQUATION

LO2 Construct the accounting equation.

The relationship between the three basic accounting elements—assets, liabilities, and owner's equity—can be expressed in the form of a simple equation known as the **accounting equation**.

The accounting equation is a very important tool to help in understanding and analyzing transactions.

Assets	=	Liabilities	+	Owner's Equity

This equation reflects the fact that both outsiders and insiders have an interest in all of the assets of a business. *Liabilities represent the outside interests of creditors. Owner's equity represents the inside interests of owners. When two elements are known, the third can always be calculated.* For example, assume that assets on December 31 total $60,400. On that same day, the business liabilities consist of $5,400 owed for equipment. Owner's equity is calculated by subtracting total liabilities from total assets, $60,400 – $5,400 = $55,000.

The left side of the equation represents the assets. The right side of the equation shows where the money came from to buy the assets.

Assets	=	Liabilities	+	Owner's Equity
$60,400	=	$5,400	+	$55,000
$60,400	=		$60,400	

LEARNING KEY: If you know two accounting elements, you can calculate the third element.

Total assets	$60,400
Total liabilities	−5,400
Owner's equity	$55,000

ANALYZING BUSINESS TRANSACTIONS

LO3 Analyze business transactions.

A **business transaction** is an economic event that has a direct impact on the business. A business transaction almost always requires an exchange between the business and another outside entity. We must be able to measure this exchange in dollars. Examples of business transactions include buying goods and services, selling goods and services, buying and selling assets, making loans, and borrowing money.

All business transactions affect the accounting equation through specific accounts. An **account** is a separate record used to summarize changes in each asset, liability, and owner's equity of a business. **Account titles** provide a description of the particular type of asset, liability, or owner's equity affected by a transaction.

Three basic questions must be answered when analyzing the effects of a business transaction on the accounting equation. These questions help address the steps in the accounting process discussed in Chapter 1.

1. **What happened?**

   ■ Make certain you understand the event that has taken place.

2. **Which accounts are affected?**

- Identify the accounts that are affected.

- Classify these accounts as assets, liabilities, or owner's equity.

3. **How is the accounting equation affected?**

- Determine which accounts have increased or decreased.

- Make certain that the accounting equation remains in balance after the transaction has been entered.

EFFECT OF TRANSACTIONS ON THE ACCOUNTING EQUATION

LO4 Show the effects of business transactions on the accounting equation.

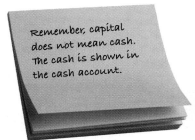

Remember, capital does not mean cash. The cash is shown in the cash account.

Each transaction affects at least two accounts and one or more of the three basic accounting elements. A transaction increases or decreases specific asset, liability, or owner's equity accounts. Assume that the following transactions occurred during June 20--, the first month of operations for Jessie Jane's Campus Delivery.

Transaction (a): Investment by owner

An Increase in an Asset Offset by an Increase in Owner's Equity. Jessica Jane opened a bank account with a deposit of $2,000 for her business. The new business now has $2,000 of the asset Cash. Since Jessie contributed the asset, the owner's equity element, Jessica Jane, Capital, increases by the same amount.

Assets (Items Owned)	=	Liabilities (Amounts Owed)	+	Owner's Equity (Owner's Investment)
Cash	=			Jessica Jane, Capital
(a) $2,000	=			$2,000

Transaction (b): Purchase of an asset for cash

An Increase in an Asset Offset by a Decrease in Another Asset. Jessie decided that the fastest and easiest way to get around campus and find parking is on a motor scooter. Thus, she bought a motor scooter (delivery equipment) for $1,200 cash. Jessie exchanged one asset, cash, for another, delivery equipment. This transaction reduces Cash and creates a new asset, Delivery Equipment.

Assets (Items Owned)			=	Liabilities (Amounts Owed)	+	Owner's Equity (Owner's Investment)
Cash	+	Delivery Equipment	=			Jessica Jane, Capital
$2,000						$2,000
(b) −1,200		+1,200				
$ 800	+	$1,200				$2,000
$2,000			=			$2,000

LEARNING KEY: If transactions are entered correctly, the accounting equation always remains in balance.

Transaction (c): Purchase of an asset on account

An Increase in an Asset Offset by an Increase in a Liability. Jessie hired a friend to work for her, which meant that a second scooter would be needed. Given Jessie's limited cash, she bought the dealer's demonstration model for $900. The seller agreed to allow Jessie to spread the payments over the next three months. This transaction increased an asset, Delivery Equipment, by $900 and increased the liability, Accounts Payable, by an equal amount.

	Assets (Items Owned)			=	Liabilities (Amounts Owed)	+	Owner's Equity (Owner's Investment)
	Cash	+	Delivery Equipment	=	Accounts Payable	+	Jessica Jane, Capital
(c)	$ 800		$1,200 + 900		+ $900		$2,000
	$ 800	+	$2,100	=	$900	+	$2,000
		$2,900				$2,900	

Transaction (d): Payment on a loan

A Decrease in an Asset Offset by a Decrease in a Liability. Jessie paid the first installment on the scooter of $300 (see transaction (c)). This payment decreased the asset, Cash, and the liability, Accounts Payable, by $300.

	Assets (Items Owned)			=	Liabilities (Amounts Owed)	+	Owner's Equity (Owner's Investment)
	Cash	+	Delivery Equipment	=	Accounts Payable	+	Jessica Jane, Capital
(d)	$ 800 −300		$2,100		$900 −300		$2,000
	$ 500	+	$2,100	=	$600	+	$2,000
		$2,600		=		$2,600	

Expanding the Accounting Equation: Revenues, Expenses, and Withdrawals

In the preceding sections, three key accounting elements of every business entity were defined and explained: assets, liabilities, and owner's equity. To complete the explanation of the accounting process, three additional elements must be added to the discussion: revenues, expenses, and withdrawals.

Revenues. Revenues represent the amount a business charges customers for products sold or services performed. Customers generally pay with cash or a credit card, or they promise to pay at a later date. Most businesses recognize revenues when earned, even if cash has not yet been received. Separate accounts are used to recognize different types of revenue. Examples include Delivery Fees; Consulting Fees; Rent Revenue, if the business rents space to others; Interest Revenue, for interest earned on bank deposits; and Sales, for sales of merchandise. *Revenues increase both assets and owner's equity.*

Expenses. Expenses represent the decrease in assets (or increase in liabilities) as a result of efforts made to produce revenues. Common examples of expenses are rent, salaries, supplies consumed, and taxes. As with revenues, separate accounts are used to maintain records for each different type of expense. Expenses are "incurred" as assets are consumed (such as supplies), cash is paid for services performed for the business, or a promise is made to pay cash at a future date for services performed for the business (such as wages). The promise to pay in the future represents a liability. *Expenses either decrease assets or increase liabilities. Expenses always reduce owner's equity.*

> **LEARNING KEY:** It is important to remember that expenses do not always reduce cash and revenues do not always increase cash right away.

The main purposes of recognizing an expense are to keep track of the amount and types of expenses incurred and to show the reduction in owner's equity. Note that an expense can cause a reduction in assets or an increase in liabilities. Wages earned by employees is a good example. If paid, the expense reduces an asset, Cash. If not paid, it increases a liability, Wages Payable. Either way, owner's equity is reduced.

If total revenues exceed total expenses of the period, the excess is the **net income** or net profit for the period.

Revenues Greater than Expenses = Net Income

On the other hand, if expenses exceed revenues of the period, the excess is a **net loss** for the period.

Expenses Greater than Revenues = Net Loss

The owner can determine the time period used in the measurement of net income or net loss. It may be a month, a quarter (three months), a year, or some other time period. The concept that income determination can be made on a periodic basis is known as the **accounting period concept**. Any accounting period of twelve months is called a **fiscal year**. The fiscal year frequently coincides with the calendar year.

Withdrawals. **Withdrawals**, or **drawing**, reduce owner's equity as a result of the owner taking cash or other assets out of the business for personal use. Since earnings are expected to offset withdrawals, this reduction is viewed as temporary.

The accounting equation is expanded to include revenues, expenses, and withdrawals. Note that revenues increase owner's equity, while expenses and drawing reduce owner's equity.

> **LEARNING KEY:**
>
> | Owner's Equity | |
> | --- | --- |
> | Decrease | Increase |
> | Expenses | Revenues |
> | Drawing | Investments |

	Assets (Items Owned)		=	Liabilities (Amounts Owed)	+	Owner's Equity (Owner's Investment + Earnings)			
	Cash	+ Delivery Equipment	=	Accounts Payable	+	Jessica Jane, Capital	− Jessica Jane, Drawing	+ Revenues	− Expenses
Balance	$ 500	+ $2,100	=	$600	+	$2,000			
		$2,600	=			$2,600			

Effect of Revenue, Expense, and Withdrawal Transactions on the Accounting Equation

To show the effects of revenue, expense, and withdrawal transactions, the example of Jessie Jane's Campus Delivery will be continued. Assume that the following transactions took place in Jessie's business during June 20--.

Transaction (e): Delivery revenues earned in cash

An Increase in an Asset Offset by an Increase in Owner's Equity Resulting from Revenue. Jessie received $500 cash from clients for delivery services. This transaction increased the asset, Cash, and increased owner's equity by $500. The increase in owner's equity is shown by increasing the revenue account, Delivery Fees, by $500.

Assets (Items Owned)		=	Liabilities (Amounts Owed)	+	Owner's Equity (Owner's Investment + Earnings)				
Cash +	Delivery Equipment	=	Accounts Payable	+	Jessica Jane, Capital	− Jessica Jane, Drawing	+ Revenues	− Expenses	Description
$ 500	$2,100		$600		$2,000				
(e) +500							+$500		Deliv. Fees
$1,000 +	$2,100	=	$600	+	$2,000		+ $500		
$3,100		=				$3,100			

Transaction (f): Paid rent for month

A Decrease in an Asset Offset by a Decrease in Owner's Equity Resulting from an Expense. Jessie rents a small office on campus. She paid $200 for office rent for June. This transaction decreased both Cash and owner's equity by $200. The decrease in owner's equity is shown by increasing an expense called Rent Expense by $200. An increase in an expense decreases owner's equity.

Assets (Items Owned)		=	Liabilities (Amounts Owed)	+	Owner's Equity (Owner's Investment + Earnings)				
Cash +	Delivery Equipment	=	Accounts Payable	+	Jessica Jane, Capital	− Jessica Jane, Drawing	+ Revenues	− Expenses	Description
$1,000	$2,100		$600		$2,000		$500		
(f) −200								+200	Rent Exp.
$ 800 +	$2,100	=	$600	+	$2,000		+ $500	− $200	
$2,900		=				$2,900			

Transaction (g): Paid telephone bill

A Decrease in an Asset Offset by a Decrease in Owner's Equity Resulting from an Expense. Jessie paid $50 in cash for telephone service. This transaction, like the previous one, decreased both Cash and owner's equity. This decrease in owner's equity is shown by increasing an expense called Telephone Expense by $50.

Assets (Items Owned)		=	Liabilities (Amounts Owed)	+	Owner's Equity (Owner's Investment + Earnings)					
Cash +	Delivery Equipment	=	Accounts Payable	+	Jessica Jane, Capital	− Jessica Jane, Drawing	+ Revenues	− Expenses	Description
$ 800	$2,100		$600		$2,000		$500	$200	
(g) − 50								+ 50	Tel. Expense
$ 750 +	$2,100	=	$600	+	$2,000		+	$500 −	$250
$2,850		=				$2,850			

Transaction (h): Delivery revenues earned on account

An Increase in an Asset Offset by an Increase in Owner's Equity Resulting from Revenue. Jessie extends credit to regular customers. Often delivery services are performed for which payment will be received later. Since revenues are recognized when earned, an increase in owner's equity must be reported by increasing the revenue account. Since no cash is received at this time, Cash cannot be increased. Instead, an increase is reported for another asset, Accounts Receivable. *The total of Accounts Receivable at any point in time reflects the amount owed to Jessie by her customers.* Deliveries made on account amounted to $600. Accounts Receivable and Delivery Fees are increased.

Assets (Items Owned)			=	Liabilities (Amounts Owed)	+	Owner's Equity (Owner's Investment + Earnings)					
Cash +	Accounts Receivable +	Delivery Equipment	=	Accounts Payable	+	Jessica Jane, Capital	− Jessica Jane, Drawing	+ Revenues	− Expenses	Description
$ 750		$2,100		$600		$2,000		$ 500	$250	
(h)	+ 600							+ 600		Deliv. Fees
$ 750 +	$ 600 +	$2,100	=	$600	+	$2,000		+	$1,100 −	$250
$3,450							$3,450			

 LEARNING KEY: Revenue is recognized when it is earned even though cash is not received.

Transaction (i): Purchase of supplies

An Increase in an Asset Offset by a Decrease in an Asset. Jessie bought pens, paper, delivery envelopes, and other supplies for $80 cash. These supplies should last for several months. Since they will generate future benefits, the supplies should be recorded as an asset. The accounting equation will show an increase in an asset, Supplies, and a decrease in Cash.

Assets (Items Owned)				=	Liabilities (Amounts Owed)	+	Owner's Equity (Owner's Investment + Earnings)					
Cash +	Accounts Receivable +	Supplies +	Delivery Equipment	=	Accounts Payable	+	Jessica Jane, Capital	− Jessica Jane, Drawing	+ Revenues	− Expenses	Description
$ 750	$ 600		$2,100		$600		$2,000		$1,100	$250	
(i) − 80		+$80									
$ 670 +	$ 600 +	$80 +	$2,100	=	$600	+	$2,000		+	$1,100 −	$250
$3,450				=				$3,450			

Transaction (j): Payment of insurance premium

An Increase in an Asset Offset by a Decrease in an Asset. Since Jessie plans to graduate and sell the business next January, she paid $200 for an eight-month liability insurance policy. Insurance is paid in advance and will provide future benefits. Thus, it is treated as an asset. We must expand the equation to include another asset, Prepaid Insurance, and show that Cash has been reduced.

	Assets (Items Owned)				=	Liabilities (Amounts Owed)	+	Owner's Equity (Owner's Investment + Earnings)					
Cash	+ Accounts Receivable	+ Supplies	+ Prepaid Insurance	+ Delivery Equipment	=	Accounts Payable	+ Jessica Jane, Capital	− Jessica Jane, Drawing	+ Revenues	− Expenses	Description
$ 670	$ 600	$80		$2,100		$600	$2,000		$1,100	$250	
(j) − 200			+$200								
$ 470 +	$ 600 +	$80 +	$200 +	$2,100	=	$600	+ $2,000		+ $1,100	− $250	
		$3,450			=			$3,450			

> **LEARNING KEY:** Both supplies and insurance are recorded as assets because they will last for several months.

As shown in transactions i, j, and k, transactions do not always affect both sides of the accounting equation.

Transaction (k): Cash receipts from prior sales on account

An Increase in an Asset Offset by a Decrease in an Asset. Jessie received $570 in cash for delivery services performed for customers earlier in the month (see transaction (h)). Receipt of this cash increases the cash account and reduces the amount due from customers reported in the accounts receivable account. *Notice that owner's equity is not affected in this transaction. Owner's equity increased in transaction (h) when revenue was recognized as it was earned, rather than now when cash is received.*

	Assets (Items Owned)				=	Liabilities (Amounts Owed)	+	Owner's Equity (Owner's Investment + Earnings)					
Cash	+ Accounts Receivable	+ Supplies	+ Prepaid Insurance	+ Delivery Equipment	=	Accounts Payable	+ Jessica Jane, Capital	− Jessica Jane, Drawing	+ Revenues	− Expenses	Description
$ 470	$ 600	$80	$200	$2,100		$600	$2,000		$1,100	$250	
(k) +570	− 570										
$1,040 +	$ 30 +	$80 +	$200 +	$2,100	=	$600	+ $2,000		+ $1,100	− $250	
		$3,450			=			$3,450			

Transaction (l): Purchase of an asset on account making a partial payment

An Increase in an Asset Offset by a Decrease in an Asset and an Increase in a Liability. With business increasing, Jessie hired a second employee and bought a third motor scooter. The scooter cost $1,500. Jessie paid $300 in cash and will spread the remaining payments over the next four months. The asset Delivery

Equipment increases by $1,500, Cash decreases by $300, and the liability Accounts Payable increases by $1,200. *Note that this transaction changes three accounts. Even so, the accounting equation remains in balance.*

	Assets (Items Owned)				=	Liabilities (Amounts Owed)	+	Owner's Equity (Owner's Investment + Earnings)				
Cash +	Accounts Receivable +	Supplies +	Prepaid Insurance +	Delivery Equipment =		Accounts Payable	+	Jessica Jane, Capital	− Jessica Jane, Drawing	+ Revenues	− Expenses	Description
$1,040 (l) −300	$30	$80	$200	$2,100 +1,500		$ 600 +1,200		$2,000		$1,100	$250	
$ 740 +	$30 +	$80 +	$200 +	$3,600 =		$1,800	+	$2,000		+ $1,100	− $250	
	$4,650				=			$4,650				

Transaction (m): Payment of wages

A Decrease in an Asset Offset by a Decrease in Owner's Equity Resulting from an Expense. Jessie paid her part-time employees $650 in wages. This represents an additional business expense. As with other expenses, Cash is reduced and owner's equity is reduced by increasing an expense.

	Assets (Items Owned)				=	Liabilities (Amounts Owed)	+	Owner's Equity (Owner's Investment + Earnings)				
Cash +	Accounts Receivable +	Supplies +	Prepaid Insurance +	Delivery Equipment =		Accounts Payable	+	Jessica Jane, Capital	− Jessica Jane, Drawing	+ Revenues	− Expenses	Description
$740 (m) − 650	$30	$80	$200	$3,600		$1,800		$2,000		$1,100	$250 +650	Wages Exp.
$ 90 +	$30 +	$80 +	$200 +	$3,600 =		$1,800	+	$2,000		+ $1,100	− $900	
	$4,000				=			$4,000				

Transaction (n): Deliveries made for cash and on account

An Increase in Two Assets Offset by an Increase in Owner's Equity. Total delivery fees for the remainder of the month amounted to $1,050: $430 in cash and $620 on account. Since all of these delivery fees have been earned, the revenue account increases by $1,050. Also, Cash increases by $430 and Accounts Receivable increases by $620. Thus, revenues increase assets and owner's equity. Note, once again, that one event impacts three accounts while the equation remains in balance.

	Assets (Items Owned)				=	Liabilities (Amounts Owed)	+	Owner's Equity (Owner's Investment + Earnings)				
Cash +	Accounts Receivable +	Supplies +	Prepaid Insurance +	Delivery Equipment =		Accounts Payable	+	Jessica Jane, Capital	− Jessica Jane, Drawing	+ Revenues	− Expenses	Description
$ 90 (n) + 430	$ 30 + 620	$80	$200	$3,600		$1,800		$2,000		$1,100 +1,050	$900	Deliv. Fees
$520 +	$650 +	$80 +	$200 +	$3,600 =		$1,800	+	$2,000		+ $2,150	− $900	
	$5,050				=			$5,050				

Transaction (o): Withdrawal of cash from business

A Decrease in an Asset Offset by a Decrease in Owner's Equity Resulting from a Withdrawal by the Owner. At the end of the month, Jessie took $150 in cash from the business to purchase books for her classes. Since the books are not business related, this is a withdrawal. Withdrawals can be viewed as the opposite of investments by the owner. Both owner's equity and Cash decrease.

Assets (Items Owned)					=	Liabilities (Amounts Owed)	+	Owner's Equity (Owner's Investment + Earnings)					
Cash +	Accounts Receivable +	Supplies +	Prepaid Insurance +	Delivery Equipment =		Accounts Payable +		Jessica Jane, Capital −	Jessica Jane, Drawing +	Revenues −	Expenses	Description	
$ 520	$650	$80	$200	$3,600		$1,800		$2,000		$2,150	$900		
(o) − 150									+$150				
$370 +	$650 +	$80 +	$200 +	$3,600 =		$1,800 +		$2,000 −	$150 +	$2,150 −	$900		
$4,900					=			$4,900					

LEARNING KEY: Withdrawals by the owner are reported in the drawing account. Withdrawals are the opposite of investments by the owner. Recall the business entity concept. The owner of the business and the business are separate economic entities. Thus, personal transactions must not be included with those of the business. If this is allowed, it will be very difficult to evaluate the performance of the business.

Figure 2-1 shows a summary of the transactions. Use this summary to test your understanding of transaction analysis by describing the economic event represented by each transaction. At the bottom of Figure 2-1, the asset accounts and their totals are compared with the liability and owner's equity accounts and their totals.

Trans-action	Cash +	Accounts Receivable +	Supplies +	Prepaid Insurance +	Delivery Equipment =	Accounts Payable +	Jessica Jane, Capital −	Jessica Jane, Drawing +	Revenues −	Expenses	Description
Assets (Items Owned)						**= Liabilities +** (Amounts Owed)	**Owner's Equity** (Owner's Investment + Earnings)				
Balance (a)	2,000						2,000				
Balance (b)	2,000 (1,200)				1,200		2,000				
Balance (c)	800				1,200 900	900	2,000				
Balance (d)	800 (300)				2,100	900 (300)	2,000				
Balance (e)	500 500				2,100	600	2,000		500		Deliv. Fees
Balance (f)	1,000 (200)				2,100	600	2,000		500	200	Rent Exp.
Balance (g)	800 (50)				2,100	600	2,000		500	200 50	Tele. Exp.
Balance (h)	750	600			2,100	600	2,000		500 600	250	Deliv. Fees
Balance (i)	750 (80)	600	80		2,100	600	2,000		1,100	250	
Balance (j)	670 (200)	600	80	200	2,100	600	2,000		1,100	250	
Balance (k)	470 570	600 (570)	80	200	2,100	600	2,000		1,100	250	
Balance (l)	1,040 (300)	30	80	200	2,100 1,500	600 1,200	2,000		1,100	250	
Balance (m)	740 (650)	30	80	200	3,600	1,800	2,000		1,100	250 650	Wages Exp.
Balance (n)	90 430	30 620	80	200	3,600	1,800	2,000		1,100 1,050	900	Deliv. Fees
Balance (o)	520 (150)	650	80	200	3,600	1,800	2,000	150	2,150	900	
Balance	**370 +**	**650 +**	**80 +**	**200 +**	**3,600 =**	**1,800 +**	**2,000 −**	**150 +**	**2,150 −**	**900**	

Cash	$ 370	Accounts Payable	$ 1,800
Accounts Receivable	650	Jessica Jane, Capital	2,000
Supplies	80	Jessica Jane, Drawing	(150)
Prepaid Insurance	200	Delivery Fees	2,150
Delivery Equipment	3,600	Rent Expense	(200)
Total assets	$ 4,900	Telephone Expense	(50)
		Wages Expense	(650)
		Total liabilities and owner's equity	$ 4,900

Amounts in ( ) are subtracted

FIGURE 2-1   Summary of Transactions Illustrated

LEARNING KEY: As with the running totals in the table, the listing immediately below the table provides proof that the accounting equation is in balance.

FINANCIAL STATEMENTS

LO5 Prepare and describe the purposes of a simple income statement, statement of owner's equity, and balance sheet.

Three financial statements commonly prepared by a business entity are the income statement, statement of owner's equity, and balance sheet. The transaction information gathered and summarized in the accounting equation may be used to prepare these financial statements. Figure 2-2 shows the following:

1. A summary of the specific revenue and expense transactions and the ending totals for the asset, liability, capital, and drawing accounts from the accounting equation.

2. The financial statements and their linkages with the accounting equation and each other.

Note that each of the financial statements in Figure 2-2 has a heading consisting of:

HEADING FOR FINANCIAL STATEMENTS	
1. The name of the company	Jessie Jane's Campus Delivery
2. The title of the statement	Income Statement, Statement of Owner's Equity, or Balance Sheet
3. The time period covered or the date of the statement	For Month Ended June 30, 20--, or June 30, 20--

The income statement and statement of owner's equity provide information concerning events covering a period of time, in this case, *the month ended* June 30, 20--. The balance sheet, on the other hand, offers a picture of the business *on a specific date*, June 30, 20--.

The Income Statement

The income statement reports the following:
Revenues   xxx
Expenses   (xx)
Net income   xx

The **income statement**, sometimes called the **profit and loss statement** or **operating statement**, reports the profitability of business operations for a specific period of time. Jessie's income statement shows the revenues earned for the month of June. Next, the expenses incurred as a result of the efforts made to earn these revenues are deducted. If the revenues are greater than the expenses, net income is reported. If the expenses are greater than the revenue, a net loss is reported.

LEARNING KEY:	Income Statement		Income Statement	
	Revenues	$500	Revenues	$500
	Expenses	← 400	Expenses	← 700
	Net income	$100	Net loss	$200

By carefully studying the income statement, it is clear that Jessie earns revenues in only one way: by making deliveries. If other types of services were offered, these revenues would also be identified on the statement. Further, the reader can see the kinds of expenses that were incurred. The reader can make a judgment as to whether these seem reasonable given the amount of revenue earned. Finally, the most important number on the statement is the net income. This is known as the "bottom line."

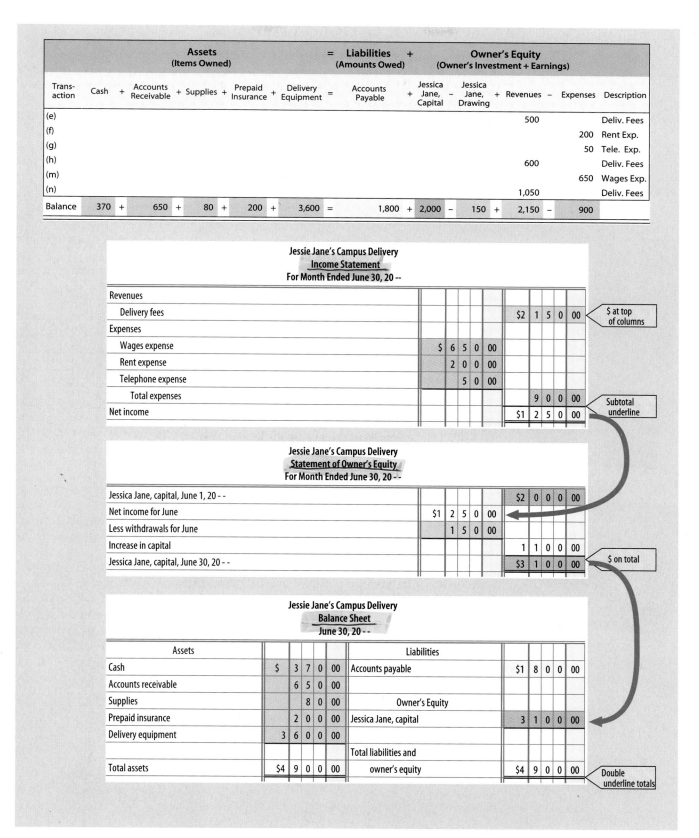

Trans-action	Cash	+	Accounts Receivable	+ Supplies +	Prepaid Insurance	+ Delivery Equipment	=	Accounts Payable	+ Jessica Jane, Capital	– Jessica Jane, Drawing	+ Revenues	– Expenses	Description
(e)											500		Deliv. Fees
(f)												200	Rent Exp.
(g)												50	Tele. Exp.
(h)											600		Deliv. Fees
(m)												650	Wages Exp.
(n)											1,050		Deliv. Fees
Balance	370	+	650	+ 80 +	200	+ 3,600	=	1,800	+ 2,000	– 150	+ 2,150	– 900	

Jessie Jane's Campus Delivery
Income Statement
For Month Ended June 30, 20 --

Revenues			
Delivery fees		$2 1 5 0 00	$ at top of columns
Expenses			
Wages expense	$ 6 5 0 00		
Rent expense	2 0 0 00		
Telephone expense	5 0 00		
Total expenses		9 0 0 00	Subtotal underline
Net income		$1 2 5 0 00	

Jessie Jane's Campus Delivery
Statement of Owner's Equity
For Month Ended June 30, 20 - -

Jessica Jane, capital, June 1, 20 - -		$2 0 0 0 00	
Net income for June	$1 2 5 0 00		
Less withdrawals for June	1 5 0 00		
Increase in capital		1 1 0 0 00	
Jessica Jane, capital, June 30, 20 - -		$3 1 0 0 00	$ on total

Jessie Jane's Campus Delivery
Balance Sheet
June 30, 20 - -

Assets		Liabilities	
Cash	$ 3 7 0 00	Accounts payable	$1 8 0 0 00
Accounts receivable	6 5 0 00		
Supplies	8 0 00	Owner's Equity	
Prepaid insurance	2 0 0 00	Jessica Jane, capital	3 1 0 0 00
Delivery equipment	3 6 0 0 00		
		Total liabilities and	
Total assets	$4 9 0 0 00	owner's equity	$4 9 0 0 00

FIGURE 2-2   **Summary and Financial Statements**

The Statement of Owner's Equity

The **statement of owner's equity** illustrated in Figure 2-2 reports on these activities for the month of June. Jessie started her business with an investment of $2,000. During the month of June she earned $1,250 in net income and withdrew $150 for personal expenses. This resulted in a net increase in Jessie's capital of $1,100. Jessie's $2,000 original investment, plus the net increase of $1,100, results in her ending capital of $3,100.

Note that Jessie's original investment and later withdrawal are taken from the accounting equation. *The net income figure could have been computed from information in the accounting equation. However, it is easier to simply transfer net income as reported on the income statement to the statement of owner's equity.* This is an important linkage between the income statement and statement of owner's equity.

If Jessie had a net loss of $500 for the month, the statement of owner's equity would be prepared as shown in Figure 2-3.

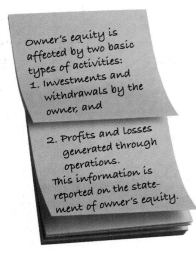

Jessie Jane's Campus Delivery Statement of Owner's Equity For Month Ended June 30, 20 - -														
Jessica Jane, capital, June 1, 20 - -									$2	0	0	0	00
Less: Net loss for June	$	5	0	0	00								
Withdrawals for June		1	5	0	00								
Decrease in capital										6	5	0	00
Jessica Jane, capital, June 30, 20 - -									$1	3	5	0	00

FIGURE 2-3   Statement of Owner's Equity with Net Loss

The Balance Sheet

The **balance sheet** reports a firm's assets, liabilities, and owner's equity on a specific date. It is called a balance sheet because it confirms that the accounting equation has remained in balance. It is also referred to as a **statement of financial position** or **statement of financial condition**.

As illustrated in Figure 2-2, the asset and liability accounts are taken from the accounting equation and reported on the balance sheet. *The total of Jessie's capital account on June 30 could have been computed from the owner's equity accounts in the accounting equation ($2,000 − $150 + $2,150 − $900). However, it is simpler to take the June 30, 20--, capital as computed on the statement of owner's equity and transfer it to the balance sheet.* This is an important linkage between these two statements.

GUIDELINES FOR PREPARING FINANCIAL STATEMENTS

1. Financial statements are prepared primarily for users not associated with the company. To make a good impression and enhance understanding, financial statements must follow a standard form with careful attention to placement, spacing, and indentations.

2. All statements have a heading with the name of the company, name of the statement, and accounting period or date.

3. Single rules (lines) indicate that the numbers above the line have been added or subtracted. Double rules (double underlines) indicate a total.

4. Dollar signs are used at the top of columns and for the first amount entered in a column beneath a ruling.

5. On the income statement, a common practice is to list expenses from highest to lowest dollar amount, with miscellaneous expense listed last.

6. On the balance sheet, assets are listed from most liquid to least liquid. **Liquidity** measures the ease with which the asset will be converted to cash. Liabilities are listed from most current to least current.

Most firms also prepare a statement of cash flows. Given the complexity of this statement, we will postpone its discussion until later in this text.

OVERVIEW OF THE ACCOUNTING PROCESS

LO6 Define the three basic phases of the accounting process.

Figure 2-4 shows the three basic phases of the accounting process in terms of input, processing, and output.

- ■ **Input.** Business transactions provide the necessary **input**.
- ■ **Processing.** Recognizing the effect of these transactions on the assets, liabilities, owner's equity, revenues, and expenses of a business is the **processing** function.
- ■ **Output.** The financial statements are the **output**.

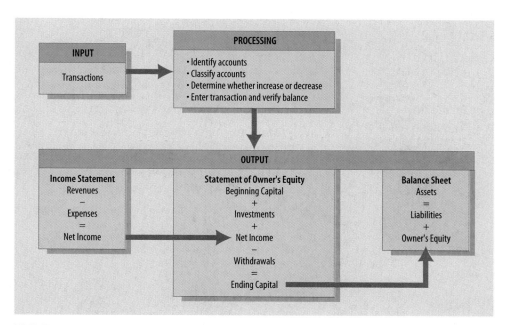

FIGURE 2-4   Input, Processing, and Output

Learning Objectives	Key Points to Remember
1 Define the accounting elements.	The three key accounting elements are assets, liabilities, and owner's equity. Owner's equity is expanded to include revenues, expenses, and drawing.
2 Construct the accounting equation.	The accounting equation is: Assets = Liabilities + Owner's Equity
3 Analyze business transactions.	Three questions must be answered in analyzing business transactions: 1. What happened? 2. Which accounts are affected? 3. How is the accounting equation affected?
4 Show the effects of business transactions on the accounting equation.	Each transaction affects at least two accounts and one or more of the three basic accounting elements. The transactions described in this chapter can be classified into five groups: 1. Increase in an asset offset by an increase in owner's equity. 2. Increase in an asset offset by a decrease in another asset. 3. Increase in an asset offset by an increase in a liability. 4. Decrease in an asset offset by a decrease in a liability. 5. Decrease in an asset offset by a decrease in owner's equity.
5 Prepare and describe the purposes of a simple income statement, statement of owner's equity, and balance sheet.	The purposes of the income statement, statement of owner's equity, and balance sheet can be summarized as follows: **STATEMENT** — **PURPOSE** Income statement — Reports net income or loss; Revenues – Expenses = Net Income or Loss Statement of owner's equity — Shows changes in the owner's capital account; Beginning Capital + Investments + Net Income – Withdrawals = Ending Capital Balance sheet — Verifies balance of accounting equation; Assets = Liabilities + Owner's Equity
6 Define the three basic phases of the accounting process.	The three basic phases of the accounting process are shown below. ▶ **Input**. Business transactions provide the necessary input. ▶ **Processing**. Recognizing the effect of these transactions on the assets, liabilities, owner's equity, revenues, and expenses of a business is the processing function. ▶ **Output**. The financial statements are the output.

Reflection: Answering the Opening Question

1. What happened?

2. Which accounts are affected?

3. How is the accounting equation affected?

KEY TERMS

account, (18)   A separate record used to summarize changes in each asset, liability, and owner's equity of a business.

account payable, (17)   An unwritten promise to pay a supplier for assets purchased or services received.

account receivable, (16)   An amount owed to a business by its customers as a result of the sale of goods or services.

account title, (18)   Provides a description of the particular type of asset, liability, owner's equity, revenue, or expense.

accounting equation, (18)   The accounting equation consists of the three basic accounting elements: assets = liabilities + owner's equity.

accounting period concept, (21)   The concept that income determination can be made on a periodic basis.

asset, (16)   An item that is owned by a business and will provide future benefits.

balance sheet, (30)   Reports assets, liabilities, and owner's equity on a specific date. It is called a balance sheet because it confirms that the accounting equation is in balance.

business entity, (16)   An individual, association, or organization that engages in economic activities and controls specific economic resources.

business entity concept, (17)   The concept that nonbusiness assets and liabilities are not included in the business entity's accounting records.

business transaction, (18)   An economic event that has a direct impact on the business.

capital, (17)   Another term for owner's equity, the amount by which the business assets exceed the business liabilities.

drawing, (21)   Withdrawals that reduce owner's equity as a result of the owner taking cash or other assets out of the business for personal use.

expenses, (20)   The decrease in assets (or increase in liabilities) as a result of efforts to produce revenues.

fiscal year, (21)   Any accounting period of twelve months' duration.

income statement, (28)   Reports the profitability of business operations for a specific period of time.

input, (31)   Business transactions provide the necessary input for the accounting information system.

liability, (16)   Something owed to another business entity.

liquidity, (31)   A measure of the ease with which an asset will be converted to cash.

net income, (21)   The excess of total revenues over total expenses for the period.

net loss, (21)   The excess of total expenses over total revenues for the period.

net worth, (17)   Another term for owner's equity, the amount by which the business assets exceed the business liabilities.

note payable, (17)   A formal written promise to pay a supplier or lender a specified sum of money at a definite future time.

operating statement, (28)   Another name for the income statement, which reports the profitability of business operations for a specific period of time.

output, (31)   The financial statements are the output of the accounting information system.

owner's equity, (17)   The amount by which the business assets exceed the business liabilities.

processing, (31)   Recognizing the effect of transactions on the assets, liabilities, owner's equity, revenues, and expenses of a business.

profit and loss statement, (28)   Another name for the income statement, which reports the profitability of business operations for a specific period of time.

revenues, (20)   The amount a business charges customers for products sold or services performed.

statement of financial condition, (30)   Another name for the balance sheet, which reports assets, liabilities, and owner's equity on a specific date.

statement of financial position, (30)   Another name for the balance sheet, which reports assets, liabilities, and owner's equity on a specific date.

statement of owner's equity, (30)   Reports beginning capital plus net income less withdrawals to compute ending capital.

withdrawals, (21)   Reduce owner's equity as a result of the owner taking cash or other assets out of the business for personal use.

DEMONSTRATION PROBLEM

GENERAL LEDGER
Peachtree

Damon Young has started his own business, Home and Away Inspections. He inspects property for buyers and sellers of real estate. Young rents office space and has a part-time assistant to answer the phone and help with inspections. The transactions for the month of September are as follows:

(a) On the first day of the month, Young invested cash by making a deposit in a bank account for the business, $15,000.

(b) Paid rent for September, $300.

(c) Bought a used truck for cash, $8,000.

(d) Purchased tools on account from Crafty Tools, $3,000.

(e) Paid electricity bill, $50.

(f) Paid two-year premium for liability insurance on truck, $600.

(g) Received cash from clients for services performed, $2,000.

(h) Paid part-time assistant (wages) for first half of month, $200.

(i) Performed inspection services for clients on account, $1,000.

(j) Paid telephone bill, $35.

(k) Bought office supplies costing $300. Paid $100 cash and will pay the balance next month, $200.

(l) Received cash from clients for inspections performed on account in (i), $300.

(m) Paid part-time assistant (wages) for last half of month, $250.

(n) Made partial payment on tools bought in (d), $1,000.

(o) Earned additional revenues amounting to $2,000: $1,400 in cash and $600 on account.

(p) Young withdrew cash at the end of the month for personal expenses, $500.

REQUIRED

1. Enter the transactions in an accounting equation similar to the one illustrated below. After each transaction, show the new amount for each account.

Assets (Items Owned)						=	Liabilities (Amounts Owed)	+	Owner's Equity (Owner's Investment + Earnings)				
Cash +	Accounts Receivable +	Supplies +	Prepaid Insurance +	Tools +	Truck =		Accounts Payable	+	Damon Young, Capital	− Damon Young, Drawing	+ Revenues	− Expenses	Description

2. Compute the ending balances for all accounts.

3. Prepare an income statement for Home and Away Inspections for the month of September 20--.

4. Prepare a statement of owner's equity for Home and Away Inspections for the month of September 20--.

5. Prepare a balance sheet for Home and Away Inspections as of September 30, 20--.

Solution

1, 2.

	Cash +	Accounts Receivable +	Supplies +	Prepaid Insurance +	Tools +	Truck =	Accounts Payable +	Damon Young, Capital −	Damon Young, Drawing +	Revenues −	Expenses	Description
Bal.												
(a)	15,000							15,000				
Bal.	15,000							15,000				
(b)	(300)										300	Rent Exp.
Bal.	14,700							15,000			300	
(c)	(8,000)					8,000						
Bal.	6,700					8,000		15,000			300	
(d)					3,000		3,000					
Bal.	6,700				3,000	8,000	3,000	15,000			300	
(e)	(50)										50	Utilities Exp.
Bal.	6,650				3,000	8,000	3,000	15,000			350	
(f)	(600)			600								
Bal.	6,050			600	3,000	8,000	3,000	15,000			350	
(g)	2,000									2,000		Inspect. Fees
Bal.	8,050			600	3,000	8,000	3,000	15,000		2,000	350	
(h)	(200)										200	Wages Exp.
Bal.	7,850			600	3,000	8,000	3,000	15,000		2,000	550	
(i)		1,000								1,000		Inspect. Fees
Bal.	7,850	1,000		600	3,000	8,000	3,000	15,000		3,000	550	
(j)	(35)										35	Tele. Exp.
Bal.	7,815	1,000		600	3,000	8,000	3,000	15,000		3,000	585	
(k)	(100)		300				200					
Bal.	7,715	1,000	300	600	3,000	8,000	3,200	15,000		3,000	585	
(l)	300	(300)										
Bal.	8,015	700	300	600	3,000	8,000	3,200	15,000		3,000	585	
(m)	(250)										250	Wages Exp.
Bal.	7,765	700	300	600	3,000	8,000	3,200	15,000		3,000	835	
(n)	(1,000)						(1,000)					
Bal.	6,765	700	300	600	3,000	8,000	2,200	15,000		3,000	835	
(o)	1,400	600								2,000		Inspect. Fees
Bal.	8,165	1,300	300	600	3,000	8,000	2,200	15,000		5,000	835	
(p)	(500)								500			
Bal.	7,665 +	1,300 +	300 +	600 +	3,000 +	8,000 =	2,200 +	15,000 −	500 +	5,000 −	835	

3.

Home and Away Inspections Income Statement For Month Ended September 30, 20 --											
Revenues											
Inspection fees							$5	0	0	0	00
Expenses											
Wages expense	$	4	5	0	00						
Rent expense		3	0	0	00						
Utilities expense			5	0	00						
Telephone expense			3	5	00						
Total expenses								8	3	5	00
Net income							$4	1	6	5	00

4.

Home and Away Inspections Statement of Owner's Equity For Month Ended September 30, 20 - -											
Damon Young, capital, September 1, 20 - -							$15	0	0	0	00
Net income for September	$4	1	6	5	00						
Less withdrawals for September		5	0	0	00						
Increase in capital								3	6	6	5	00
Damon Young, capital, September 30, 20 - -							$18	6	6	5	00

5.

Home and Away Inspections Balance Sheet September 30, 20 - -											
Assets						Liabilities					
Cash	$ 7	6	6	5	00	Accounts payable	$ 2	2	0	0	00
Accounts receivable	1	3	0	0	00						
Supplies		3	0	0	00	Owner's Equity					
Prepaid insurance		6	0	0	00	Damon Young, capital	18	6	6	5	00
Tools	3	0	0	0	00						
Truck	8	0	0	0	00	Total liabilities and					
Total assets	$20	8	6	5	00	owner's equity	$20	8	6	5	00

REVIEW QUESTIONS

1. Why is it necessary to distinguish between business assets and liabilities and nonbusiness assets and liabilities of a single proprietor?

2. List the three basic questions that must be answered when analyzing the effects of a business transaction on the accounting equation.

3. Name and define the six major elements of the accounting equation.

4. What is the function of an income statement?

5. What is the function of a statement of owner's equity?

6. What is the function of a balance sheet?

7. What are the three basic phases of the accounting process?

MANAGING YOUR WRITING

Write a brief memo that explains the differences and similarities between expenses and withdrawals.

SERIES A EXERCISES

EXERCISE 2-1A   **(LO1)**   **ACCOUNTING ELEMENTS** Label each of the following accounts as an asset (A), a liability (L), or owner's equity (OE), using the following format.

Item	Account	Classification
Money in bank	Cash	
Office supplies	Supplies	
Money owed	Accounts Payable	
Office chairs	Office Furniture	
Net worth of owner	John Smith, Capital	
Money withdrawn by owner	John Smith, Drawing	
Money owed by customers	Accounts Receivable	

EXERCISE 2-2A   **(LO2)**   **THE ACCOUNTING EQUATION** Using the accounting equation, compute the missing elements.

Assets	=	Liabilities	+	Owner's Equity
_____	=	$24,000	+	$10,000
$25,000	=	$18,000	+	_____
$40,000	=	_____	+	$15,000

EXERCISE 2-3A   (LO3/4)   **EFFECTS OF TRANSACTIONS (BALANCE SHEET ACCOUNTS)** Alice Stern started a business. During the first month (February 20--), the following transactions occurred. Show the effect of each transaction on the accounting equation: *Assets = Liabilities + Owner's Equity.* After each transaction, show the new account totals.

(a) Invested cash in the business, $20,000.

(b) Bought office equipment on account, $3,500.

(c) Bought office equipment for cash, $1,200.

(d) Paid cash on account to supplier in (b), $1,500.

EXERCISE 2-4A   (LO3/4)   **EFFECTS OF TRANSACTIONS (REVENUE, EXPENSE, WITHDRAWALS)** Assume Alice Stern completed the following additional transactions during February. Show the effect of each transaction on the basic elements of the expanded accounting equation: *Assets = Liabilities + Owner's Equity [Capital – Drawing + Revenues – Expenses].* After each transaction show the new account totals.

(e) Received cash from a client for professional services, $2,500.

(f) Paid office rent for February, $900.

(g) Paid February telephone bill, $73.

(h) Withdrew cash for personal use, $500.

(i) Performed services for clients on account, $1,000.

(j) Paid wages to part-time employee, $600.

(k) Received cash for services performed on account in (i), $600.

EXERCISE 2-5A   (LO1/5)   **FINANCIAL STATEMENT ACCOUNTS** Label each of the following accounts as an asset (A), liability (L), owner's equity (OE), revenue (R), or expense (E). Indicate the financial statement on which the account belongs — income statement (IS), statement of owner's equity (SOE), or balance sheet (BS) — in a format similar to the following.

Account	Classification	Financial Statement
Cash		
Rent Expense		
Accounts Payable		
Service Fees		
Supplies		
Wages Expense		
Ramon Martinez, Drawing		
Ramon Martinez, Capital		
Prepaid Insurance		
Accounts Receivable		

EXERCISE 2-6A   **(LO5)**   **STATEMENT OF OWNER'S EQUITY REPORTING NET INCOME** Betsy Ray started an accounting service on June 1, 20--, by investing $20,000. Her net income for the month was $10,000 and she withdrew $8,000. Prepare a statement of owner's equity for the month of June.

EXERCISE 2-7A   **(LO5)**   **STATEMENT OF OWNER'S EQUITY REPORTING NET LOSS** Based on the information provided in Exercise 2-6A, prepare a statement of owner's equity assuming Ray had a net loss of $3,000.

SERIES A PROBLEMS

PROBLEM 2-1A   **(LO1/2)**   **THE ACCOUNTING EQUATION** Dr. John Schleper is a chiropractor. As of December 31, he owned the following property that related to his professional practice:

Cash	$ 4,750
Office Equipment	$ 6,200
X-ray Equipment	$11,680
Laboratory Equipment	$ 7,920

He also owes the following business suppliers:

Chateau Gas Company	$2,420
Aloe Medical Supply Company	$3,740

REQUIRED

1. From the preceding information, compute the accounting elements and enter them in the accounting equation shown as follows.

Assets	=	Liabilities	+	Owner's Equity
_____	=	_____	+	_____

2. During January, the assets increase by $7,290, and the liabilities increase by $4,210. Compute the resulting accounting equation.

3. During February, the assets decrease by $2,920, and the liabilities increase by $2,200. Compute the resulting accounting equation.

PROBLEM 2-2A   **(LO3/4)**   **EFFECT OF TRANSACTIONS ON ACCOUNTING EQUATION** Jay Pembroke started a business. During the first month (April 20--), the following transactions occurred:

(a) Invested cash in business, $18,000.

(b) Bought office supplies for $4,600: $2,000 in cash and $2,600 on account.

(c) Paid one-year insurance premium, $1,200.

(d) Earned revenues totaling $3,300: $1,300 in cash and $2,000 on account.

(e) Paid cash on account to the company that supplied the office supplies in (b), $2,300.

(f) Paid office rent for the month, $750.

(g) Withdrew cash for personal use, $100.

REQUIRED

Show the effect of each transaction on the basic elements of the accounting equation: *Assets = Liabilities + Owner's Equity [Capital – Drawing + Revenues – Expenses]*. After each transaction, show the new account totals.

PROBLEM 2-3A   (LO5)   **INCOME STATEMENT** Based on Problem 2-2A, prepare an income statement for Jay Pembroke for the month of April 20--.

PROBLEM 2-4A   (LO5)   **STATEMENT OF OWNER'S EQUITY** Based on Problem 2-2A, prepare a statement of owner's equity for Jay Pembroke for the month of April 20--.

PROBLEM 2-5A   (LO5)   **BALANCE SHEET** Based on Problem 2-2A, prepare a balance sheet for Jay Pembroke as of April 30, 20--.

SERIES B EXERCISES

EXERCISE 2-1B   (LO1)   **ACCOUNTING ELEMENTS** Label each of the following accounts as an asset (A), liability (L), or owner's equity (OE) using the following format.

Account	Classification
Cash	
Accounts Payable	
Supplies	
Bill Jones, Drawing	
Prepaid Insurance	
Accounts Receivable	
Bill Jones, Capital	

EXERCISE 2-2B   (LO2)   **THE ACCOUNTING EQUATION** Using the accounting equation, compute the missing elements.

Assets	=	Liabilities	+	Owner's Equity
_____	=	$20,000	+	$5,000
$30,000	=	$15,000	+	_____
$20,000	=	_____	+	$10,000

EXERCISE 2-3B   (LO3/4)   **EFFECTS OF TRANSACTIONS (BALANCE SHEET ACCOUNTS)** Jon Wallace started a business. During the first month (March 20--), the following transactions occurred. Show the effect of each transaction on the accounting equation: *Assets = Liabilities + Owner's Equity*. After each transaction, show the new account totals.

(a) Invested cash in the business, $30,000.

(b) Bought office equipment on account, $4,500.

(c) Bought office equipment for cash, $1,600.

(d) Paid cash on account to supplier in (b), $2,000.

EXERCISE 2-4B (LO3/4) **EFFECTS OF TRANSACTIONS (REVENUE, EXPENSE, WITHDRAWALS)** Assume Jon Wallace completed the following additional transactions during March. Show the effect of each transaction on the basic elements of the expanded accounting equation: *Assets = Liabilities + Owner's Equity [Capital – Drawing + Revenues – Expenses]*. After each transaction show the new account totals.

(e) Performed services and received cash, $3,000.

(f) Paid rent for March, $1,000.

(g) Paid March telephone bill, $68.

(h) Jon Wallace withdrew cash for personal use, $800.

(i) Performed services for clients on account, $900.

(j) Paid wages to part-time employee, $500.

(k) Received cash for services performed on account in (i), $500.

EXERCISE 2-5B (LO1/5) **FINANCIAL STATEMENT ACCOUNTS** Label each of the following accounts as an asset (A), liability (L), owner's equity (OE), revenue (R), or expense (E). Indicate the financial statement on which the account belongs—income statement (IS), statement of owner's equity (SOE), or balance sheet (BS)—in a format similar to the following.

Account	Classification	Financial Statement
Cash		
Rent Expense		
Accounts Payable		
Service Fees		
Supplies		
Wages Expense		
Amanda Wong, Drawing		
Amanda Wong, Capital		
Prepaid Insurance		
Accounts Receivable		

EXERCISE 2-6B (LO5) **STATEMENT OF OWNER'S EQUITY REPORTING NET INCOME** Efran Lopez started a financial consulting service on June 1, 20--, by investing $15,000. His net income for the month was $6,000 and he withdrew $7,000 for personal use. Prepare a statement of owner's equity for the month of June.

EXERCISE 2-7B (LO5) **STATEMENT OF OWNER'S EQUITY REPORTING NET LOSS** Based on the information provided in Exercise 2-6B, prepare a statement of owner's equity assuming Lopez had a net loss of $2,000.

SERIES B PROBLEMS

PROBLEM 2-1B   (LO1/2)   **THE ACCOUNTING EQUATION** Dr. Patricia Parsons is a dentist. As of January 31, Parsons owned the following property that related to her professional practice:

Cash	$3,560
Office Equipment	$4,600
X-ray Equipment	$8,760
Laboratory Equipment	$5,940

She also owes the following business suppliers:

Cupples Gas Company	$1,815
Swan Dental Lab	$2,790

REQUIRED

1. From the preceding information, compute the accounting elements and enter them in the accounting equation as shown below.

Assets	=	Liabilities	+	Owner's Equity
_____	=	_____	+	_____

2. During February, the assets increase by $4,565, and the liabilities increase by $3,910. Compute the resulting accounting equation.

3. During March, the assets decrease by $2,190, and the liabilities increase by $1,650. Compute the resulting accounting equation.

PROBLEM 2-2B   (LO3/4)   **EFFECT OF TRANSACTIONS ON ACCOUNTING EQUATION** David Segal

started a business. During the first month (October 20--), the following transactions occurred.

(a) Invested cash in the business, $15,000.

(b) Bought office supplies for $3,800: $1,800 in cash and $2,000 on account.

(c) Paid one-year insurance premium, $1,000.

(d) Earned revenues amounting to $2,700: $1,700 in cash and $1,000 on account.

(e) Paid cash on account to the company that supplied the office supplies in (b), $1,800.

(f) Paid office rent for the month, $650.

(g) Withdrew cash for personal use, $150.

REQUIRED

Show the effect of each transaction on the basic elements of the accounting equation: *Assets = Liabilities + Owner's Equity [Capital – Drawing + Revenues – Expenses]*. After each transaction, show the new account totals.

PROBLEM 2-3B   (LO5)   **INCOME STATEMENT** Based on Problem 2-2B, prepare an income statement for David Segal for the month of October 20--.

PROBLEM 2-4B   (LO5)   **STATEMENT OF OWNER'S EQUITY** Based on Problem 2-2B, prepare a statement of owner's equity for David Segal for the month of October 20--.

PROBLEM 2-5B   (LO5)   **BALANCE SHEET** Based on Problem 2-2B, prepare a balance sheet for David Segal as of October 31, 20--.

CHALLENGE PROBLEM

In this chapter you learned about three important financial statements: the income statement, statement of owner's equity, and balance sheet. As mentioned in the margin note on page 31, most firms also prepare a statement of cash flows. Part of this statement reports the **cash received** from customers, and **cash paid** for goods and services.

REQUIRED

Take another look at the Demonstration Problem for Damon Young's "Home and Away Inspections." Note that when revenues are measured based on the amount earned, and expenses are measured based on the amount incurred, net income for the period was $4,165. Now, compute the difference between cash received from customers and cash paid to suppliers of goods and services by completing the form provided below. Are these measures different? Which provides a better measure of profitability?

Cash from customers   _____

Cash paid for wages   _____

Cash paid for rent   _____

Cash paid for utilities   _____

Cash paid for insurance   _____

Cash paid for supplies   _____

Cash paid for telephone   _____

Total cash paid for operating items   _____

Difference between cash received from
    customers and cash paid for goods
    and services   ========

MASTERY PROBLEM

Lisa Vozniak started her own business, We Do Windows. She offers interior and exterior window cleaning for local area residents. Lisa rents a garage to store her tools and cleaning supplies and has a part-time assistant to answer the phone and handle third-story work. (Lisa is afraid of heights.) The transactions for the month of July are as follows:

(a) On the first day of the month, Vozniak invested cash by making a deposit in a bank account for the business, $8,000.

(b) Paid rent for July, $150.

(c) Purchased a used van for cash, $5,000.

(d) Purchased tools on account from Clean Tools, $600.

(e) Purchased cleaning supplies that cost $300. Paid $200 cash and will pay the balance next month, $100.

(f) Paid part-time assistant (wages) for first half of month, $100.

(g) Paid for advertising, $75.

(h) Paid two-year premium for liability insurance on van, $480.

(i) Received cash from clients for services performed, $800.

(j) Performed cleaning services for clients on account, $500.

(k) Paid telephone bill, $40.

(l) Received cash from clients for window cleaning performed on account in (j), $200.

(m) Paid part-time assistant (wages) for last half of month, $150.

(n) Made partial payment on tools purchased in (d), $200.

(o) Earned additional revenues amounting to $800: $600 in cash and $200 on account.

(p) Vozniak withdrew cash at the end of the month for personal expenses, $100.

REQUIRED

1. Enter the above transactions in an accounting equation similar to the one illustrated below. After each transaction, show the new amount for each account.

Assets (Items Owned)						=	Liabilities (Amounts Owed)	+	Owner's Equity (Owner's Investment + Earnings)				
Cash	+ Accounts Receivable	+ Supplies	+ Prepaid Insurance	+ Tools	+ Van	=	Accounts Payable	+	Lisa Vozniak Capital	− Lisa Vozniak, Drawing	+ Revenues	− Expenses	Description

2. Compute the ending balances for all accounts.

3. Prepare an income statement for We Do Windows for the month of July 20--.

4. Prepare a statement of owner's equity for We Do Windows for the month of July 20--.

5. Prepare a balance sheet for We Do Windows as of July 31, 20--.

Self-Study Test Questions

True/False

1. Assets are items that are owned by the business and are expected to provide future benefits.

2. Accounts Payable is an example of an asset account.

3. According to the business entity concept, nonbusiness assets and liabilities are not included in the business's accounting records.

4. The accounting equation (assets = liabilities + owner's equity) must always be in balance.

5. When an asset increases, a liability must also increase.

6. When total revenues exceed total expenses, the difference is called net loss.

7. Expenses represent outflows of assets or increases in liabilities as a result of efforts to produce revenues.

Multiple Choice

1. An increase to which of these accounts will increase owner's equity?

   (a) Accounts Payable   (c) Client Fees
   (b) Drawing   (d) Rent Expense

2. When delivery revenue is earned in cash, which accounts increase and decrease?

   (a) Cash increases; Revenue increases.
   (b) Cash decreases; Revenue increases.
   (c) Cash decreases; Revenue decreases.
   (d) Cash does not change; owner's equity increases.

3. When delivery revenue is earned on account, which accounts increase and decrease?

   (a) Cash increases; Revenue increases.
   (b) Accounts Receivable increases; Revenue increases.
   (c) Accounts Receivable increases; Revenue decreases.
   (d) Accounts Receivable decreases; Revenue decreases.

4. When payment is made on an existing debt, which accounts increase and decrease?

   (a) Cash increases; Accounts Receivable increases.
   (b) Cash decreases; Accounts Payable increases.
   (c) Cash increases; Accounts Payable increases.
   (d) Cash decreases; Accounts Payable decreases.

5. The process of entering information into the accounting system is called

   (a) analyzing.   (c) classifying.
   (b) recording.   (d) summarizing.

The answers to the Self-Study Test Questions are at the end of the text.

3

The Double-Entry Framework

How do you keep track of your personal finances? Perhaps you make a list of your earnings and other cash inflows. Then you prepare a list of how the money was spent. Jessie needs to do this, too. However, since businesses earn and spend money in many different ways, and enter thousands of transactions, a systematic approach must be followed. This is called the double-entry framework. Could you use this double-entry system for your personal finances, or for a small business that you might start?

Careful study of this chapter should enable you to:

LO1 Define the parts of a T account.

LO2 Foot and balance a T account.

LO3 Describe the effects of debits and credits on specific types of accounts.

LO4 Use T accounts to analyze transactions.

LO5 Prepare a trial balance and explain its purposes and linkages with the financial statements.

The terms asset, liability, owner's equity, revenue, and expense were explained in Chapter 2. Examples showed how individual business transactions change one or more of these basic accounting elements. Each transaction had a dual effect. An increase or decrease in any asset, liability, owner's equity, revenue, or expense was *always* accompanied by an offsetting change within the basic accounting elements. The fact that each transaction has a dual effect upon the accounting elements provides the basis for what is called **double-entry accounting.** To understand double-entry accounting, it is important to learn how T accounts work and the role of debits and credits in accounting.

THE T ACCOUNT

LO1 Define the parts of a T account.

The assets of a business may consist of a number of items, such as cash, accounts receivable, equipment, buildings, and land. The liabilities may consist of one or more items, such as accounts payable and notes payable. Similarly, owner's equity may consist of the owner's investments and various revenue and expense items. A separate account is used to record the increases and decreases in each type of asset, liability, owner's equity, revenue, and expense.

The T account gets its name from the fact that it resembles the letter T. As shown below, there are three major parts of an account:

1. the title,

2. the debit, or left side, and

3. the credit, or right side.

Title	
Debit = Left	Credit = Right

The debit side is always on the left and the credit side is always on the right. This is true for all types of asset, liability, owner's equity, revenue, and expense accounts.

 LEARNING KEY: Debit means left and credit means right.

BALANCING A T ACCOUNT

LO2 Foot and balance a T account.

To determine the balance of a T account at any time, simply total the dollar amounts on the debit and credit sides. These totals are known as **footings.** The difference between the footings is called the **balance** of the account. This amount is then written on the side with the larger footing.

In Chapter 2, the accounting equation was used to analyze business transactions. This required columns in which to record the increases and decreases in various accounts. Let's compare this approach with the use of a T account for the transactions affecting cash. When a T account is used, increases in cash are recorded on the debit side and decreases are recorded on the credit side. Transactions for Jessie Jane's Campus Delivery are shown in Figure 3-1.

COLUMNAR SUMMARY (From Chapter 2, page 27)		T ACCOUNT FORM				
				Cash		
Transaction	Cash	(a)	2,000	(b)	1,200	
(a)	2,000	(e)	500	(d)	300	
(b)	(1,200)	(k)	570	(f)	200	
(d)	(300)	(n)	430	(g)	50	
(e)	500	footing →	**3,500**	(i)	80	
(f)	(200)			(j)	200	
(g)	(50)			(l)	300	
(i)	(80)			(m)	650	
(j)	(200)			(o)	150	
(k)	570	Balance →	370		**3,130** ← footing	
(l)	(300)					
(m)	(650)					
(n)	430					
(o)	(150)					
Balance	370					

FIGURE 3-1   Cash T Account

DEBITS AND CREDITS

LO3 Describe the effects of debits and credits on specific types of accounts.

Abbreviations:
Often debit and credit are abbreviated as:
Dr. = Debit
Cr. = Credit
(based on the Latin terms "debere" and "credere")

To **debit** an account means to enter an amount on the left or debit side of the account. To **credit** an account means to enter an amount on the right or credit side of the account. *Debits may increase or decrease the balances of specific accounts. This is also true for credits. To learn how to use debits and credits, it is best to reflect on the accounting equation.*

Assets		=	Liabilities		+	Owner's Equity	
Debit	**Credit**		**Debit**	**Credit**		**Debit**	**Credit**
+	–		–	+		–	+

← memorize →

Assets

Assets are on the left side of the accounting equation. Therefore, increases are entered on the left (debit) side of an asset account and decreases are entered on the right (credit) side.

Liabilities and Owner's Equity

Liabilities and owner's equity are on the right side of the equation. Therefore, increases are entered on the right (credit) side and decreases are entered on the left (debit) side.

LEARNING KEY: Debits increase assets and decrease liabilities and owner's equity. Credits decrease assets and increase liabilities and owner's equity.

Normal Balances

A **normal balance** is the side of an account that is increased. Since assets are debited for increases, these accounts normally have **debit balances**. Since liability and owner's equity accounts are credited for increases, these accounts normally have **credit balances**. Figure 3-2 shows the relationship between normal balances and debits and credits.

ACCOUNT	SIDE OF ACCOUNTING EQUATION	INCREASE	DECREASE	NORMAL BALANCE
Assets	Left	Debit	Credit	Debit
Liabilities	Right	Credit	Debit	Credit
Owner's Equity	Right	Credit	Debit	Credit

FIGURE 3-2 **Normal Balances**

Expanding the accounting equation helps illustrate the use of debits and credits for revenue, expense, and drawing accounts. Since these accounts affect owner's equity, they are shown under the "umbrella" of owner's equity in the accounting equation in Figure 3-3.

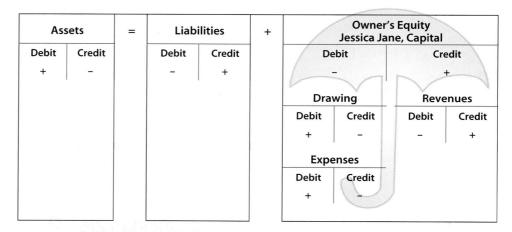

FIGURE 3-3 **The Accounting Equation and the Owner's Equity Umbrella**

Revenues

Revenues increase owner's equity. Revenues could be recorded directly on the credit side of the owner's capital account. However, readers of financial statements are interested in the specific types of revenues earned. Therefore, specific revenue accounts, like Delivery Fees, Sales, and Service Fees, are used. These specific accounts are credited when revenue is earned.

Expenses

Expenses decrease owner's equity. Expenses could be recorded on the debit side of the owner's capital account. However, readers of financial statements want to see the types of expenses incurred during the accounting period. Thus, specific expense accounts are maintained for items like rent, wages, advertising, and utilities. These specific accounts are debited as expenses are incurred.

LEARNING KEY: You could credit the owner's capital account for revenues and debit the capital account for expenses and withdrawals. However, this is not a good idea. Using specific accounts provides additional information. Remember: an increase in an expense decreases owner's equity.

Drawing

Withdrawals of cash and other assets by the owner for personal reasons decrease owner's equity. Withdrawals could be debited directly to the owner's capital account. However, readers of financial statements want to know the amount of withdrawals for the accounting period. Thus, this information is kept in a separate account.

Normal Balances for the Owner's Equity Umbrella

Since expense and drawing accounts are debited for increases, these accounts normally have debit balances. Since revenue accounts are credited for increases, these accounts normally have credit balances. Figure 3-4 shows the normal balances for the owner's equity accounts.

ACCOUNT	SIDE OF OWNER'S EQUITY UMBRELLA	INCREASE	DECREASE	NORMAL
Revenues	Right	Credit	Debit	Credit
Expenses	Left	Debit	Credit	Debit
Drawing	Left	Debit	Credit	Debit

FIGURE 3-4   **Normal Balances for the Owner's Equity Umbrella**

TRANSACTION ANALYSIS

LO4 Use T accounts to analyze transactions.

In Chapter 2, you learned how to analyze transactions by using the accounting equation. Here, we continue to use the accounting equation, but add debits and credits by using T accounts. As shown in Figure 3-5, the three basic questions that must be answered when analyzing a transaction are essentially the same, but are expanded slightly to address the use of the owner's equity umbrella and T accounts. You must determine the location of the account within the accounting equation and/or the owner's equity umbrella. You must also determine whether the accounts should be debited or credited.

---

1. **What happened?**
   Make certain you understand the event that has taken place.

2. **Which accounts are affected?**
   Once you have determined what happened, you must:
   ■ Identify the accounts that are affected.
   ■ Classify these accounts as assets, liabilities, owner's equity, revenues, or expenses.
   ■ Identify the location of the accounts in the accounting equation and/or the owner's equity umbrella—left or right.

3. **How is the accounting equation affected?**
   ■ Determine whether the accounts have increased or decreased.
   ■ Determine whether the accounts should be debited or credited.
   ■ Make certain that the accounting equation remains in balance after the transaction has been entered.
   (1) Assets = Liabilities + Owner's Equity.
   (2) Debits = Credits for every transaction.

FIGURE 3-5 Steps in Transaction Analysis

LEARNING KEY: If you have a debit, you must always have at least one credit. If you have a credit, you must always have at least one debit.

Debits and Credits: Asset, Liability, and Owner's Equity Accounts

Transactions (a) through (d) from Jessie Jane's Campus Delivery (Chapter 2) demonstrate the double-entry process for transactions affecting asset, liability, and owner's equity accounts.

As you study each transaction, answer the three questions: (1) What happened? (2) Which accounts are affected? and (3) How is the accounting equation affected? The transaction statement tells you what happened. The analysis following the illustration of each transaction tells which accounts are affected. The illustration shows you how the accounting equation is affected.

Transaction (a): Investment by owner
Jessica Jane opened a bank account with a deposit of $2,000 for her business (Figure 3-6).

Analysis: As a result of this transaction, the business acquired an asset, Cash. In exchange for the asset, the business gave Jessica Jane owner's equity. The owner's equity account is called Jessica Jane, Capital. The transaction is entered as an increase in an asset and an increase in owner's equity. Debit Cash and credit Jessica Jane, Capital for $2,000.

Assets		=	Liabilities		+	Owner's Equity	
Debit	**Credit**		**Debit**	**Credit**		**Debit**	**Credit**
+	–		–	+		–	+
Cash						*Jessica Jane, Capital*	
(a) 2,000							(a) 2,000
$2,000		**=**				**$2,000**	

ACCOUNT AFFECTED	CLASSIFICATION	LOCATION IN EQUATION	INCREASE OR DECREASE	DEBIT OR CREDIT
Cash	Asset	Left	Increase	Debit
Capital	Owner's Equity	Right	Increase	Credit

FIGURE 3-6   **Transaction (a): Investment by Owner**

Transaction (b): Purchase of an asset for cash
Jessie bought a motor scooter (delivery equipment) for $1,200 cash (Figure 3-7).

Analysis: Jessie exchanged one asset, Cash, for another, Delivery Equipment. Debit Delivery Equipment and credit Cash for $1,200. Notice that the total assets are still $2,000 as they were following transaction (a). Transaction (b) shifted assets from cash to delivery equipment, but total assets remained the same.

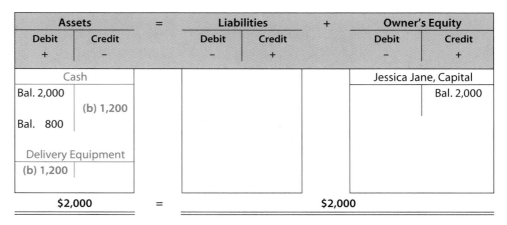

Assets		=	Liabilities		+	Owner's Equity	
Debit	**Credit**		**Debit**	**Credit**		**Debit**	**Credit**
+	–		–	+		–	+
Cash						*Jessica Jane, Capital*	
Bal. 2,000							Bal. 2,000
	(b) 1,200						
Bal. 800							
Delivery Equipment							
(b) 1,200							
$2,000		**=**				**$2,000**	

ACCOUNT AFFECTED	CLASSIFICATION	LOCATION IN EQUATION	INCREASE OR DECREASE	DEBIT OR CREDIT
Delivery Equipment	Asset	Left	Increase	Debit
Cash	Asset	Left	Decrease	Credit

FIGURE 3-7   **Transaction (b): Purchase of an Asset for Cash**

Transaction (c): Purchase of an asset on account
Jessie bought a second motor scooter on account for $900 (Figure 3-8).

Analysis: The asset, Delivery Equipment, increases by $900 and the liability, Accounts Payable, increases by the same amount. Thus, debit Delivery Equipment and credit Accounts Payable for $900.

Assets		=	Liabilities		+	Owner's Equity	
Debit	**Credit**		**Debit**	**Credit**		**Debit**	**Credit**
+	−		−	+		−	+
Cash			Accounts Payable			Jessica Jane, Capital	
Bal. 800				(c) 900			Bal. 2,000
Delivery Equipment							
Bal. 1,200							
(c) 900							
Bal. 2,100							
$2,900		=		$2,900			

ACCOUNT AFFECTED	CLASSIFICATION	LOCATION IN EQUATION	INCREASE OR DECREASE	DEBIT OR CREDIT
Delivery Equipment	Asset	Left	Increase	Debit
Accounts Payable	Liability	Right	Increase	Credit

FIGURE 3-8   Transaction (c): Purchase of an Asset on Account

Transaction (d): Payment on a loan
Jessie made the first $300 payment on the scooter purchased in transaction (c) (Figure 3-9).

Analysis: This payment decreases the asset, Cash, and decreases the liability, Accounts Payable. Debit Accounts Payable and credit Cash for $300.

Assets		=	Liabilities		+	Owner's Equity	
Debit	**Credit**		**Debit**	**Credit**		**Debit**	**Credit**
+	−		−	+		−	+
Cash			Accounts Payable			Jessica Jane, Capital	
Bal. 800				Bal. 900			Bal. 2,000
	(d) 300		(d) 300				
Bal. 500				Bal. 600			
Delivery Equipment							
Bal. 2,100							
$2,600		=		$2,600			

ACCOUNT AFFECTED	CLASSIFICATION	LOCATION IN EQUATION	INCREASE OR DECREASE	DEBIT OR CREDIT
Accounts Payable	Liability	Right	Decrease	Debit
Cash	Asset	Left	Decrease	Credit

FIGURE 3-9   **Transaction (d): Payment on a Loan**

Notice that for transactions (a) through (d), the debits equal credits and the accounting equation is in balance. Review transactions (a) through (d). Again, identify the accounts that were affected and how they were classified (assets, liabilities, or owner's equity). Finally, note each account's location within the accounting equation.

Debits and Credits: Including Revenues, Expenses, and Drawing

Transactions (a) through (d) involved only assets, liabilities, and the owner's capital account. To complete the illustration of Jessie Jane's Campus Delivery, the equation is expanded to include revenues, expenses, and drawing. Remember, revenues increase owner's equity and are shown under the credit side of the capital account. Expenses and drawing decrease owner's equity and are shown under the debit side of the capital account. The expanded equation is shown in Figure 3-10.

LEARNING KEY: Credits increase the capital account. Revenues increase capital. Thus, revenues are shown under the credit side of the capital account. Debits decrease the capital account. Expenses and drawing reduce owner's equity. Thus, they are shown under the debit side of the capital account.

Assets		=	Liabilities		+	Owner's Equity (Jessica Jane, Capital)			
Debit	Credit		Debit	Credit		Debit		Credit	
+	–		–	+		–		+	

Drawing		Expenses		Revenues	
Debit	Credit	Debit	Credit	Debit	Credit
+	–	+	–	–	+

FIGURE 3-10   **The Expanded Accounting Equation**

Transaction (e): Delivery revenues earned in cash
Jessie made deliveries and received $500 cash from clients (Figure 3-11).

Analysis: The asset, Cash, and the revenue, Delivery Fees, increase. Debit Cash and credit Delivery Fees for $500.

Assets		=	Liabilities		+	Owner's Equity		
Debit	Credit		Debit	Credit		Debit	Credit	
+	–		–	+		–	+	

Cash			Accounts Payable	
Bal. 500				Bal. 600
(e) 500				
Bal. 1,000				

Jessica Jane, Capital	
	Bal. 2,000

Delivery Equipment	
Bal. 2,100	

Drawing		Expenses		Revenues	
Debit	Credit	Debit	Credit	Debit	Credit
+	–	+	–	–	+

	Delivery Fees	
		(e) 500

$3,100 =	**$3,100**

ACCOUNT AFFECTED	CLASSIFICATION	LOCATION IN EQUATION	INCREASE OR DECREASE	DEBIT OR CREDIT
Cash	Asset	Left	Increase	Debit
Delivery Fees	Revenue	Right O.E.—Right Side	Increase	Credit

FIGURE 3-11 Transaction (e): Delivery Revenues Earned in Cash

Transaction (f): Paid rent for month
Jessie paid $200 for office rent for June (Figure 3-12).

Analysis: Rent Expense increases and Cash decreases. Debit Rent Expense and credit Cash for $200.

A debit to an expense account increases that expense and decreases owner's equity. Notice that the placement of the plus and minus signs for expenses are opposite the placement of the signs for owner's equity. Note also that expenses are located on the left (debit) side of the owner's equity umbrella.

Assets		=	Liabilities		+	Owner's Equity		
Debit	Credit		Debit	Credit		Debit	Credit	
+	–		–	+		–	+	

Cash			Accounts Payable	
Bal. 1,000				Bal. 600
	(f) 200			
Bal. 800				

Jessica Jane, Capital	
	Bal. 2,000

Delivery Equipment	
Bal. 2,100	

Drawing		Expenses		Revenues	
Debit	Credit	Debit	Credit	Debit	Credit
+	–	+	–	–	+

Rent Expense		Delivery Fees	
(f) 200			Bal. 500

$2,900 =	**$2,900**

ACCOUNT AFFECTED	CLASSIFICATION	LOCATION IN EQUATION	INCREASE OR DECREASE	DEBIT OR CREDIT
Rent Expense	Expense	Right O.E.—Left Side	Exp.— Increases; O.E.— Decreases	Debit
Cash	Asset	Left	Decrease	Credit

FIGURE 3-12   **Transaction (f): Paid Rent for Month**

Transaction (g): Paid telephone bill
Jessie paid for telephone service, $50 (Figure 3-13).

Analysis: This transaction, like the previous one, increases an expense and decreases an asset. Debit Telephone Expense and credit Cash for $50.

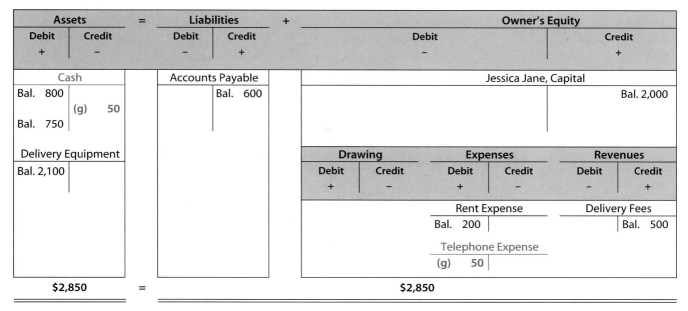

ACCOUNT AFFECTED	CLASSIFICATION	LOCATION IN EQUATION	INCREASE OR DECREASE	DEBIT OR CREDIT
Tele. Expense	Expense	Right O.E.—Left Side	Exp.— Increases; O.E.— Decreases	Debit
Cash	Asset	Left	Decrease	Credit

FIGURE 3-13 **Transaction (g): Paid Telephone Bill**

Transaction (h): Delivery revenues earned on account
Jessie made deliveries on account for $600 (Figure 3-14).

Analysis: As discussed in Chapter 2, delivery services are performed for which payment will be received later. This is called offering services "on account" or "on credit." Instead of receiving cash, Jessie receives a promise that her customers will pay cash in the future. Therefore, the asset, Accounts Receivable, increases. Since revenues are recognized when earned, the revenue account, Delivery Fees, also increases. Debit Accounts Receivable and credit Delivery Fees for $600.

Assets		=	Liabilities		+	Owner's Equity			
Debit +	Credit −		Debit −	Credit +		Debit −		Credit +	

Cash		Accounts Payable		Jessica Jane, Capital	
Bal. 750			Bal. 600		Bal. 2,000

Accounts Receivable	
(h) 600	

Drawing		Expenses		Revenues	
Debit +	Credit −	Debit +	Credit −	Debit −	Credit +

Delivery Equipment	
Bal. 2,100	

Rent Expense		Delivery Fees	
Bal. 200			Bal. 500
			(h) 600
			Bal. 1,100

Telephone Expense	
Bal. 50	

$3,450 = **$3,450**

ACCOUNT AFFECTED	CLASSIFICATION	LOCATION IN EQUATION	INCREASE OR DECREASE	DEBIT OR CREDIT
Accounts Rec.	Asset	Left	Increase	Debit
Delivery Fees	Revenue	Right O.E.—Right Side	Increase	Credit

FIGURE 3-14   Transaction (h): Delivery Revenues Earned on Account

Review transactions (e) through (h). Two of these transactions are expenses and two are revenue transactions. Each of these transactions affected the owner's equity umbrella. Three transactions affected Cash and one transaction affected Accounts Receivable. Keep in mind that expense and revenue transactions do not always affect cash.

Notice that the debits equal credits and the accounting equation is in balance after each transaction. As you review transactions (e) through (h), identify the accounts that were affected and classify each account (assets, liabilities, owner's equity, revenue, or expense). Notice each account's location within the accounting equation and the owner's equity umbrella.

Upcoming transactions (i) and (j) both involve an exchange of cash for another asset. As you analyze these two transactions and answer the three questions about these transactions, you may wonder why prepaid insurance and supplies are assets while the rent and telephone bill in transactions (f) and (g) are expenses. Prepaid insurance and supplies are assets because they will last for more than one month. Jessie pays her rent and her telephone bill each month so they are classified as expenses. If Jessie paid her rent only once every three months, she would need to set up an asset account called Prepaid Rent. She would debit this account when she paid the rent.

Transaction (i): Purchase of supplies

Jessie bought pens, paper, delivery envelopes, and other supplies for $80 cash (Figure 3-15).

Analysis: These supplies will last for several months. Since they will generate future benefits, the supplies should be recorded as an asset. An asset, Supplies, increases, and an asset, Cash, decreases. Debit Supplies and credit Cash for $80.

Assets		=	Liabilities		+	Owner's Equity	
Debit +	Credit −		Debit −	Credit +		Debit −	Credit +

Cash
Bal. 750
(i) 80
Bal. 670

Accounts Receivable
Bal. 600

Supplies
(i) 80

Delivery Equipment
Bal. 2,100

Accounts Payable
Bal. 600

Jessica Jane, Capital
Bal. 2,000

	Drawing		Expenses		Revenues	
	Debit +	Credit −	Debit +	Credit −	Debit −	Credit +

Rent Expense
Bal. 200

Delivery Fees
Bal. 1,100

Telephone Expense
Bal. 50

$3,450   = $3,450

ACCOUNT AFFECTED	CLASSIFICATION	LOCATION IN EQUATION	INCREASE OR DECREASE	DEBIT OR CREDIT
Supplies	Asset	Left	Increase	Debit
Cash	Asset	Left	Decrease	Credit

FIGURE 3-15   Transaction (i): Purchase of Supplies

A BROADER VIEW

Supplies—Asset or Expense?

When businesses buy office supplies from Staples or other suppliers, the supplies are initially recorded as assets. This is done because the supplies will provide future benefits. Those still remaining at the end of the accounting period are reported on the balance sheet as assets. Supplies actually used during the period are recognized as an expense on the income statement. We will discuss how to account for the expense in Chapter 5.

PROFILES IN ACCOUNTING
Jeanette Anderson, Factory Accounting Clerk

Jeanette Anderson earned a 4.0 GPA and membership in Phi Theta Kappa while completing her Associate Degree in Business at Eastern Wyoming College. While on campus, she held a work-study job as an Instructor Assistant. In this position Jeanette demonstrated a sound work ethic, an ability to get along well with others, and competence.

After graduation, she went to work for Imperial/Holly Sugar Corp. in Torrington, WY. Her duties include working with automated accounts payable, accounts receivable, and inventory control. During the annual harvest campaign, she supervises data entry clerks.

Jeanette believes the key to her success has been her understanding of double-entry accounting combined with her computer skills. Possessing problem-solving skills and being flexible are also important.

Source: Jack Kappeler, Eastern Wyoming College

Transaction (j): Payment of insurance premium
Jessie paid $200 for an eight-month liability insurance policy (Figure 3-16).

Analysis: Since insurance is paid in advance and will provide future benefits, it is treated as an asset. Therefore, one asset, Prepaid Insurance, increases and another, Cash, decreases. Debit Prepaid Insurance and credit Cash for $200.

Assets		=	Liabilities		+	Owner's Equity	
Debit	Credit		Debit	Credit		Debit	Credit
+	−		−	+		−	+

Cash		Accounts Payable		Jessica Jane, Capital	
Bal. 670			Bal. 600		Bal. 2,000
	(j) 200				
Bal. 470					

Accounts Receivable	
Bal. 600	

Supplies	
Bal. 80	

Prepaid Insurance	
(j) 200	

Delivery Equipment	
Bal. 2,100	

Drawing		Expenses		Revenues	
Debit	Credit	Debit	Credit	Debit	Credit
+	−	+	−	−	+

		Rent Expense		Delivery Fees	
		Bal. 200		Bal. 1,100	

		Telephone Expense	
		Bal. 50	

$3,450 = $3,450

ACCOUNT AFFECTED	CLASSIFICATION	LOCATION IN EQUATION	INCREASE OR DECREASE	DEBIT OR CREDIT
Prepaid Insurance	Asset	Left	Increase	Debit
Cash	Asset	Left	Decrease	Credit

FIGURE 3-16   **Transaction (j): Payment of Insurance Premium**

Transaction (k): Cash receipts from prior sales on account
Jessie received $570 in cash for delivery services performed for customers earlier in the month (see transaction (h)) (Figure 3-17).

Analysis: This transaction increases Cash and reduces the amount due from customers reported in Accounts Receivable. Debit Cash and credit Accounts Receivable $570.

As you analyze transaction (k), notice which accounts are affected and the location of these accounts in the accounting equation. Jessie received cash, but this transaction did not affect revenue. The revenue was recorded in transaction (h). Transaction (k) is an exchange of one asset (Accounts Receivable) for another asset (Cash).

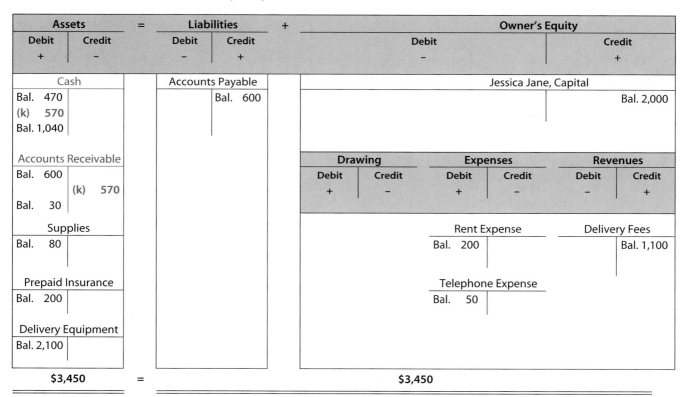

ACCOUNT AFFECTED	CLASSIFICATION	LOCATION IN EQUATION	INCREASE OR DECREASE	DEBIT OR CREDIT
Cash	Asset	Left	Increase	Debit
Accounts Rec.	Asset	Left	Decrease	Credit

FIGURE 3-17   **Transaction (k): Cash Receipts from Prior Sales on Account**

As you analyze transactions (l) through (o), make certain that you understand what has happened in each transaction. Identify the accounts that are affected and the locations of these accounts within the accounting equation. Notice that the accounting equation remains in balance after every transaction and debits equal credits for each transaction.

Transaction (l): Purchase of an asset on credit making a partial payment
Jessie bought a third motor scooter for $1,500. Jessie made a down payment of $300 and spread the remaining payments over the next four months (Figure 3-18).

Analysis: The asset, Delivery Equipment, increases by $1,500, Cash decreases by $300, and the liability, Accounts Payable, increases by $1,200. Thus, debit Delivery Equipment for $1,500, credit Cash for $300, and credit Accounts Payable for $1,200. This transaction requires one debit and two credits. Even so, total debits ($1,500) equal the total credits ($1,200 + $300) and the accounting equation remains in balance.

Assets		=	Liabilities		+	Owner's Equity		
Debit +	Credit –		Debit –	Credit +		Debit –		Credit +

Cash		Accounts Payable		Jessica Jane, Capital	
Bal. 1,040	(l) 300		Bal. 600		Bal. 2,000
Bal. 740			(l) 1,200		
			Bal. 1,800		

Accounts Receivable	
Bal. 30	

Drawing		Expenses		Revenues	
Debit +	Credit –	Debit +	Credit –	Debit –	Credit +

Supplies	
Bal. 80	

Rent Expense		Delivery Fees	
Bal. 200		Bal. 1,100	

Prepaid Insurance	
Bal. 200	

Telephone Expense	
Bal. 50	

Delivery Equipment	
Bal. 2,100	
(l) 1,500	
Bal. 3,600	

$4,650 = $4,650

ACCOUNT AFFECTED	CLASSIFICATION	LOCATION IN EQUATION	INCREASE OR DECREASE	DEBIT OR CREDIT
Delivery Equip.	Asset	Left	Increase	Debit
Cash	Asset	Left	Decrease	Credit
Accounts Payable	Liability	Right	Increase	Credit

FIGURE 3-18 Transaction (l): Purchase of an Asset on Credit Making a Partial Payment

Transaction (m): Payment of wages
Jessie paid her part-time employees $650 in wages (Figure 3-19).

Analysis: This is an additional business expense. Wages Expense increases and Cash decreases. Debit Wages Expense and credit Cash for $650.

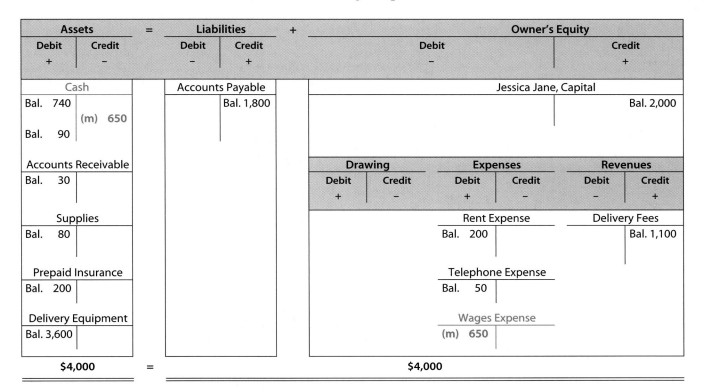

ACCOUNT AFFECTED	CLASSIFICATION	LOCATION IN EQUATION	INCREASE OR DECREASE	DEBIT OR CREDIT
Wages Expense	Expense	Right O.E.— Left Side	Exp.— Increases; O.E.— Decreases	Debit
Cash	Asset	Left	Decrease	Credit

FIGURE 3-19   Transaction (m): Payment of Wages

Transaction (n): Deliveries made for cash and credit
Total delivery fees for the remainder of the month amounted to $1,050: $430 in cash and $620 on account (Figure 3-20).

Analysis: Since the delivery fees have been earned, the revenue account increases by $1,050. Also, Cash increases by $430 and Accounts Receivable increases by $620. Note once again that one event impacts three accounts. This time we have debits of $430 to Cash and $620 to Accounts Receivable, and a credit of $1,050 to Delivery Fees. As before, the total debits ($430 + $620) equal the total credits ($1,050) and the accounting equation remains in balance.

Assets		=	Liabilities		+	Owner's Equity	
Debit +	Credit −		Debit −	Credit +		Debit −	Credit +

Cash		**Accounts Payable**		**Jessica Jane, Capital**	
Bal. 90			Bal. 1,800		Bal. 2,000
(n) 430					
Bal. 520					

Accounts Receivable	
Bal. 30	
(n) 620	
Bal. 650	

Drawing		**Expenses**		**Revenues**	
Debit +	Credit −	Debit +	Credit −	Debit −	Credit +

Supplies	
Bal. 80	

Rent Expense		**Delivery Fees**	
Bal. 200			Bal. 1,100
			(n) 1,050
			Bal. 2,150

Prepaid Insurance	
Bal. 200	

Telephone Expense	
Bal. 50	

Delivery Equipment	
Bal. 3,600	

Wages Expense	
Bal. 650	

$5,050   = $5,050

ACCOUNT AFFECTED	CLASSIFICATION	LOCATION IN EQUATION	INCREASE OR DECREASE	DEBIT OR CREDIT
Cash	Asset	Left	Increase	Debit
Accounts Rec.	Asset	Left	Increase	Debit
Delivery Fees	Revenue	Right O.E.—Right Side	Increase	Credit

FIGURE 3-20   **Transaction (n): Deliveries Made for Cash and Credit**

Transaction (o): Withdrawal of cash from business
At the end of the month, Jessie withdrew $150 in cash from the business to purchase books for her classes (Figure 3-21).

Analysis: Cash withdrawals decrease owner's equity and decrease cash. Debit Jessica Jane, Drawing and credit Cash for $150.

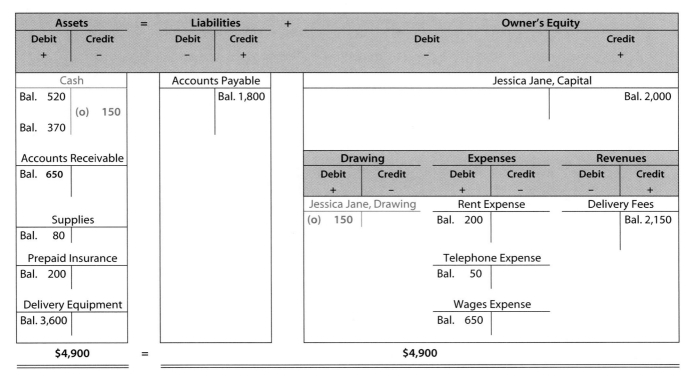

ACCOUNT AFFECTED	CLASSIFICATION	LOCATION IN EQUATION	INCREASE OR DECREASE	DEBIT OR CREDIT
Drawing	Drawing	Right O.E.— Left Side	Drawing— Increases; O.E.— Decreases	Debit
Cash	Asset	Left	Decrease	Credit

FIGURE 3-21 Transaction (o): Withdrawal of Cash from Business

Withdrawals are reported in the drawing account. Withdrawals by an owner are the opposite of an investment. You could debit the owner's capital account for withdrawals. However, using a specific account tells the user of the accounting information how much was withdrawn for the period.

Summary of Transactions

In illustrating transactions (a) through (o), each T account for Jessie Jane's Campus Delivery shows a balance before and after each transaction. To focus your attention on the transaction being explained, only a single entry was shown. In practice, this is not done. Instead, each account gathers all transactions for a period. Jessie's accounts, with all transactions listed, are shown in Figure 3-22. Note the following:

1. The footings are directly under the debit (left) and credit (right) sides of the T account for those accounts with more than one debit or credit.

2. The balance is shown on the side with the larger footing.

3. The footing serves as the balance for accounts with entries on only one side of the account.

4. If an account has only a single entry, it is not necessary to enter a footing or balance.

Assets		=	Liabilities		+	Owner's Equity	
Debit	**Credit**		**Debit**	**Credit**		**Debit**	**Credit**
+	−		−	+		−	+

Cash

(a)	2,000	(b)	1,200
(e)	500	(d)	300
(k)	570	(f)	200
(n)	430	(g)	50
	3,500	(i)	80
		(j)	200
		(l)	300
		(m)	650
		(o)	150
			3,130
Bal.	370		

Accounts Receivable

(h)	600	(k)	570
(n)	620		
	1,220		
Bal.	650		

Supplies

(i)	80	

Prepaid Insurance

(j)	200	

Delivery Equipment

(b)	1,200	
(c)	900	
(l)	1,500	
Bal.	3,600	

Accounts Payable

(d)	300	(c)	900
		(l)	1,200
			2,100
		Bal.	1,800

Jessica Jane, Capital

		(a)	2,000

Drawing		Expenses		Revenues	
Debit	**Credit**	**Debit**	**Credit**	**Debit**	**Credit**
+	−	+	−	−	+

Jessica Jane, Drawing

(o)	150	

Rent Expense

(f)	200	

Delivery Fees

		(e)	500
		(h)	600
		(n)	1,050
		Bal.	2,150

Telephone Expense

(g)	50	

Wages Expense

(m)	650	

$4,900	=	$4,900

FIGURE 3-22   **Summary of Transactions (a) Through (o)**

THE TRIAL BALANCE

LO5 Prepare a trial balance and explain its purposes and linkages with the financial statements.

Recall the two very important rules in double-entry accounting:

1. The sum of the debits must equal the sum of the credits. This means that at least two accounts are affected by each transaction. This rule is so important that many computer accounting programs will not permit a transaction to be entered into the accounting system unless the debits equal the credits.

2. The accounting equation must remain in balance.

In illustrating the transactions for Jessie Jane's Campus Delivery, the equality of the accounting equation was verified after each transaction. Because of the large number of transactions entered each day, this is not done in practice. Instead, a trial balance is prepared periodically to determine the equality of the debits and credits. A **trial balance** is a list of all accounts showing the title and balance of each account. By totaling the debits and credits, their equality can be tested.

A trial balance of Jessie's accounts, taken on June 30, 20--, is shown in Figure 3-23. This date is shown on the third line of the heading. The trial balance shows that the debit and credit totals are equal in amount. This is proof that (1) in entering transactions (a) through (o), the total of the debits was equal to the total of the credits, and (2) the accounting equation has remained in balance.

 LEARNING KEY: A trial balance provides proof that total debits equal total credits and shows that the accounting equation is in balance.

A trial balance is not a formal statement or report. Normally, only the accountant sees it. As shown in Figure 3-24, a trial balance can be used as an aid in preparing the financial statements.

Since a trial balance is not a formal statement, dollar signs are not used.

Jessie Jane's Campus Delivery																
Trial Balance																
June 30, 20 - -																
ACCOUNT TITLE					DEBIT BALANCE						CREDIT BALANCE					
Cash						3	7	0	00							
Accounts Receivable						6	5	0	00							
Supplies							8	0	00							
Prepaid Insurance						2	0	0	00							
Delivery Equipment					3	6	0	0	00							
Accounts Payable											1	8	0	0	00	
Jessica Jane, Capital											2	0	0	0	00	
Jessica Jane, Drawing						1	5	0	00							
Delivery Fees											2	1	5	0	00	
Rent Expense						2	0	0	00							
Telephone Expense							5	0	00							
Wages Expense						6	5	0	00							
					5	9	5	0	00		5	9	5	0	00	

FIGURE 3-23 Trial Balance

Jessie Jane's Campus Delivery
Trial Balance
June 30, 20 - -

ACCOUNT TITLE	DEBIT BALANCE	CREDIT BALANCE
Cash	3 7 0 00	
Accounts Receivable	6 5 0 00	
Supplies	8 0 00	
Prepaid Insurance	2 0 0 00	
Delivery Equipment	3 6 0 0 00	
Accounts Payable		1 8 0 0 00
Jessica Jane, Capital		2 0 0 0 00
Jessica Jane, Drawing	1 5 0 00	
Delivery Fees		2 1 5 0 00
Rent Expense	2 0 0 00	
Telephone Expense	5 0 00	
Wages Expense	6 5 0 00	
	5 9 5 0 00	5 9 5 0 00

Jessie Jane's Campus Delivery
Income Statement
For Month Ended June 30, 20 --

Revenue:		
Delivery fees		$2 1 5 0 00
Expenses:		
Wages expense	$ 6 5 0 00	
Rent expense	2 0 0 00	
Telephone expense	5 0 00	
Total expenses		9 0 0 00
Net income		$1 2 5 0 00

Jessie Jane's Campus Delivery
Statement of Owner's Equity
For Month Ended June 30, 20 - -

Jessica Jane, capital, June 1, 20 - -		$2 0 0 0 00
Net income for June	$1 2 5 0 00	
Less withdrawals for June	1 5 0 00	
Increase in capital		1 1 0 0 00
Jessica Jane, capital, June 30, 20 - -		$3 1 0 0 00

Jessie Jane's Campus Delivery
Balance Sheet
June 30, 20 - -

Assets		Liabilities	
Cash	$ 3 7 0 00	Accounts payable	$1 8 0 0 00
Accounts receivable	6 5 0 00		
Supplies	8 0 00	Owner's Equity	
Prepaid insurance	2 0 0 00	Jessica Jane, capital	3 1 0 0 00
Delivery equipment	3 6 0 0 00		
		Total liabilities and	
Total assets	$4 9 0 0 00	owner's equity	$4 9 0 0 00

FIGURE 3-24 Linkages Between the Trial Balance and Financial Statements

Learning Objectives	Key Points to Remember
1 Define the parts of a T account.	The parts of a T account are: 1. the title, 2. the debit or left side, and 3. the credit or right side. **Title** Debit = Left | Credit = Right
2 Foot and balance a T account.	Rules for footing and balancing T accounts are: 1. The footings are directly under the debit (left) and credit (right) sides of the T account for those accounts with more than one debit or credit. 2. The balance is shown on the side with the larger footing. 3. The footing serves as the balance for accounts with entries on only one side of the account. 4. If an account has only a single entry, it is not necessary to enter a footing or balance.
3 Describe the effects of debits and credits on specific types of accounts.	Rules for debits and credits. (See illustration below.) 1. Assets are on the left side of the accounting equation. Therefore, increases are entered on the left (debit) side of an asset account and decreases are entered on the right (credit) side. 2. Liabilities and owner's equity are on the right side of the accounting equation. Therefore, increases are entered on the right (credit) side and decreases are entered on the left (debit) side. 3. Revenues are on the right side of the owner's equity umbrella. Therefore, increases are entered on the right (credit) side and decreases are entered on the left (debit) side. 4. Expenses and drawing are on the left side of the owner's equity umbrella. Therefore, increases are entered on the left (debit) side and decreases are entered on the right (credit) side. **Accounting Equation with Owner's Equity Umbrella**
4 Use T accounts to analyze transactions.	Picture the accounting equation in your mind as you analyze transactions. When entering transactions in T accounts: 1. The sum of the debits must equal the sum of the credits. 2. At least two accounts are affected by each transaction. 3. When finished, the accounting equation must remain in balance.
5 Prepare a trial balance and explain its purposes and linkages with the financial statements.	A trial balance shows that the debit and credit totals are equal. A trial balance also can be used in preparing the financial statements.

Reflection: Answering the Opening Question

The beauty of the double-entry system illustrated in this chapter is that it can be used for businesses of all kinds (service, merchandising, and manufacturing), ownership interests (proprietorship, partnership, corporation), and sizes, including your own personal finances.

KEY TERMS

balance, (48)   The difference between the footings of an account.

credit, (49)   To enter an amount on the right side of an account.

credit balance, (50)   The normal balance of liability, owner's equity, and revenue accounts.

debit, (49)   To enter an amount on the left side of an account.

debit balance, (50)   The normal balance of asset, expense, and drawing accounts.

double-entry accounting, (48)   A system in which each transaction has a dual effect on the accounting elements.

footings, (48)   The total dollar amounts on the debit and credit sides of an account.

normal balance, (50)   The side of an account that is increased.

trial balance, (67)   A list of accounts, showing the title and balance of each account, used to prove that the debits equal the credits in the general ledger.

DEMONSTRATION PROBLEM

Celia Pints opened We-Buy, You-Pay Shopping Services. For a fee that is based on the amount of research and shopping time required, Pints and her associates will shop for almost anything from groceries to home furnishings. Business is particularly heavy around Christmas and in early summer. The business operates from a rented store front. The associates receive a commission based on the revenues they produce and a mileage reimbursement for the use of their personal automobiles for shopping trips. Pints decided to use the following accounts to record transactions:

Assets
    Cash
    Accounts Receivable
    Office Equipment
    Computer Equipment
Liabilities
    Accounts Payable
    Notes Payable

Owner's Equity
    Celia Pints, Capital
    Celia Pints, Drawing
Revenue
    Shopping Fees
Expenses
    Rent Expense
    Telephone Expense
    Commissions Expense
    Utilities Expense
    Travel Expense

The following transactions are for the month of December 20--.

(a) Pints invested cash in the business, $30,000.

(b) Bought office equipment for $10,000. Paid $2,000 in cash and promised to pay the balance over the next four months.

(c) Paid rent for December, $500.

(d) Provided shopping services for customers on account, $5,200.

(e) Paid telephone bill, $90.

(f) Borrowed cash from the bank by signing a note payable, $5,000.

(g) Bought a computer and printer, $4,800.

(h) Collected cash from customers for services performed on account, $4,000.

(i) Paid commissions to associates for revenues generated during the first half of the month, $3,500.

(j) Paid utility bill, $600.

(k) Paid cash on account for the office equipment purchased in transaction (b), $2,000.

(l) Earned shopping fees of $13,200: $6,000 in cash and $7,200 on account.

(m) Paid commissions to associates for last half of month, $7,000.

(n) Paid mileage reimbursements for the month, $1,500.

(o) Paid cash on note payable to bank, $1,000.

(p) Pints withdrew cash for personal use, $2,000.

REQUIRED

1. Enter the transactions for December in T accounts. Use the accounting equation as a guide for setting up the T accounts.

2. Foot the T accounts and determine their balances as necessary.

3. Prepare a trial balance of the accounts as of December 31 of the current year.

4. Prepare an income statement for the month ended December 31 of the current year.

5. Prepare a statement of owner's equity for the month ended December 31 of the current year.

6. Prepare a balance sheet as of December 31 of the current year.

Solution

1, 2.

Assets	=	Liabilities	+	Owner's Equity	
Debit / Credit		Debit / Credit		Debit	Credit
+ / −		− / +		−	+

Cash

(a) 30,000	(b) 2,000
(f) 5,000	(c) 500
(h) 4,000	(e) 90
(l) 6,000	(g) 4,800
45,000	(i) 3,500
	(j) 600
	(k) 2,000
	(m) 7,000
	(n) 1,500
	(o) 1,000
	(p) 2,000
	24,990
Bal. 20,010	

Accounts Receivable

(d) 5,200	(h) 4,000
(l) 7,200	
12,400	
Bal. 8,400	

Office Equipment

(b) 10,000	

Computer Equipment

(g) 4,800	

Accounts Payable

(k) 2,000	(b) 8,000
	Bal. 6,000

Notes Payable

(o) 1,000	(f) 5,000
	Bal. 4,000

Celia Pints, Capital

	(a) 30,000

Drawing		Expenses		Revenues	
Debit	Credit	Debit	Credit	Debit	Credit
+	−	+	−	−	+

Celia Pints, Drawing

(p) 2,000	

Rent Expense

(c) 500	

Shopping Fees

	(d) 5,200
	(l) 13,200
	Bal. 18,400

Telephone Expense

(e) 90	

Commissions Expense

(i) 3,500	
(m) 7,000	
Bal. 10,500	

Utilities Expense

(j) 600	

Travel Expense

(n) 1,500	

$43,210 = $43,210

3.

We-Buy, You-Pay Shopping Services Trial Balance December 31, 20 - -										
ACCOUNT TITLE	DEBIT BALANCE					CREDIT BALANCE				
Cash	20	0	1	0	00					
Accounts Receivable	8	4	0	0	00					
Office Equipment	10	0	0	0	00					
Computer Equipment	4	8	0	0	00					
Accounts Payable						6	0	0	0	00
Notes Payable						4	0	0	0	00
Celia Pints, Capital						30	0	0	0	00
Celia Pints, Drawing	2	0	0	0	00					
Shopping Fees						18	4	0	0	00
Rent Expense		5	0	0	00					
Telephone Expense			9	0	00					
Commissions Expense	10	5	0	0	00					
Utilities Expense		6	0	0	00					
Travel Expense	1	5	0	0	00					
	58	4	0	0	00	58	4	0	0	00

4.

We-Buy, You-Pay Shopping Services Income Statement For Month Ended December 31, 20 - -										
Revenue:										
Shopping fees						$18	4	0	0	00
Expenses:										
Commissions expense	$10	5	0	0	00					
Travel expense	1	5	0	0	00					
Utilities expense		6	0	0	00					
Rent expense		5	0	0	00					
Telephone expense			9	0	00					
Total expenses						13	1	9	0	00
Net income						$ 5	2	1	0	00

5.

We-Buy, You-Pay Shopping Services Statement of Owner's Equity For Month Ended December 31, 20 - -										
Celia Pints, capital, December 1, 20 - -						$30	0	0	0	00
Net income for December	$5	2	1	0	00					
Less withdrawals for December	2	0	0	0	00					
Increase in capital						3	2	1	0	00
Celia Pints, capital, December 31, 20 - -						$33	2	1	0	00

(continued)

6.

We-Buy, You-Pay Shopping Services										
Balance Sheet										
December 31, 20 - -										
Assets						Liabilities					
Cash	$ 20	0	1	0	00	Accounts payable	$ 6	0	0	0	00
Accounts receivable	8	4	0	0	00	Notes payable	4	0	0	0	00
Office equipment	10	0	0	0	00	Total liabilities	$10	0	0	0	00
Computer equipment	4	8	0	0	00						
						Owner's Equity					
						Celia Pints, capital	33	2	1	0	00
						Total liabilities and					
Total assets	$43	2	1	0	00	owner's equity	$43	2	1	0	00

REVIEW QUESTIONS

1. What are the three major parts of a T account?

2. What is the left side of the T account called? the right side?

3. What is a footing?

4. What is the relationship between the revenue and expense accounts and the owner's equity account?

5. What is the function of the trial balance?

MANAGING YOUR WRITING

Write a one-page memo to your instructor explaining how you could use the double-entry system to maintain records of your personal finances. What types of accounts would you use for the accounting elements?

SERIES A EXERCISES

EXERCISE 3-1A   (LO2)   **FOOT AND BALANCE A T ACCOUNT** Foot and balance the cash T account shown.

Cash	
500	100
400	200
600	

EXERCISE 3-2A   (LO3)   **DEBIT AND CREDIT ANALYSIS** Complete the following questions using either "debit" or "credit."

(a) The cash account is increased with a _____ .

(b) The owner's capital account is increased with a _____ .

(c) The delivery equipment account is increased with a _____ .

(d) The cash account is decreased with a _____.

(e) The liability account Accounts Payable is increased with a _____.

(f) The revenue account Delivery Fees is increased with a _____.

(g) The asset account Accounts Receivable is increased with a _____.

(h) The rent expense account is increased with a _____.

(i) The owner's drawing account is increased with a _____.

EXERCISE 3-3A   **(LO2/3/4)**   **ANALYSIS OF T ACCOUNTS** Jim Arnold began a business called Arnold's Shoe Repair.

1. Create T accounts for Cash; Supplies; Jim Arnold, Capital; and Utilities Expense. Identify the following transactions by letter and place them on the proper side of the T accounts.

    (a) Arnold invested cash in the business, $5,000.

    (b) Purchased supplies for cash, $800.

    (c) Paid utility bill, $1,500.

2. Foot the T account for cash and enter the ending balance.

EXERCISE 3-4A   **(LO3)**   **NORMAL BALANCE OF ACCOUNT** Indicate the normal balance (debit or credit) for each of the following accounts.

1. Cash

2. Wages Expense

3. Accounts Payable

4. Owner's Drawing

5. Supplies

6. Owner's Capital

7. Equipment

EXERCISE 3-5A   **(LO4)**   **TRANSACTION ANALYSIS** Sheryl Hansen started a business on May 1, 20--. Analyze the following transactions for the first month of business using T accounts. Label each T account with the title of the account affected and then place the transaction letter and the dollar amount on the debit or credit side.

(a) Hansen invested cash in the business, $4,000.

(b) Bought equipment for cash, $500.

(c) Bought equipment on account, $800.

(d) Paid cash on account for equipment purchased in transaction (c), $300.

(e) Hansen withdrew cash for personal use, $700.

EXERCISE 3-6A   **(LO2)**   **FOOT AND BALANCE A T ACCOUNT** Foot and balance the cash T account prepared in Exercise 3-5A.

EXERCISE 3-7A   (LO2/4)   **ANALYSIS OF TRANSACTIONS** Charles Chadwick opened a business called Charlie's Detective Service in January 20--. Set up T accounts for the following accounts: Cash; Accounts Receivable; Office Supplies; Computer Equipment; Office Furniture; Accounts Payable; Charles Chadwick, Capital; Charles Chadwick, Drawing; Professional Fees; Rent Expense; and Utilities Expense.

The following transactions occurred during the first month of business. Record these transactions in T accounts. After all transactions are recorded, foot and balance the accounts if necessary.

(a) Chadwick invested cash in the business, $30,000.

(b) Bought office supplies for cash, $300.

(c) Bought office furniture for cash, $5,000.

(d) Purchased computer and printer on account, $8,000.

(e) Received cash from clients for services, $3,000.

(f) Paid cash on account for computer and printer purchased in transaction (d), $4,000.

(g) Earned professional fees on account during the month, $9,000.

(h) Paid cash for office rent for January, $1,500.

(i) Paid utility bills for the month, $800.

(j) Received cash from clients billed in transaction (g), $6,000.

(k) Chadwick withdrew cash for personal use, $3,000.

EXERCISE 3-8A   (LO5)   **TRIAL BALANCE** Based on the transactions recorded in Exercise 3-7A, prepare a trial balance for Charlie's Detective Service as of January 31, 20--.

EXERCISE 3-9A   (LO5)   **TRIAL BALANCE** The following accounts have normal balances. Prepare a trial balance for Juanita's Delivery Service as of September 30, 20--.

Cash	$ 5,000
Accounts Receivable	3,000
Supplies	800
Prepaid Insurance	600
Delivery Equipment	8,000
Accounts Payable	2,000
Juanita Raye, Capital	10,000
Juanita Raye, Drawing	1,000
Delivery Fees	9,400
Wages Expense	2,100
Rent Expense	900

EXERCISE 3-10A   (LO5)   **INCOME STATEMENT** From the information in Exercise 3-9A, prepare an income statement for Juanita's Delivery Service for the month ended September 30, 20--.

EXERCISE 3-11A   (LO5)   **STATEMENT OF OWNER'S EQUITY** From the information in Exercise 3-9A, prepare a statement of owner's equity for Juanita's Delivery Service for the month ended September 30, 20--.

EXERCISE 3-12A   (LO5)   **BALANCE SHEET** From the information in Exercise 3-9A, prepare a balance sheet for Juanita's Delivery Service as of September 30, 20--.

SERIES A PROBLEMS

PROBLEM 3-1A　(LO2/4/5)　**T ACCOUNTS AND TRIAL BALANCE** Harold Long started a business in May 20-- called Harold's Home Repair. Long hired a part-time college student as an assistant. Long has decided to use the following accounts for recording transactions:

Assets	Owner's Equity
Cash	Harold Long, Capital
Accounts Receivable	Harold Long, Drawing
Office Supplies	Revenue
Prepaid Insurance	Service Fees
Equipment	Expenses
Van	Rent Expense
Liabilities	Wages Expense
Accounts Payable	Telephone Expense
	Gas and Oil Expense

The following transactions occurred during May:

(a) Long invested cash in the business, $20,000.

(b) Purchased a used van for cash, $7,000.

(c) Purchased equipment on account, $5,000.

(d) Received cash for services rendered, $6,000.

(e) Paid cash on account owed from transaction (c), $2,000.

(f) Paid rent for the month, $900.

(g) Paid telephone bill, $200.

(h) Earned revenue on account, $4,000.

(i) Purchased office supplies for cash, $120.

(j) Paid wages to student, $600.

(k) Purchased insurance, $1,200.

(l) Received cash from services performed in transaction (h), $3,000.

(m) Paid cash for gas and oil expense on the van, $160.

(n) Purchased additional equipment for $3,000, paying $1,000 cash and spreading the remaining payments over the next 10 months.

(o) Service fees earned for the remainder of the month amounted to $3,200: $1,800 in cash and $1,400 on account.

(p) Long withdrew cash at the end of the month, $2,800.

REQUIRED

1. Enter the transactions in T accounts, identifying each transaction with its corresponding letter.

2. Foot and balance the accounts where necessary.

3. Prepare a trial balance as of May 31, 20--.

PROBLEM 3-2A (LO5) **NET INCOME AND CHANGE IN OWNER'S EQUITY** Refer to the trial balance of Harold's Home Repair in Problem 3-1A to determine the following information. Use the format provided below.

1. a.   Total revenue for the month   _____

    b.   Total expenses for the month   _____

    c.   Net income for the month   _____

2. a.   Harold Long's original investment   _____
         in the business

         + the net income for the month   _____

         – owner's drawing   _____

         Increase (decrease) in capital   _____

         = ending owner's equity   _____

    b.   End of month accounting equation:

Assets	=	Liabilities	+	Owner's Equity
_____	=	_____	+	_____

PROBLEM 3-3A (LO5) **FINANCIAL STATEMENTS** Refer to the trial balance in Problem 3-1A and to the analysis of the change in owner's equity in Problem 3-2A.

REQUIRED

1. Prepare an income statement for Harold's Home Repair for the month ended May 31, 20--.

2. Prepare a statement of owner's equity for Harold's Home Repair for the month ended May 31, 20--.

3. Prepare a balance sheet for Harold's Home Repair as of May 31, 20--.

SERIES B EXERCISES

EXERCISE 3-1B (LO2) **FOOT AND BALANCE A T ACCOUNT** Foot and balance the accounts payable T account shown.

Accounts Payable	
300	450
250	350
	150

EXERCISE 3-2B (LO3) **DEBIT AND CREDIT ANALYSIS** Complete the following questions using either "debit" or "credit."

(a) The asset account Prepaid Insurance is increased with a _____ .

(b) The owner's drawing account is increased with a _____ .

(c) The asset account Accounts Receivable is decreased with a _____ .

(d) The liability account Accounts Payable is decreased with a _____ .

(e) The owner's capital account is increased with a _____ .

(f) The revenue account Professional Fees is increased with a _____ .

(g) The expense account Repair Expense is increased with a _____ .

(h) The asset account Cash is decreased with a _____ .

(i) The asset account Delivery Equipment is decreased with a _____ .

EXERCISE 3-3B   (LO2/3/4)   **ANALYSIS OF T ACCOUNTS** Roberto Alvarez began a business called Roberto's Fix-It Shop.

1. Create T accounts for Cash; Supplies; Roberto Alvarez, Capital; and Utilities Expense. Identify the following transactions by letter and place them on the proper side of the T accounts.

    (a) Alvarez invested cash in the business, $6,000.

    (b) Purchased supplies for cash, $1,200.

    (c) Paid utility bill, $900.

2. Foot the T account for cash and enter the ending balance.

EXERCISE 3-4B   (LO3)   **NORMAL BALANCE OF ACCOUNT** Indicate the normal balance (debit or credit) for each of the following accounts.

1. Cash

2. Rent Expense

3. Notes Payable

4. Owner's Drawing

5. Accounts Receivable

6. Owner's Capital

7. Tools

EXERCISE 3-5B   (LO4)   **TRANSACTION ANALYSIS** George Atlas started a business on June 1, 20--. Analyze the following transactions for the first month of business using T accounts. Label each T account with the title of the account affected and then place the transaction letter and the dollar amount on the debit or credit side.

(a) Atlas invested cash in the business, $7,000.

(b) Purchased equipment for cash, $900.

(c) Purchased equipment on account, $1,500.

(d) Paid cash on account for equipment purchased in transaction (c), $800.

(e) Atlas withdrew cash for personal use, $1,100.

EXERCISE 3-6B   (LO2)   **FOOT AND BALANCE A T ACCOUNT** Foot and balance the cash T account prepared in Exercise 3-5B.

EXERCISE 3-7B   (LO2/4)   **ANALYSIS OF TRANSACTIONS** Nicole Lawrence opened a business called Nickie's Neat Ideas in January 20--. Set up T accounts for the following accounts: Cash; Accounts Receivable; Office Supplies; Computer Equipment; Office Furniture; Accounts Payable; Nicole Lawrence, Capital; Nicole Lawrence, Drawing; Professional Fees; Rent Expense; and Utilities Expense.

(continued)

The following transactions occurred during the first month of business. Record these transactions in T accounts. After all transactions have been recorded, foot and balance the accounts if necessary.

(a) Lawrence invested cash in the business, $18,000.

(b) Purchased office supplies for cash, $500.

(c) Purchased office furniture for cash, $8,000.

(d) Purchased computer and printer on account, $5,000.

(e) Received cash from clients for services, $4,000.

(f) Paid cash on account for computer and printer purchased in transaction (d), $2,000.

(g) Earned professional fees on account during the month, $7,000.

(h) Paid office rent for January, $900.

(i) Paid utility bills for the month, $600.

(j) Received cash from clients that were billed previously in transaction (g), $3,000.

(k) Lawrence withdrew cash for personal use, $4,000.

EXERCISE 3-8B **(LO5)** **TRIAL BALANCE** Based on the transactions recorded in Exercise 3-7B, prepare a trial balance for Nickie's Neat Ideas as of January 31, 20--.

EXERCISE 3-9B **(LO5)** **TRIAL BALANCE** The following accounts have normal balances. Prepare a trial balance for Bill's Delivery Service as of September 30, 20--.

Cash	$ 7,000
Accounts Receivable	4,000
Supplies	600
Prepaid Insurance	900
Delivery Equipment	9,000
Accounts Payable	3,000
Bill Swift, Capital	12,000
Bill Swift, Drawing	2,000
Delivery Fees	12,500
Wages Expense	3,000
Rent Expense	1,000

EXERCISE 3-10B **(LO5)** **INCOME STATEMENT** From the information in Exercise 3-9B, prepare an income statement for Bill's Delivery Service for the month ended September 30, 20--.

EXERCISE 3-11B **(LO5)** **STATEMENT OF OWNER'S EQUITY** From the information in Exercise 3-9B, prepare a statement of owner's equity for Bill's Delivery Service for the month ended September 30, 20--.

EXERCISE 3-12B **(LO5)** **BALANCE SHEET** From the information in Exercise 3-9B, prepare a balance sheet for Bill's Delivery Service as of September 30, 20--.

SERIES B PROBLEMS

PROBLEM 3-1B   (LO2/4/5)   **T ACCOUNTS AND TRIAL BALANCE** Sue Jantz started a business in August 20-- called Jantz Plumbing Service. Jantz hired a part-time college student as an administrative assistant. Jantz has decided to use the following accounts:

Assets	Owner's Equity
Cash	Sue Jantz, Capital
Accounts Receivable	Sue Jantz, Drawing
Office Supplies	Revenue
Prepaid Insurance	Service Fees
Plumbing Equipment	Expenses
Van	Rent Expense
Liabilities	Wages Expense
Accounts Payable	Telephone Expense
	Advertising Expense

The following transactions occurred during August:

(a) Jantz invested cash in the business, $30,000.

(b) Purchased a used van for cash, $8,000.

(c) Purchased plumbing equipment on account, $4,000.

(d) Received cash for services rendered, $3,000.

(e) Paid cash on account owed from transaction (c), $1,000.

(f) Paid rent for the month, $700.

(g) Paid telephone bill, $100.

(h) Earned revenue on account, $4,000.

(i) Purchased office supplies for cash, $300.

(j) Paid wages to student, $500.

(k) Purchased insurance, $800.

(l) Received cash from services performed in transaction (h), $3,000.

(m) Paid cash for advertising expense, $2,000.

(n) Purchased additional plumbing equipment for $2,000, paying $500 cash and spreading the remaining payments over the next six months.

(o) Revenue earned from services for the remainder of the month amounted to $2,800: $1,100 in cash and $1,700 on account.

(p) Jantz withdrew cash at the end of the month, $3,000.

REQUIRED

1. Enter the transactions in T accounts, identifying each transaction with its corresponding letter.

2. Foot and balance the accounts where necessary.

3. Prepare a trial balance as of August 31, 20--.

PROBLEM 3-2B   **(LO5)**   **NET INCOME AND CHANGE IN OWNER'S EQUITY** Refer to the trial balance of Jantz Plumbing Service in Problem 3-1B to determine the following information. Use the format provided below.

1.   a.   Total revenue for the month   _____

     b.   Total expenses for the month   _____

     c.   Net income for the month   _____

2.   a.   Sue Jantz's original investment   _____
         in the business

           + the net income for the month   _____

           – owner's drawing   _____

           Increase (decrease) in capital   _____

           = ending owner's equity   _____

     b.   End of month accounting equation:

Assets	=	Liabilities	+	Owner's Equity
_____	=	_____	+	_____

PROBLEM 3-3B   **(LO5)**   **FINANCIAL STATEMENTS** Refer to the trial balance in Problem 3-1B and to the analysis of the change in owner's equity in Problem 3-2B.

REQUIRED

1. Prepare an income statement for Jantz Plumbing Service for the month ended August 31, 20--.

2. Prepare a statement of owner's equity for Jantz Plumbing Service for the month ended August 31, 20--.

3. Prepare a balance sheet for Jantz Plumbing Service as of August 31, 20--.

CHALLENGE PROBLEM

Your friend, Chris Stevick, started a part-time business in June and has been keeping her own accounting records. She has been preparing monthly financial statements. At the end of August, she stopped by to show you her performance for the most recent month. She prepared the following income statement and balance sheet.

Income Statement		Balance	End of	Beginning
Revenues	$500	Sheet	Month	of Month
Expenses	200	Cash	$600	$400
Net Income	$300	Capital	$600	$400

Chris has also heard that there is a statement of owner's equity, but is not familiar with that statement. She asks if you can help her prepare one. After confirming that she has no assets other than cash, no liabilities, and made no additional investments in the business in August, you agree.

REQUIRED

1. Prepare the statement of owner's equity for your friend's most recent month.

2. What suggestions might you make to Chris that would make her income statement more useful?

MASTERY PROBLEM

Craig Fisher started a lawn service called Craig's Quick Cut to earn money over the summer months. Fisher has decided to use the following accounts for recording transactions:

Assets
- Cash
- Accounts Receivable
- Mowing Equipment
- Lawn Tools

Liabilities
- Accounts Payable
- Notes Payable

Owner's Equity
- Craig Fisher, Capital
- Craig Fisher, Drawing

Revenue
- Lawn Fees

Expenses
- Rent Expense
- Wages Expense
- Telephone Expense
- Gas and Oil Expense
- Transportation Expense

Transactions for the month of June are listed below.

(a) Fisher invested cash in the business, $3,000.

(b) Bought mowing equipment for $1,000: paid $200 in cash and promised to pay the balance over the next four months.

(c) Paid garage rent for June, $50.

(d) Provided lawn services for customers on account, $520.

(e) Paid telephone bill, $30.

(f) Borrowed cash from the bank by signing a note payable, $500.

(g) Bought lawn tools, $480.

(h) Collected cash from customers for services performed on account in transaction (d), $400.

(i) Paid associates for lawn work done during the first half of the month, $350.

(j) Paid for gas and oil for the equipment, $60.

(k) Paid cash on account for the mowing equipment purchased in transaction (b), $200.

(l) Earned lawn fees of $1,320: $600 in cash and $720 on account.

(m) Paid associates for last half of month, $700.

(n) Reimbursed associates for expenses associated with using their own vehicles for transportation, $150.

(o) Paid on note payable to bank, $100.

(p) Fisher withdrew cash for personal use, $200.

(continued)

REQUIRED

1. Enter the transactions for June in T accounts. Use the accounting equation as a guide for setting up the T accounts.

2. Foot and balance the T accounts where necessary.

3. Prepare a trial balance of the accounts as of June 30, 20--.

4. Prepare an income statement for the month ended June 30, 20--.

5. Prepare a statement of owner's equity for the month ended June 30, 20--.

6. Prepare a balance sheet as of June 30, 20--.

Self-Study Test Questions

True/False

1. To debit an account is to enter an amount on the left side of the account.

2. Liability accounts normally have debit balances.

3. Increases in owner's equity are entered as credits.

4. Revenue accounts normally have debit balances.

5. To credit an account is to enter an amount on the right side of the account.

6. A debit to an asset account will decrease it.

Multiple Choice

1. A common example of an asset is

   (a) Professional Fees.
   (b) Rent Expense.
   (c) Accounts Receivable.
   (d) Accounts Payable.

2. To record the payment of rent expense, an accountant would

   (a) debit Cash; credit Rent Expense.
   (b) debit Rent Expense; debit Cash.
   (c) debit Rent Expense; credit Cash.
   (d) credit Rent Expense; credit Cash.

3. The accounting equation may be expressed as

   (a) Assets = Liabilities − Owner's Equity.
   (b) Assets = Liabilities + Owner's Equity.
   (c) Liabilities = Owner's Equity − Assets.
   (d) all of the above.

4. Liability, owner's equity, and revenue accounts normally have

   (a) debit balances.
   (b) large balances.
   (c) negative balances.
   (d) credit balances.

5. An investment of cash by the owner will

   (a) increase assets and owner's equity.
   (b) increase assets and liabilities.
   (c) increase liabilities and owner's equity.
   (d) increase owner's equity; decrease liabilities.

The answers to the Self-Study Test Questions are at the end of the text.

4

Journalizing and Posting Transactions

W̲ith business picking up, Jessie realized that she needed help maintaining records of her business trans-

actions. Since she has not studied accounting and prefers to spend her time making deliveries and meeting with

new clients, she hired an accounting student, Mitch, to help her "keep the books." After a few days on the job,

Mitch and Jessie sat down to discuss the business events that had taken place and the entries made by Mitch. As

might be expected, Mitch had misunderstood a few transactions and had entered them improperly. Jessie

suggested that they go through the journal and ledger to erase the errors and make the corrections. Is this the

best way to make corrections?

Careful study of this chapter should enable you to:

LO1 Describe the flow of data from source documents through the trial balance.

LO2 Describe the chart of accounts as a means of classifying financial information.

LO3 Describe and explain the purpose of source documents.

LO4 Journalize transactions.

LO5 Post to the general ledger.

LO6 Explain how to find and correct errors.

The double-entry framework of accounting was explained and illustrated in Chapter 3. To demonstrate the use of debits and credits, business transactions were entered directly into T accounts. Now we will take a more detailed look at the procedures used to account for business transactions.

FLOW OF DATA

LO1 Describe the flow of data from source documents through the trial balance.

This chapter traces the flow of financial data from the source documents through the accounting information system. This process includes the following steps:

1. Analyze what happened by using information from source documents and the firm's chart of accounts.

2. Enter business transactions in the general journal in the form of journal entries.

3. Post these journal entries to the accounts in the general ledger.

4. Prepare a trial balance.

The flow of data from the source documents through the preparation of a trial balance is shown in Figure 4-1.

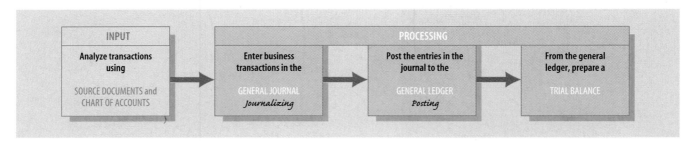

FIGURE 4-1 Flow of Data from Source Documents through Trial Balance

THE CHART OF ACCOUNTS

LO2 Describe the chart of accounts as a means of classifying financial information.

You learned in Chapters 2 and 3 that there are three basic questions that must be answered when analyzing transactions:

1. What happened?
2. Which accounts are affected?
3. How is the accounting equation affected?

To determine which accounts are affected (step 2), the accountant must know the accounts being used by the business. A list of all accounts used by a business is called a **chart of accounts.**

The chart of accounts includes the account titles in numeric order for all assets, liabilities, owner's equity, revenues, and expenses. The numbering should follow a consistent pattern. In Jessie Jane's Campus Delivery, asset accounts begin with "1," liability accounts begin with "2," owner's equity accounts begin with "3," revenue accounts begin with "4," and expense accounts begin with "5." Jessie uses three-digit numbers for all accounts.

A chart of accounts for Jessie Jane's Campus Delivery is shown in Figure 4-2. Jessie would not need many accounts initially because the business is new. Additional accounts can easily be added as needed. Note that the accounts are arranged according to the accounting equation.

JESSIE JANE'S CAMPUS DELIVERY CHART OF ACCOUNTS			
Assets	**(100–199)**	**Revenues**	**(400–499)**
101	Cash	401	Delivery Fees
122	Accounts Receivable		
141	Supplies	**Expenses**	**(500–599)**
145	Prepaid Insurance	511	Wages Expense
185	Delivery Equipment	521	Rent Expense
		525	Telephone Expense
Liabilities	**(200–299)**		
202	Accounts Payable		
Owner's Equity	**(300–399)**		
311	Jessica Jane, Capital		
312	Jessica Jane, Drawing		

FIGURE 4-2   **Chart of Accounts**

SOURCE DOCUMENTS

L03 **Describe and explain the purpose of source documents.**

Almost any document that provides information about a business transaction can be called a **source document**. A source document triggers the analysis of what happened. It begins the process of entering transactions in the accounting system. Examples of source documents are shown in Figure 4-3. These source documents provide information that is useful in determining the effect of business transactions on specific accounts.

In addition to serving as input for transaction analysis, source documents serve as objective evidence of business transactions. If anyone questions the accounting records, these documents may be used as objective, verifiable evidence of the accuracy of the accounting records. For this reason, source documents are filed for possible future reference. *Having objective, verifiable evidence that a transaction occurred is an important accounting concept.*

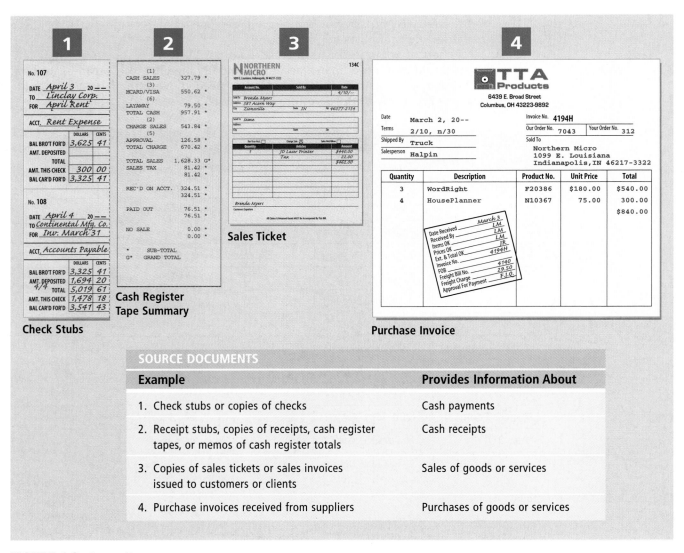

Check Stubs

Cash Register Tape Summary

Sales Ticket

Purchase Invoice

SOURCE DOCUMENTS	
Example	**Provides Information About**
1. Check stubs or copies of checks	Cash payments
2. Receipt stubs, copies of receipts, cash register tapes, or memos of cash register totals	Cash receipts
3. Copies of sales tickets or sales invoices issued to customers or clients	Sales of goods or services
4. Purchase invoices received from suppliers	Purchases of goods or services

FIGURE 4-3   Source Documents

A BROADER VIEW

Electronic Source Documents

With the ability to go shopping in cyberspace, more transactions are being initiated electronically. Even Sears, known for its low prices and excellent in-store service, has "online" shopping at www.Sears.com. Customers can place orders and these orders can be filled, all based on electronic communications. This means that more and more "source documents" will be in an electronic form.

THE GENERAL JOURNAL

LO4 Journalize transactions.

A day-by-day listing of the transactions of a business is called a **journal.** The purpose of a journal is to provide a record of all transactions completed by the business. The journal shows the date of each transaction, titles of the accounts to be debited and credited, and the amounts of the debits and credits.

> **LEARNING KEY:** A journal provides a day-by-day listing of all transactions completed by the business.

A journal is commonly referred to as a **book of original entry** because it is here that the first formal accounting record of a transaction is made. Although many types of journals are used in business, the simplest journal form is a two-column general journal (Figure 4-4). Any kind of business transaction may be entered into a general journal.

A **two-column general journal** is so-named because it has only two amount columns, one for debit amounts and one for credit amounts. Journal pages are numbered in the upper right-hand corner. The five column numbers in Figure 4-4 are explained in Figure 4-5.

GENERAL JOURNAL | PAGE 1

	DATE	DESCRIPTION	POST REF.	DEBIT	CREDIT	
1	20-- 1	2	3	4	5	1
2						2
3						3

FIGURE 4-4   Two-Column General Journal

Column 1 Date	The year is entered in small figures at the top of the column immediately below the column heading. The year is repeated only at the top of each new page. The month is entered for the first entry on the page and for the first transaction of the month. The day of the month is recorded for every transaction, even if it is the same as the prior entry.
Column 2 Description	The *Description* or *Explanation* column is used to enter the titles of the accounts affected by each transaction, and to provide a very brief description of the transaction. Each transaction affects two or more accounts. The account(s) to be debited are entered first at the extreme left of the column. The account(s) to be credited are listed after the debits and indented. The description should be entered immediately following the last credit entry with an additional indentation.
Column 3 Posting Reference	No entries are made in the *Posting Reference* column during journalizing. Entries are made in this column when the debits and credits are copied to the proper accounts in the ledger. This process will be explained in detail later in this chapter.
Column 4 Debit Amount	The *Debit amount column* is used to enter the amount to be debited to an account. The amount should be entered on the same line as the title of that account.
Column 5 Credit Amount	The *Credit amount column* is used to enter the amount to be credited to an account. The amount should be entered on the same line as the title of that account.

FIGURE 4-5   The Columns in a Two-Column General Journal

Journalizing

Entering the transactions in a journal is called **journalizing**. For every transaction, the entry should include the date, the title of each account affected, the amounts, and a brief description.

To illustrate the journalizing process, transactions for the first month of operations of Jessie Jane's Campus Delivery will be journalized. The transactions are listed in Figure 4-6. Since you analyzed these transactions in Chapters 2 and 3, the journalizing process should be easier to understand. Let's start with a close look at the steps followed when journalizing the first transaction, Jessie's initial investment of $2,000.

LEARNING KEY: When journalizing, the exact account titles shown in the chart of accounts must be used. Refer to the chart of accounts in Figure 4-2 as you review the entries for Jessie Jane's Campus Delivery.

		SUMMARY OF TRANSACTIONS JESSIE JANE'S CAMPUS DELIVERY		

Transaction

(a)	June 1	Jessica Jane invested cash in her business, $2,000.
(b)	3	Bought delivery equipment for cash, $1,200.
(c)	5	Bought delivery equipment on account from Big Red Scooters, $900.
(d)	6	Paid first installment from transaction (c) to Big Red Scooters, $300.
(e)	6	Received cash for delivery services rendered, $500.
(f)	7	Paid cash for June office rent, $200.
(g)	15	Paid telephone bill, $50.
(h)	15	Made deliveries on account for a total of $600: Accounting Department ($400) and the School of Music ($200).
(i)	16	Bought supplies for cash, $80.
(j)	18	Paid cash for an eight-month liability insurance policy, $200. Coverage began on June 1.
(k)	20	Received $570 in cash for services performed in transaction (h): $400 from the Accounting Department and $170 from the School of Music.
(l)	25	Bought a third scooter from Big Red Scooters, $1,500. Paid $300 cash, with the remaining payments expected over the next four months.
(m)	27	Paid wages of part-time employees, $650.
(n)	30	Earned delivery fees for the remainder of the month amounting to $1,050: $430 in cash and $620 on account. Deliveries on account: Accounting Department ($250) and Athletic Ticket Office ($370).
(o)	30	Jessie withdrew cash for personal use, $150.

FIGURE 4-6   **Summary of Transactions**

Transaction (a)

June 1   Jessica Jane opened a bank account with a deposit of $2,000 for her business.

STEP 1   **Enter the date.** Since this is the first entry on the journal page, the year is entered on the first line of the Date column (in small print at the top of the line). The month and day are entered on the same line, below the year, in the Date column.

	DATE		DESCRIPTION	POST REF.	DEBIT	CREDIT	
	20--						
1	June	1					1
2							2

GENERAL JOURNAL   PAGE 1

STEP 2   **Enter the debit.** Cash is entered on the first line at the extreme left of the Description column. The amount of the debit, $2,000, is entered on the same line in the Debit column. Since this is not a formal financial statement, dollar signs are not used.

		GENERAL JOURNAL				PAGE 1
	DATE	DESCRIPTION	POST REF.	DEBIT	CREDIT	
1	20-- June 1	Cash		2 0 0 0 00		1
2						2

STEP 3   **Enter the credit.** The title of the account to be credited, Jessica Jane, Capital, is entered on the second line, indented one-half inch from the left side of the Description column. The amount of the credit, $2,000, is entered on the same line in the Credit column.

		GENERAL JOURNAL				PAGE 1
	DATE	DESCRIPTION	POST REF.	DEBIT	CREDIT	
1	20-- June 1	Cash		2 0 0 0 00		1
2		Jessica Jane, Capital			2 0 0 0 00	2

STEP 4   **Enter the explanation.** The explanation of the entry is entered on the next line, indented an additional one-half inch. The second line of the explanation, if needed, is also indented the same distance as the first.

		GENERAL JOURNAL				PAGE 1
	DATE	DESCRIPTION	POST REF.	DEBIT	CREDIT	
1	20-- June 1	Cash		2 0 0 0 00		1
2		Jessica Jane, Capital			2 0 0 0 00	2
3		Owner's original investment in				3
4		delivery business				4

To enter transaction (b), the purchase of a motor scooter for $1,200 cash, we skip a line and follow the same four steps. *To help prevent inappropriate changes to entries, you probably would not skip a line in practice.* Note that the month and year do not need to be repeated. The day of the month must, however, be entered.

GENERAL JOURNAL   PAGE 1

	DATE		DESCRIPTION	POST REF.	DEBIT	CREDIT	
	20--						
1	June	1	Cash		2 0 0 0 00		1
2			Jessica Jane, Capital			2 0 0 0 00	2
3			Owner's original investment in				3
4			delivery business				4
5							5
6		3	Delivery Equipment		1 2 0 0 00		6
7			Cash			1 2 0 0 00	7
8			Purchased delivery equipment for cash				8

Skip a line (pointing to line 5)

The journal entries for the month of June are shown in Figure 4-7. Note that the entries on June 25 and June 30 affect more than two accounts. Entries requiring more than one debit and/or one credit are called **compound entries**. The entry on June 25 has two credits. The credits are listed after the debit, indented and listed one under the other. The entry on June 30 has two debits. They are aligned with the left margin of the Description column and listed one under the other. In both cases, the debits equal the credits.

GENERAL JOURNAL   PAGE 1

	DATE		DESCRIPTION	POST REF.	DEBIT	CREDIT	
	20--						
1	June	1	Cash		2 0 0 0 00		1
2			Jessica Jane, Capital			2 0 0 0 00	2
3			Owner's original investment in				3
4			delivery business				4
5							5
6			Delivery Equipment		1 2 0 0 00		6
7			Cash			1 2 0 0 00	7
8			Purchased delivery equipment for cash				8
9							9
10		5	Delivery Equipment		9 0 0 00		10
11			Accounts Payable			9 0 0 00	11
12			Purchased delivery equipment on account				12
13			from Big Red Scooters				13
14							14
15		6	Accounts Payable		3 0 0 00		15
16			Cash			3 0 0 00	16
17			Made partial payment to Big Red Scooters				17
18							18
19		6	Cash		5 0 0 00		19
20			Delivery Fees			5 0 0 00	20
21			Received cash for delivery services				21

Annotations: *List debits first* (line 1 Cash); *List credits second and indented.* (line 2 Jessica Jane, Capital); *Explanation is third and indented.* (line 3); *Space to make entries easier to read. To prevent improper changes to entries, the extra spacing might not be used in practice.*

FIGURE 4-7   General Journal Entries

		GENERAL JOURNAL											PAGE 1	
	DATE	DESCRIPTION	POST REF.		DEBIT				CREDIT					
23	7	Rent Expense			2	0	0	00						23
24		Cash							2	0	0	00		24
25		Paid office rent for June												25
26														26
27	15	Telephone Expense				5	0	00						27
28		Cash								5	0	00		28
29		Paid telephone bill for June												29
30														30
31	15	Accounts Receivable			6	0	0	00						31
32		Delivery Fees							6	0	0	00		32
33		Deliveries made on account for Accounting												33
34		Department ($400) and School of Music ($200)												34
35														35

		GENERAL JOURNAL											PAGE 2	
	DATE	DESCRIPTION	POST REF.		DEBIT				CREDIT					
	20--													
1	June 16	Supplies				8	0	00						1
2		Cash								8	0	00		2
3		Purchased supplies for cash												3
4														4
5	18	Prepaid Insurance			2	0	0	00						5
6		Cash							2	0	0	00		6
7		Paid premium for eight-month												7
8		insurance policy												8
9														9
10	20	Cash			5	7	0	00						10
11		Accounts Receivable							5	7	0	00		11
12		Received cash on account from Accounting												12
13		Department ($400) and School of Music ($170)												13
14														14
15	25	Delivery Equipment		1	5	0	0	00						15
16		Accounts Payable							1	2	0	0	00	16
17		Cash								3	0	0	00	17
18		Purchased scooter with down payment;												18
19		balance on account with Big Red Scooters												19
20														20
21	27	Wages Expense			6	5	0	00						21
22		Cash							6	5	0	00		22
23		Paid employees												23
24														24

Compound entry

Line up credits

Debits = Credits

FIGURE 4-7 General Journal Entries (continued)

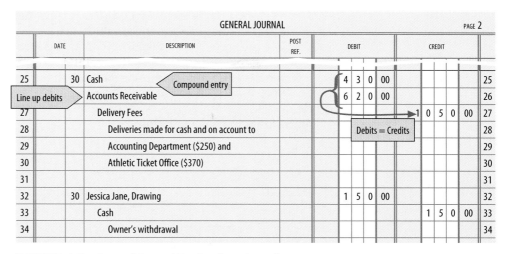

	GENERAL JOURNAL						PAGE 2	
	DATE	DESCRIPTION	POST REF.	DEBIT		CREDIT		
25	30	Cash ◁ Compound entry		4 3 0 00				25
26	Line up debits ▷	Accounts Receivable		6 2 0 00				26
27		Delivery Fees				1 0 5 0 00		27
28		Deliveries made for cash and on account to		Debits = Credits				28
29		Accounting Department ($250) and						29
30		Athletic Ticket Office ($370)						30
31								31
32	30	Jessica Jane, Drawing		1 5 0 00				32
33		Cash				1 5 0 00		33
34		Owner's withdrawal						34

FIGURE 4-7   **General Journal Entries** *(continued)*

THE GENERAL LEDGER

LO5 Post to the general ledger.

The journal provides a day-by-day record of business transactions. To determine the current balance of specific accounts, however, the information in the journal must be transferred to accounts similar to the T accounts illustrated in Chapter 3. This process is called posting.

A complete set of all the accounts used by a business is known as the **general ledger**. The general ledger accumulates a complete record of the debits and credits made to each account as a result of entries made in the journal. The accounts are numbered and arranged in the same order as the chart of accounts. That is, accounts are numbered and grouped by classification: assets, liabilities, owner's equity, revenues, and expenses.

> **LEARNING KEY:** While the journal provides a day-by-day record of business transactions, the ledger provides a record of the transactions entered in each account.

Four-Column Account

For purposes of illustration, the T account was introduced in Chapter 3. In practice, businesses are more likely to use a version of the account called the **four-column account**. Figure 4-8 compares the cash T account from Chapter 3 for Jessie Jane's Campus Delivery and a four-column cash account summarizing the same cash transactions. A four-column account contains columns for the debit or credit transaction and columns for the debit or credit running balance. In addition, there are columns for the date, description of the item, and posting reference. The Item column is used to provide descriptions of special entries. For example, "Balance" is written in this column when the balance of an account is transferred to a new page. The Posting Reference column is used to indicate the journal page from which an entry was posted, or a check mark (✔) is inserted to indicate that no posting was required.

As shown in Figure 4-8, the primary advantage of the T account is that the debit and credit sides of the account are easier to identify. Thus, for demonstration purposes and analyzing what happened, T accounts are very helpful. However, computing the balance of a T account is cumbersome. The primary advantage of the four-column account is that it maintains a running balance.

Note that the heading for the four-column account has the account title and an account number. The account number is taken from the chart of accounts and is used in the posting process.

Cash

(a)	2,000	(b)	1,200
(e)	500	(d)	300
(k)	570	(f)	200
(n)	430	(g)	50
	3,500	(i)	80
		(j)	200
		(l)	300
		(m)	650
		(o)	150
Bal.	370		3,130

GENERAL LEDGER

ACCOUNT: Cash *Asset* *liability* ACCOUNT NO. 101

DATE	ITEM	POST REF.	DEBIT	CREDIT	BALANCE DEBIT	BALANCE CREDIT
20— June 1			2000 00		2000 00	
3				1200 00	800 00	
6				300 00	500 00	
6			500 00		1000 00	
7				200 00	800 00	
15				50 00	750 00	
16				80 00	670 00	
18				200 00	470 00	
20			570 00		1040 00	
25				300 00	740 00	
27				650 00	90 00	
30			430 00		520 00	
30				150 00	370 00	

└─ Transaction Amount ─┘ └─ Running Balance ─┘

FIGURE 4-8 Comparison of T Account and Four-Column Account

LEARNING KEY: The four-column account is similar to the T account, but makes it easier to maintain a running balance.

Posting to the General Ledger

The process of copying the debits and credits from the journal to the ledger accounts is known as **posting**. All amounts entered in the journal must be posted to the general ledger accounts.

LEARNING KEY: Posting is simply the copying of the exact dates and dollar amounts from the journal to the ledger.

Posting from the journal to the ledger is done daily or at frequent intervals. There are five steps.

Steps in the Posting Process

In the ledger account:

STEP 1   Enter the date of the transaction in the Date column. There is no need to repeat the month and year, but the day must be entered even if it is the same date as in the previous transaction.

STEP 2   Enter the amount of the debit or credit in the Debit or Credit column.

STEP 3   Enter the new balance in the Balance columns under Debit or Credit. If the balance of the account is zero, draw a line through the debit and credit columns.

STEP 4   Enter the journal page number from which each transaction is posted in the Posting Reference column.

In the journal:

STEP 5   Enter the ledger account number in the Posting Reference column of the journal for each transaction that is posted.

Step 5 is the last step in the posting process. After this step is completed, the posting references will indicate which journal entries have been posted to the ledger accounts. This is very helpful, particularly if you are interrupted during the posting process. The information in the Posting Reference columns of the journal and ledger provides a link between the journal and ledger known as a **cross-reference**.

LEARNING KEY: Posting references indicate that a journal entry has been posted to the general ledger.

To illustrate the posting process, the first journal entry for Jessie Jane's Campus Delivery will be posted step-by-step. First, let's post the debit to Cash (Figure 4-9).

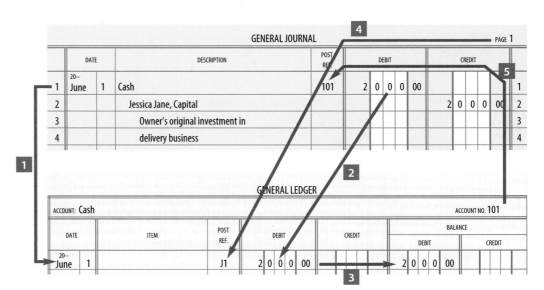

FIGURE 4-9   **Posting a Debit**

In the ledger account:

STEP 1   Enter the year, "20--," the month, "June," and the day, "1," in the Date column of the cash account.

STEP 2   Enter the amount, "$2,000," in the Debit column. Again, since this is not a formal financial statement, dollar signs are not used.

STEP 3   Enter the $2,000 balance in the Balance columns under Debit.

STEP 4   Enter "J1" in the Posting Reference column since the posting came from page 1 of the *J*ournal.

     The Item column is left blank, except for special reasons such as indicating the beginning balance.

In the journal:

STEP 5   Enter the account number for Cash, 101 (see chart of accounts in Figure 4-2 on page 89), in the Posting Reference column of the journal on the same line as the debit to Cash for $2,000.

     Now let's post the credit portion of the first entry (Figure 4-10).

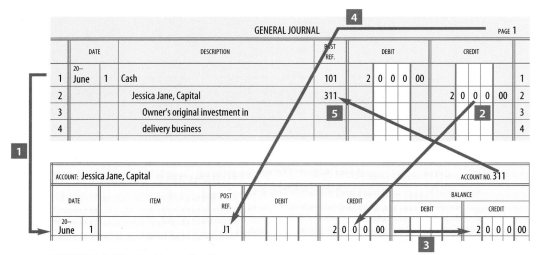

FIGURE 4-10   Posting a Credit

In the ledger account:

STEP 1   Enter the year, "20--," the month, "June," and the day, "1," in the Date column of the Jessica Jane, Capital account.

STEP 2   Enter the amount, "$2,000," in the Credit column.

STEP 3   Enter the $2,000 balance in the Balance columns under Credit.

STEP 4   Enter "J1" in the Posting Reference column since the posting came from Page 1 of the *J*ournal.

In the journal:

STEP 5   Enter the account number for Jessica Jane, Capital, 311, in the Posting Reference column.

After posting the journal entries for Jessie Jane's Campus Delivery for the month of June, the general journal and general ledger should appear as illustrated in Figures 4-11 and 4-12 on pages 101–104. *Note that the Posting Reference column of the journal has been filled in because the entries have been posted.*

	DATE		DESCRIPTION	POST REF.	DEBIT					CREDIT					
	20--														
1	June	1	Cash	101	2	0	0	0	00						1
2			Jessica Jane, Capital	311						2	0	0	0	00	2
3			Owner's original investment in												3
4			delivery business												4
5															5
6		3	Delivery Equipment	185	1	2	0	0	00						6
7			Cash	101						1	2	0	0	00	7
8			Purchased delivery equipment for cash												8
9															9
10		5	Delivery Equipment	185		9	0	0	00						10
11			Accounts Payable	202							9	0	0	00	11
12			Purchased delivery equipment on account												12
13			from Big Red Scooters												13
14															14
15		6	Accounts Payable	202		3	0	0	00						15
16			Cash	101							3	0	0	00	16
17			Made partial payment to Big Red Scooters												17
18															18
19		6	Cash	101		5	0	0	00						19
20			Delivery Fees	401							5	0	0	00	20
21			Received cash for delivery services												21
22															22
23		7	Rent Expense	521		2	0	0	00						23
24			Cash	101							2	0	0	00	24
25			Paid office rent for June												25
26															26
27		15	Telephone Expense	525			5	0	00						27
28			Cash	101								5	0	00	28
29			Paid telephone bill for June												29
30															30
31		15	Accounts Receivable	122		6	0	0	00						31
32			Delivery Fees	401							6	0	0	00	32
33			Deliveries made on account for Accounting												33
34			Department ($400) and School of Music ($200)												34
35															35

GENERAL JOURNAL — PAGE 1

FIGURE 4-11   General Journal After Posting

	DATE		DESCRIPTION	POST REF.	DEBIT				CREDIT				
	20--												
1	June	16	Supplies	141		8	0	00					1
2			Cash	101						8	0	00	2
3			Purchased supplies for cash										3
4													4
5		18	Prepaid Insurance	145	2	0	0	00					5
6			Cash	101					2	0	0	00	6
7			Paid premium for eight-month										7
8			insurance policy										8
9													9
10		20	Cash	101	5	7	0	00					10
11			Accounts Receivable	122					5	7	0	00	11
12			Received cash on account from Accounting										12
13			Department ($400) and School of Music ($170)										13
14													14
15		25	Delivery Equipment	185	1 5	0	0	00					15
16			Accounts Payable	202					1 2	0	0	00	16
17			Cash	101					3	0	0	00	17
18			Purchased scooter with down payment;										18
19			balance on account with Big Red Scooters										19
20													20
21		27	Wages Expense	511	6	5	0	00					21
22			Cash	101					6	5	0	00	22
23			Paid employees										23
24													24
25		30	Cash	101	4	3	0	00					25
26			Accounts Receivable	122	6	2	0	00					26
27			Delivery Fees	401					1 0	5	0	00	27
28			Deliveries made for cash and on account to										28
29			Accounting Department ($250) and										29
30			Athletic Ticket Office ($370)										30
31													31
32		30	Jessica Jane, Drawing	312	1	5	0	00					32
33			Cash	101					1	5	0	00	33
34			Owner's withdrawal										34

FIGURE 4-11 **General Journal After Posting** *(continued)*

GENERAL LEDGER

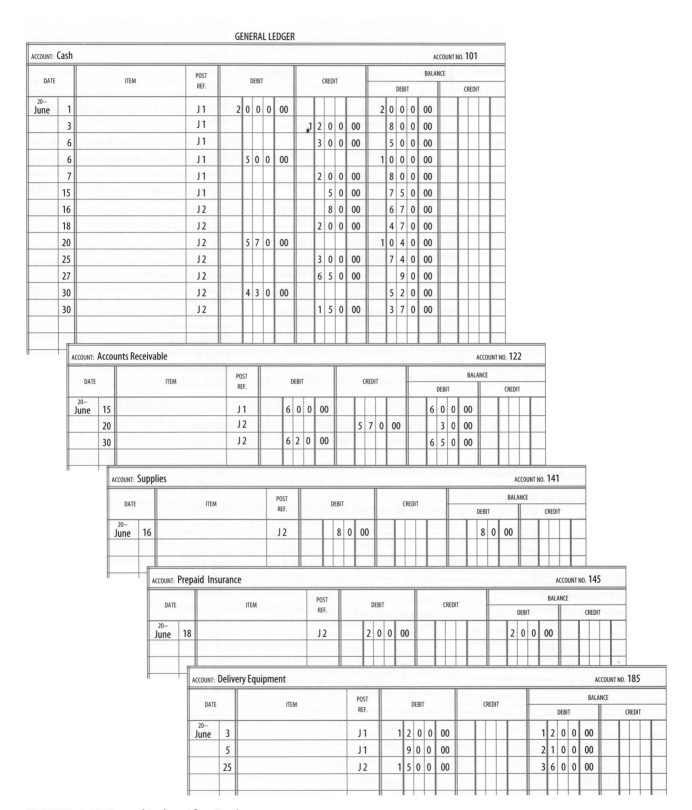

ACCOUNT: Cash   ACCOUNT NO. 101

DATE	ITEM	POST REF.	DEBIT	CREDIT	BALANCE DEBIT	BALANCE CREDIT
20-- June 1		J 1	2 0 0 0 00		2 0 0 0 00	
3		J 1		1 2 0 0 00	8 0 0 00	
6		J 1		3 0 0 00	5 0 0 00	
6		J 1	5 0 0 00		1 0 0 0 00	
7		J 1		2 0 0 00	8 0 0 00	
15		J 1		5 0 00	7 5 0 00	
16		J 2		8 0 00	6 7 0 00	
18		J 2		2 0 0 00	4 7 0 00	
20		J 2	5 7 0 00		1 0 4 0 00	
25		J 2		3 0 0 00	7 4 0 00	
27		J 2		6 5 0 00	9 0 00	
30		J 2	4 3 0 00		5 2 0 00	
30		J 2		1 5 0 00	3 7 0 00	

ACCOUNT: Accounts Receivable   ACCOUNT NO. 122

DATE	ITEM	POST REF.	DEBIT	CREDIT	BALANCE DEBIT	BALANCE CREDIT
20-- June 15		J 1	6 0 0 00		6 0 0 00	
20		J 2		5 7 0 00	3 0 00	
30		J 2	6 2 0 00		6 5 0 00	

ACCOUNT: Supplies   ACCOUNT NO. 141

DATE	ITEM	POST REF.	DEBIT	CREDIT	BALANCE DEBIT	BALANCE CREDIT
20-- June 16		J 2	8 0 00		8 0 00	

ACCOUNT: Prepaid Insurance   ACCOUNT NO. 145

DATE	ITEM	POST REF.	DEBIT	CREDIT	BALANCE DEBIT	BALANCE CREDIT
20-- June 18		J 2	2 0 0 00		2 0 0 00	

ACCOUNT: Delivery Equipment   ACCOUNT NO. 185

DATE	ITEM	POST REF.	DEBIT	CREDIT	BALANCE DEBIT	BALANCE CREDIT
20-- June 3		J 1	1 2 0 0 00		1 2 0 0 00	
5		J 1	9 0 0 00		2 1 0 0 00	
25		J 2	1 5 0 0 00		3 6 0 0 00	

FIGURE 4-12 General Ledger After Posting

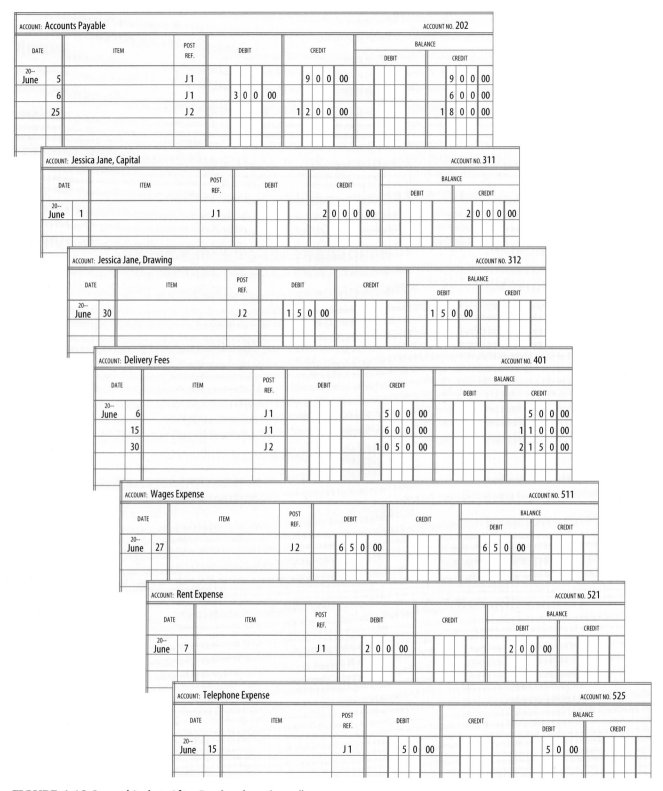

FIGURE 4-12 General Ledger After Posting (continued)

The Trial Balance

In Chapter 3, a **trial balance** was used to prove that the totals of the debit and credit balances in the T accounts were equal. In this chapter, a trial balance is used to prove the equality of the debits and credits in the ledger accounts. A trial balance can be prepared daily, weekly, monthly, or whenever desired. Before preparing a trial balance, all transactions should be journalized and posted so that the effect of all transactions will be reflected in the ledger accounts.

The trial balance for Jessie Jane's Campus Delivery shown in Figure 4-13 was prepared from the balances in the general ledger in Figure 4-12. The accounts are listed in the order used in the chart of accounts. This order is also often used when preparing financial statements. In Chapter 2, we pointed out that many firms list expenses from highest to lowest amounts. Some firms list expenses according to the chart of accounts, which is the method we will follow.

 LEARNING KEY: The chart of accounts determines the order for listing accounts in the general ledger and trial balance. This order may also be used when preparing financial statements.

ACCOUNT TITLE	ACCOUNT NO.	DEBIT BALANCE	CREDIT BALANCE
Jessie Jane's Campus Delivery — Trial Balance — June 30, 20 - -			
Cash	101	3 7 0 00	
Accounts Receivable	122	6 5 0 00	
Supplies	141	8 0 00	
Prepaid Insurance	145	2 0 0 00	
Delivery Equipment	185	3 6 0 0 00	
Accounts Payable	202		1 8 0 0 00
Jessica Jane, Capital	311		2 0 0 0 00
Jessica Jane, Drawing	312	1 5 0 00	
Delivery Fees	401		2 1 5 0 00
Wages Expense	511	6 5 0 00	
Rent Expense	521	2 0 0 00	
Telephone Expense	525	5 0 00	
		5 9 5 0 00	5 9 5 0 00

FIGURE 4-13   Trial Balance

Even though the trial balance indicates that the ledger is in balance, the ledger can still contain errors. For example, if a journal entry was made debiting or crediting the wrong accounts, or if an item was posted to the wrong account, the ledger will still be in balance. It is important, therefore, to be very careful in preparing the journal entries and in posting them to the ledger accounts.

FINDING AND CORRECTING ERRORS IN THE TRIAL BALANCE

LO6 **Explain how to find and correct errors.**

Tips are available to help if your trial balance has an error. Figure 4-14 offers hints for finding the error when your trial balance does not balance.

1. Double check your addition. Review balances to see if they are too large or small, relative to other accounts, or entered in the wrong column.

2. Find the difference between the debits and the credits.

    a. If the difference is equal to the amount of a specific transaction, perhaps you forgot to post the debit or credit portion of this transaction.

    b. Divide the difference by 2. If the difference is evenly divisible by 2, you may have posted two debits or two credits for a transaction. If a debit were posted as a credit, it would mean that one transaction had two credits and no debits. The difference between the total debits and credits would be twice the amount of the debit that was posted as a credit.

    c. Divide the difference by 9. If the difference is evenly divisible by 9, you may have committed a **slide error** or a **transposition error**. A slide occurs when debit or credit amounts "slide" a digit or two to the left or right when entered. For example, if *$250* was entered as *$25*:

$250	−	25	=	$225
$225	÷	9	=	$25

    The difference is evenly divisible by 9.

    A transposition occurs when two digits are reversed. For example, if *$250* was entered as *$520*:

$520	−	250	=	$270
$270	÷	9	=	$30

    Again, the difference is evenly divisible by 9.

FIGURE 4-14   **Tips for Finding Errors in the Trial Balance**

If the tips in Figure 4-14 don't work, you must retrace your steps through the accounting process. Double check your addition for the ledger accounts. Also trace all postings. Be patient as you search for your error. Use this process as an opportunity to reinforce your understanding of the flow of information through the accounting system. Much can be learned while looking for an error.

Once you have found an error, there are two methods of making the correction. Although you may want to erase when correcting your homework, this is not acceptable in practice. An erasure may suggest that you are trying to hide something. Instead you should use the ruling method or make a correcting entry.

Ruling Method

The **ruling method** should be used to correct two types of errors:

1. When an incorrect journal entry has been made, but not yet posted.

2. When a proper entry has been made but posted to the wrong account or for the wrong amount.

When using the ruling method, draw a single line through the incorrect account title or amount and write the correct information directly above the line. Corrections should be initialed by someone authorized to make such changes. This is done so the source and reason for the correction can be traced. This type of correction may be made in the journal or ledger accounts, as shown in Figure 4-15.

GENERAL JOURNAL   PAGE 2

	DATE		DESCRIPTION	POST REF.	DEBIT	CREDIT	
1	20-- Sept.	17	~~Entertainment Expense~~ Wages Expense MP		6 5 0 00		1
2			Cash			6 5 0 00	2
3			Paid employees				3
4							4
5		18	Prepaid Insurance		MP 2 0 0 00 ~~2 0 00~~		5
6			Cash			MP 2 0 0 00 ~~2 0 00~~	6
7			Paid premium for eight-month				7
8			insurance policy				8
9							9

Slide

GENERAL LEDGER

ACCOUNT: Accounts Payable   ACCOUNT NO. 202

DATE		ITEM	POST REF.	DEBIT	CREDIT	BALANCE DEBIT	BALANCE CREDIT
20-- Sept.	8		J 1		7 0 0 00		7 0 0 00
	15		J 1	2 0 0 00			5 0 0 00
	25		J 2		1 2 0 0 00 ~~2 1 0 0 00~~ MP	MP 1 7 0 0 00 ~~2 6 0 0 00~~

Transposition

FIGURE 4-15   Ruling Method of Making a Correction

Correcting Entry Method

If an incorrect entry has been journalized and posted to the wrong account, a **correcting entry** should be made. For example, assume that a $400 payment for Rent Expense was incorrectly debited to Repair Expense and correctly credited to Cash. This requires a correcting entry and explanation as shown in Figure 4-16. Figure 4-17 shows the effects of the correcting entry on the ledger accounts. Generally, "Correcting" is written in the Item column of the general ledger account.

GENERAL JOURNAL   PAGE 6

	DATE		DESCRIPTION	POST REF.	DEBIT	CREDIT	
1	20-- Sept.	25	Rent Expense	521	4 0 0 00		1
2			Repair Expense	537		4 0 0 00	2
3			To correct error in which payment for rent				3
4			was debited to Repair Expense				4
5							5

FIGURE 4-16   Correcting Entry Method

GENERAL LEDGER

ACCOUNT: Rent Expense   ACCOUNT NO. 521

DATE		ITEM	POST REF.	DEBIT	CREDIT	BALANCE DEBIT	BALANCE CREDIT
20-- Sept.	25	Correcting	J 6	4 0 0 00		4 0 0 00	

ACCOUNT: Repair Expense   ACCOUNT NO. 537

DATE		ITEM	POST REF.	DEBIT	CREDIT	BALANCE DEBIT	BALANCE CREDIT
20-- Sept.	10		J 5	5 0 00		5 0 00	
	15		J 5	4 0 0 00		4 5 0 00	
	25	Correcting	J 6		4 0 0 00	5 0 00	

FIGURE 4-17   Effects of Correcting Entry on Ledger Accounts

Learning Objectives	Key Points to Remember
1 **Describe the flow of data from source documents through the trial balance.**	The flow of data from the source documents through the trial balance is: 1. Analyze business transactions. 2. Journalize transactions in the general journal. 3. Post journal entries to the general ledger. 4. Prepare a trial balance.
2 **Describe the chart of accounts as a means of classifying financial information.**	The chart of accounts includes the account titles in numerical order for all assets, liabilities, owner's equity, revenues, and expenses. The chart of accounts is used in classifying information about transactions.
3 **Describe and explain the purpose of source documents.**	Source documents trigger the analysis of business transactions and the entries into the accounting system.
4 **Journalize transactions.**	A journal provides a day-by-day listing of transactions. The journal shows the date, titles of the accounts to be debited or credited, and the amounts of the debits and credits. The steps in the journalizing process are: 1. Enter the date. 2. Enter the debit. Accounts to be debited are entered first. 3. Enter the credit. Accounts to be credited are entered after the debits and are indented one-half inch. 4. Enter the explanation. A brief explanation of the transaction should be entered in the description column on the line following the last credit. The explanation should be indented an additional one-half inch.
5 **Post to the general ledger.**	The general ledger is a complete set of all accounts used by the business. The steps in posting from the general journal to the general ledger are: In the general ledger: 1. Enter the date of each transaction. 2. Enter the amount of each debit or credit in the Debit or Credit column. 3. Enter the new balance. 4. Enter the journal page number from which each transaction is posted in the Posting Reference column. In the journal: 5. Enter the account number to which each transaction is posted in the Posting Reference column.
6 **Explain how to find and correct errors.**	Errors may be found by verifying your addition, by dividing the difference between the debits and credits by 2 or 9, and by retracing your steps through the accounting process. Use the ruling method or the correcting entry method to correct the error.

Reflection: Answering the Opening Question

Corrections should not be made by erasing the original entry. Erasing could create suspicion over what was changed and the reasons for the change. Instead, use the ruling method or make a correcting entry as discussed in the chapter.

KEY TERMS

book of original entry, (91)   The journal or the first formal accounting record of a transaction.

chart of accounts, (89)   A list of all accounts used by a business.

compound entry, (95)   A general journal entry that affects more than two accounts.

correcting entry, (108)   An entry to correct an incorrect entry that has been journalized and posted to the wrong account.

cross-reference, (99)   The information in the Posting Reference columns of the journal and ledger that provides a link between the journal and ledger.

four-column account, (97)   An account with columns for the debit or credit transaction and columns for the debit or credit running balance.

general ledger, (97)   A complete set of all the accounts used by a business. The general ledger accumulates a complete record of the debits and credits made to each account as a result of entries made in the journal.

journal, (91)   A day-by-day listing of the transactions of a business.

journalizing, (92)   Entering the transactions in a journal.

posting, (98)   Copying the debits and credits from the journal to the ledger accounts.

ruling method, (107)   A method of correcting an entry in which a line is drawn through the error and the correct information is placed above it.

slide error, (106)   An error that occurs when debit or credit amounts "slide" a digit or two to the left or right.

source document, (90)   Any document that provides information about a business transaction.

transposition error, (106)   An error that occurs when two digits are reversed.

trial balance, (105)   A list used to prove that the totals of the debit and credit balances in the ledger accounts are equal.

two-column general journal, (91)   A journal with only two amount columns, one for debit amounts and one for credit amounts.

DEMONSTRATION PROBLEM

George Fielding is a financial planning consultant. He provides budgeting, estate planning, tax planning, and investing advice for professional golfers. He developed the following chart of accounts for his business.

Assets	Revenues
101 Cash	401 Professional Fees
142 Office Supplies	

Liabilities	Expenses
202 Accounts Payable	511 Wages Expense
	521 Rent Expense
Owner's Equity	525 Telephone Expense
311 George Fielding, Capital	533 Utilities Expense
312 George Fielding, Drawing	534 Charitable Contributions Expense
	538 Automobile Expense

The following transactions took place during the month of December of the current year.

Dec. 1	Fielding invested cash to start the business, $20,000.
3	Paid Bollhorst Real Estate for December office rent, $1,000.
4	Received cash from Aaron Patton, a client, for services, $2,500.
6	Paid T. Z. Anderson Electric for December heating and light, $75.
7	Received cash from Andrew Conder, a client, for services, $2,000.
12	Paid Fichter's Super Service for gasoline and oil purchases for the company car, $60.
14	Paid Hillenburg Staffing for temporary secretarial services during the past two weeks, $600.
17	Bought office supplies from Bowers Office Supply on account, $280.
20	Paid Mitchell Telephone Co. for business calls during the past month, $100.
21	Fielding withdrew cash for personal use, $1,100.
24	Made donation to the National Multiple Sclerosis Society, $100.
27	Received cash from Billy Walters, a client, for services, $2,000.
28	Paid Hillenburg Staffing for temporary secretarial services during the past two weeks, $600.
29	Made payment on account to Bowers Office Supply, $100.

REQUIRED

1. Record the preceding transactions in a general journal.

2. Post the entries to the general ledger.

3. Prepare a trial balance.

(continued)

Solution

1.

	DATE		DESCRIPTION	POST REF.	DEBIT					CREDIT					
	20--														
1	Dec.	1	Cash	101	20	0	0	0	00						1
2			George Fielding, Capital	311						20	0	0	0	00	2
3			Owner's original investment in												3
4			consulting business												4
5															5
6		3	Rent Expense	521	1	0	0	0	00						6
7			Cash	101						1	0	0	0	00	7
8			Paid rent for December												8
9															9
10		4	Cash	101	2	5	0	0	00						10
11			Professional Fees	401						2	5	0	0	00	11
12			Received cash for services rendered												12
13															13
14		6	Utilities Expense	533			7	5	00						14
15			Cash	101								7	5	00	15
16			Paid utilities												16
17															17
18		7	Cash	101	2	0	0	0	00						18
19			Professional Fees	401						2	0	0	0	00	19
20			Received cash for services rendered												20
21															21
22		12	Automobile Expense	538			6	0	00						22
23			Cash	101								6	0	00	23
24			Paid for gas and oil												24
25															25
26		14	Wages Expense	511		6	0	0	00						26
27			Cash	101							6	0	0	00	27
28			Paid temporary secretaries												28
29															29
30		17	Office Supplies	142		2	8	0	00						30
31			Accounts Payable	202							2	8	0	00	31
32			Purchased office supplies on account from												32
33			Bowers Office Supply												33
34															34
35															35

GENERAL JOURNAL PAGE 1

GENERAL JOURNAL   PAGE 2

	DATE		DESCRIPTION	POST REF.	DEBIT					CREDIT					
	20--														
1	Dec.	20	Telephone Expense	525		1	0	0	00						1
2			Cash	101							1	0	0	00	2
3			Paid telephone bill												3
4															4
5		21	George Fielding, Drawing	312	1	1	0	0	00						5
6			Cash	101						1	1	0	0	00	6
7			Owner's withdrawal												7
8															8
9		24	Charitable Contributions Expense	534		1	0	0	00						9
10			Cash	101							1	0	0	00	10
11			Contribution to National Multiple												11
12			Sclerosis Society												12
13															13
14		27	Cash	101	2	0	0	0	00						14
15			Professional Fees	401						2	0	0	0	00	15
16			Received cash for services rendered												16
17															17
18		28	Wages Expense	511		6	0	0	00						18
19			Cash	101							6	0	0	00	19
20			Paid temporary secretaries												20
21															21
22		29	Accounts Payable	202		1	0	0	00						22
23			Cash	101							1	0	0	00	23
24			Payment on account to Bowers Office Supply												24

2.

GENERAL LEDGER

ACCOUNT: **Cash**   ACCOUNT NO. **101**

DATE		ITEM	POST REF.	DEBIT					CREDIT					BALANCE									
														DEBIT					CREDIT				
20--																							
Dec.	1		J 1	20	0	0	0	00						20	0	0	0	00					
	3		J 1						1	0	0	0	00	19	0	0	0	00					
	4		J 1	2	5	0	0	00						21	5	0	0	00					
	6		J 1							7	5	00		21	4	2	5	00					
	7		J 1	2	0	0	0	00						23	4	2	5	00					
	12		J 1							6	0	00		23	3	6	5	00					
	14		J 1						6	0	0	00		22	7	6	5	00					
	20		J 2						1	0	0	00		22	6	6	5	00					
	21		J 2						1	1	0	0	00	21	5	6	5	00					
	24		J 2						1	0	0	00		21	4	6	5	00					
	27		J 2	2	0	0	0	00						23	4	6	5	00					
	28		J 2						6	0	0	00		22	8	6	5	00					
	29		J 2						1	0	0	00		22	7	6	5	00					

(continued)

ACCOUNT: Office Supplies · ACCOUNT NO. 142

DATE	ITEM	POST REF.	DEBIT	CREDIT	BALANCE DEBIT	BALANCE CREDIT
20-- Dec. 17		J1	2 8 0 00		2 8 0 00	

ACCOUNT: Accounts Payable · ACCOUNT NO. 202

DATE	ITEM	POST REF.	DEBIT	CREDIT	BALANCE DEBIT	BALANCE CREDIT
20-- Dec. 17		J1		2 8 0 00		2 8 0 00
29		J2	1 0 0 00			1 8 0 00

ACCOUNT: George Fielding, Capital · ACCOUNT NO. 311

DATE	ITEM	POST REF.	DEBIT	CREDIT	BALANCE DEBIT	BALANCE CREDIT
20-- Dec. 1		J1		20 0 0 0 00		20 0 0 0 00

ACCOUNT: George Fielding, Drawing · ACCOUNT NO. 312

DATE	ITEM	POST REF.	DEBIT	CREDIT	BALANCE DEBIT	BALANCE CREDIT
20-- Dec. 21		J2	1 1 0 0 00		1 1 0 0 00	

ACCOUNT: Professional Fees · ACCOUNT NO. 401

DATE	ITEM	POST REF.	DEBIT	CREDIT	BALANCE DEBIT	BALANCE CREDIT
20-- Dec. 4		J1		2 5 0 0 00		2 5 0 0 00
7		J1		2 0 0 0 00		4 5 0 0 00
27		J2		2 0 0 0 00		6 5 0 0 00

ACCOUNT: Wages Expense · ACCOUNT NO. 511

DATE	ITEM	POST REF.	DEBIT	CREDIT	BALANCE DEBIT	BALANCE CREDIT
20-- Dec. 14		J1	6 0 0 00		6 0 0 00	
28		J2	6 0 0 00		1 2 0 0 00	

ACCOUNT: Rent Expense · ACCOUNT NO. 521

DATE	ITEM	POST REF.	DEBIT	CREDIT	BALANCE DEBIT	BALANCE CREDIT
20-- Dec. 3		J1	1 0 0 0 00		1 0 0 0 00	

ACCOUNT: Telephone Expense   ACCOUNT NO. 525

DATE		ITEM	POST REF.	DEBIT	CREDIT	BALANCE	
						DEBIT	CREDIT
20-- Dec.	20		J2	1 0 0 00		1 0 0 00	

ACCOUNT: Utilities Expense   ACCOUNT NO. 533

DATE		ITEM	POST REF.	DEBIT	CREDIT	BALANCE	
						DEBIT	CREDIT
20-- Dec.	6		J1	7 5 00		7 5 00	

ACCOUNT: Charitable Contributions Expense   ACCOUNT NO. 534

DATE		ITEM	POST REF.	DEBIT	CREDIT	BALANCE	
						DEBIT	CREDIT
20-- Dec.	24		J2	1 0 0 00		1 0 0 00	

ACCOUNT: Automobile Expense   ACCOUNT NO. 538

DATE		ITEM	POST REF.	DEBIT	CREDIT	BALANCE	
						DEBIT	CREDIT
20-- Dec.	12		J1	6 0 00		6 0 00	

3.

George Fielding, Financial Planning Consultant
Trial Balance
December 31, 20 - -

ACCOUNT TITLE	ACCOUNT NO.	DEBIT BALANCE	CREDIT BALANCE
Cash	101	22 7 6 5 00	
Office Supplies	142	2 8 0 00	
Accounts Payable	202		1 8 0 00
George Fielding, Capital	311		20 0 0 0 00
George Fielding, Drawing	312	1 1 0 0 00	
Professional Fees	401		6 5 0 0 00
Wages Expense	511	1 2 0 0 00	
Rent Expense	521	1 0 0 0 00	
Telephone Expense	525	1 0 0 00	
Utilities Expense	533	7 5 00	
Charitable Contributions Expense	534	1 0 0 00	
Automobile Expense	538	6 0 00	
		26 6 8 0 00	26 6 8 0 00

REVIEW QUESTIONS

1. Trace the flow of accounting information through the accounting system.

2. Explain the purpose of a chart of accounts.

3. Name the five types of financial statement classifications for which it is ordinarily desirable to keep separate accounts.

4. Name a source document that provides information about each of the following types of business transactions:
   a. Cash payment
   b. Cash receipt
   c. Sale of goods or services
   d. Purchase of goods or services

5. Where is the first formal accounting record of a business transaction usually made?

6. Describe the four steps required to journalize a business transaction in a general journal.

7. In what order are the accounts customarily placed in the ledger?

8. Explain the primary advantage of a four-column ledger account.

9. Explain the five steps required when posting the journal to the ledger.

10. What information is entered in the Posting Reference column of the journal as an amount is posted to the proper account in the ledger?

11. Explain why the ledger can still contain errors even though the trial balance is in balance. Give examples of two such types of errors.

12. What is a slide error?

13. What is a transposition error?

14. What is the ruling method of correcting an error?

15. What is the correcting entry method?

MANAGING YOUR WRITING

You are a public accountant with many small business clients. During a recent visit to a client's business, the bookkeeper approached you with a problem. The columns of the trial balance were not equal. You helped the bookkeeper find and correct the error, but believe you should go one step further. Write a memo to all of your clients that explains the purpose of the double-entry framework, the importance of maintaining the equality of the accounting equation, the errors that might cause an inequality, and suggestions for finding the errors.

SERIES A EXERCISES

EXERCISE 4-1A   (LO3)   **SOURCE DOCUMENTS** Source documents trigger the analysis of events requiring an accounting entry. Match the following source documents with the type of information they provide.

1. Check stubs or check register
2. Purchase invoice from suppliers (vendors)
3. Sales tickets or invoices to customers
4. Receipts or cash register tapes

a. A good or service has been sold.
b. Cash has been received by the business.
c. Cash has been paid by the business.
d. Goods or services have been purchased by the business.

EXERCISE 4-2A   (LO4)   **GENERAL JOURNAL ENTRIES** For each of the following transactions, list the account to be debited and the account to be credited in the general journal.

1. Invested cash in the business, $5,000.
2. Paid office rent, $500.
3. Purchased office supplies on account, $300.
4. Received cash for services rendered (fees), $400.
5. Paid cash on account, $50.
6. Rendered services on account, $300.
7. Received cash for an amount owed by a customer, $100.

EXERCISE 4-3A   (LO5)   **GENERAL LEDGER ACCOUNTS** Set up T accounts for each of the general ledger accounts needed for Exercise 4-2A and post debits and credits to the accounts. Foot the accounts and enter the balances. Prove that total debits equal total credits.

EXERCISE 4-4A   (LO4)   **GENERAL JOURNAL ENTRIES** Jean Jones has opened Jones Consulting. Journalize the following transactions that occurred during January of the current year. Use the following journal pages: January 1–10, page 1 and January 11–29, page 2. Use the chart of accounts provided below.

Chart of Accounts

Assets	Revenues
101 Cash	401 Consulting Fees
142 Office Supplies	
181 Office Equipment	Expenses
	511 Wages Expense
Liabilities	521 Rent Expense
202 Accounts Payable	525 Telephone Expense
	533 Utilities Expense
Owner's Equity	549 Miscellaneous Expense
311 Jean Jones, Capital	
312 Jean Jones, Drawing	

(continued)

Jan.	1	Jones invested cash in the business, $10,000.
	2	Paid office rent, $500.
	3	Purchased office equipment on account, $1,500.
	5	Received cash for services rendered, $750.
	8	Paid telephone bill, $65.
	10	Paid for a magazine subscription (miscellaneous expense), $15.
	11	Purchased office supplies on account, $300.
	15	Made a payment on account (see Jan. 3 transaction), $150.
	18	Paid part-time employee, $500.
	21	Received cash for services rendered, $350.
	25	Paid utilities bill, $85.
	27	Jones withdrew cash for personal use, $100.
	29	Paid part-time employee, $500.

EXERCISE 4-5A   (LO5)   **GENERAL LEDGER ACCOUNTS; TRIAL BALANCE** Set up four-column general ledger accounts using the chart of accounts provided in Exercise 4-4A. Post the transactions from Exercise 4-4A to the general ledger accounts and prepare a trial balance.

EXERCISE 4-6A   **FINANCIAL STATEMENTS** From the information in Exercises 4-4A and 4-5A, prepare an income statement, a statement of owner's equity, and a balance sheet.

EXERCISE 4-7A   **FINANCIAL STATEMENTS** From the following trial balance taken after one month of operation, prepare an income statement, a statement of owner's equity, and a balance sheet. Assume that TJ Ulza made no additional investments in the business during the month.

<table>
<tr><th colspan="8">TJ's Paint Service
Trial Balance
July 31, 20 - -</th></tr>
<tr><th rowspan="2">ACCOUNT TITLE</th><th rowspan="2">ACCOUNT NO.</th><th colspan="3">DEBIT BALANCE</th><th colspan="3">CREDIT BALANCE</th></tr>
<tr></tr>
<tr><td>Cash</td><td>101</td><td colspan="3">4 3 0 0 00</td><td colspan="3"></td></tr>
<tr><td>Accounts Receivable</td><td>122</td><td colspan="3">1 1 0 0 00</td><td colspan="3"></td></tr>
<tr><td>Supplies</td><td>141</td><td colspan="3">8 0 0 00</td><td colspan="3"></td></tr>
<tr><td>Paint Equipment</td><td>183</td><td colspan="3">9 0 0 00</td><td colspan="3"></td></tr>
<tr><td>Accounts Payable</td><td>202</td><td colspan="3"></td><td colspan="3">2 1 5 0 00</td></tr>
<tr><td>TJ Ulza, Capital</td><td>311</td><td colspan="3"></td><td colspan="3">3 2 0 5 00</td></tr>
<tr><td>TJ Ulza, Drawing</td><td>312</td><td colspan="3">5 0 0 00</td><td colspan="3"></td></tr>
<tr><td>Painting Fees</td><td>401</td><td colspan="3"></td><td colspan="3">3 6 0 0 00</td></tr>
<tr><td>Wages Expense</td><td>511</td><td colspan="3">9 0 0 00</td><td colspan="3"></td></tr>
<tr><td>Rent Expense</td><td>521</td><td colspan="3">2 5 0 00</td><td colspan="3"></td></tr>
<tr><td>Telephone Expense</td><td>525</td><td colspan="3">5 0 00</td><td colspan="3"></td></tr>
<tr><td>Transportation Expense</td><td>526</td><td colspan="3">6 0 00</td><td colspan="3"></td></tr>
<tr><td>Utilities Expense</td><td>533</td><td colspan="3">7 0 00</td><td colspan="3"></td></tr>
<tr><td>Miscellaneous Expense</td><td>549</td><td colspan="3">2 5 00</td><td colspan="3"></td></tr>
<tr><td></td><td></td><td colspan="3">8 9 5 5 00</td><td colspan="3">8 9 5 5 00</td></tr>
</table>

EXERCISE 4-8A   **(LO6)**   **FINDING AND CORRECTING ERRORS** Joe Adams bought $500 worth of office supplies on account. The following entry was recorded on May 17. Find the error(s) and correct it (them) using the ruling method.

14													14
15	20-- May	17	Office Equipment			4	0	0	00				15
16			Cash							4	0	0	00	16
17			Purchased copy paper										17

On May 25, after the transactions had been posted, Adams discovered that the following entry contains an error. The cash received represents a collection on account, rather than new service fees. Correct the error in the general journal using the correcting entry method.

22														22
23	20-- May	23	Cash	101	1	0	0	0	00					23
24			Service Fees	401						1	0	0	0	00	24
25			Received cash for services previously earned											25

SERIES A PROBLEMS

PROBLEM 4-1A   **(LO4/5)**   **JOURNALIZING AND POSTING TRANSACTIONS** Jim Andrews opened a delivery business in March. He rented a small office and has a part-time assistant. His trial balance shows accounts for the first three months of business.

Jim's Quick Delivery Trial Balance May 31, 20 - -										
ACCOUNT TITLE	ACCOUNT NO.	DEBIT BALANCE				CREDIT BALANCE				
Cash	101	3	8	2	6	00				
Accounts Receivable	122	1	2	1	2	00				
Office Supplies	142		6	4	8	00				
Office Equipment	181	2	1	0	0	00				
Delivery Truck	185	8	0	0	0	00				
Accounts Payable	202						6	0	0	0	00
Jim Andrews, Capital	311						4	4	7	8	00
Jim Andrews, Drawing	312	1	8	0	0	00				
Delivery Fees	401						9	8	8	0	00
Wages Expense	511	1	2	0	0	00				
Advertising Expense	512		9	0	0	00				
Rent Expense	521		9	0	0	00				
Telephone Expense	525		1	2	6	00				
Electricity Expense	533		9	8	00					
Charitable Contributions Expense	534		6	0	00					
Gas and Oil Expense	538		1	8	6	00				
Miscellaneous Expense	549		1	1	2	00				
		20	3	5	8	00	20	3	5	8	00

(continued)

Andrews' transactions for the month of June are as follows:

June 1	Paid rent, $300.
2	Performed delivery services for $300: $100 in cash and $200 on account.
4	Paid for newspaper advertising, $15.
6	Purchased office supplies on account, $180.
7	Received cash for delivery services rendered, $260.
9	Paid cash on account (truck payment), $200.
10	Purchased a copier (office equipment) for $700: paid $100 in cash and put $600 on account.
11	Made a contribution to the Red Cross (charitable contributions), $20.
12	Received cash for delivery services rendered, $380.
13	Received cash on account for services previously rendered, $100.
15	Paid a part-time worker, $200.
16	Paid electric bill, $36.
18	Paid telephone bill, $46.
19	Received cash on account for services previously rendered, $100.
20	Andrews withdrew cash for personal use, $200.
21	Paid for gas and oil, $32.
22	Made payment on account (for office supplies), $40.
24	Received cash for services rendered, $340.
26	Paid for a magazine subscription (miscellaneous expense), $15.
27	Received cash for services rendered, $180.
27	Received cash on account for services previously rendered, $100.
29	Paid for gasoline, $24.
30	Paid a part-time worker, $200.

REQUIRED

1. Set up four-column general ledger accounts by entering the balances as of June 1.

2. Journalize the transactions for June in a two-column general journal. Use the following journal pages: June 1–10, page 7; June 11–20, page 8; June 21–30, page 9.

3. Post the entries from the general journal.

4. Prepare a trial balance.

PROBLEM 4-2A   (LO4/5)

JOURNALIZING AND POSTING TRANSACTIONS Annette Creighton opened Creighton Consulting. She rented a small office and paid a part-time worker to answer the telephone and make deliveries. Her chart of accounts is as follows:

Chart of Accounts

Assets	Revenues
101 Cash	401 Consulting Fees
142 Office Supplies	
181 Office Equipment	Expenses
	511 Wages Expense
Liabilities	512 Advertising Expense
202 Accounts Payable	521 Rent Expense
	525 Telephone Expense
Owner's Equity	526 Transportation Expense
311 Annette Creighton, Capital	533 Utilities Expense
312 Annette Creighton, Drawing	549 Miscellaneous Expense

Creighton's transactions for the first month of business are as follows:

Jan. 1   Creighton invested cash in the business, $10,000.

1   Paid rent, $500.

2   Purchased office supplies on account, $300.

4   Purchased office equipment on account, $1,500.

6   Received cash for services rendered, $580.

7   Paid telephone bill, $42.

8   Paid utilities bill, $38.

10   Received cash for services rendered, $360.

12   Made payment on account, $50.

13   Paid for car rental while visiting an out-of-town client (transportation expense), $150.

15   Paid part-time worker, $360.

17   Received cash for services rendered, $420.

18   Creighton withdrew cash for personal use, $100.

20   Paid for a newspaper ad, $26.

22   Reimbursed part-time employee for cab fare incurred delivering materials to clients (transportation expense), $35.

24   Paid for books on consulting practices (miscellaneous expense), $28.

25   Received cash for services rendered, $320.

27   Made payment on account for office equipment purchased, $150.

29   Paid part-time worker, $360.

30   Received cash for services rendered, $180.

(continued)

REQUIRED

1. Set up four-column general ledger accounts from the chart of accounts.

2. Journalize the transactions for January in a two-column general journal. Use the following journal page numbers: January 1–10, page 1; January 12–24, page 2; January 25–30, page 3.

3. Post the transactions from the general journal.

4. Prepare a trial balance.

5. Prepare an income statement and a statement of owner's equity for the month of January, and a balance sheet as of January 31, 20--.

PROBLEM 4-3A **(LO6)** **CORRECTING ERRORS** Assuming that all entries have been posted, prepare correcting entries for each of the following errors:

1. The following entry was made to record the purchase of $500 in supplies on account:

Supplies	142	500	
Cash	101		500

2. The following entry was made to record the payment of $300 in wages:

Rent Expense	521	300	
Cash	101		300

3. The following entry was made to record a $200 payment to a supplier on account:

Supplies	142	100	
Cash	101		100

SERIES B EXERCISES

EXERCISE 4-1B **(LO3)** **SOURCE DOCUMENTS** What type of information is found on each of the following source documents?

1. Cash register tape

2. Sales ticket (issued to customer)

3. Purchase invoice (received from supplier or vendor)

4. Check stub

EXERCISE 4-2B **(LO4)** **GENERAL JOURNAL ENTRIES** For each of the following transactions, list the account to be debited and the account to be credited in the general journal.

1. Invested cash in the business, $1,000.

2. Performed services on account, $200.

3. Purchased office equipment on account, $500.

4. Received cash on account for services previously rendered, $200.

5. Made a payment on account, $100.

EXERCISE 4-3B   (LO5)   **GENERAL LEDGER ACCOUNTS** Set up T accounts for each of the general ledger accounts needed for Exercise 4-2B and post debits and credits to the accounts. Foot the accounts and enter the balances. Prove that total debits equal total credits.

EXERCISE 4-4B   (LO4)   **GENERAL JOURNAL ENTRIES** Sengel Moon opened The Bike Doctor. Journalize the following transactions that occurred during the month of October of the current year. Use the following journal pages: October 1–12, page 1 and October 14–29, page 2. Use the chart of accounts provided below.

Chart of Accounts

Assets	Revenues
101 Cash	401 Repair Fees
141 Bicycle Parts	
142 Office Supplies	Expenses
	511 Wages Expense
Liabilities	521 Rent Expense
202 Accounts Payable	525 Telephone Expense
	533 Utilities Expense
Owner's Equity	549 Miscellaneous Expense
311 Sengel Moon, Capital	
312 Sengel Moon, Drawing	

Oct. 1   Moon invested cash in the business, $15,000.

2   Paid shop rental for the month, $300.

3   Purchased bicycle parts on account, $2,000.

5   Purchased office supplies on account, $250.

8   Paid telephone bill, $38.

9   Received cash for services, $140.

11   Paid a sports magazine subscription (miscellaneous expense), $15.

12   Made payment on account (see Oct. 3 transaction), $100.

14   Paid part-time employee, $300.

15   Received cash for services, $350.

16   Paid utilities bill, $48.

19   Received cash for services, $250.

23   Moon withdrew cash for personal use, $50.

25   Made payment on account (see Oct. 5 transaction), $50.

29   Paid part-time employee, $300.

EXERCISE 4-5B   (LO5)   **GENERAL LEDGER ACCOUNTS; TRIAL BALANCE** Set up four-column general ledger accounts using the chart of accounts provided in Exercise 4-4B. Post the transactions from Exercise 4-4B to the general ledger accounts and prepare a trial balance.

EXERCISE 4-6B   **FINANCIAL STATEMENTS** From the information in Exercises 4-4B and 4-5B, prepare an income statement, a statement of owner's equity, and a balance sheet.

EXERCISE 4-7B

FINANCIAL STATEMENTS From the following trial balance taken after one month of operation, prepare an income statement, a statement of owner's equity, and a balance sheet. Assume that no additional investments were made during the month.

AT's Speaker's Bureau Trial Balance March 31, 20 - -												
ACCOUNT TITLE	ACCOUNT NO.	DEBIT BALANCE					CREDIT BALANCE					
Cash	101	6	6	0	0	00						
Accounts Receivable	122	2	8	0	0	00						
Office Supplies	142	1	0	0	0	00						
Office Equipment	181	1	5	0	0	00						
Accounts Payable	202							3	0	0	0	00
AT Speaker, Capital	311							6	0	9	8	00
AT Speaker, Drawing	312		8	0	0	00						
Speaking Fees	401							4	8	0	0	00
Wages Expense	511		4	0	0	00						
Rent Expense	521		2	0	0	00						
Telephone Expense	525			3	5	00						
Travel Expense	526		4	5	0	00						
Utilities Expense	533			8	8	00						
Miscellaneous Expense	549			2	5	00						
		13	8	9	8	00		13	8	9	8	00

EXERCISE 4-8B (LO6)

FINDING AND CORRECTING ERRORS Mary Smith purchased $350 worth of office equipment on account. The following entry was recorded on April 6. Find the error(s) and correct it (them) using the ruling method.

7															7
8	20-- Apr.	6	Office Supplies			5	3	0	00						8
9			Cash							5	3	0	00		9
10			Purchased office equipment												10

On April 25, after the transactions had been posted, Smith discovered the following entry contains an error. When her customer received services, Cash was debited, but no cash was received. Correct the error in the journal using the correcting entry method.

27															27
28	20-- Apr.	21	Cash	101		3	0	0	00						28
29			Service Fees	401						3	0	0	00		29
30			Revenue earned from services												30
31			previously rendered												31

SERIES B PROBLEMS

PROBLEM 4-1B   (LO4/5)   **JOURNALIZING AND POSTING TRANSACTIONS** Ann Tailor owns a suit tailoring shop. She opened business in September. She rented a small work space and has an assistant to receive job orders and process claim tickets. Her trial balance shows her account balances for the first two months of business.

ACCOUNT TITLE	ACCOUNT NO.	DEBIT BALANCE	CREDIT BALANCE
Cash	101	6 2 1 1 00	
Accounts Receivable	122	4 8 4 00	
Tailoring Supplies	141	1 0 0 0 00	
Tailoring Equipment	183	3 8 0 0 00	
Accounts Payable	202		4 1 2 5 00
Ann Tailor, Capital	311		6 1 3 0 00
Ann Tailor, Drawing	312	8 0 0 00	
Tailoring Fees	401		3 6 0 0 00
Wages Expense	511	8 0 0 00	
Advertising Expense	512	3 4 00	
Rent Expense	521	6 0 0 00	
Telephone Expense	525	6 0 00	
Electricity Expense	533	4 4 00	
Miscellaneous Expense	549	2 2 00	
		13 8 5 5 00	13 8 5 5 00

Tailor Tailoring / Trial Balance / October 31, 20- -

Tailor's transactions for November are as follows:

Nov. 1   Paid rent, $300.

2   Purchased tailoring supplies on account, $150.

3   Purchased a new button hole machine on account, $300.

5   Earned first week's revenue, $400: $100 in cash and $300 on account.

8   Paid for newspaper advertising, $13.

9   Paid telephone bill, $28.

10   Paid electric bill, $21.

11   Received cash on account from customers, $200.

12   Earned second week's revenue, $450: $200 in cash and $250 on account.

15   Paid assistant, $400.

16   Made payment on account, $100.

17   Paid for magazine subscription (miscellaneous expense), $12.

19   Earned third week's revenue, $450: $300 in cash, $150 on account.

23   Received cash on account from customers, $300.

24   Paid for newspaper advertising, $13.

26   Paid for postage (miscellaneous expense), $12.

(continued)

27 Earned fourth week's revenue, $600: $200 in cash and $400 on account.

30 Received cash on account from customers, $400.

REQUIRED

1. Set up four-column general ledger accounts by entering the balances as of November 1, 20--.

2. Journalize the transactions for November in a two-column general journal. Use the following journal page numbers: November 1–11, page 7; November 12–24, page 8; November 26–30, page 9.

3. Post the entries from the general journal.

4. Prepare a trial balance.

PROBLEM 4-2B (LO4/5)

JOURNALIZING AND POSTING TRANSACTIONS Benito Mendez opened Mendez Appraisals. He rented office space and has a part-time secretary to answer the telephone and make appraisal appointments. His chart of accounts is as follows:

Chart of Accounts

Assets	Revenues
101 Cash	401 Appraisal Fees
122 Accounts Receivable	
142 Office Supplies	Expenses
181 Office Equipment	511 Wages Expense
	512 Advertising Expense
Liabilities	521 Rent Expense
202 Accounts Payable	525 Telephone Expense
	526 Transportation Expense
Owner's Equity	533 Electricity Expense
311 Benito Mendez, Capital	549 Miscellaneous Expense
312 Benito Mendez, Drawing	

Mendez's transactions for the first month of business are as follows:

May 1 Mendez invested cash in the business, $5,000.

2 Paid rent, $500.

3 Purchased office supplies, $100.

4 Purchased office equipment on account, $2,000.

5 Received cash for services rendered, $280.

8 Paid telephone bill, $38.

9 Paid electric bill, $42.

10 Received cash for services rendered, $310.

13 Paid part-time employee, $500.

14 Paid car rental for out-of-town trip, $200.

15 Paid for newspaper ad, $30.

18 Received cash for services rendered, $620.

19 Paid mileage reimbursement for part-time employee's use of personal car for business deliveries (transportation expense), $22.

21   Mendez withdrew cash for personal use, $50.

23   Made payment on account for office equipment purchased earlier, $200.

24   Earned appraisal fee, which will be paid in a week, $500.

26   Paid for newspaper ad, $30.

27   Paid for local softball team sponsorship (miscellaneous expense), $15.

28   Paid part-time employee, $500.

29   Received cash on account, $250.

30   Received cash for services rendered, $280.

31   Paid cab fare (transportation expense), $13.

REQUIRED

1.   Set up four-column general ledger accounts from the chart of accounts.

2.   Journalize the transactions for May in a two-column general journal. Use the following journal page numbers: May 1–10, page 1; May 13–24, page 2; May 26–31, page 3.

3.   Post the transactions from the general journal.

4.   Prepare a trial balance.

5.   Prepare an income statement and a statement of owner's equity for the month of May, and a balance sheet as of May 31, 20--.

PROBLEM 4-3B   (LO6)   **CORRECTING ERRORS** Assuming that all entries have been posted, prepare correcting entries for each of the following errors:

1.   The following entry was made to record the purchase of $400 in equipment on account:

Supplies	142	400	
Cash	101		400

2.   The following entry was made to record the payment of $200 for advertising:

Repair Expense	537	200	
Cash	101		200

3.   The following entry was made to record a $600 payment to a supplier on account:

Prepaid Insurance	145	400	
Cash	101		400

CHALLENGE PROBLEM

Journal entries and a trial balance for Fred Phaler Consulting are provided below. As you will note, the trial balance does not balance, suggesting that there are errors. Recall that the chapter offers tips on identifying individual posting errors. These techniques are not as effective when there are two or more errors. Thus, you will need to first carefully inspect the trial balance to see if you can identify any obvious errors either due to amounts that look out of proportion or simply reported in the wrong place. Then, you will need to carefully evaluate the other amounts by using the techniques offered in the text, or tracing the journal entries to the amounts reported on the trial balance. (Hint: four errors were made in the posting process and preparation of the trial balance.)

	DATE		DESCRIPTION	POST REF.	DEBIT	CREDIT	
	20--						
1	June	1	Cash	101	10 0 0 0 00		1
2			Fred Phaler, Capital	311		10 0 0 0 00	2
3							3
4		2	Rent Expense	521	5 0 0 00		4
5			Cash	101		5 0 0 00	5
6							6
7		3	Cash	101	4 0 0 0 00		7
8			Professional Fees	401		4 0 0 0 00	8
9							9
10		4	Utilities Expense	533	1 0 0 00		10
11			Cash	101		1 0 0 00	11
12							12
13		7	Cash	101	3 0 0 0 00		13
14			Professional Fees	401		3 0 0 0 00	14
15							15
16		12	Automobile Expense	526	5 0 00		16
17			Cash	101		5 0 00	17
18							18
19		14	Wages Expense	511	5 0 0 00		19
20			Cash	101		5 0 0 00	20
21							21
22		14	Office Supplies	142	2 5 0 00		22
23			Accounts Payable	202		2 5 0 00	23
24							24
25		20	Telephone Expense	525	1 0 0 00		25
26			Cash	101		1 0 0 00	26
27							27
28		21	Fred Phaler, Drawing	312	1 2 0 0 00		28
29			Cash	101		1 2 0 0 00	29
30							30
31		24	Accounts Receivable	122	2 0 0 0 00		31
32			Professional Fees	401		2 0 0 0 00	32
33							33
34		25	Accounts Payable	202	1 0 0 0 00		34
35			Cash	101		1 0 0 0 00	35
36							36
37		30	Wages Expense	511	3 0 0 00		37
38			Wages Payable	219		3 0 0 00	38

GENERAL JOURNAL — PAGE 1

Fred Phaler Consulting Trial Balance June 30, 20 - -			
ACCOUNT TITLE	ACCOUNT NO.	DEBIT BALANCE	CREDIT BALANCE
Cash	101		14 2 0 0 00
Accounts Receivable	122	2 0 0 0 00	
Office Supplies	142	2 5 0 00	
Accounts Payable	202	1 0 0 00	
Wages Payable	219		3 0 0 00
Fred Phaler, Capital	311		10 0 0 0 00
Fred Phaler, Drawing	312	2 1 0 0 00	
Professional Fees	401		9 0 0 0 00
Wages Expense	511	8 0 0 00	
Rent Expense	521	5 0 0 00	
Telephone Expense	525	1 0 0 00	
Automobile Expense	526	50 0 0 0 00	
Utilities Expense	533	1 0 0 00	
		55 9 5 0 00	33 5 0 0 00

REQUIRED

1. Find the errors.

2. Explain what caused the errors.

MASTERY PROBLEM

Barry Bird opened the Barry Bird Basketball Camp for children ages 10 through 18. Campers typically register for one week in June or July, arriving on Sunday and returning home the following Saturday. College players serve as cabin counselors and assist the local college and high school coaches who run the practice sessions. The registration fee includes a room, meals at a nearby restaurant, and basketball instruction. In the off-season, the facilities are used for weekend retreats and coaching clinics. Bird developed the following chart of accounts for his service business.

Chart of Accounts

Assets
101 Cash
142 Office Supplies
183 Athletic Equipment
184 Basketball Facilities

Liabilities
202 Accounts Payable

Owner's Equity
311 Barry Bird, Capital
312 Barry Bird, Drawing

Revenues
401 Registration Fees

Expenses
511 Wages Expense
512 Advertising Expense
524 Food Expense
525 Telephone Expense
533 Utilities Expense
536 Postage Expense

The following transactions took place during the month of June.

June 1	Bird invested cash in the business, $10,000.
1	Purchased basketballs and other athletic equipment, $3,000.
2	Paid Hite Advertising for flyers that had been mailed to prospective campers, $5,000.
2	Collected registration fees, $15,000.
2	Rogers Construction completed work on a new basketball court that cost $12,000. Arrangements were made to pay the bill in July.
5	Purchased office supplies on account from Gordon Office Supplies, $300.
6	Received bill from Magic's Restaurant for meals served to campers on account, $5,800.
7	Collected registration fees, $16,200.
10	Paid wages to camp counselors, $500.
14	Collected registration fees, $13,500.
14	Received bill from Magic's Restaurant for meals served to campers on account, $6,200.
17	Paid wages to camp counselors, $500.
18	Paid postage, $85.
21	Collected registration fees, $15,200.
22	Received bill from Magic's Restaurant for meals served to campers on account, $6,500.
24	Paid wages to camp counselors, $500.
28	Collected registration fees, $14,000.
30	Received bill from Magic's Restaurant for meals served to campers on account, $7,200.
30	Paid wages to camp counselors, $500.
30	Paid Magic's Restaurant on account, $25,700.
30	Paid utility bill, $500.
30	Paid telephone bill, $120.
30	Bird withdrew cash for personal use, $2,000.

REQUIRED

1. Enter the above transactions in a general journal. Use the following journal pages: June 1–6, page 1; June 7–22, page 2; June 24–30, page 3.

2. Post the entries to the general ledger.

3. Prepare a trial balance.

Self-Study Test Questions

True/False

1. Source documents serve as historical evidence of business transactions. _____

2. No entries are made in the Posting Reference column at the time of journalizing. _____

3. When entering the credit item in a general journal, it should be listed after all debits and indented. _____

4. The chart of accounts lists capital accounts first, followed by liabilities, assets, expenses, and revenue. _____

5. When an incorrect entry has been journalized and posted to the wrong account, a correcting entry should be made. _____

Multiple Choice

1. The process of copying debits and credits from the journal to the ledger is called _____

   (a) journalizing.   (c) cross-referencing.
   (b) posting.   (d) sliding.

2. To purchase an asset such as office equipment on account, you would credit which account? _____

   (a) Cash   (c) Accounts Payable
   (b) Accounts Receivable (d) Capital

3. When fees are earned but will be paid later, which account is debited? _____

   (a) Cash   (c) Accounts Payable
   (b) Accounts Receivable (d) Capital

4. When the correct numbers are used but are in the wrong order, the error is called a _____

   (a) transposition.   (c) ruling.
   (b) slide.   (d) correcting entry.

5. A revenue account will begin with the number _____ in the chart of accounts. _____

   (a) 1   (c) 3
   (b) 2   (d) 4

The answers to the Self-Study Test Questions are at the end of the text.

5

Adjusting Entries and the Work Sheet

At the end of the first month of operations, Jessie and Mitch were looking over the trial balance. "These accounts don't look right," said Jessie. "Don't worry, I just need to make a few adjustments before we prepare the financial statements," replied Mitch. Does it seem appropriate to make adjustments prior to issuing financial statements?

Careful study of this chapter should enable you to:

LO1 Prepare end-of-period adjustments.

LO2 Prepare a work sheet.

LO3 Describe methods for finding errors on the work sheet.

LO4 Journalize adjusting entries.

LO5 Post adjusting entries to the general ledger.

Up to this point, you have learned how to journalize business transactions, post to the ledger, and prepare a trial balance. Now it is time to learn how to make end-of-period adjustments to the accounts listed in the trial balance. This chapter explains the need for adjustments and illustrates how they are made using a work sheet.

END-OF-PERIOD ADJUSTMENTS

LO1 Prepare end-of-period adjustments.

Transactions are entered as they occur throughout the year. Adjustments are made to reflect changes in account balances that are not the direct

result of an exchange with an outside party. Adjustments are made at the end of the accounting period.

Throughout the accounting period, business transactions are entered in the accounting system. These transactions are based on exchanges between the business and other companies and individuals. During the accounting period, other changes occur that affect the business's financial condition. For example, equipment is wearing out, prepaid insurance and supplies are being used up, and employees are earning wages that have not yet been paid. Since these events have not been entered into the accounting system, **adjusting entries** must be made prior to the preparation of financial statements.

The **matching principle** in accounting requires the matching of revenues earned during an accounting period with the expenses incurred to produce the revenues. This approach offers the best measure of net income. The income statement reports earnings for a specific period of time and the balance sheet reports the assets, liabilities, and owner's equity on a specific date. Thus, to follow the matching principle, the accounts must be brought up to date before financial statements are prepared. This requires adjusting some of the accounts listed in the trial balance. Figure 5-1 lists reasons to adjust the trial balance.

LEARNING KEY: Matching revenues earned with expenses incurred as a result of efforts to produce those revenues offers the best measure of net income.

1. To report all revenues earned during the accounting period.

2. To report all expenses incurred to produce the revenues earned in this accounting period.

3. To accurately report the assets on the balance sheet date. Some assets may have been used up during the accounting period.

4. To accurately report the liabilities on the balance sheet date. Expenses may have been incurred but not yet paid.

FIGURE 5-1 **Reasons to Adjust the Trial Balance**

Generally, adjustments are made and financial statements prepared at the end of a twelve-month period called a **fiscal year**. This period does not need to be the same as a calendar year. In fact, many businesses schedule their fiscal year end for a time when business is slow. In this chapter we continue the illustration of Jessie Jane's Campus Delivery and will prepare adjustments at the end of the first month of operations. We will focus on the following accounts: Supplies, Prepaid Insurance, Delivery Equipment, and Wages Expense.

Supplies

During June, Jessie purchased supplies consisting of paper, pens, and delivery envelopes for $80. *Since these supplies were expected to provide future benefits, Supplies, an asset, was debited at the time of the purchase.* No other entries were made to the supplies account during June. As reported on the trial balance in Figure 5-2, the $80 balance remains in the supplies account at the end of the month.

As supplies are used, an expense is incurred. However, it is not practical to make a journal entry to recognize this expense and the reduction in the supplies account every time someone uses an envelope. It is more efficient to wait until the end of the accounting period to make one adjusting entry to reflect the expense incurred for the use of supplies for the entire month.

A BROADER VIEW

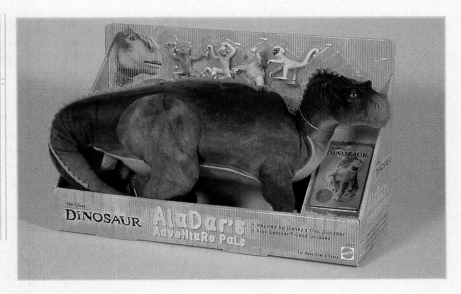

Adjusting Entries

Are adjusting entries important? The Walt Disney Company and Mattel, Inc. probably think so. The Walt Disney Company granted Mattel, Inc. the right to make and sell toys based on Disney characters. In return, Mattel agreed to make payments to Disney as the toys were sold. One of the issues in a court case was whether Mattel should have made an adjusting entry when it fell behind on these payments. The entry would have been:

Royalty Expense on Disney Characters	17,000,000	
Accounts Payable (Disney)		17,000,000

This adjusting entry would have reduced Mattel's fourth quarter earnings for that year by more than 15%. Following an investigation by the Securities and Exchange Commission, Mattel eventually agreed to make an adjustment to later financial statements.

Jessie Jane's Campus Delivery
Trial Balance
June 30, 20 - -

ACCOUNT TITLE	ACCOUNT NO.	DEBIT BALANCE					CREDIT BALANCE				
Cash	101		3	7	0	00					
Accounts Receivable	122		6	5	0	00					
Supplies	141			8	0	00					
Prepaid Insurance	145		2	0	0	00					
Delivery Equipment	185	3	6	0	0	00					
Accounts Payable	202						1	8	0	0	00
Jessica Jane, Capital	311						2	0	0	0	00
Jessica Jane, Drawing	312		1	5	0	00					
Delivery Fees	401						2	1	5	0	00
Wages Expense	511		6	5	0	00					
Rent Expense	521		2	0	0	00					
Telephone Expense	525			5	0	00					
		5	9	5	0	00	5	9	5	0	00

FIGURE 5-2   Trial Balance

At the end of the month, an inventory, or physical count, of the remaining supplies is taken. The inventory shows that supplies costing $20 were still unused at the end of June. Since Jessie bought supplies costing $80, and only $20 worth remain, supplies costing $60 must have been used ($80 − $20 = $60). Thus, supplies expense for the month is $60. (Trial balance is abbreviated as TB in Figure 5-3 and other T account illustrations.)

Since $60 worth of supplies have been used, Supplies Expense is debited and Supplies (asset) is credited for $60 (Figure 5-3). Thus, as shown in Figure 5-4, supplies with a cost of $20 will be reported as an asset on the balance sheet and a supplies expense of $60 will be reported on the income statement. The adjusting entry affected an income statement account (Supplies Expense) and a balance sheet account (Supplies).

LEARNING KEY: Since it is not practical to make a journal entry for supplies expense each time supplies are used, one adjusting entry is made at the end of the accounting period.

Assets		=	Liabilities		+	Owner's Equity					
Debit	Credit		Debit	Credit			Debit			Credit	
+	−		−	+			−			+	

			Drawing		Expenses		Revenues	
			Debit	Credit	Debit	Credit	Debit	Credit
			+	−	+	−	−	+

Supplies				Supplies Expense	
TB 80				Adj. 60	
	Adj. 60				
Bal. 20					

FIGURE 5-3   Adjustment for Supplies

LEARNING KEY: By making an adjusting entry that debits Supplies Expense and credits Supplies, you are taking the amount of supplies used out of Supplies and putting it in Supplies Expense.

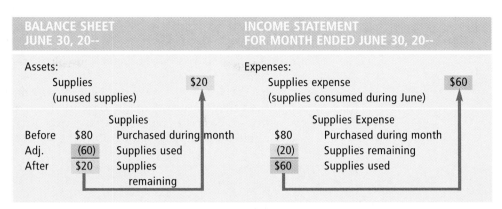

FIGURE 5-4   **Effect of Adjusting Entry for Supplies on Financial Statements**

Prepaid Insurance

On June 18, Jessie paid $200 for an eight-month liability insurance policy with coverage beginning on June 1. *Prepaid Insurance, an asset, was debited because the insurance policy is expected to provide future benefits.* The $200 balance is reported on the trial balance. As the insurance policy expires with the passage of time, the asset should be reduced and an expense recognized.

Since the $200 premium covers eight months, the cost of the expired coverage for June is $25 ($200 ÷ 8 months). As shown in Figure 5-5, the adjusting entry is to debit Insurance Expense for $25 and credit Prepaid Insurance for $25. Figure 5-6 shows that the unexpired portion of the insurance premium will be reported on the balance sheet as Prepaid Insurance of $175. The expired portion will be reported on the income statement as Insurance Expense of $25.

LEARNING KEY: The $200 premium covers eight months. The cost for June is $25 ($200 ÷ 8 months).

Assets		=	Liabilities		+	Owner's Equity			
Debit	**Credit**		**Debit**	**Credit**		**Debit**		**Credit**	
+	–		–	+		–		+	

		Drawing		Expenses		Revenues	
		Debit	**Credit**	**Debit**	**Credit**	**Debit**	**Credit**
		+	–	+	–	–	+

Prepaid Insurance				Insurance Expense	
TB 200				Adj. 25	
	Adj. 25				
Bal. 175					

FIGURE 5-5   **Adjustment for Expired Insurance**

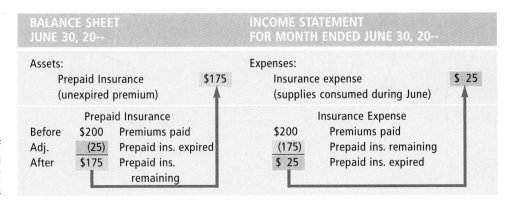

FIGURE 5-6   **Effect of Adjusting Entry for Prepaid Insurance on Financial Statements**

Wages Expense

Jessie paid her part-time employees $650 on June 27. Since then, they have earned an additional $50, but have not yet been paid. The additional wages expense must be recognized.

Since the employees have not been paid, Wages Payable, a liability, should be established. Thus, Wages Expense is debited and Wages Payable is credited for $50 in Figure 5-7. Note in Figure 5-8 that Wages Expense of $700 is reported on the income statement and Wages Payable of $50 is reported on the balance sheet.

Assets		=	Liabilities		+	Owner's Equity					
Debit	**Credit**		**Debit**	**Credit**		**Debit**				**Credit**	
+	−		−	+		−				+	
							Drawing		**Expenses**		**Revenues**
							Debit | **Credit**		**Debit** | **Credit**		**Debit** | **Credit**
							+ | −		+ | −		− | +

	Wages Payable		Wages Expense	
		Adj. 50	TB 650	
			Adj. 50	
			Bal. 700	

FIGURE 5-7   Adjustment for Unpaid Wages

BALANCE SHEET JUNE 30, 20--		INCOME STATEMENT FOR MONTH ENDED JUNE 30, 20--	
Liabilities:		Expenses:	
Wages Payable (owed to employees)	$ 50	Wages expense (incurred for June)	$700

	Wages Payable			Wages Expense	
$700	Total wages expense incurred		Before	$650	Wages paid
(650)	Paid to employees		Adj.	50	Wages owed
$ 50	Owed to employees		After	$700	Total wages expense

FIGURE 5-8   Effect of Adjusting Entry for Wages on Financial Statements

PROFILES IN ACCOUNTING

Jeff Clifton, Account Supervisor

Jeff Clifton maintained a 4.0 GPA with nearly perfect attendance while earning an Associate Degree in Accounting Automation. He performed an externship with Brooke County Taxing Authority and then began working as an accounts receivable clerk with the DeBartolo Properties Management, Inc., in Youngstown, OH.

He was promoted and is now an account supervisor. His duties include managing accounts receivable for 20 development properties across the United States, supervising five employees, and interviewing prospective employees.

According to Jeff, being self-motivated is the main key to success. You need to work hard and success will come. Accounting interested Jeff because he enjoys working with numbers and considers himself to be very analytical.

Depreciation Expense

During the month of June, Jessie purchased three motor scooters. Since the scooters will provide future benefits, they were recorded as assets in the delivery equipment account. Under the **historical cost principle**, assets are recorded at their actual cost, in this case $3,600. This cost remains on the books as long as the business owns the asset. No adjustments are made for changes in the market value of the asset. It does not matter whether the firm got a "good buy" or paid "too much" when the asset was purchased.

> **LEARNING KEY:** The historical cost principle is an important accounting concept. Assets are recorded at their actual cost. This historical cost is not adjusted for changes in market values.

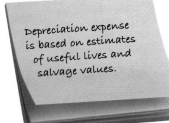

Depreciation expense is based on estimates of useful lives and salvage values.

The period of time that an asset is expected to help produce revenues is called its **useful life**. The asset's useful life expires as a result of wear and tear or because it no longer satisfies the needs of the business. For example, as Jessie adds miles to her scooters, they will become less reliable and will eventually fail to run. As this happens, depreciation expense should be recognized and the value of the asset should be reduced. **Depreciation** is a method of *matching* an asset's original cost against the revenues produced over its useful life. There are many depreciation methods. In our example, we will use the **straight-line method**.

Let's assume that Jessie's motor scooters have estimated useful lives of three years and will have no salvage value at the end of that time period. **Salvage value** (also called scrap value, or residual value) is the expected **market value** or selling price of the asset at the end of its useful life. The **depreciable cost** of these scooters is the original cost, less salvage value, or $3,600. It is this amount that is subject to depreciation. Let's also assume that a full month's depreciation is recognized in the month in which an asset is purchased.

The depreciable cost is spread over 36 months (3 years × 12 months). Thus, the straight-line depreciation expense for the month of June is $100 ($3,600 ÷ 36 months).

Straight-Line Depreciation					
Original Cost	−	Salvage Value	=	Depreciable Cost	
$\dfrac{\text{Depreciable Cost}}{\text{Estimated Useful Life}}$	=	$\dfrac{\$3,600}{36 \text{ months}}$	=	$100 per month	

When we made adjustments for supplies and prepaid insurance, the asset accounts were credited to show that they had been consumed. Assets of a durable nature that are expected to provide benefits over several years or more, called **plant assets**, require a different approach. The business maintains a record of the original cost and the amount of depreciation taken since the asset was acquired. By comparing these two amounts, the reader can estimate the relative age of the assets. Thus, instead of crediting Delivery Equipment for the amount of depreciation, a contra-asset account, Accumulated Depreciation—Delivery Equipment, is credited. "Contra" means opposite or against. Thus, a **contra-asset** has a credit balance (the opposite of an asset) and is deducted from the related asset account on the balance sheet.

LEARNING KEY: Depreciable assets provide benefits over more than one year. Therefore, the historical cost of the asset remains in the asset account. To show that it has been depreciated, a *contra-asset* account is used.

As shown in Figure 5-9, the appropriate adjusting entry consists of a debit to Depreciation Expense—Delivery Equipment and a credit to Accumulated Depreciation—Delivery Equipment. Note the position of the accumulated depreciation account in the accounting equation. It is shown in the asset section, directly beneath Delivery Equipment. Contra-asset accounts should always be shown along with the related asset account. Therefore, Delivery Equipment and Accumulated Depreciation—Delivery Equipment are shown together.

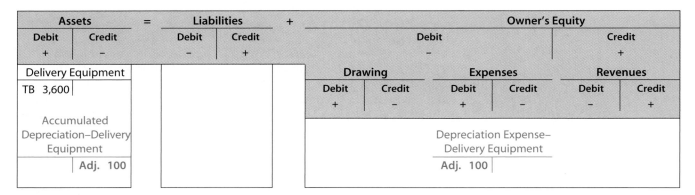

FIGURE 5-9 Adjustment for Depreciation of Delivery Equipment

The same concept is used on the balance sheet. Note in Figure 5-10 that Accumulated Depreciation is reported immediately beneath Delivery Equipment as a deduction. The difference between these accounts is known as the **book value**, or **undepreciated cost**, of the delivery equipment. Book value simply means the value carried on the books or in the accounting records. It does *not* represent the market value, or selling price, of the asset.

LEARNING KEY: Book Value = Cost of Plant Assets − Accumulated Depreciation. There is no individual account that reports book value. It must be computed as shown below.

BALANCE SHEET JUNE 30, 20--			INCOME STATEMENT FOR MONTH ENDED JUNE 30, 20--	
Assets:			Expenses:	
Delivery equipment	$3,600		Depreciation expense	$100
Less: Accumulated			(Expired cost for June)	
depreciation	100	$3,500		
		(Book value)		

FIGURE 5-10 Effect of Adjusting Entry for Depreciation on Financial Statements for June

If no delivery equipment is bought or sold during the next month, the same adjusting entry would be made at the end of July. If an income statement for the month of July and a balance sheet as of July 31 were prepared, the amounts shown in Figure 5-11 would be reported for the delivery equipment.

BALANCE SHEET JULY 31, 20--			INCOME STATEMENT FOR MONTH ENDED JULY 31, 20--	
Assets:			Expenses:	
Delivery equipment	$3,600		Depreciation expense	$100
Less: Accumulated			(Expired cost for July)	
depreciation	200	$3,400		
		(Book value)		

FIGURE 5-11   **Effect of Adjusting Entry for Depreciation on Financial Statements for July**

The cost ($3,600) remains unchanged, but the accumulated depreciation has increased to $200. This represents *the depreciation that has accumulated* since the delivery equipment was purchased ($100 in June and $100 in July). The depreciation expense for July is $100, the same as reported for June. Depreciation expense is reported for a specific time period. It does not accumulate across reporting periods.

Expanded Chart of Accounts

Several new accounts were needed to make the adjusting entries. New accounts are easily added to the chart of accounts, as shown in Figure 5-12. Note the close relationship between assets and contra-assets in the numbering of the accounts. Contra-accounts carry the same number as the related asset account with a ".1" suffix. For example, Delivery Equipment is account number 185 and the contra-asset account, Accumulated Depreciation—Delivery Equipment, is account number 185.1.

JESSIE JANE'S CAMPUS DELIVERY CHART OF ACCOUNTS				
Assets			**Revenue**	
101	Cash		401	Delivery Fees
122	Accounts Receivable			
141	Supplies		**Expenses**	
145	Prepaid Insurance		511	Wages Expense
185	Delivery Equipment		521	Rent Expense
185.1	Accumulated Depr.—		523	Supplies Expense
	Delivery Equipment		525	Telephone Expense
			535	Insurance Expense
Liabilities			541	Depr. Expense—
202	Accounts Payable			Delivery Equipment
219	Wages Payable			
Owner's Equity				
311	Jessica Jane, Capital			
312	Jessica Jane, Drawing			

FIGURE 5-12   **Expanded Chart of Accounts**

THE WORK SHEET

LO2 Prepare a work sheet.

A **work sheet** pulls together all of the information needed to enter adjusting entries and prepare the financial statements. Work sheets are not financial statements and are not a formal part of the accounting system. Ordinarily, only the accountant uses a work sheet. For this reason, a work sheet is usually prepared in pencil or as a spreadsheet on a computer.

The Ten-Column Work Sheet

Although a work sheet can take several forms, a common format has a column for account titles and ten amount columns grouped into five pairs. The work sheet format and the five steps in preparing the work sheet are illustrated in Figure 5-13. As with financial statements, the work sheet has a heading consisting of the name of the company, name of the working paper, and the date of the accounting period just ended. The five major column headings for the work sheet are Trial Balance, Adjustments, Adjusted Trial Balance, Income Statement, and Balance Sheet.

Preparing the Work Sheet

Let's apply the five steps required for the preparation of a work sheet to Jessie Jane's Campus Delivery.

STEP 1

Prepare the Trial Balance. As shown in Figure 5-14, the first pair of amount columns is for the trial balance. The trial balance assures the equality of the debits and credits before the adjustment process begins. The columns should be double ruled to show that they are equal.

> You are already familiar with a trial balance. Here we are simply copying a trial balance to a different form, called a work sheet.

Note that all accounts listed in the expanded chart of accounts are included in the Trial Balance columns of the work sheet. This is done even though some accounts have zero balances. The accounts with zero balances could be added to the bottom of the list as they are needed for adjusting entries. However, it is easier to include them now, especially if preparing the work sheet on an electronic spreadsheet. Listing the accounts within their proper classifications (assets, liabilities, etc.) also makes it easier to extend the amounts to the proper columns.

STEP 2

Prepare the Adjustments. As shown in Figure 5-15, the second pair of amount columns is used to prepare the adjusting entries. Enter the adjustments directly in these columns. When an account is debited or credited, the amount is entered on the same line as the name of the account and in the appropriate Adjustments Debit or Credit column. A small letter in parentheses identifies each adjusting entry made on the work sheet.

LEARNING KEY: For adjustments (a), (b), and (d), we are simply recognizing that assets have been used. When this happens, the asset must be decreased and an expense recognized. Note that the reported amount for delivery equipment is reduced by crediting a contra-asset.

ADJUSTMENT (a):
Supplies costing $60 were used during June.

	Debit	Credit
Supplies Expense	60	
Supplies		60

FIGURE 5-13 **Steps in Preparing the Work Sheet**

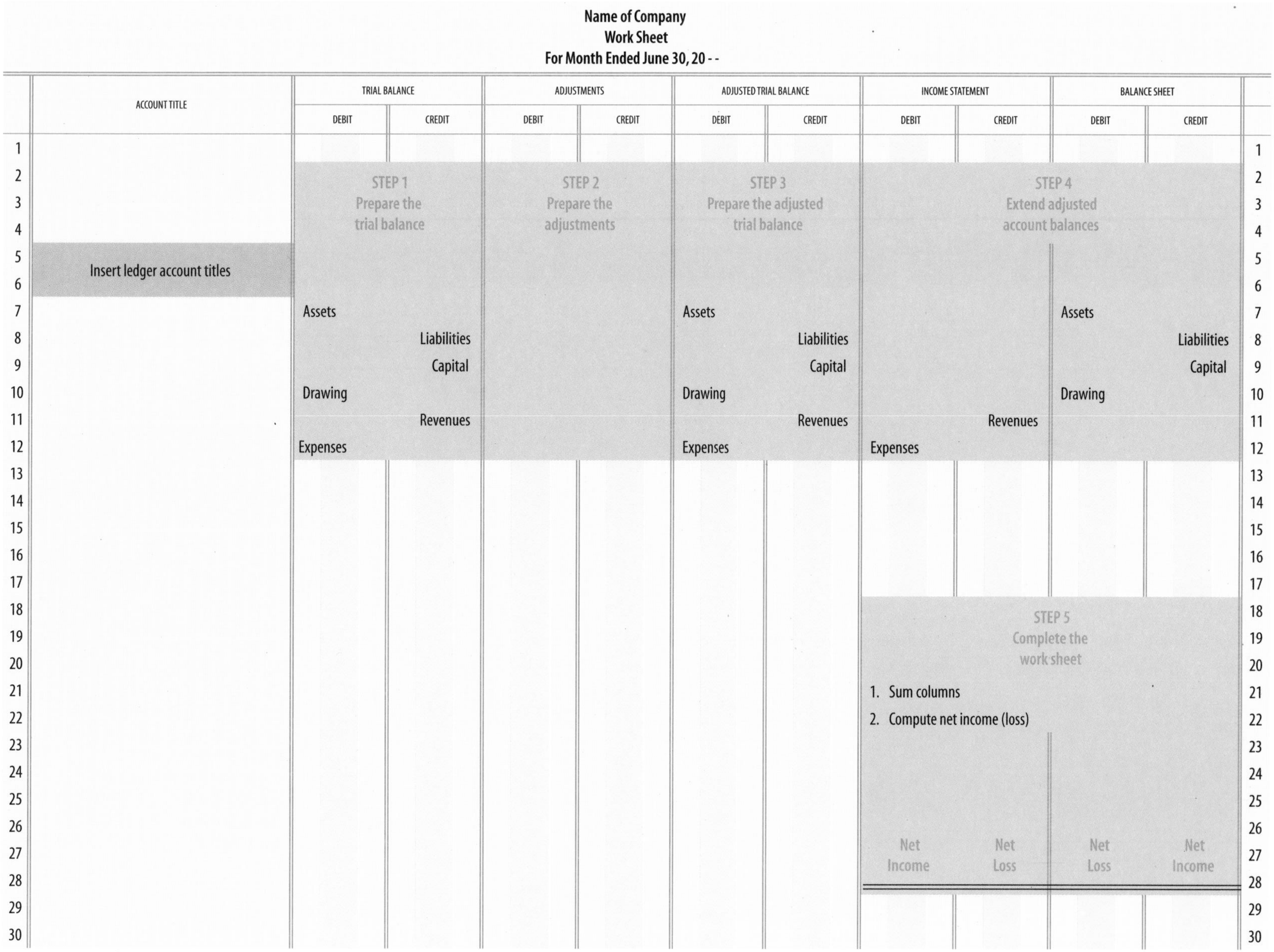

Name of Company
Work Sheet
For Month Ended June 30, 20 - -

ACCOUNT TITLE

Insert ledger account titles

TRIAL BALANCE — DEBIT / CREDIT
STEP 1 — Prepare the trial balance
Assets, Liabilities, Capital, Drawing, Revenues, Expenses

ADJUSTMENTS — DEBIT / CREDIT
STEP 2 — Prepare the adjustments

ADJUSTED TRIAL BALANCE — DEBIT / CREDIT
STEP 3 — Prepare the adjusted trial balance
Assets, Liabilities, Capital, Drawing, Revenues, Expenses

INCOME STATEMENT — DEBIT / CREDIT
STEP 4 — Extend adjusted account balances
Expenses, Revenues

BALANCE SHEET — DEBIT / CREDIT
Assets, Liabilities, Drawing, Capital

STEP 5 — Complete the work sheet
1. Sum columns
2. Compute net income (loss)

Net Income / Net Loss

FIGURE 5-14 Step 1—Prepare the Trial Balance

Jessica Jane's Campus Delivery
Work Sheet
For Month Ended June 30, 20 - -

	ACCOUNT TITLE	TRIAL BALANCE DEBIT	TRIAL BALANCE CREDIT	ADJUSTMENTS DEBIT	ADJUSTMENTS CREDIT	ADJUSTED TRIAL BALANCE DEBIT	ADJUSTED TRIAL BALANCE CREDIT	INCOME STATEMENT DEBIT	INCOME STATEMENT CREDIT	BALANCE SHEET DEBIT	BALANCE SHEET CREDIT	
1	Cash	3 7 0 00										1
2	Accounts Receivable	6 5 0 00										2
3	Supplies	8 0 00										3
4	Prepaid Insurance	2 0 0 00										4
5	Delivery Equipment	3 6 0 0 00										5
6	Accum. Depr.—Delivery Equipment											6
7	Accounts Payable		1 8 0 0 00									7
8	Wages Payable											8
9	Jessica Jane, Capital		2 0 0 0 00									9
10	Jessica Jane, Drawing	1 5 0 00										10
11	Delivery Fees		2 1 5 0 00									11
12	Wages Expense	6 5 0 00										12
13	Rent Expense	2 0 0 00										13
14	Supplies Expense											14
15	Telephone Expense	5 0 00										15
16	Insurance Expense											16
17	Depr. Expense—Delivery Equipment											17
18		5 9 5 0 00	5 9 5 0 00									18
19												19
20												20
21												21
22												22
23												23
24												24
25												25
26												26
27												27
28												28
29												29
30												30

STEP 1

Preparing the Work Sheet

STEP 1   Prepare the Trial Balance.

- Write the heading, account titles, and the debit and credit amounts from the general ledger.
- Place a single rule across the Trial Balance columns and total the debit and credit amounts.
- Place a double rule under the columns to show that they are equal.

STEP 2   Prepare the Adjustments.

- Record the adjustments.

  Hint: Make certain that each adjustment is on the same line as the account name and in the appropriate column.

  Hint: Identify each adjusting entry by a letter in parentheses.

- Rule the Adjusted Trial Balance columns.
- Total the debit and credit columns and double rule the columns to show equality.

STEP 3   Prepare the Adjusted Trial Balance.

- Extend those debits and credits that are not adjusted directly to the appropriate Adjusted Trial Balance column.
- Enter the adjusted balances in the appropriate Adjusted Trial Balance column.

  Hint: If an account has a debit and a credit, subtract the adjustment. If an account has two debits or two credits, add the adjustment.

- Single rule the Adjusted Trial Balance columns. Total and double rule the debit and credit columns.

STEP 4   Extend Adjusted Balances to the Income Statement and Balance Sheet Columns.

- Extend all revenue accounts to the Income Statement Credit column.
- Extend all expense accounts to the Income Statement Debit column.
- Extend the asset and drawing accounts to the Balance Sheet Debit column.
- Extend the liability and owner's capital accounts to the Balance Sheet Credit column.

STEP 5   Complete the Work Sheet.

- Rule and total the Income Statement and Balance Sheet columns.
- Calculate the difference between the Income Statement Debit and Credit columns.
- Calculate the difference between the Balance Sheet Debit and Credit columns.

  Hint: If the Income Statement credits exceed debits, net income has occurred; otherwise a net loss has occurred. If the Balance Sheet debits exceed the credits, the difference is net income; otherwise a net loss has occurred.

  Hint: The difference between the Balance Sheet columns should be the same as the difference between the Income Statement columns.

- Add the net income to the Income Statement Debit column or add the net loss to the Income Statement Credit column. Add the net income to the Balance Sheet Credit column or the net loss to the Balance Sheet Debit column.
- Total and double rule the columns.

ADJUSTMENT (b):
One month's insurance premium has expired.

	Debit	Credit
Insurance Expense	25	
Prepaid Insurance		25

ADJUSTMENT (c):
Employees earned $50 that has not yet been paid.

	Debit	Credit
Wages Expense	50	
Wages Payable		50

> **LEARNING KEY:** Adjustment (c) recognizes an economic event that has not required an actual transaction yet. Employees earned wages, but have not been paid. The adjustment recognizes an expense and a liability.

ADJUSTMENT (d):
Depreciation on the motor scooters is recognized.

	Debit	Credit
Depreciation Expense—Delivery Equipment	100	
Accumulated Depreciation—Delivery Equipment		100

When all adjustments have been entered on the work sheet, each column should be totaled to assure that the debits equal the credits for all entries. After balancing the columns, they should be double ruled.

STEP 3 **Prepare the Adjusted Trial Balance.** As shown in Figure 5-16, the third pair of amount columns on the work sheet are the **Adjusted Trial Balance columns**. When an account balance is not affected by entries in the Adjustments columns, the amount in the Trial Balance columns is extended directly to the Adjusted Trial Balance columns. *When affected by an entry in the Adjustments columns, the balance to be entered in the Adjusted Trial Balance columns increases or decreases by the amount of the adjusting entry.*

For example, in Jessica Jane's business, Supplies is listed in the Trial Balance Debit column as $80. Since the entry of $60 is in the Adjustments Credit column, the amount extended to the Adjusted Trial Balance Debit column is $20 ($80 – $60).

Wages Expense is listed in the Trial Balance Debit column as $650. Since $50 is in the Adjustments Debit column, the amount extended to the Adjusted Trial Balance Debit column is $700 ($650 + $50).

After all extensions have been made, the Adjusted Trial Balance columns are totaled to prove the equality of the debits and the credits. Once balanced, the columns are double ruled.

STEP 4 **Extend Adjusted Balances to the Income Statement and Balance Sheet Columns.** As shown in Figure 5-17, each account listed in the Adjusted Trial Balance must be extended to either the Income Statement or Balance Sheet columns. The **Income Statement columns** show the amounts that will be reported in the income statement. All revenue accounts are extended to the Income Statement Credit column and expense accounts are extended to the Income Statement Debit column.

The asset, liability, drawing, and capital accounts are extended to the **Balance Sheet columns**. Although called the Balance Sheet columns, these columns of the work sheet show the amounts that will be reported in the balance sheet and the statement of owner's equity. The asset and drawing accounts are extended to the Balance Sheet Debit column. The liability and owner's capital accounts are extended to the Balance Sheet Credit column.

 LEARNING KEY: The Balance Sheet columns show the amounts for both the balance sheet and the statement of owner's equity.

STEP 5   **Complete the Work Sheet.** To complete the work sheet, first total the Income Statement columns. If the total of the credits (revenues) exceeds the total of the debits (expenses), the difference represents net income. If the total of the debits exceeds the total of the credits, the difference represents a net loss.

The Income Statement columns of Jessie's work sheet in Figure 5-18 show total credits of $2,150 and total debits of $1,135. The difference, $1,015, is the net income for the month of June. This amount should be added to the debit column to balance the Income Statement columns. "Net Income" should be written on the same line in the Account Title column. If the business had a net loss, the amount of the loss would be added to the Income Statement Credit column and the words "Net Loss" would be written in the Account Title column. Once balanced, the columns should be double ruled.

Finally, the Balance Sheet columns are totaled. The difference between the totals of these columns also is the amount of net income or net loss for the accounting period. If the total debits exceed the total credits, the difference is net income. If the total credits exceed the total debits, the difference is a net loss. This difference should be the same as the difference we found for the Income Statement columns.

 LEARNING KEY: In the Balance Sheet columns of the work sheet, total debits minus total credits equals net <u>income</u> if greater than zero and equals net <u>loss</u> if less than zero.

The Balance Sheet columns of Jessie's work sheet show total debits of $4,965 and total credits of $3,950. The difference of $1,015 represents the amount of net income for the month. This amount is added to the credit column to balance the Balance Sheet columns. If the business had a net loss, this amount would be added to the Balance Sheet Debit column. Once balanced, the columns should be double ruled.

A trick for remembering the appropriate placement of the net income and net loss is the following: Net Income *apart*; Net Loss *together*. Figure 5-19 illustrates this learning aid.

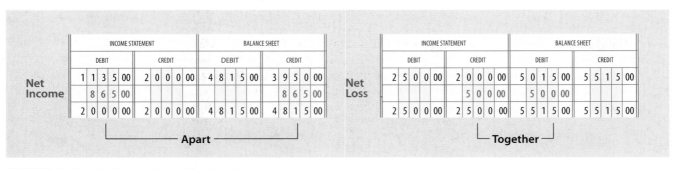

FIGURE 5-19   **Net Income Apart, Net Loss Together**

FINDING ERRORS ON THE WORK SHEET

LO3 **Describe methods for finding errors on the work sheet.**

If any of the columns on the work sheet do not balance, you must find the error before you continue. Once you are confident that the work sheet is accurate, you are ready to journalize the adjusting entries and prepare financial statements. Figure 5-20 offers tips for finding errors on the work sheet.

TIPS FOR FINDING ERRORS ON THE WORK SHEET
1.   Check the addition of all columns.
2.   Check the addition and subtraction required when extending to the Adjusted Trial Balance columns.
3.   Make sure the adjusted account balances have been extended to the appropriate columns.
4.   Make sure that the net income or net loss has been added to the appropriate columns.

FIGURE 5-20   **Finding Errors on the Work Sheet**

JOURNALIZING ADJUSTING ENTRIES

LO4 **Journalize adjusting entries.**

Keep in mind that the work sheet simply helps the accountant organize the end-of-period work. *Writing the adjustments on the work sheet has no effect on the ledger accounts in the accounting system. The only way to change the balance of a ledger account is to make a journal entry.* Once the adjustments have been entered on the work sheet, simply copy the adjustments from the work sheet to the journal.

Jessie's adjusting entries are illustrated in Figure 5-21 as they would appear in a general journal. Note that the last day of the accounting period, June 30, has been entered in the date column and "*Adjusting Entries*" is written in the Description column prior to the first adjusting entry. No explanation is required in the Description column for individual adjusting entries. We simply label them as adjusting entries.

POSTING ADJUSTING ENTRIES

LO5 **Post adjusting entries to the general ledger.**

Adjusting entries are posted to the general ledger in the same manner as all other entries, except that "*Adjusting*" is written in the Item column of the general ledger. Figure 5-22 shows the posting of the adjusting entry for supplies. The posting reference numbers are inserted as each entry is posted.

GENERAL JOURNAL PAGE 3

	DATE		DESCRIPTION	POST REF.	DEBIT	CREDIT	
1			Adjusting Entries				1
2	20-- June	30	Supplies Expense	523	6 0 00		2
3			Supplies	141		6 0 00	3
4							4
5		30	Insurance Expense	535	2 5 00		5
6			Prepaid Insurance	145		2 5 00	6
7							7
8		30	Wages Expense	511	5 0 00		8
9			Wages Payable	219		5 0 00	9
10							10
11		30	Depr. Expense — Delivery Equipment	541	1 0 0 00		11
12			Accum. Depr. — Delivery Equipment	185.1		1 0 0 00	12

FIGURE 5-21   Adjusting Entries

GENERAL LEDGER

ACCOUNT: Supplies   ACCOUNT NO. 141

DATE	ITEM	POST REF.	DEBIT	CREDIT	BALANCE DEBIT	BALANCE CREDIT
20-- June 16		J1	8 0 00		8 0 00	
30	Adjusting	J3		6 0 00	2 0 00	

ACCOUNT: Supplies Expense   ACCOUNT NO. 523

DATE	ITEM	POST REF.	DEBIT	CREDIT	BALANCE DEBIT	BALANCE CREDIT
20-- June 30	Adjusting	J3	6 0 00		6 0 00	

FIGURE 5-22   Posting the Adjusting Entry for Supplies

Learning Objectives	Key Points to Remember
1 **Prepare end-of-period adjustments.**	End-of-period adjustments are necessary to bring the general ledger accounts up to date prior to preparing financial statements. Reasons to adjust the trial balance are: 1. To report all revenues earned during the accounting period. 2. To report all expenses incurred to produce the revenues during the accounting period. 3. To accurately report the assets on the balance sheet. Some assets may have expired, depreciated, or been used up during the accounting period. 4. To accurately report the liabilities on the balance sheet date. Expenses may have been incurred, but not yet paid.
2 **Prepare a work sheet.**	Steps in preparing the work sheet are: 1. Prepare the trial balance. 2. Prepare the adjustments. 3. Prepare the adjusted trial balance. 4. Extend the adjusted account balances to the Income Statement and Balance Sheet columns. 5. Total the Income Statement and Balance Sheet columns to compute the net income or net loss.
3 **Describe methods for finding errors on the work sheet.**	Tips for finding errors on the work sheet include: 1. Check the addition of all columns. 2. Check the addition and subtraction required when extending to the Adjusted Trial Balance columns. 3. Make sure the adjusted account balances have been extended to the appropriate columns. 4. Make sure that the net income or net loss has been added to the appropriate columns.
4 **Journalize adjusting entries.**	The adjustments are copied from the work sheet to the journal. The last day of the accounting period is entered in the Date column and "Adjusting Entries" is written in the Description column.
5 **Post adjusting entries to the general ledger.**	Adjusting entries are posted to the general ledger in the same manner as all other entries, except that "Adjusting" is written in the Item column of the general ledger.

Reflection: Answering the Opening Question

As discussed in the chapter, it is essential to make appropriate adjustments prior to the preparation of financial statements.

KEY TERMS

Adjusted Trial Balance columns, (143)   The third pair of amount columns on the work sheet. They are used to prove the equality of the debits and credits in the general ledger accounts after making all end-of-period adjustments.

adjusting entries, (134)   Journal entries made at the end of an accounting period to reflect changes in account balances that are not the direct result of an exchange with an outside party.

Balance Sheet columns, (143)   The work sheet columns that show the amounts that will be reported in the balance sheet and the statement of owner's equity.

book value, (140)   The difference between the asset account and its related accumulated depreciation account. The value reflected by the accounting records.

contra-asset, (139)   An account with a credit balance that is deducted from the related asset account on the balance sheet.

depreciable cost, (139)   The cost of an asset that is subject to depreciation.

depreciation, (139)   A method of matching an asset's original cost against the revenues produced over its useful life.

fiscal year, (134)   A twelve-month period for which financial reports are prepared.

historical cost principle, (139)   A principle that requires assets to be recorded at their actual cost.

Income Statement columns, (143)   The work sheet columns that show the amounts that will be reported in the income statement.

market value, (139)   The amount an item can be sold for under normal economic conditions.

matching principle, (134)   A principle that requires the matching of revenues earned during an accounting period with the expenses incurred to produce the revenues.

plant assets, (139)   Assets of a durable nature that will be used for operations over several years. Examples include buildings and equipment.

salvage value, (139)   The expected market value of an asset at the end of its useful life.

straight-line method, (139)   A depreciation method in which the depreciable cost is divided by the estimated useful life.

undepreciated cost, (140)   The difference between the asset account and its related accumulated depreciation account. Also known as book value.

useful life, (139)   The period of time that an asset is expected to help produce revenues.

work sheet, (142)   A form used to pull together all of the information needed to enter adjusting entries and prepare the financial statements.

DEMONSTRATION PROBLEM

Justin Park is a lawyer specializing in corporate tax law. He began his practice on January 1. A chart of accounts and trial balance taken on December 31, 20-- are provided below.

Information for year-end adjustments:

(a) Office supplies on hand at year end amounted to $300.

(b) On January 1, 20--, Park purchased office equipment costing $15,000 with an expected life of five years and no salvage value.

(c) Computer equipment costing $6,000 with an expected life of three years and no salvage value was purchased on July 1, 20--. Assume that Park computes depreciation to the nearest full month.

(d) A premium of $1,200 for a one-year insurance policy was paid on December 1, 20--.

(e) Wages earned by Park's part-time secretary, which have not yet been paid, amount to $300.

REQUIRED

1. Prepare the work sheet for the year ended December 31, 20--.

2. Prepare adjusting entries in a general journal.

JUSTIN PARK LEGAL SERVICES CHART OF ACCOUNTS			
Assets		**Revenue**	
101	Cash	401	Client Fees
142	Office Supplies		
145	Prepaid Insurance	**Expenses**	
181	Office Equipment	511	Wages Expense
181.1	Accumulated Depr.—	521	Rent Expense
	Office Equipment	523	Office Supplies Expense
187	Computer Equipment	525	Telephone Expense
187.1	Accumulated Depr.—	533	Utilities Expense
	Computer Equipment	535	Insurance Expense
Liabilities		541	Depr. Expense—
201	Notes Payable		Office Equipment
202	Accounts Payable	542	Depr. Expense—
219	Wages Payable		Computer Equipment
Owner's Equity			
311	Justin Park, Capital		
312	Justin Park, Drawing		

				Justin Park Legal Services												
				Trial Balance												
				December 31, 20 - -												

ACCOUNT TITLE	ACCOUNT NO.	DEBIT BALANCE					CREDIT BALANCE				
Cash	101	7	0	0	0	00					
Office Supplies	142		8	0	0	00					
Prepaid Insurance	145	1	2	0	0	00					
Office Equipment	181	15	0	0	0	00					
Computer Equipment	187	6	0	0	0	00					
Notes Payable	201						5	0	0	0	00
Accounts Payable	202							5	0	0	00
Justin Park, Capital	311						11	4	0	0	00
Justin Park, Drawing	312	5	0	0	0	00					
Client Fees	401						40	0	0	0	00
Wages Expense	511	12	0	0	0	00					
Rent Expense	521	5	0	0	0	00					
Telephone Expense	525	1	0	0	0	00					
Utilities Expense	533	3	9	0	0	00					
		56	9	0	0	00	56	9	0	0	00

(continued)

Solution

1.

Justin Park Legal Services
Work Sheet
For Month Ended December 31, 20 --

Line	Account Title	TB Debit	TB Credit	Adj. Debit	Adj. Credit	Adj. TB Debit	Adj. TB Credit	Inc. Stmt. Debit	Inc. Stmt. Credit	Bal. Sheet Debit	Bal. Sheet Credit
1	Cash	7 0 0 0 00				7 0 0 0 00				7 0 0 0 00	
2	Office Supplies	8 0 0 00			(a) 5 0 0 00	3 0 0 00				3 0 0 00	
3	Prepaid Insurance	1 2 0 0 00			(d) 1 0 0 00	1 1 0 0 00				1 1 0 0 00	
4	Office Equipment	15 0 0 0 00				15 0 0 0 00				15 0 0 0 00	
5	Accum. Depr.—Office Equip.				(b) 3 0 0 00		3 0 0 00				3 0 0 00
6	Computer Equipment	6 0 0 0 00				6 0 0 0 00				6 0 0 0 00	
7	Accum. Depr.—Computer Equip.				(c) 1 0 0 00		1 0 0 00				1 0 0 00
8	Notes Payable		5 0 0 0 00				5 0 0 0 00				5 0 0 0 00
9	Accounts Payable		5 0 0 00				5 0 0 00				5 0 0 00
10	Wages Payable				(e) 3 0 0 00		3 0 0 00				3 0 0 00
11	Justin Park, Capital		15 0 0 0 00				15 0 0 0 00				15 0 0 0 00
12	Justin Park, Drawing	5 0 0 0 00				5 0 0 0 00				5 0 0 0 00	
13	Client Fees		40 0 0 0 00				40 0 0 0 00		40 0 0 0 00		
14	Wages Expense	15 6 0 0 00		(e) 3 0 0 00		15 9 0 0 00		15 9 0 0 00			
15	Rent Expense	5 0 0 0 00				5 0 0 0 00		5 0 0 0 00			
16	Office Supplies Expense			(a) 5 0 0 00		5 0 0 00		5 0 0 00			
17	Telephone Expense	1 0 0 0 00				1 0 0 0 00		1 0 0 0 00			
18	Utilities Expense	3 9 0 0 00				3 9 0 0 00		3 9 0 0 00			
19	Insurance Expense			(d) 1 0 0 00		1 0 0 00		1 0 0 00			
20	Depr. Expense—Office Equip.			(b) 3 0 0 00		3 0 0 00		3 0 0 00			
21	Depr. Expense—Computer Equip.			(c) 1 0 0 00		1 0 0 00		1 0 0 00			
22		60 5 0 0 00	60 5 0 0 00	1 3 0 0 00	1 3 0 0 00	61 2 0 0 00	61 2 0 0 00	26 8 0 0 00	40 0 0 0 00	34 4 0 0 00	21 2 0 0 00
23	Net Income							13 2 0 0 00			13 2 0 0 00
24								40 0 0 0 00	40 0 0 0 00	34 4 0 0 00	34 4 0 0 00
25											
26											
27											
28											
29											
30											

2.

	DATE		DESCRIPTION	POST REF.	DEBIT					CREDIT					
1			Adjusting Entries												1
2	20-- Dec.	31	Office Supplies Expense		5	0	0	00							2
3			Office Supplies							5	0	0	00		3
4															4
5		31	Depr. Expense—Office Equipment		3	0	0	0	00						5
6			Accum. Depr.—Office Equipment							3	0	0	0	00	6
7															7
8		31	Depr. Expense—Computer Equipment		1	0	0	0	00						8
9			Accum. Depr—Computer Equipment							1	0	0	0	00	9
10															10
11		31	Insurance Expense		1	0	0	00							11
12			Prepaid Insurance							1	0	0	00		12
13															13
14		31	Wages Expense		3	0	0	00							14
15			Wages Payable							3	0	0	00		15

GENERAL JOURNAL   PAGE **11**

REVIEW QUESTIONS

1. Explain the matching principle.

2. Explain the historical cost principle.

3. Describe a plant asset.

4. What is a contra-asset?

5. What is the useful life of an asset?

6. What is the purpose of depreciation?

7. What is an asset's depreciable cost?

8. What is the book value of an asset?

9. Explain the purpose of the work sheet.

10. Identify the five major column headings on a work sheet.

11. List the five steps taken in preparing a work sheet.

12. Describe four tips for finding errors on the work sheet.

MANAGING YOUR WRITING

Delia Alvarez, owner of Delia's Lawn Service, wants to borrow money to buy new lawn equipment. A local bank has asked for financial statements. Alvarez has asked you to prepare financial statements for the year ended December 31, 20--. You have been given the unadjusted trial balance shown below and suspect that Alvarez expects you to base your statements on this information. You are concerned, however, that some of the account balances may need to be adjusted. Write a memo to Alvarez explaining what additional information you need before you can prepare the financial statements. Alvarez is not familiar with accounting issues. Therefore, explain in your memo why you need this information, the potential impact of this information on the financial statements, and the importance of making these adjustments before approaching the bank for a loan.

Delia's Lawn Service Trial Balance December 31, 20 - -				
ACCOUNT TITLE	ACCOUNT NO.	DEBIT BALANCE		CREDIT BALANCE
Cash	101	7 7 0 00		
Accounts Receivable	122	1 7 0 0 00		
Supplies	142	2 8 0 00		
Prepaid Insurance	145	4 0 0 00		
Lawn Equipment	183	13 8 0 0 00		
Accounts Payable	202			2 2 0 0 00
Delia Alvarez, Capital	311			3 0 0 0 00
Delia Alvarez, Drawing	312	3 5 0 00		
Lawn Cutting Fees	401			52 4 0 0 00
Wages Expense	511	35 8 5 0 00		
Rent Expense	521	1 2 0 0 00		
Gas and Oil Expense	538	3 2 5 0 00		
		57 6 0 0 00		57 6 0 0 00

SERIES A EXERCISES

EXERCISE 5-1A (LO1) **ADJUSTMENT FOR SUPPLIES** On December 31, the trial balance indicates that the supplies account has a balance, prior to the adjusting entry, of $320. A physical count of the supplies inventory shows that $90 of supplies remain. Analyze this adjustment for supplies using T accounts, and then formally enter this adjustment in the general journal.

EXERCISE 5-2A (LO1) **ADJUSTMENT FOR INSURANCE** On December 1, a six-month liability insurance policy was purchased for $900. Analyze the required adjustment as of December 31 using T accounts, and then formally enter this adjustment in the general journal.

EXERCISE 5-3A (LO1) **ADJUSTMENT FOR WAGES** On December 31, the trial balance shows wages expense of $600. An additional $200 of wages was earned by the employees, but has not yet been paid. Analyze this adjustment for wages, and then formally enter this adjustment in the general journal.

EXERCISE 5-4A   **(LO1)**   **ADJUSTMENT FOR DEPRECIATION OF ASSET** On December 1, delivery equipment was purchased for $7,200. The delivery equipment has an estimated useful life of four years (48 months) and no salvage value. Using the straight-line depreciation method, prepare the necessary adjusting entry as of December 31 (one month), and then formally enter this adjustment in the general journal.

EXERCISE 5-5A   **(LO1)**   **CALCULATION OF BOOK VALUE** On June 1, 20--, a depreciable asset was acquired for $5,400. The asset has an estimated useful life of five years (60 months) and no salvage value. Using the straight-line depreciation method, calculate the book value as of December 31, 20--.

EXERCISE 5-6A   **(LO1)**   **ANALYSIS OF ADJUSTING ENTRY FOR SUPPLIES** Analyze each situation and indicate the correct dollar amount for the adjusting entry. (Trial balance is abbreviated as TB.)

1.   Ending inventory of supplies is $130.

(Balance Sheet) Supplies	(Income Statement) Supplies Expense
TB 460	
Adj. _____	Adj. _____
Bal. _____	

2.   Amount of supplies used is $320.

(Balance Sheet) Supplies	(Income Statement) Supplies Expense
TB 545	
Adj. _____	Adj. _____
Bal. _____	

EXERCISE 5-7A   **(LO1)**   **ANALYSIS OF ADJUSTING ENTRY FOR INSURANCE** Analyze each situation and indicate the correct dollar amount for the adjusting entry.

1.   Amount of insurance expired is $900.

(Balance Sheet) Prepaid Insurance	(Income Statement) Insurance Expense
TB 1,300	
Adj. _____	Adj. _____
Bal. _____	

2.   Amount of unexpired insurance is $185.

(Balance Sheet) Prepaid Insurance	(Income Statement) Insurance Expense
TB 860	
Adj. _____	Adj. _____
Bal. _____	

EXERCISE 5-8A   **(LO2)**   **WORK SHEET AND ADJUSTING ENTRIES** A partial work sheet for Jim Jacob's furniture repair is shown as follows. Indicate by letters (a) through (d) the four adjustments in the Adjustments columns of the work sheet, properly matching each debit and credit. Complete the Adjustments columns.

Jim Jacob's Furniture Repair
Work Sheet (Partial)
For Month Ended December 31, 20 - -

	ACCOUNT TITLE	TRIAL BALANCE DEBIT	TRIAL BALANCE CREDIT	ADJUSTMENTS DEBIT	ADJUSTMENTS CREDIT	ADJUSTED TRIAL BALANCE DEBIT	ADJUSTED TRIAL BALANCE CREDIT	
1	Cash	1 0 0 00				1 0 0 00		1
2	Supplies	8 5 0 00				2 0 0 00		2
3	Prepaid Insurance	9 0 0 00				3 0 0 00		3
4	Delivery Equipment	3 6 0 0 00				3 6 0 0 00		4
5	Accum. Depr.— Delivery Equipment		6 0 0 00				8 0 0 00	5
6	Wages Payable						1 0 0 00	6
7	Jim Jacob, Capital		4 0 0 0 00				4 0 0 0 00	7
8	Repair Fees		1 6 5 0 00				1 6 5 0 00	8
9	Wages Expense	6 0 0 00				7 0 0 00		9
10	Advertising Expense	2 0 0 00				2 0 0 00		10
11	Supplies Expense					6 5 0 00		11
12	Insurance Expense					6 0 0 00		12
13	Depr. Expense—Delivery Equipment					2 0 0 00		13
14		6 2 5 0 00	6 2 5 0 00			6 5 5 0 00	6 5 5 0 00	14

EXERCISE 5-9A   **(LO4)**   **JOURNALIZING ADJUSTING ENTRIES** From the adjustments columns in Exercise 5-8A, journalize the four adjusting entries, as of December 31, in proper general journal format.

EXERCISE 5-10A   **(LO2)**   **EXTENDING ADJUSTED BALANCES TO THE INCOME STATEMENT AND BALANCE SHEET COLUMNS** Indicate with an "x" whether each account total should be extended to the Income Statement Debit or Credit or to the Balance Sheet Debit or Credit columns on the work sheet.

	Income Statement Debit	Income Statement Credit	Balance Sheet Debit	Balance Sheet Credit
Cash				
Accounts Receivable				
Supplies				
Prepaid Insurance				
Delivery Equipment				
Accum. Depr.—Delivery Equipment				
Accounts Payable				
Wages Payable				
Owner, Capital				
Owner, Drawing				
Delivery Fees				
Wages Expense				
Rent Expense				
Supplies Expense				
Insurance Expense				
Depr. Exp.—Delivery Equipment				

EXERCISE 5-11A   **(LO2)**   **ANALYSIS OF NET INCOME OR NET LOSS ON THE WORK SHEET** Indicate with an "x" in which columns, Income Statement Debit or Credit or Balance Sheet Debit or Credit, a net income or a net loss would appear on a work sheet.

	Income Statement		Balance Sheet	
	Debit	Credit	Debit	Credit
Net Income	_____	_____	_____	_____
Net Loss	_____	_____	_____	_____

EXERCISE 5-12A   **(LO5)**   **POSTING ADJUSTING ENTRIES** Two adjusting entries are in the following general journal. Post these adjusting entries to the four general ledger accounts. The following account numbers were taken from the chart of accounts: 141, Supplies; 219, Wages Payable; 511, Wages Expense; and 523, Supplies Expense. If you are not using the working papers that accompany this text, enter the following balances before posting the entries: Supplies, $200 Dr.; Wages Expense, $1,200 Dr.

GENERAL JOURNAL   PAGE 9

	DATE		DESCRIPTION	POST REF.	DEBIT	CREDIT	
1			Adjusting Entries				1
2	20-- Dec.	31	Supplies Expense		8 5 00		2
3			Supplies			8 5 00	3
4							4
5		31	Wages Expense		2 2 0 00		5
6			Wages Payable			2 2 0 00	6

SERIES A PROBLEMS

PROBLEM 5-1A   **(LO1/2)**   **ADJUSTMENTS AND WORK SHEET SHOWING NET INCOME** The trial balance after one month of operation for Mason's Delivery Service as of September 30, 20--, is shown below. Data to complete the adjustments are as follows:

(a) Supplies inventory as of September 30, $165.
(b) Insurance expired (used), $800.
(c) Depreciation on delivery equipment, $400.
(d) Wages earned by employees, but not paid as of September 30, $225.

(continued)

REQUIRED

1. Enter the adjustments in the Adjustments columns of the work sheet.

2. Complete the work sheet.

Mason's Delivery Service
Work Sheet
For Month Ended September 30, 20 - -

	ACCOUNT TITLE	TRIAL BALANCE		ADJUSTMENTS		
		DEBIT	CREDIT	DEBIT	CREDIT	
1	Cash	1 6 0 0 00				1
2	Accounts Receivable	9 4 0 00				2
3	Supplies	6 3 5 00				3
4	Prepaid Insurance	1 2 0 0 00				4
5	Delivery Equipment	6 4 0 0 00				5
6	Accum. Depr.—Delivery Equipment					6
7	Accounts Payable		1 2 2 0 00			7
8	Wages Payable					8
9	Jill Mason, Capital		8 0 0 0 00			9
10	Jill Mason, Drawing	1 4 0 0 00				10
11	Delivery Fees		6 2 0 0 00			11
12	Wages Expense	1 5 0 0 00				12
13	Advertising Expense	4 6 0 00				13
14	Rent Expense	8 0 0 00				14
15	Supplies Expense					15
16	Telephone Expense	1 6 5 00				16
17	Insurance Expense					17
18	Repair Expense	2 3 0 00				18
19	Oil and Gas Expense	9 0 00				19
20	Depr. Expense—Delivery Equipment					20
21		15 4 2 0 00	15 4 2 0 00			21

PROBLEM 5-2A (LO1/2) **ADJUSTMENTS AND WORK SHEET SHOWING A NET LOSS** Jason Armstrong started a business called Campus Escort Service. After the first month of operations, the trial balance as of November 30, 20--, is as shown on the next page.

REQUIRED

1. Analyze the following adjustments and enter them on the work sheet.

   (a) Ending inventory of supplies on November 30, $185.

   (b) Unexpired (remaining) insurance as of November 30, $800.

   (c) Depreciation expense on van, $300.

   (d) Wages earned, but not paid as of November 30, $190.

2. Complete the work sheet.

Campus Escort Service
Work Sheet
For Month Ended November 30, 20 - -

	ACCOUNT TITLE	TRIAL BALANCE		ADJUSTMENTS		
		DEBIT	CREDIT	DEBIT	CREDIT	
1	Cash	9 8 0 00				1
2	Accounts Receivable	5 9 0 00				2
3	Supplies	5 7 5 00				3
4	Prepaid Insurance	1 3 0 0 00				4
5	Van	5 8 0 0 00				5
6	Accum. Depr.—Van					6
7	Accounts Payable		9 6 0 00			7
8	Wages Payable					8
9	Jason Armstrong, Capital		10 0 0 0 00			9
10	Jason Armstrong, Drawing	6 0 0 00				10
11	Escort Fees		2 6 0 0 00			11
12	Wages Expense	1 8 0 0 00				12
13	Advertising Expense	3 8 0 00				13
14	Rent Expense	9 0 0 00				14
15	Supplies Expense					15
16	Telephone Expense	2 2 0 00				16
17	Insurance Expense					17
18	Repair Expense	3 1 5 00				18
19	Oil and Gas Expense	1 0 0 00				19
20	Depr. Expense—Van					20
21		13 5 6 0 00	13 5 6 0 00			21

PROBLEM 5-3A   (LO4/5)

JOURNALIZE AND POST ADJUSTING ENTRIES FROM THE WORK SHEET
Refer to Problem 5-2A and the following additional information.

Account Name	Account Number	Balance in Account Before Adjusting Entry
Supplies	141	$ 575
Prepaid Insurance	145	1,300
Accum. Depr.—Van	185.1	0
Wages Payable	219	0
Wages Expense	511	1,800
Supplies Expense	523	0
Insurance Expense	535	0
Depr. Expense—Van	541	0

REQUIRED

1. Journalize the adjusting entries on page 5 of the general journal.

2. Post the adjusting entries to the general ledger. (If you are not using the working papers that accompany this text, enter the balances provided in this problem before posting the adjusting entries.)

PROBLEM 5-4A **(LO3)** **CORRECTING WORK SHEET WITH ERRORS** A beginning accounting student tried to complete a work sheet for Joyce Lee's Tax Service. The following adjusting entries were to have been analyzed and entered onto the work sheet. The work sheet is shown on page 159.

(a) Ending inventory of supplies as of March 31, $160.

(b) Unexpired insurance as of March 31, $520.

(c) Depreciation of office equipment, $275.

(d) Wages earned, but not paid as of March 31, $110.

REQUIRED

The accounting student made a number of errors. Review the work sheet for addition mistakes, transpositions, and other errors and make all necessary corrections.

SERIES B EXERCISES

EXERCISE 5-1B **(LO1)** **ADJUSTMENT FOR SUPPLIES** On July 31, the trial balance indicates that the supplies account has a balance, prior to the adjusting entry, of $430. A physical count of the supplies inventory shows that $120 of supplies remain. Analyze the adjustment for supplies using T accounts, and then formally enter this adjustment in the general journal.

EXERCISE 5-2B **(LO1)** **ADJUSTMENT FOR INSURANCE** On July 1, a six-month liability insurance policy was purchased for $750. Analyze the required adjustment as of July 31 using T accounts, and then formally enter this adjustment in the general journal.

EXERCISE 5-3B **(LO1)** **ADJUSTMENT FOR WAGES** On July 31, the trial balance shows wages expense of $800. An additional $150 of wages was earned by the employees but has not yet been paid. Analyze the required adjustment using T accounts, and then formally enter this adjustment in the general journal.

EXERCISE 5-4B **(LO1)** **ADJUSTMENT FOR DEPRECIATION OF ASSET** On July 1, delivery equipment was purchased for $4,320. The delivery equipment has an estimated useful life of 3 years (36 months) and no salvage value. Using the straight-line depreciation method, prepare the necessary adjusting entry as of July 31 (one month), and then formally enter this adjustment in the general journal.

EXERCISE 5-5B **(LO1)** **CALCULATION OF BOOK VALUE** On January 1, 20--, a depreciable asset was acquired for $5,760. The asset has an estimated useful life of four years (48 months) and no salvage value. Use the straight-line depreciation method to calculate the book value as of July 1, 20--.

PROBLEM 5-4A

Joyce Lee's Tax Service
Work Sheet
For Month Ended March 31, 20--

	Account Title	Trial Balance Debit	Trial Balance Credit	Adjustments Debit	Adjustments Credit	Adjusted Trial Balance Debit	Adjusted Trial Balance Credit	Income Statement Debit	Income Statement Credit	Balance Sheet Debit	Balance Sheet Credit	
1	Cash	1 7 2 5 00				1 7 2 5 00				1 7 5 2 00		1
2	Accounts Receivable	9 6 0 00				9 6 0 00				9 6 00		2
3	Supplies	5 2 5 00			(a) 1 6 0 00	3 6 5 00				3 6 5 00		3
4	Prepaid Insurance	9 3 0 00			(b) 4 1 0 00	5 4 0 00				5 4 0 00		4
5	Office Equipment	5 4 5 0 00			(c) 2 7 5 00	5 1 7 5 00				5 1 7 5 00		5
6	Accum. Depr.—Office Equipment											6
7	Accounts Payable		4 8 0 00				4 8 0 00				4 8 0 00	7
8	Wages Payable				(d) 1 1 0 00		1 1 0 00		1 1 0 00			8
9	Joyce Lee, Capital		7 5 0 0 00				7 5 0 0 00				7 5 0 0 00	9
10	Joyce Lee, Drawing	1 1 2 5 00				1 1 2 5 00		1 1 2 5 00				10
11	Professional Fees		5 7 0 0 00				5 7 0 0 00		5 7 0 0 00			11
12	Wages Expense	1 4 2 0 00		(d) 1 1 0 00		1 4 2 0 00		1 4 2 0 00				12
13	Advertising Expense	3 5 0 00				3 5 0 00		3 5 0 00				13
14	Rent Expense	7 0 0 00				7 0 0 00		7 0 0 00				14
15	Supplies Expense			(a) 1 6 0 00		1 6 0 00		1 6 0 00				15
16	Telephone Expense	1 3 0 00				1 3 0 00		1 3 0 00				16
17	Utilities Expense	1 9 0 00				1 9 0 00		1 9 0 00				17
18	Insurance Expense			(b) 4 1 0 00		4 1 0 00		4 1 00				18
19	Depr. Expense—Office Equipment			(c) 2 7 5 00		2 7 5 00		2 7 5 00				19
20	Miscellaneous Expense	1 7 5 00				1 7 5 00		1 7 5 00				20
21												21
22		13 6 8 0 00	13 6 8 0 00	9 5 5 00	9 5 5 00	13 1 6 0 00	13 7 9 0 00	4 5 6 6 00	5 8 1 0 00	9 5 0 8 00	7 9 8 0 00	22
23								1 2 4 4 00			1 5 2 8 00	23
24								5 8 1 0 00	5 8 1 0 00	9 5 0 8 00	9 5 0 8 00	24
25												25
26												26
27												27
28												28
29												29
30												30

This work sheet contains errors.

EXERCISE 5-6B   **(LO1)**   **ANALYSIS OF ADJUSTING ENTRY FOR SUPPLIES** Analyze each situation and indicate the correct dollar amount for the adjusting entry.

1. Ending inventory of supplies is $95.

(Balance Sheet) Supplies		(Income Statement) Supplies Expense
TB 540	Adj. _____	Adj. _____
Bal. _____		

2. Amount of supplies used is $280.

(Balance Sheet) Supplies		(Income Statement) Supplies Expense
TB 330	Adj. _____	Adj. _____
Bal. _____		

EXERCISE 5-7B   **(LO1)**   **ANALYSIS OF ADJUSTING ENTRY FOR INSURANCE** Analyze each situation and indicate the correct dollar amount for the adjusting entry.

1. Amount of insurance expired (used) is $830.

(Balance Sheet) Prepaid Insurance		(Income Statement) Insurance Expense
TB 960	Adj. _____	Adj. _____
Bal. _____		

2. Amount of unexpired (remaining) insurance is $340.

(Balance Sheet) Prepaid Insurance		(Income Statement) Insurance Expense
TB 1,135	Adj. _____	Adj. _____
Bal. _____		

EXERCISE 5-8B   **(LO2)**   **WORK SHEET AND ADJUSTING ENTRIES** Page 161 shows a partial work sheet for Jasmine Kah's Auto Detailing. Indicate by letters (a) through (d) the four adjustments in the Adjustments columns of the work sheet, properly matching each debit and credit. Complete the Adjustments columns.

Jasmine Kah's Auto Detailing
Work Sheet (Partial)
For Month Ended June 30, 20 - -

	ACCOUNT TITLE	TRIAL BALANCE		ADJUSTMENTS		ADJUSTED TRIAL BALANCE		
		DEBIT	CREDIT	DEBIT	CREDIT	DEBIT	CREDIT	
1	Cash	1 5 0 00				1 5 0 00		1
2	Supplies	5 2 0 00				9 0 00		2
3	Prepaid Insurance	7 5 0 00				2 0 0 00		3
4	Cleaning Equipment	5 4 0 0 00				5 4 0 0 00		4
5	Accum. Depr.— Cleaning Equipment		8 5 0 00				1 1 5 0 00	5
6	Wages Payable						2 5 0 00	6
7	Jasmine Kah, Capital		4 6 0 0 00				4 6 0 0 00	7
8	Detailing Fees		2 2 2 0 00				2 2 2 0 00	8
9	Wages Expense	7 0 0 00				9 5 0 00		9
10	Advertising Expense	1 5 0 00				1 5 0 00		10
11	Supplies Expense					4 3 0 00		11
12	Insurance Expense					5 5 0 00		12
13	Depr. Expense—Cleaning Equipment					3 0 0 00		13
14		7 6 7 0 00	7 6 7 0 00			8 2 2 0 00	8 2 2 0 00	14

EXERCISE 5-9B   (LO4)   **JOURNALIZING ADJUSTING ENTRIES** From the Adjustments columns in Exercise 5-8B, journalize the four adjusting entries as of June 30, in proper general journal format.

EXERCISE 5-10B   (LO2)   **EXTENDING ADJUSTED BALANCES TO THE INCOME STATEMENT AND BALANCE SHEET COLUMNS** Indicate with an "x" whether each account total should be extended to the Income Statement Debit or Credit or to the Balance Sheet Debit or Credit columns on the work sheet.

	Income Statement		Balance Sheet	
	Debit	Credit	Debit	Credit
Cash	_____	_____	_____	_____
Accounts Receivable	_____	_____	_____	_____
Supplies	_____	_____	_____	_____
Prepaid Insurance	_____	_____	_____	_____
Automobile	_____	_____	_____	_____
Accum. Depr.—Automobile	_____	_____	_____	_____
Accounts Payable	_____	_____	_____	_____
Wages Payable	_____	_____	_____	_____
Owner, Capital	_____	_____	_____	_____
Owner, Drawing	_____	_____	_____	_____
Service Fees	_____	_____	_____	_____
Wages Expense	_____	_____	_____	_____
Supplies Expense	_____	_____	_____	_____
Utilities Expense	_____	_____	_____	_____
Insurance Expense	_____	_____	_____	_____
Depr. Exp.—Automobile	_____	_____	_____	_____

EXERCISE 5-11B (LO2) **ANALYSIS OF NET INCOME OR NET LOSS ON THE WORK SHEET** Insert the dollar amounts where the net income or net loss would appear on the work sheet.

	Income Statement		Balance Sheet	
	Debit	Credit	Debit	Credit
Net Income: $2,500	_____	_____	_____	_____
Net Loss: $1,900	_____	_____	_____	_____

EXERCISE 5-12B (LO5) **POSTING ADJUSTING ENTRIES** Two adjusting entries are shown in the following general journal. Post these adjusting entries to the four general ledger accounts. The following account numbers were taken from the chart of accounts: 145, Prepaid Insurance; 183.1, Accumulated Depreciation—Cleaning Equipment; 541, Depreciation Expense—Cleaning Equipment; and 535, Insurance Expense. If you are not using the working papers that accompany this text, enter the following balances before posting the entries: Prepaid Insurance, $960 Dr.; Accumulated Depr.—Cleaning Equip., $870 Cr.

GENERAL JOURNAL   PAGE 7

	DATE		DESCRIPTION	POST REF.	DEBIT	CREDIT	
1			Adjusting Entries				1
2	20-- July	31	Insurance Expense		3 2 0 00		2
3			Prepaid Insurance			3 2 0 00	3
4							4
5		31	Depr. Expense—Cleaning Equipment		1 4 5 00		5
6			Accum. Depr.—Cleaning Equipment			1 4 5 00	6

SERIES B PROBLEMS

PROBLEM 5-1B   (LO1/2)   **ADJUSTMENTS AND WORK SHEET SHOWING NET INCOME** Louie Long started a business called Louie's Lawn Service. The trial balance as of March 31, after the first month of operation, is shown below.

Louie's Lawn Service
Work Sheet
For Month Ended March 31, 20 - -

	ACCOUNT TITLE	TRIAL BALANCE		ADJUSTMENTS		
		DEBIT	CREDIT	DEBIT	CREDIT	
1	Cash	1 3 7 5 00				1
2	Accounts Receivable	8 8 0 00				2
3	Supplies	4 9 0 00				3
4	Prepaid Insurance	8 0 0 00				4
5	Lawn Equipment	5 7 0 0 00				5
6	Accum. Depr.—Lawn Equipment					6
7	Accounts Payable		7 8 0 00			7
8	Wages Payable					8
9	Louie Long, Capital		6 5 0 0 00			9
10	Louie Long, Drawing	1 2 5 0 00				10
11	Lawn Service Fees		6 1 0 0 00			11
12	Wages Expense	1 1 4 5 00				12
13	Advertising Expense	5 4 0 00				13
14	Rent Expense	7 2 5 00				14
15	Supplies Expense					15
16	Telephone Expense	1 6 0 00				16
17	Insurance Expense					17
18	Repair Expense	2 5 0 00				18
19	Depr. Expense—Lawn Equipment					19
20	Miscellaneous Expense	6 5 00				20
21		13 3 8 0 00	13 3 8 0 00			21

REQUIRED

1. Analyze the following adjustments and enter them on a work sheet.

    (a)   Ending supplies inventory as of March 31, $165.

    (b)   Insurance expired (used), $100.

    (c)   Depreciation of lawn equipment, $200.

    (d)   Wages earned, but not paid as of March 31, $180.

2. Complete the work sheet.

PROBLEM 5-2B (LO1/2) **ADJUSTMENTS AND WORK SHEET SHOWING A NET LOSS** Val Nolan started a business called Nolan's Home Appraisals. The trial balance as of October 31, after the first month of operations, is shown below.

Nolan's Home Appraisals
Work Sheet
For Month Ended October 31, 20 - -

	ACCOUNT TITLE	TRIAL BALANCE DEBIT	TRIAL BALANCE CREDIT	ADJUSTMENTS DEBIT	ADJUSTMENTS CREDIT	
1	Cash	8 3 0 00				1
2	Accounts Receivable	7 6 0 00				2
3	Supplies	6 2 5 00				3
4	Prepaid Insurance	9 5 0 00				4
5	Automobile	6 5 0 0 00				5
6	Accum. Depr.—Automobile					6
7	Accounts Payable		1 5 0 0 00			7
8	Wages Payable					8
9	Val Nolan, Capital		9 9 0 0 00			9
10	Val Nolan, Drawing	1 1 0 0 00				10
11	Appraisal Fees		3 0 0 0 00			11
12	Wages Expense	1 5 6 0 00				12
13	Advertising Expense	4 2 0 00				13
14	Rent Expense	1 0 5 0 00				14
15	Supplies Expense					15
16	Telephone Expense	2 5 5 00				16
17	Insurance Expense					17
18	Repair Expense	2 7 0 00				18
19	Oil and Gas Expense	8 0 00				19
20	Depr. Expense—Automobile					20
21		14 4 0 0 00	14 4 0 0 00			21

REQUIRED

1. Analyze the following adjustments and enter them on the work sheet.

    (a) Supplies inventory as of October 31, $210.

    (b) Unexpired (remaining) insurance as of October 31, $800.

    (c) Depreciation of automobile, $250.

    (d) Wages earned, but not paid as of October 31, $175.

2. Complete the work sheet.

PROBLEM 5-3B   (LO4/5)

JOURNALIZE AND POST ADJUSTING ENTRIES FROM THE WORK SHEET
Refer to Problem 5-2B and the following additional information.

Account Name	Account Number	Balance in Account Before Adjusting Entry
Supplies	141	$ 625
Prepaid Insurance	145	950
Accum. Depr.—Automobile	185.1	0
Wages Payable	219	0
Wages Expense	511	1,560
Supplies Expense	523	0
Insurance Expense	535	0
Depr. Expense—Automobile	541	0

REQUIRED

1. Journalize the adjusting entries on page 3 of the general journal.

2. Post the adjusting entries to the general ledger. (If you are not using the working papers that accompany this text, enter the balances provided in this problem before posting the adjusting entries.)

PROBLEM 5-4B   (LO3)

CORRECTING WORK SHEET WITH ERRORS A beginning accounting student tried to complete a work sheet for Dick Ady's Bookkeeping Service. The following adjusting entries were to have been analyzed and entered in the work sheet.

(a) Ending inventory of supplies on July 31, $130.

(b) Unexpired insurance on July 31, $420.

(c) Depreciation of office equipment, $325.

(d) Wages earned, but not paid as of July 31, $95.

REQUIRED

Review the work sheet shown on page 166 for addition mistakes, transpositions, and other errors and make all necessary corrections.

PROBLEM 5-4B

Dick Ady's Bookkeeping Service
Work Sheet
For Month Ended July 31, 20 - -

#	ACCOUNT TITLE	TRIAL BALANCE DEBIT	TRIAL BALANCE CREDIT	ADJUSTMENTS DEBIT	ADJUSTMENTS CREDIT	ADJUSTED TRIAL BALANCE DEBIT	ADJUSTED TRIAL BALANCE CREDIT	INCOME STATEMENT DEBIT	INCOME STATEMENT CREDIT	BALANCE SHEET DEBIT	BALANCE SHEET CREDIT
1	Cash	1 3 6 5 00				1 3 6 5 00				1 3 5 6 00	
2	Accounts Receivable	8 4 5 00				8 4 5 00					
3	Supplies	6 2 0 00			(a) 4 9 0 00	1 3 0 00				1 3 0 00	
4	Prepaid Insurance	1 1 5 0 00			(b) 4 2 0 00	7 3 0 00				7 3 0 00	
5	Office Equipment	6 4 0 0 00				6 7 2 5 00			8 4 5 00	6 7 2 5 00	
6	Accum. Depr.—Office Equipment				(c) 3 2 5 00						
7	Accounts Payable		7 3 5 00				7 3 5 00				7 3 5 00
8	Wages Payable				(d) 9 5 00		9 5 00				5 9 0 00
9	Dick Ady, Capital		7 8 0 0 00				7 8 0 0 00				7 8 0 0 00
10	Dick Ady, Drawing	1 2 0 0 00				1 2 0 0 00				1 2 0 0 00	
11	Professional Fees		6 3 5 0 00				6 3 5 0 00		6 3 5 0 00		
12	Wages Expense	1 4 9 5 00		(d) 9 5 00		1 5 9 0 00		1 5 9 0 00			
13	Advertising Expense	3 8 0 00				3 8 0 00		3 8 0 00			
14	Rent Expense	8 5 0 00				8 5 0 00		8 5 0 00			
15	Supplies Expense			(a) 4 9 0 00		4 9 0 00		4 9 0 00			
16	Telephone Expense	2 0 5 00				2 0 5 00		2 0 5 00			
17	Utilities Expense	2 8 5 00				2 8 5 00		2 8 5 00			
18	Insurance Expense			(b) 4 2 0 00		4 2 0 00		4 2 0 00			
19	Depr. Expense—Office Equipment			(c) 3 2 5 00		3 2 5 00		3 2 5 00			
20	Miscellaneous Expense	9 0 00				9 0 00		9 0 00			
21	Net Income	14 8 8 5 00	14 8 8 5 00	1 3 3 0 00	1 3 3 0 00	15 6 3 0 00	14 9 8 0 00	4 8 8 0 00	7 1 9 5 00	10 1 4 1 00	8 5 9 4 00
22								2 3 1 5 00			1 5 4 7 00
23								7 1 9 5 00	7 1 9 5 00	10 1 4 1 00	10 1 4 1 00
24											
25											
26											
27											
28											
29											

Contains Errors

This work sheet contains errors.

CHALLENGE PROBLEM

GENERAL LEDGER

Your friend, Diane Kiefner, teaches elementary school and operates her own wilderness kayaking tours in the summers. She thinks she has been doing fine financially, but has never really measured her profits. Until this year, her business has always had more money at the end of the summer than at the beginning. She enjoys kayaking and as long as she came out a little ahead, that was fine. Unfortunately, Diane had to dip into her savings to make up for "losses" on her kayaking tours this past summer. Hearing that you have been studying accounting, she brought a list of cash receipts and expenditures and would like you to try to figure out what happened.

Cash balance beginning of summer		$15,000
Cash receipts from kayakers over the summer	$10,000	
Cash expenditures over the summer	13,500	
Amount taken from savings		($3,500)
Cash balance end of summer		$11,500

When asked for more details on the expenditures and the kayaking gear that you saw in her garage, Diane provided the following information.

Expenditures were made on the following items:
Brochures used to advertise her services (Diane only used about 1/4 of them and plans to use the remainder over the next three summers.) $1,000
Food for trips (nothing left) 2,000
Rent on equipment used by kayakers on trips 3,000
Travel expenses 4,000
A new kayak and paddles (At the beginning of the summer, Diane bought a new kayak and paddles. Up to this time, she had always borrowed her father's. Diane expects to use the equipment for about five years. At that time she expects it to have no value.) 3,500

A trial balance based on the above information is provided below. As you will note, Diane's trial balance is not consistent with some of the concepts discussed in this chapter.

Diane Kiefner's Wilderness Kayaking Tours
Work Sheet
For Summer Ended 20 - -

	ACCOUNT TITLE	TRIAL BALANCE DEBIT	TRIAL BALANCE CREDIT	ADJUSTMENTS DEBIT	ADJUSTMENTS CREDIT	ADJUSTED TRIAL BALANCE DEBIT	ADJUSTED TRIAL BALANCE CREDIT	INCOME STATEMENT DEBIT	INCOME STATEMENT CREDIT	BALANCE SHEET DEBIT	BALANCE SHEET CREDIT	
1	Cash	11 5 0 0 00										1
2	Diane Kiefner, Capital		15 0 0 0 00									2
3	Tour Revenue		10 0 0 0 00									3
4	Advertising Supplies Expense	1 0 0 0 00										4
5	Food Expense	2 0 0 0 00										5
6	Equipment Rental Expense	3 0 0 0 00										6
7	Travel Expense	4 0 0 0 00										7
8	Kayak Expense	3 5 0 0 00										8
9		25 0 0 0 00	25 0 0 0 00									9

(continued)

REQUIRED

1. Complete Diane's work sheet by making appropriate adjustments and extensions. Note: (a) You may need to add new accounts. (b) Some of the adjustments you need to make are actually "corrections of errors" Diane has made in classifying certain items.

2. What is your best measure of Diane's net income for the summer of 20--?

MASTERY PROBLEM

Kristi Williams offers family counseling services specializing in financial and marital problems. A chart of accounts and a trial balance taken on December 31, 20-1, are provided below.

KRISTI WILLIAMS FAMILY COUNSELING SERVICES CHART OF ACCOUNTS			
Assets		**Revenue**	
101	Cash	401	Client Fees
142	Office Supplies		
145	Prepaid Insurance	**Expenses**	
181	Office Equipment	511	Wages Expense
181.1	Accumulated Depr.—	521	Rent Expense
	Office Equipment	523	Office Supplies Expense
187	Computer Equipment	533	Utilities Expense
187.1	Accumulated Depr.—	535	Insurance Expense
	Computer Equipment	541	Depr. Expense—
			Office Equipment
Liabilities		542	Depr. Expense—
201	Notes Payable		Computer Equipment
202	Accounts Payable	549	Miscellaneous Expense
Owner's Equity			
311	Kristi Williams, Capital		
312	Kristi Williams, Drawing		

Kristi Williams Family Counseling Services Trial Balance December 31, 20 - 1											
ACCOUNT TITLE	ACCOUNT NO.	DEBIT BALANCE					CREDIT BALANCE				
Cash	101	8	7	3	0	00					
Office Supplies	142		7	0	0	00					
Prepaid Insurance	145		6	0	0	00					
Office Equipment	181	18	0	0	0	00					
Computer Equipment	187	6	0	0	0	00					
Notes Payable	201						8	0	0	0	00
Accounts Payable	202							5	0	0	00
Kristi Williams, Capital	311						11	4	0	0	00
Kristi Williams, Drawing	312	3	0	0	0	00					
Client Fees	401						35	8	0	0	00
Wages Expense	511	9	5	0	0	00					
Rent Expense	521	6	0	0	0	00					
Utilities Expense	533	2	1	7	0	00					
Miscellaneous Expense	549	1	0	0	0	00					
		55	7	0	0	00	55	7	0	0	00

Information for year-end adjustments:

(a) Office supplies on hand at year end amounted to $100.

(b) On January 1, 20-1, Williams purchased office equipment that cost $18,000. It has an expected useful life of ten years and no salvage value.

(c) On July 1, 20-1, Williams purchased computer equipment costing $6,000. It has an expected useful life of three years and no salvage value. Assume that Williams computes depreciation to the nearest full month.

(d) On December 1, 20-1, Williams paid a premium of $600 for a six-month insurance policy.

REQUIRED

1. Prepare the work sheet for the year ended December 31, 20-1.

2. Prepare adjusting entries in a general journal.

Self-Study Test Questions

True/False

1. The matching principle in accounting requires the matching of debits and credits. _____

2. Adjusting entries are required at the end of the accounting period because of mistakes in the journal and ledger. _____

3. As part of the adjustment of supplies, an expense account is debited and Supplies is credited for the amount of supplies used during the accounting period. _____

4. Depreciable cost is the difference between the original cost of the asset and its accumulated depreciation. _____

5. The purpose of depreciation is to record the asset's market value in the accounting records. _____

Multiple Choice

1. The purpose of depreciation is to _____

    (a) spread the cost of an asset over its useful life.
    (b) show the current market value of an asset.
    (c) set up a reserve fund to purchase a new asset.
    (d) expense the asset in the year it was purchased.

2. Depreciable cost is the _____

    (a) difference between original cost and accumulated depreciation.
    (b) difference in actual cost and true market value.
    (c) difference between original cost and estimated salvage value.
    (d) difference between estimated salvage value and the actual salvage value.

3. Book value is the _____

    (a) difference between market value and estimated value.
    (b) difference between market value and historical cost.
    (c) difference between original cost and salvage value.
    (d) difference between original cost and accumulated depreciation.

4. The adjustment for wages earned but not yet paid is _____

    (a) debit Wages Payable and credit Wages Expense.
    (b) debit Wages Expense and credit Cash.
    (c) debit Wages Expense and credit Wages Payable.
    (d) debit Wages Expense and credit Accounts Receivable.

5. The first step in preparing a work sheet is to _____

    a) prepare the trial balance.
    (b) prepare the adjustments.
    (c) prepare the adjusted trial balance.
    (d) extend the amounts from the Adjusted Trial Balance to the Income Statement and Balance Sheet columns.

The answers to the Self-Study Test Questions are at the end of the text.

Careful study of this appendix should enable you to:

LO1 Prepare a depreciation schedule using the straight-line method.

LO2 Prepare a depreciation schedule using the sum-of-the-years'-digits method.

LO3 Prepare a depreciation schedule using the double-declining-balance method.

LO4 Prepare a depreciation schedule for tax purposes using the Modified Accelerated Cost Recovery System.

Chapter 5 Appendix
Depreciation Methods

In Chapter 5, we introduced the straight-line method of depreciation. Here, we will review this method and illustrate three others: sum-of-the-years'-digits; double-declining-balance; and, for tax purposes, the Modified Accelerated Cost Recovery System. For all illustrations, we will assume that a delivery van was purchased for $40,000. It has a five-year useful life and salvage value of $4,000.

STRAIGHT-LINE METHOD

LO1 Prepare a depreciation schedule using the straight-line method.

Under the straight-line method, an equal amount of depreciation will be taken each period. First, compute the depreciable cost by subtracting the salvage value from the cost of the asset. This is done because we expect to sell the asset for $4,000 at the end of its useful life. Thus, the total cost to be recognized as an expense over the five years is $36,000, not $40,000.

Cost	–	Salvage Value	=	Depreciable Cost
$40,000	–	$4,000	=	$36,000

Next, we divide the depreciable cost by the expected life of the asset, five years.

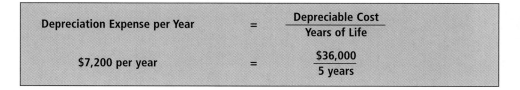

$$\text{Depreciation Expense per Year} = \frac{\text{Depreciable Cost}}{\text{Years of Life}}$$

$$\$7,200 \text{ per year} = \frac{\$36,000}{5 \text{ years}}$$

When preparing a depreciation schedule, it is often convenient to use a depreciation rate per year. In this case it would be 20% (100% ÷ 5 years of life). Figure 5A-1 shows the depreciation expense, accumulated depreciation, and book value for each of the five years.

STRAIGHT-LINE DEPRECIATION					
Year	Depreciable Cost[a] ×	Rate[b] =	Depreciation Expense	Accumulated Depreciation (End of Year)	Book Value[c] (End of Year)
1	$36,000	20%	$7,200	$ 7,200	$32,800
2	36,000	20%	7,200	14,400	25,600
3	36,000	20%	7,200	21,600	18,400
4	36,000	20%	7,200	28,800	11,200
5	36,000	20%	7,200	36,000	4,000

[a] Depreciable Cost = Cost − Salvage Value ($40,000 − $4,000 = $36,000)
[b] Rate = 1 year ÷ 5 years of life × 100 = 20%
[c] Book Value = Cost ($40,000) − Accumulated Depreciation

FIGURE 5A-1 Depreciation Schedule Using Straight-Line Method

SUM-OF-THE-YEARS'-DIGITS

LO2 Prepare a depreciation schedule using the sum-of-the-years'-digits method.

Under the sum-of-the-years'-digits method, depreciation is determined by multiplying the depreciable cost by a schedule of fractions. The numerator of the fraction for a specific year is the number of years of remaining useful life for the asset, measured from the beginning of the year. The denominator for all fractions is determined by adding the digits that represent the years of the estimated life of the asset. The calculation for our delivery van with a five-year useful life is shown below.

> **Sum-of-the-Years'-Digits = 5 + 4 + 3 + 2 + 1 = 15**

A depreciation schedule using these fractions is shown in Figure 5A-2.

SUM-OF-THE-YEARS' DIGITS					
Year	Depreciable Cost[a] ×	Rate[b] =	Depreciation Expense	Accumulated Depreciation (End of Year)	Book Value[c] (End of Year)
1	$36,000	5/15	$12,000	$12,000	$28,000
2	36,000	4/15	9,600	21,600	18,400
3	36,000	3/15	7,200	28,800	11,200
4	36,000	2/15	4,800	33,600	6,400
5	36,000	1/15	2,400	36,000	4,000

[a] Depreciable Cost = Cost − Salvage Value ($40,000 − $4,000 = $36,000)
[b] Rate = Number of Years of Remaining Useful Life ÷ Sum-of-the-Years'-Digits
[c] Book Value = Cost ($40,000) − Accumulated Depreciation

FIGURE 5A-2 Depreciation Schedule Using Sum-of-the-Years'-Digits Method

DOUBLE-DECLINING-BALANCE METHOD

LO3 Prepare a depreciation schedule using the double-declining-balance method.

Under this method, the book value is multiplied by a fixed rate, often double the straight-line rate. The van has a five-year life, so the straight-line rate is $1 \div 5$, or 20%. Double the straight-line rate is $2 \times 20\%$, or 40%. The double-declining-balance depreciation schedule is shown in Figure 5A-3. Note that the rate is applied to the book value of the asset. Once the book value is reduced to the expected salvage value, $4,000, no more depreciation may be recognized.

LEARNING KEY:
Double means double the straight-line rate. Declining-balance means that the rate is multiplied by the *book value* (not depreciable cost) at the beginning of each year. This amount is *declining* each year.

DOUBLE-DECLINING-BALANCE METHOD

Year	Book Value[a] (Beginning of Year)	×	Rate[b]	=	Depreciation Expense	Accumulated Depreciation (End of Year)	Book Value[a] (End of Year)
1	$40,000		40%		$16,000	$16,000	$24,000
2	24,000		40%		9,600	25,600	14,400
3	14,400		40%		5,760	31,360	8,640
4	8,640		40%		3,456	34,816	5,184
5	5,184				1,184	36,000	4,000

[a] Book Value = Cost ($40,000) − Accumulated Depreciation
[b] Rate = Double the straight-line rate ($1/5 \times 2 = 2/5$ or 40%)

FIGURE 5A-3   Depreciation Schedule Using Double-Declining-Balance Method

MODIFIED ACCELERATED COST RECOVERY SYSTEM

LO4 Prepare a depreciation schedule for tax purposes using the Modified Accelerated Cost Recovery System.

For assets purchased since 1986, many firms use the Modified Accelerated Cost Recovery System (MACRS) for tax purposes. Under this method, the Internal Revenue Service (IRS) classifies various assets according to useful life and sets depreciation rates for each year of the asset's life. These rates are then multiplied by the cost of the asset. Even though the van is expected to have a useful life of five years, and a salvage value of $4,000, the IRS schedule, shown in Figure 5A-4, spreads the depreciation over a six-year period and assumes no salvage value.

MODIFIED ACCELERATED COST RECOVERY SYSTEM

Year	Cost	×	Rate[a]	=	Depreciation Expense	Accumulated Depreciation (End of Year)	Book Value[b] (End of Year)
1	$40,000		20.00%		$ 8,000	$ 8,000	$32,000
2	40,000		32.00%		12,800	20,800	19,200
3	40,000		19.20%		7,680	28,480	11,520
4	40,000		11.52%		4,608	33,088	6,912
5	40,000		11.52%		4,608	37,696	2,304
6	40,000		5.76%		2,304	40,000	0

[a] Rates set by IRS
[b] Book Value = Cost ($40,000) − Accumulated Depreciation

FIGURE 5A-4   Depreciation Schedule Using Modified Accelerated Cost Recovery System

SERIES A EXERCISES

EXERCISE 5Apx-1A (LO1)   **STRAIGHT-LINE DEPRECIATION** A small delivery truck was purchased on January 1 at a cost of $25,000. It has an estimated useful life of four years and an estimated salvage value of $5,000. Prepare a depreciation schedule showing the depreciation expense, accumulated depreciation, and book value for each year under the straight-line method.

EXERCISE 5Apx-2A (LO2)   **SUM-OF-THE-YEARS'-DIGITS DEPRECIATION** Using the information given in Exercise 5Apx-1A, prepare a depreciation schedule showing the depreciation expense, accumulated depreciation, and book value for each year under the sum-of-the-years'-digits method.

EXERCISE 5Apx-3A (LO3)   **DOUBLE-DECLINING-BALANCE DEPRECIATION** Using the information given in Exercise 5Apx-1A, prepare a depreciation schedule showing the depreciation expense, accumulated depreciation, and book value for each year under the double-declining-balance method.

EXERCISE 5Apx-4A (LO4)   **MODIFIED ACCELERATED COST RECOVERY SYSTEM** Using the information given in Exercise 5Apx-1A and the rates shown in Figure 5A-4, prepare a depreciation schedule showing the depreciation expense, accumulated depreciation, and book value for each year under the Modified Accelerated Cost Recovery System. For tax purposes, assume that the truck has a useful life of five years. (The IRS schedule will spread depreciation over 6 years.)

SERIES B EXERCISES

EXERCISE 5Apx-1B (LO1)   **STRAIGHT-LINE DEPRECIATION** A computer was purchased on January 1 at a cost of $5,000. It has an estimated useful life of five years and an estimated salvage value of $500. Prepare a depreciation schedule showing the depreciation expense, accumulated depreciation, and book value for each year under the straight-line method.

EXERCISE 5Apx-2B (LO2)   **SUM-OF-THE-YEARS'-DIGITS DEPRECIATION** Using the information given in Exercise 5Apx-1B, prepare a depreciation schedule showing the depreciation expense, accumulated depreciation, and book value for each year under the sum-of-the-years'-digits method.

EXERCISE 5Apx-3B (LO3)   **DOUBLE-DECLINING-BALANCE DEPRECIATION** Using the information given in Exercise 5Apx-1B, prepare a depreciation schedule showing the depreciation expense, accumulated depreciation, and book value for each year under the double-declining-balance method.

EXERCISE 5Apx-4B (LO4)   **MODIFIED ACCELERATED COST RECOVERY SYSTEM** Using the information given in Exercise 5Apx-1B and the rates shown in Figure 5A-4, prepare a depreciation schedule showing the depreciation expense, accumulated depreciation, and book value for each year under the Modified Accelerated Cost Recovery System. For tax purposes, assume that the computer has a useful life of five years. (The IRS schedule will spread depreciation over six years.)

6

Financial Statements and the Closing Process

"Come on Jessie, let's get busy. We have to close the books before we go to the New Year's Eve party," said Mitch. But after seeing the disappointed look on Jessie's face, Mitch changed his mind. "What the heck. Let's do it on the 2nd, while we recover from watching all of those bowl games." "Great," said Jessie, "let's get out of here." Will Mitch and Jessie be in trouble for not closing the books before the end of the year?

LO1 Prepare financial statements with the aid of a work sheet.

LO2 Journalize and post closing entries.

LO3 Prepare a post-closing trial balance.

LO4 List and describe the steps in the accounting cycle.

The work sheet, introduced in Chapter 5, is used for three major end-of-period activities:

1. journalizing adjusting entries,

2. preparing financial statements, and

3. journalizing closing entries.

This chapter illustrates the use of the work sheet for preparing financial statements and closing entries. In addition, the post-closing trial balance is explained and illustrated. All of these activities take place at the end of the firm's fiscal year. However, to continue our illustration of Jessie Jane's Campus Delivery, we demonstrate these activities at the end of the first month of operations.

THE FINANCIAL STATEMENTS

LO1 Prepare financial statements with the aid of a work sheet.

Since Jessie made no additional investments during the month, the work sheet prepared in Chapter 5 supplies all of the information needed to prepare an income statement, a statement of owner's equity, and a balance sheet. The statements and work sheet columns from which they are derived for Jessie Jane's Campus Delivery are shown in Figures 6-1 and 6-2.

As you refer to the financial statements in Figures 6-1 and 6-2, notice the placement of dollar signs, single rulings, and double rulings. Dollar signs are placed at the top of each column and beneath rulings. Single rulings indicate addition or subtraction, and double rulings are placed under totals. Notice that each statement heading contains three lines: (1) company name, (2) statement title, and (3) period ended or date.

Multiple columns are used on the financial statements to make them easier to read. There are no debit or credit columns on the financial statements.

The Income Statement

Figure 6-1 shows how the Income Statement columns of the work sheet provide the information needed to prepare an income statement. Revenue is shown first, followed by an itemized and totaled list of expenses. Then, net income is calculated to double check the accuracy of the work sheet. It is presented with a double ruling as the last item in the statement.

The expenses could be listed in the same order that they appear in the chart of accounts or in descending order by dollar amount. The second approach helps the reader identify the most important expenses.

The Statement of Owner's Equity

Figure 6-2 shows that the Balance Sheet columns of the work sheet provide the information needed to prepare a statement of owner's equity. Jessie's capital account balance and the drawing account balance are in the Balance Sheet columns of the work sheet. The net income for the year can be found either on the work sheet at the bottom of the Income Statement (see Figure 6-1) and Balance Sheet columns or on the income statement. With these three items of information, the statement of owner's equity can be prepared.

FIGURE 6-1   Linkages Between the Work Sheet and Income Statement

Jessie Jane's Campus Delivery
Work Sheet (Partial)
For Month Ended June 30, 20 --

	ACCOUNT TITLE	INCOME STATEMENT DEBIT	INCOME STATEMENT CREDIT
1	Cash		
2	Accounts Receivable		
3	Supplies		
4	Prepaid Insurance		
5	Delivery Equipment		
6	Accum. Depr.—Delivery Equipment		
7	Accounts Payable		
8	Wages Payable		
9	Jessica Jane, Capital		
10	Jessica Jane, Drawing		
11	Delivery Fees		2 1 5 0 00
12	Wages Expense	7 0 0 00	
13	Rent Expense	2 0 0 00	
14	Supplies Expense	6 0 00	
15	Telephone Expense	5 0 00	
16	Insurance Expense	2 5 00	
17	Depr. Expense—Delivery Equipment	1 0 0 00	
18		1 1 3 5 00	2 1 5 0 00
19	Net Income	1 0 1 5 00	2 1 5 0 00
20		2 1 5 0 00	
21			
22			
23			
24			
25			
26			
27			
28			
29			

Prepare 1st →

Jessie Jane's Campus Delivery
Income Statement
For Month Ended June 30, 20 --

Revenue:		
Delivery fees		$ 2 1 5 0 00
Expenses:		
Wages expense	$ 7 0 0 00	
Rent expense	2 0 0 00	
Supplies expense	6 0 00	
Telephone expense	5 0 00	
Insurance expense	2 5 00	
Depr. expense—delivery equip.	1 0 0 00	
Total expenses		1 1 3 5 00
Net income		$ 1 0 1 5 00

Name of company
Title of statement
Accounting period ended

Revenues listed first

Expenses listed second by amount (largest to smallest), or in chart of accounts order. Amounts are itemized in left column, subtotaled in right column.

Dollar signs used at top of columns and under rulings.

Single rulings indicate addition or subtraction.

Double rulings indicate totals.

FIGURE 6-2   Linkages Between the Work Sheet, Statement of Owner's Equity, and Balance Sheet

Note: The Statement of Owner's Equity is prepared before the Balance Sheet. The S.O.E. is shown below the B.S. to enhance the illustration of the linkages between the work sheet and financial statements.

Jessie Jane's Campus Delivery
Work Sheet (Partial)
For Month Ended June 30, 20 --

	ACCOUNT TITLE	BALANCE SHEET DEBIT	BALANCE SHEET CREDIT
1	Cash	3 7 0 00	
2	Accounts Receivable	6 5 0 00	
3	Supplies	2 0 00	
4	Prepaid Insurance	1 7 5 00	
5	Delivery Equipment	3 6 0 0 00	
6	Accum. Depr.—Delivery Equip.		1 0 0 00
7	Accounts Payable		1 8 0 0 00
8	Wages Payable		5 0 00
9	Jessica Jane, Capital		2 0 0 0 00
10	Jessica Jane, Drawing	1 5 0 00	
11	Delivery Fees		
12	Wages Expense		
13	Rent Expense		
14	Supplies Expense		
15	Telephone Expense		
16	Insurance Expense		
17	Depr. Expense—Delivery Equip.		
18		4 9 6 5 00	3 9 5 0 00
19	Net Income		1 0 1 5 00
20		4 9 6 5 00	4 9 6 5 00
21			

Prepare 3rd

Jessie Jane's Campus Delivery
Balance Sheet
June 30, 20 --

Assets			
Current assets:			
Cash		$ 3 7 0 00	
Accounts receivable		6 5 0 00	
Supplies		2 0 00	
Prepaid insurance		1 7 5 00	
Total current assets			$ 1 2 1 5 00
Property, plant, and equipment:			
Delivery equipment	$3 6 0 0 00		
Less accumulated depreciation	1 0 0 00		3 5 0 0 00
Total assets			$ 4 7 1 5 00
Liabilities			
Current liabilities:			
Accounts payable	$1 8 0 0 00		
Wages payable	5 0 00		
Total current liabilities		$ 1 8 5 0 00	
Owner's Equity			
Jessica Jane, capital		2 8 6 5 00	
Total liabilities and owner's equity		$ 4 7 1 5 00	

Prepare 2nd

Jessie Jane's Campus Delivery
Statement of Owner's Equity
For Month Ended June 30, 20 --

Jessica Jane, capital, June 1, 20--		$ 2 0 0 0 00	
Net income for June	$ 1 0 1 5 00		
Less withdrawals for June	1 5 0 00		
Increase in capital		8 6 5 00	
Jessica Jane, capital, June 30, 20--		$ 2 8 6 5 00	

Name of company
Title of statement
Accounting period ended

Current assets: cash and items that will be converted to cash or consumed within a year.

Property, plant, and equipment: durable assets that will help produce revenues for several years.

Current liabilities: amounts owed that will be paid within a year (will require the use of current assets).

Ending capital is not taken from work sheet. It is computed on the statement of owner's equity.

Dollar signs used at top of columns and beneath rulings.

Single rulings indicate addition or subtraction.

Double rulings indicate totals.

LEARNING KEY: The owner's capital account in the general ledger must be reviewed to determine if additional investments were made during the accounting period.

Be careful when using the capital account balance reported in the balance sheet columns of the work sheet. This account balance is the beginning balance *plus any additional investments made during the period.* Since Jessie made no additional investments during June, the $2,000 balance may be used as the beginning balance on the statement of owner's equity.

The Balance Sheet

As shown in Figure 6-2, the work sheet and the statement of owner's equity are used to prepare Jessie's balance sheet. The asset and liability amounts can be found in the Balance Sheet columns of the work sheet. The ending balance in Jessica Jane, Capital has been computed on the statement of owner's equity. This amount should be copied from the statement of owner's equity to the balance sheet.

Two important features of the balance sheet in Figure 6-2 should be noted. First, it is a **report form of balance sheet**, which means that the liabilities and owner's equity sections are shown below the assets section. It differs from an **account form of balance sheet** in which the assets are on the left and the liabilities and owner's equity sections are on the right. (See Jessie's balance sheet illustrated in Figure 2-2 on page 29 in Chapter 2.)

Second, it is a **classified balance sheet**, which means that similar items are grouped together on the balance sheet. Assets are classified as current assets and property, plant, and equipment. Similarly, liabilities are broken down into current and long-term sections. The following major balance sheet classifications are generally used.

Current Assets. **Current assets** include cash and assets that will be converted into cash or consumed within either one year or the normal operating cycle of the business, whichever is longer. Examples include cash, accounts receivable, supplies, and prepaid insurance. An **operating cycle** is the period of time required to purchase supplies and services and convert them back into cash.

Property, Plant, and Equipment. **Property, plant, and equipment**, also called **plant assets** or **long-term assets**, represent assets that are expected to serve the business for many years. Examples include land, buildings, and equipment.

Current Liabilities. **Current liabilities** are due within either one year or the normal operating cycle of the business, whichever is longer. They will be paid out of current assets. Accounts payable and wages payable are classified as current liabilities.

Long-Term Liabilities. **Long-term liabilities**, or **long-term debt**, are obligations that are not expected to be paid within a year and do not require the use of current assets. A mortgage on an office building is an example of a long-term liability. Jessie has no long-term debts. If she did, they would be listed on the balance sheet in the long-term liabilities section immediately following the current liabilities.

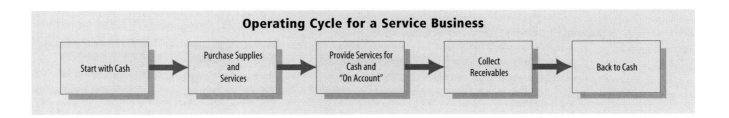

Additional Investments by the Owner

If the owner of a business made additional investments during the accounting period, the owner's capital reported in the Balance Sheet columns of the work sheet would represent the beginning balance plus any additional investments made during the accounting period. If this amount were used as the beginning balance on the statement of owner's equity, it would not equal the ending balance from last period and would create confusion for those comparing the two statements. In addition, the statement would not reflect all of the activities affecting the owner's capital account during the period.

Thus, we must also review the owner's capital account in the general ledger to get the information needed to prepare the statement of owner's equity. Figure 6-3 illustrates this situation for another business, Ramon's Shopping Service. The $5,000 balance of July 1, 20--, in Ramon Balboa's general ledger capital account is used as the beginning balance on the statement of owner's equity. Note that this is also the ending balance on June 30, 20--. The additional investment of $3,000 made on July 5 and posted to Balboa's general ledger capital account is reported by writing "add additional investments" on the line immediately after the beginning balance. The beginning balance plus the additional investment equals the total investment by the owner in the business and is the amount reported in the Balance Sheet columns of the work sheet. From this point, the preparation of the statement is the same as for businesses without additional investments.

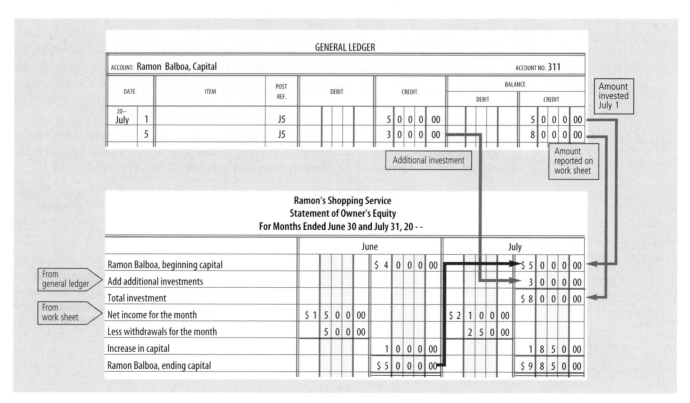

FIGURE 6-3 **Statement of Owner's Equity with Additional Investment**

THE CLOSING PROCESS

LO2 Journalize and post closing entries.

Assets, liabilities, and the owner's capital account accumulate information across accounting periods. Their balances are brought forward for each new period. For example, the amount of cash at the end of one accounting period must be the same as the amount of cash at the beginning of the next period. Thus, the balance reported for Cash is a result of all cash transactions since the business first opened. This is true for all accounts reported on the balance sheet. For this reason, they are called **permanent accounts**.

LEARNING KEY: Permanent accounts contain the results of all transactions since the business started. Their balances are carried forward to each new accounting period.

Revenue, expense, and drawing accounts accumulate information *for a specific accounting period*. At the end of the fiscal year, these accounts must be *closed*. The **closing process** gives these accounts zero balances so they are prepared to accumulate new information for the next accounting period. Since these accounts do not accumulate information across accounting periods, they are called **temporary accounts**. The drawing account and all accounts reported in the income statement are temporary accounts and must be closed at the end of each accounting period.

LEARNING KEY: Temporary accounts contain information for one accounting period. These accounts are closed at the end of each accounting period.

The income summary account is not really needed for the closing process. Some businesses simply close the revenue and expense accounts directly to the owner's capital account. One benefit of using the income summary account is that its balance before closing to the capital account equals

the net income or net loss for the period. Thus, it can serve as a check of the accuracy of the closing entries for revenues and expenses. Of course, computer programs post the closing entries to the owner's capital account automatically.

The closing process is most clearly demonstrated by returning to the accounting equation and T accounts. As shown in Figure 6-4, revenue, expense, and drawing accounts impact owner's equity and should be considered "under the umbrella" of the capital account. The effect of these accounts on owner's equity is formalized at the end of the accounting period when the balances of the temporary accounts are transferred to the owner's capital account (a permanent account) during the closing process.

The four basic steps in the closing process are illustrated in Figure 6-4. As you can see, a new account, **Income Summary**, is used in the closing process. This account may also be called *Expense and Revenue Summary*. This temporary account is used to close the revenue and expense accounts. After closing the revenues and expenses to Income Summary, the balance of this account is equal to the net income. This is why it is called Income Summary. Income Summary is opened during the closing process. Then it is closed to the owner's capital account. It does not appear on any financial statement. The four steps in the closing process are explained below.

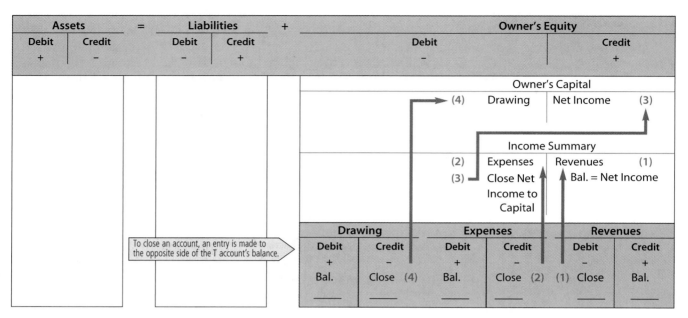

FIGURE 6-4   The Closing Process

STEPS IN THE CLOSING PROCESS

STEP 1   **Close Revenue Accounts to Income Summary.** Revenues have credit balances and increase owner's equity. Therefore, the revenue account is debited to create a zero balance. Income Summary is credited for the same amount.

STEP 2   **Close Expense Accounts to Income Summary.** Expenses have debit balances and reduce owner's equity. Therefore, the expense accounts are credited to create a zero balance. Income Summary must be debited for the total of the expenses.

STEP 3   **Close Income Summary to Capital.** The balance in Income Summary represents the net income (credit balance) or net loss (debit balance) for the period. This balance is transferred to the owner's capital account. If net income has been earned, Income Summary is debited to create a zero balance, and the owner's capital account is credited. If a net loss has been incurred, the owner's capital account is debited and Income Summary is credited to create a zero balance. Figure 6-5 shows examples for closing net income and net loss.

STEP 4   **Close Drawing to Capital.** Drawing has a debit balance and reduces owner's equity. Therefore, it is credited to create a zero balance. The owner's capital account is debited.

LEARNING KEY: The owner can make withdrawals from the business for any amount and at any time, as long as the assets are available. These withdrawals are for personal reasons and have nothing to do with measuring the profitability of the firm. Thus, they are closed directly to the owner's capital account.

NET INCOME				
Capital				
		1,000	STEP 3	
			(Net Income)	
Income Summary				
(Expenses)	4,000	5,000	(Revenues)	
STEP 3 to close	1,000	1,000	(Bal. before closing)	

NET LOSS				
Capital				
STEP 3		2,000		
(Net Loss)				
Income Summary				
(Expenses)	6,000	4,000	(Revenues)	
(Bal. before closing)	2,000	2,000	STEP 3 to close	

FIGURE 6-5   Step 3: Closing Net Income and Closing Net Loss

Upon completion of these four steps, all temporary accounts have zero balances. The earnings and withdrawals for the period have been transferred to the owner's capital account.

Journalize Closing Entries

Of course, to actually change the ledger accounts, the closing entries must be journalized and posted to the general ledger. As shown in Figure 6-6, the balances of the accounts to be closed are readily available from the Income Statement and Balance Sheet columns of the work sheet. These balances are used to illustrate the

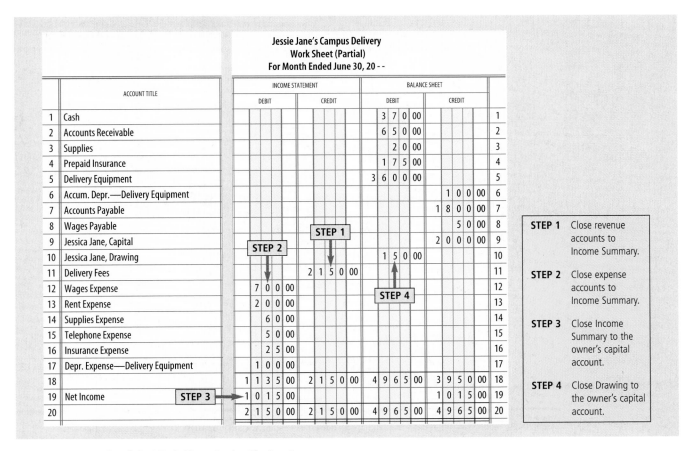

FIGURE 6-6   Role of the Work Sheet in the Closing Process

Rulings are entered on the debit and credit sides of the T accounts to indicate a zero balance.

closing entries for Jessie Jane's Campus Delivery, in T account and general journal form, in Figures 6-7 and 6-8, respectively. Remember: Closing entries are made at the end of the *fiscal year*. Closing entries made at the end of June are illustrated here so you can see the completion of the accounting cycle for Jessie Jane's Campus Delivery.

Like adjusting entries, the closing entries are made on the last day of the accounting period. "Closing Entries" is written in the Description column before the first entry and no explanations are required. Note that it is best to make one compound entry to close the expense accounts.

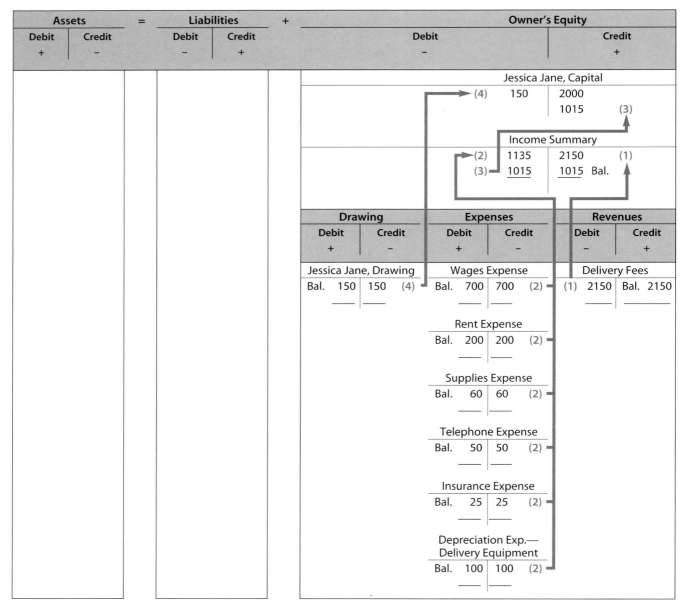

FIGURE 6-7   Closing Entries in T Account Form

 LEARNING KEY: Each individual revenue, expense, and drawing account must be closed.

A BROADER VIEW

Importance of Earnings to the Stock Market

Investors in the stock market pay close attention to earnings reported on the income statement. This information is so important that corporate officials often announce expected earnings before the financial statements are actually distributed to the public. If the announcement is different from what investors are expecting, the price of the stock may go up or down.

For example, when Aetna, a leader in the managed health care industry, warned that earnings would be about 27 percent lower than expected by stock analysts, its stock price fell more than 10 percent.

	DATE		DESCRIPTION	POST REF.	DEBIT	CREDIT	
1			Closing Entries				1
STEP 1 2	20-- June	30	Delivery Fees	401	2 1 5 0 00		2
3			Income Summary	313		2 1 5 0 00	3
4							4
STEP 2 5		30	Income Summary	313	1 1 3 5 00		5
6			Wages Expense	511		7 0 0 00	6
7			Rent Expense	521		2 0 0 00	7
8			Supplies Expense	523		6 0 00	8
9			Telephone Expense	525		5 0 00	9
10			Insurance Expense	535		2 5 00	10
11			Depr. Expense—Delivery Equipment	541		1 0 0 00	11
12							12
STEP 3 13		30	Income Summary	313	1 0 1 5 00		13
14			Jessica Jane, Capital	311		1 0 1 5 00	14
15							15
STEP 4 16		30	Jessica Jane, Capital	311	1 5 0 00		16
17			Jessica Jane, Drawing	312		1 5 0 00	17
18							18
19							19

GENERAL JOURNAL — PAGE 4

Compund Entry (between rows 7 and 8)

No explanations are necessary (between rows 16 and 17)

FIGURE 6-8   Closing Entries in General Journal

Post the Closing Entries

The account numbers have been entered in the Posting Reference column of the journal to show that the entries have been posted to the ledger accounts illustrated in Figure 6-9. Note that "Closing" has been written in the Item column of each account to identify the closing entries. Zero account balances are recorded by drawing a line in both the debit and credit Balance columns.

GENERAL LEDGER

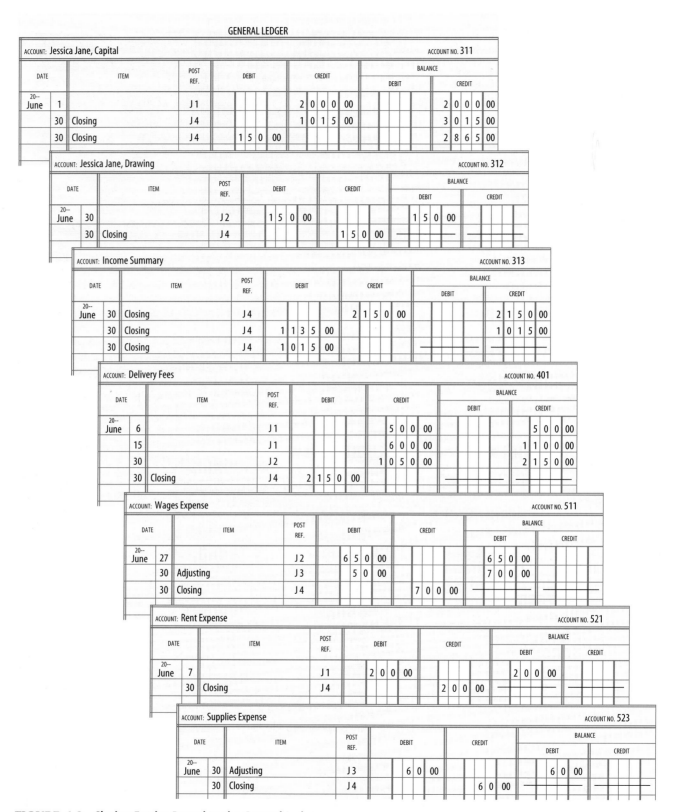

ACCOUNT: Jessica Jane, Capital ACCOUNT NO. 311

DATE		ITEM	POST REF.	DEBIT	CREDIT	BALANCE DEBIT	BALANCE CREDIT
20-- June	1		J 1		2 0 0 0 00		2 0 0 0 00
	30	Closing	J 4		1 0 1 5 00		3 0 1 5 00
	30	Closing	J 4	1 5 0 00			2 8 6 5 00

ACCOUNT: Jessica Jane, Drawing ACCOUNT NO. 312

DATE		ITEM	POST REF.	DEBIT	CREDIT	BALANCE DEBIT	BALANCE CREDIT
20-- June	30		J 2	1 5 0 00		1 5 0 00	
	30	Closing	J 4		1 5 0 00	—	

ACCOUNT: Income Summary ACCOUNT NO. 313

DATE		ITEM	POST REF.	DEBIT	CREDIT	BALANCE DEBIT	BALANCE CREDIT
20-- June	30	Closing	J 4		2 1 5 0 00		2 1 5 0 00
	30	Closing	J 4	1 1 3 5 00			1 0 1 5 00
	30	Closing	J 4	1 0 1 5 00		—	—

ACCOUNT: Delivery Fees ACCOUNT NO. 401

DATE		ITEM	POST REF.	DEBIT	CREDIT	BALANCE DEBIT	BALANCE CREDIT
20-- June	6		J 1		5 0 0 00		5 0 0 00
	15		J 1		6 0 0 00		1 1 0 0 00
	30		J 2		1 0 5 0 00		2 1 5 0 00
	30	Closing	J 4	2 1 5 0 00		—	—

ACCOUNT: Wages Expense ACCOUNT NO. 511

DATE		ITEM	POST REF.	DEBIT	CREDIT	BALANCE DEBIT	BALANCE CREDIT
20-- June	27		J 2	6 5 0 00		6 5 0 00	
	30	Adjusting	J 3	5 0 00		7 0 0 00	
	30	Closing	J 4		7 0 0 00	—	

ACCOUNT: Rent Expense ACCOUNT NO. 521

DATE		ITEM	POST REF.	DEBIT	CREDIT	BALANCE DEBIT	BALANCE CREDIT
20-- June	7		J 1	2 0 0 00		2 0 0 00	
	30	Closing	J 4		2 0 0 00	—	

ACCOUNT: Supplies Expense ACCOUNT NO. 523

DATE		ITEM	POST REF.	DEBIT	CREDIT	BALANCE DEBIT	BALANCE CREDIT
20-- June	30	Adjusting	J 3	6 0 00		6 0 00	
	30	Closing	J 4		6 0 00		

FIGURE 6-9   Closing Entries Posted to the General Ledger

ACCOUNT: Telephone Expense							ACCOUNT NO. 525	
DATE	ITEM	POST REF.	DEBIT	CREDIT	BALANCE			
					DEBIT		CREDIT	
20-- June 15		J 1	5 0 00		5 0 00			
30	Closing	J 4		5 0 00	—		—	

ACCOUNT: Insurance Expense							ACCOUNT NO. 535	
DATE	ITEM	POST REF.	DEBIT	CREDIT	BALANCE			
					DEBIT		CREDIT	
20-- June 30	Adjusting	J 3	2 5 00		2 5 00			
30	Closing	J 4		2 5 00	—		—	

ACCOUNT: Depreciation Expense—Delivery Equipment							ACCOUNT NO. 541	
DATE	ITEM	POST REF.	DEBIT	CREDIT	BALANCE			
					DEBIT		CREDIT	
20-- June 30	Adjusting	J 3	1 0 0 00		1 0 0 00			
30	Closing	J 4		1 0 0 00	—		—	

FIGURE 6-9   Closing Entries Posted to the General Ledger *(continued)*

LEARNING KEY: Once the closing entries are posted, the general ledger account balances will agree with the amounts reported on the balance sheet.

POST-CLOSING TRIAL BALANCE

LO3 Prepare a post-closing trial balance.

After posting the closing entries, a **post-closing trial balance** should be prepared to prove the equality of the debit and credit balances in the general ledger accounts. The ending balance of each general ledger account that remains open at the end of the year is listed. Remember: Only the permanent accounts remain open after the closing process is completed. Figure 6-10 shows the post-closing trial balance for Jessie's ledger.

Jessie Jane's Campus Delivery
Post-Closing Trial Balance
June 30, 20 - -

ACCOUNT TITLE	ACCOUNT NO.	DEBIT BALANCE	CREDIT BALANCE
Cash	101	3 7 0 00	
Accounts Receivable	122	6 5 0 00	
Supplies	141	2 0 00	
Prepaid Insurance	145	1 7 5 00	
Delivery Equipment	185	3 6 0 0 00	
Accumulated Depreciation—Delivery Equipment	185.1		1 0 0 00
Accounts Payable	202		1 8 0 0 00
Wages Payable	219		5 0 00
Jessica Jane, Capital	311		2 8 6 5 00
		4 8 1 5 00	4 8 1 5 00

FIGURE 6-10   Post-Closing Trial Balance

Note that all amounts reflected on the post-closing trial balance are the same as reported in the Balance Sheet columns of the work sheet except Drawing and Owner's Capital. Drawing was closed. Owner's Capital was updated to reflect revenues, expenses, and drawing for the accounting period.

THE ACCOUNTING CYCLE

LO4 List and describe the steps in the accounting cycle.

The steps involved in accounting for all of the business activities during an accounting period are called the **accounting cycle**. The cycle begins with the analysis of source documents and ends with a post-closing trial balance. A brief summary of the steps in the cycle follows.

STEPS IN THE ACCOUNTING CYCLE

During Accounting Period

STEP 1   Analyze source documents.

STEP 2   Journalize the transactions.

STEP 3   Post to the ledger accounts.

End of Accounting Period

STEP 4   Prepare a trial balance.

STEP 5   Determine and prepare the needed adjustments on the work sheet.

STEP 6   Complete an end-of-period work sheet.

STEP 7   Prepare an income statement, statement of owner's equity, and balance sheet.

STEP 8   Journalize and post the adjusting entries.

STEP 9   Journalize and post the closing entries.

STEP 10   Prepare a post-closing trial balance.

 LEARNING KEY: Properly analyzing and journalizing transactions is very important. A mistake made in step 1 is carried through the entire accounting cycle.

Steps 4 through 10 in the preceding list are performed *as of* the last day of the accounting period. This does not mean that they are actually done on the last day. The accountant may not be able to do any of these things until the first few days (sometimes weeks) of the next period. Nevertheless, the work sheet, statements, and entries are prepared as of the closing date.

COMPUTERS AND ACCOUNTING

Accounting Software—Gary P. Schneider

In recent years, people have come to use computers to help them do many common, everyday tasks. For example, instead of writing a homework assignment using pen and paper or even using a typewriter, many students today use word-processing software on a personal computer to create the homework assignment. If the homework requires calculations, students might use spreadsheet software to perform those calculations and paste the results into the word processed document. If the homework requires a figure or other artwork, students might use a graphics program to create the art and, again, paste the results into the word processed document. Some students will print the assignment on a computer printer and carry it to class. Other students may even use the computer to handle the delivery chore. They can use their e-mail software to attach the document file to an e-mail message and send it to their teacher's e-mail account.

Similarly, accountants have been using computers to make their jobs easier in recent years. It is possible to create journals and ledgers for a small business using spreadsheet software or even word processing software. However, most accountants use software created to help them perform the accounting tasks you have learned about thus far in this book.

Many different companies make accounting software—and some of those companies make more than one accounting software package. The needs of a small business are quite different from the needs of a major international company. Thus, different accounting software products are available for businesses of different sizes. Although the accounting software used by larger companies is often more complex and can do more things than the software used by smaller companies, the accounting tasks that the software must accomplish are very much the same in any size company. In addition, the accounting software does not change any of the fundamental principles that you have learned in this book—it just makes the work easier for accountants.

Good software can make accountants' jobs easier in two ways. The software can do some tasks automatically and it can reduce the likelihood of errors in tasks that accountants must still do themselves. For example, assume an accountant needs to make adjusting journal entries such as those you learned about in Chapter 5. At the end of the accounting period, the accountant must adjust the amount of prepaid expenses to reflect the insurance expense that has expired during the period. In a manual bookkeeping system, the accountant would debit insurance expense and credit prepaid expenses for the amount of the prepaid insurance that is used up in the period. The accountant would make this entry in the General Journal. Figure A on the next page shows how one popular accounting software package, Peachtree, accomplishes this task.

As you can see in the figure, $856.12 of the prepaid insurance has expired and is being recorded as an expense. The accountant has entered a date and a reference number. The reference number is a unique number that identifies this particular entry. In a computerized accounting system, unique identifiers are used to track every entry. This can be very important in larger companies that have thousands or millions of entries every year.

Next, the accountant has entered account numbers for Insurance Expense and Prepaid Expenses. When the account number is entered (or selected from a drop down list), the computer displays and enters the corresponding account

Figure A

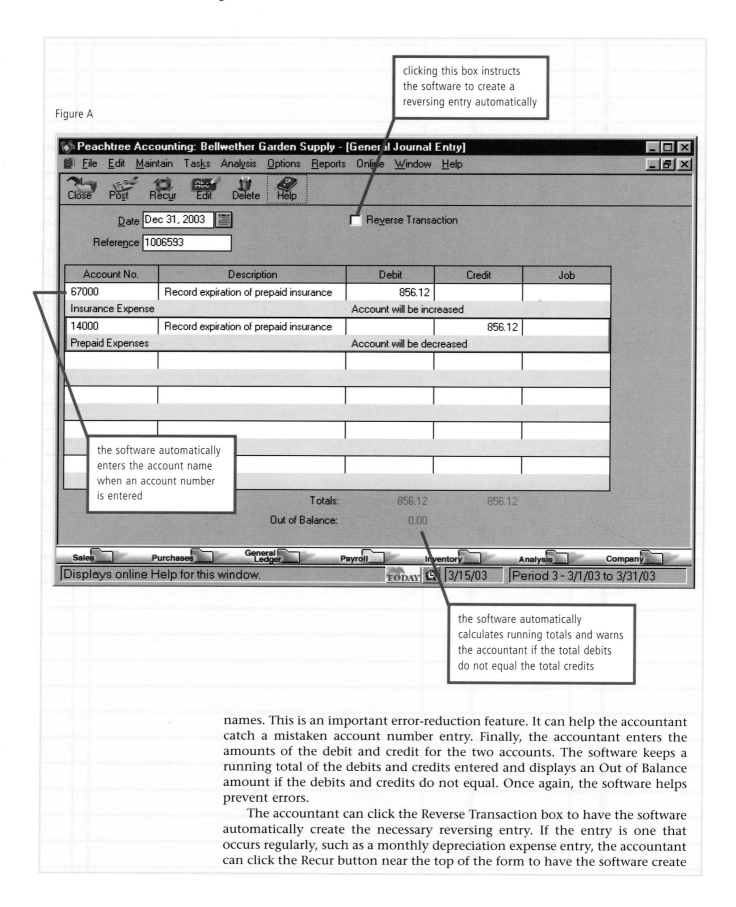

clicking this box instructs the software to create a reversing entry automatically

the software automatically enters the account name when an account number is entered

the software automatically calculates running totals and warns the accountant if the total debits do not equal the total credits

names. This is an important error-reduction feature. It can help the accountant catch a mistaken account number entry. Finally, the accountant enters the amounts of the debit and credit for the two accounts. The software keeps a running total of the debits and credits entered and displays an Out of Balance amount if the debits and credits do not equal. Once again, the software helps prevent errors.

The accountant can click the Reverse Transaction box to have the software automatically create the necessary reversing entry. If the entry is one that occurs regularly, such as a monthly depreciation expense entry, the accountant can click the Recur button near the top of the form to have the software create

Figure B

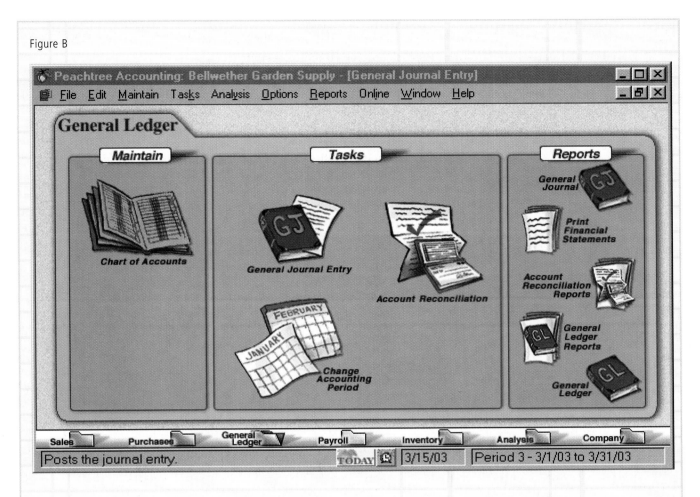

the entry automatically every month. When the accountant has reviewed the entry and made sure that the accounts are correct and the debits and credits balance, he or she can click the Post button to record the debits and credits in the General Ledger. Figure B shows the General Ledger task and report options in the Peachtree accounting software package.

By clicking on the icons that appear in Figure B, the accountant can use the software to perform the same kinds of tasks that are necessary in any accounting system, manual or computerized. In every accounting system, someone must create and maintain the chart of accounts and make entries in the General Journal. Although accountants rarely change the accounting periods of their companies, it is something that the software must be capable of doing. Finally, the reports that the software can produce include printouts of the General Journal and the General Ledger, along with the standard financial statements. This software package also gives the accountant the ability to create reconciliation reports and customized reports based on numbers in the General Ledger.

Learning Objectives	Key Points to Remember
1 **Prepare financial statements with the aid of a work sheet.**	The work sheet is used as an aid in preparing: 1. adjusting entries, 2. financial statements, and 3. closing entries The following classifications are used for accounts reported on the balance sheet. ■ *Current assets* include cash and assets that will be converted into cash or consumed within either one year or the normal operating cycle of the business, whichever is longer. An *operating cycle* is the time required to purchase supplies and services and convert them back into cash. ■ *Property, plant, and equipment,* also called *plant assets* or *long-term assets,* represent assets that are expected to serve the business for many years. ■ *Current liabilities* are liabilities that are due within either one year or the normal operating cycle of the business, whichever is longer, and that are to be paid out of current assets. ■ *Long-term liabilities,* or *long-term debt,* are obligations that are not expected to be paid within a year and do not require the use of current assets.
2 **Journalize and post closing entries.**	Steps in the closing process are: 1. Close revenue accounts to Income Summary. 2. Close expense accounts to Income Summary. 3. Close Income Summary to Capital. 4. Close Drawing to Capital.

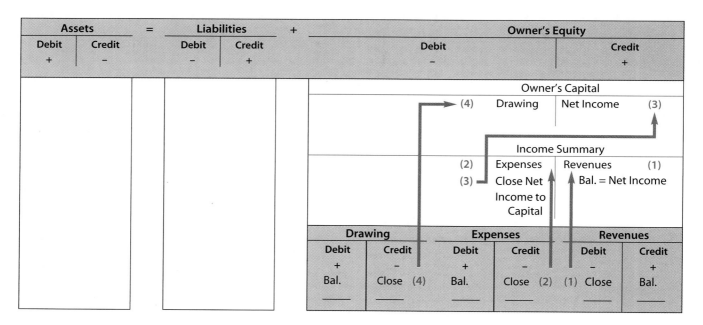

Learning Objectives	Key Points to Remember
3 **Prepare a post-closing trial balance.**	After posting the closing entries, a post-closing trial balance should be prepared to prove the equality of the debit and credit balances in the general ledger accounts. The accounts shown in the post-closing trial balance are the permanent accounts.

4 **List and describe the steps in the accounting cycle.**	Steps in the accounting cycle are:
	
	During Accounting Period
	  1. Analyze source documents.
	  2. Journalize the transactions.
	  3. Post to the ledger accounts.
	
	End of Accounting Period
	  4. Prepare a trial balance.
	  5. Determine and prepare the needed adjustments on the work sheet.
	  6. Complete an end-of-period work sheet.
	  7. Prepare an income statement, statement of owner's equity, and balance sheet.
	  8. Journalize and post the adjusting entries.
	  9. Journalize and post the closing entries.
	  10. Prepare a post-closing trial balance.

Reflection: Answering the Opening Question

The accounting records are closed "as of" December 31, or another fiscal year end chosen by the firm. The actual adjustments, closing entries, and financial statements are generally prepared several weeks after the official closing date. However, it is important to include all transactions occurring prior to year end in the current year's financial statements. Similarly, transactions taking place after year end must be included in the next year's financial statements. Improper timing of the recognition of transactions taking place around the end of the year can have major effects on the reported profits. For example, some firms have been found to "leave the books open" for a few days to include a major sale, or other profitable transactions, that actually took place after the end of the year. If undetected, the good news could be reported on the current year's statements, rather than in the following year. Similarly, a firm could be tempted to "close early" to avoid recognizing unprofitable events occurring during the last few days of the year. Thus, proper treatment of transactions taking place around the end of the year is carefully monitored by auditors.

KEY TERMS

account form of balance sheet, (179)   A balance sheet in which the assets are on the left and the liabilities and the owner's equity sections are on the right.

accounting cycle, (188)   The steps involved in accounting for all of the business activities during an accounting period.

classified balance sheet, (179)   A balance sheet with separate categories for current assets; property, plant, and equipment; current liabilities; and long-term liabilities.

closing process, (181)   The process of giving zero balances to the temporary accounts so that they can accumulate information for the next accounting period.

current assets, (179)   Cash and assets that will be converted into cash or consumed within either one year or the normal operating cycle of the business, whichever is longer.

current liabilities, (179)   Liabilities that are due within either one year or the normal operating cycle of the business, whichever is longer, and that are to be paid out of current assets.

Income Summary, (181)   A temporary account used in the closing process to summarize the effects of all revenue and expense accounts.

long-term assets, (179)   See property, plant, and equipment.

long-term debt, (179)   See long-term liabilities.

long-term liabilities, (179)   Obligations that are not expected to be paid within a year and do not require the use of current assets. Also called long-term debt.

operating cycle, (179)   The period of time required to purchase supplies and services and convert them back into cash.

permanent accounts, (181)   Accounts that accumulate information across accounting periods; all accounts reported on the balance sheet.

plant assets, (179)   See property, plant, and equipment.

post-closing trial balance, (187)   Prepared after posting the closing entries to prove the equality of the debit and credit balances in the general ledger accounts.

property, plant, and equipment, (179)   Assets that are expected to serve the business for many years. Also called plant assets or long-term assets.

report form of balance sheet, (179)   A balance sheet in which the liabilities and the owner's equity sections are shown below the assets section.

temporary accounts, (181)   Accounts that do not accumulate information across accounting periods but are closed, such as the drawing account and all income statement accounts.

DEMONSTRATION PROBLEM

Timothy Chang owns and operates Hard Copy Printers. A work sheet for the year ended December 31, 20--, is provided on the next page. Chang made no additional investments during the year.

REQUIRED

1. Prepare financial statements.

2. Prepare closing entries.

Hard Copy Printers
Work Sheet
For Year Ended December 31, 20--

	Trial Balance		Adjustments		Adjusted Trial Balance		Income Statement		Balance Sheet	
ACCOUNT TITLE	DEBIT	CREDIT	DEBIT	CREDIT	DEBIT	CREDIT	DEBIT	CREDIT	DEBIT	CREDIT
1 Cash	11 8 0 0 00				11 8 0 0 00				11 8 0 0 00	
2 Paper Supplies	3 6 0 0 00			(a) 3 5 5 0 00	5 0 00				5 0 00	
3 Prepaid Insurance	1 0 0 0 00			(b) 5 0 5 00	4 9 5 00				4 9 5 00	
4 Printing Equipment	5 8 0 0 00				5 8 0 0 00				5 8 0 0 00	
5 Accum. Depr.—Printing Equipment				(d) 1 2 0 0 00		1 2 0 0 00				1 2 0 0 00
6 Accounts Payable		5 0 0 00				5 0 0 00				5 0 0 00
7 Wages Payable				(c) 3 0 00		3 0 00				3 0 00
8 Timothy Chang, Capital		10 0 0 0 00				10 0 0 0 00				10 0 0 0 00
9 Timothy Chang, Drawing	13 0 0 0 00				13 0 0 0 00				13 0 0 0 00	
10 Printing Fees		35 1 0 0 00				35 1 0 0 00		35 1 0 0 00		
11 Wages Expense	11 9 7 0 00		(c) 3 0 00		12 0 0 0 00		12 0 0 0 00			
12 Rent Expense	7 5 0 0 00				7 5 0 0 00		7 5 0 0 00			
13 Paper Supplies Expense			(a) 3 5 5 0 00		3 5 5 0 00		3 5 5 0 00			
14 Telephone Expense	5 5 0 0 00				5 5 0 0 00		5 5 0 0 00			
15 Utilities Expense	1 0 0 0 00				1 0 0 0 00		1 0 0 0 00			
16 Insurance Expense			(b) 5 0 5 00		5 0 5 00		5 0 5 00			
17 Depr. Expense—Printing Equipment			(d) 1 2 0 0 00		1 2 0 0 00		1 2 0 0 00			
18	45 6 0 0 00	45 6 0 0 00	5 2 8 5 00	5 2 8 5 00	46 8 3 0 00	46 8 3 0 00	26 3 0 5 00	35 1 0 0 00	20 5 2 5 00	11 7 3 0 00
19 Net Income							8 7 9 5 00			8 7 9 5 00
20							35 1 0 0 00	35 1 0 0 00	20 5 2 5 00	20 5 2 5 00

Solution

1.

Hard Copy Printers Income Statement For Year Ended December 31, 20 - -														
Revenue:														
Printing fees								$ 35	1	0	0	00
Expenses:												
Wages expense	$ 12	0	0	0	00							
Rent expense	7	5	0	0	00							
Paper supplies expense	3	5	5	0	00							
Telephone expense		5	5	0	00							
Utilities expense	1	0	0	0	00							
Insurance expense		5	0	5	00							
Depreciation expense—printing equipment	1	2	0	0	00							
Total expenses								26	3	0	5	00
Net income								$ 8	7	9	5	00

Hard Copy Printers Statement of Owner's Equity For Year Ended December 31, 20 - -														
Timothy Chang, capital, Jan. 1, 20 - -								$ 10	0	0	0	00
Net income for 20 - -	$ 8	7	9	5	00							
Less withdrawals for 20 - -	13	0	0	0	00							
Decrease in capital								(4	2	0	5	00)
Timothy Chang, capital, Dec. 31, 20 - -								$ 5	7	9	5	00

Hard Copy Printers Balance Sheet December 31, 20 - -														
Assets												
Current assets:												
Cash	$ 1	1	8	0	00							
Paper supplies			5	0	00							
Prepaid insurance		4	9	5	00							
Total current assets								$ 1	7	2	5	00
Property, plant and equipment:												
Printing equipment	$ 5	8	0	0	00							
Less accumulated depreciation	1	2	0	0	00			4	6	0	0	00
Total assets								$ 6	3	2	5	00
Liabilities												
Current liabilities:												
Accounts payable	$	5	0	0	00							
Wages payable			3	0	00							
Total current liabilities								$	5	3	0	00
Owner's Equity												
Timothy Chang, capital									5	7	9	5	00
Total liabilities and owner's equity								$ 6	3	2	5	00

2.

GENERAL JOURNAL   PAGE 4

	DATE		DESCRIPTION	POST REF.	DEBIT	CREDIT	
1			Closing Entries				1
2	20-- Dec.	31	Printing Fees		35 1 0 0 00		2
3			Income Summary			35 1 0 0 00	3
4							4
5		31	Income Summary		26 3 0 5 00		5
6			Wages Expense			12 0 0 0 00	6
7			Rent Expense			7 5 0 0 00	7
8			Paper Supplies Expense			3 5 5 0 00	8
9			Telephone Expense			5 5 0 00	9
10			Utilities Expense			1 0 0 0 00	10
11			Insurance Expense			5 0 5 00	11
12			Depr. Expense—Printing Equipment			1 2 0 0 00	12
13							13
14		31	Income Summary		8 7 9 5 00		14
15			Timothy Chang, Capital			8 7 9 5 00	15
16							16
17		31	Timothy Chang, Capital		13 0 0 0 00		17
18			Timothy Chang, Drawing			13 0 0 0 00	18
19							19

REVIEW QUESTIONS

1. Identify the source of the information needed to prepare the income statement.

2. Describe two approaches to listing the expenses in the income statement.

3. Identify the sources of the information needed to prepare the statement of owner's equity.

4. If additional investments were made during the year, what information in addition to the work sheet would be needed to prepare the statement of owner's equity?

5. Identify the sources of the information needed to prepare the balance sheet.

6. What is a permanent account? On which financial statement are permanent accounts reported?

7. Name three types of temporary accounts.

8. List the four steps for closing the temporary accounts.

9. Describe the net effect of the four closing entries on the balance of the owner's capital account. Where else is this same amount calculated?

10. What is the purpose of the post-closing trial balance?

11. List the ten steps in the accounting cycle.

MANAGING YOUR WRITING

At lunch, two bookkeepers got into a heated discussion about whether closing entries should be made before or after preparing the financial statements. They have come to you to resolve this issue and have agreed to accept your position. Write a memo explaining the purpose of closing entries and whether they should be made before or after preparing the financial statements.

SERIES A EXERCISES

EXERCISE 6-1A   (LO1)   INCOME STATEMENT From the partial work sheet for Case Advising, prepare an income statement.

Case Advising
Work Sheet (Partial)
For Month Ended January 31, 20 - -

	ACCOUNT TITLE	INCOME STATEMENT DEBIT	INCOME STATEMENT CREDIT	BALANCE SHEET DEBIT	BALANCE SHEET CREDIT	
1	Cash			1 2 1 2 00		1
2	Accounts Receivable			8 9 6 00		2
3	Supplies			4 8 2 00		3
4	Prepaid Insurance			9 0 0 00		4
5	Office Equipment			3 0 0 0 00		5
6	Accum. Depr.—Office Equipment				1 0 0 00	6
7	Accounts Payable				1 0 0 0 00	7
8	Wages Payable				2 0 0 00	8
9	Bill Case, Capital				4 0 0 0 00	9
10	Bill Case, Drawing			8 0 0 00		10
11	Advising Fees		3 7 9 3 00			11
12	Wages Expense	8 0 0 00				12
13	Advertising Expense	8 0 00				13
14	Rent Expense	5 0 0 00				14
15	Supplies Expense	1 2 0 00				15
16	Telephone Expense	5 8 00				16
17	Electricity Expense	4 4 00				17
18	Insurance Expense	3 0 00				18
19	Gas and Oil Expense	3 8 00				19
20	Depr. Expense—Office Equipment	1 0 0 00				20
21	Miscellaneous Expense	3 3 00				21
22		1 8 0 3 00	3 7 9 3 00	7 2 9 0 00	5 3 0 0 00	22
23	Net Income	1 9 9 0 00			1 9 9 0 00	23
24		3 7 9 3 00	3 7 9 3 00		7 2 9 0 00	24

EXERCISE 6-2A   (LO1)   STATEMENT OF OWNER'S EQUITY From the partial work sheet in Exercise 6-1A, prepare a statement of owner's equity, assuming no additional investment was made by the owner.

EXERCISE 6-3A   (LO1)   BALANCE SHEET From the partial work sheet in Exercise 6-1A, prepare a balance sheet.

EXERCISE 6-4A   **(LO2)**   **CLOSING ENTRIES (NET INCOME)** Set up T accounts for Case Advising based on the work sheet in Exercise 6-1A and the chart of accounts provided below. Enter the existing balance for each account. Prepare closing entries in general journal form. Then post the closing entries to the T accounts.

Chart of Accounts

Assets		Revenues	
101	Cash	401	Advising Fees
122	Accounts Receivable		
141	Supplies	**Expenses**	
145	Prepaid Insurance	511	Wages Expense
181	Office Equipment	512	Advertising Expense
181.1	Accum. Depr.—Office Equip.	521	Rent Expense
		524	Supplies Expense
Liabilities		525	Telephone Expense
202	Accounts Payable	533	Electricity Expense
219	Wages Payable	535	Insurance Expense
		538	Gas and Oil Expense
Owner's Equity		541	Depr. Exp.—Office Equip.
311	Bill Case, Capital	549	Miscellaneous Expense
312	Bill Case, Drawing		
313	Income Summary		

EXERCISE 6-5A   **(LO2)**   **CLOSING ENTRIES (NET LOSS)** Using the following T accounts, prepare closing entries in general journal form dated January 31, 20--. Then post the closing entries to the T accounts.

Accum. Depr.—Del. Equip. 185.1	Wages Expense 511	Electricity Expense 533
Bal. 100	Bal. 1,800	Bal. 44

Wages Payable 219	Advertising Expense 512	Insurance Expense 535
Bal. 200	Bal. 80	Bal. 30

Saburo Goto, Capital 311	Rent Expense 521	Gas and Oil Expense 538
Bal. 4,000	Bal. 500	Bal. 38

Saburo Goto, Drawing 312	Supplies Expense 523	Depr. Exp.—Del. Equip. 541
Bal. 800	Bal. 120	Bal. 100

Income Summary 313	Telephone Expense 525	Miscellaneous Expense 549
	Bal. 58	Bal. 33

Delivery Fees 401
Bal. 2,200

SERIES A PROBLEMS

PROBLEM 6-1A (LO1) **FINANCIAL STATEMENTS** The following page shows a work sheet for Monte's Repairs. No additional investments were made by the owner during the month.

REQUIRED

1. Prepare an income statement.

2. Prepare a statement of owner's equity.

3. Prepare a balance sheet.

PROBLEM 6-2A (LO1) **STATEMENT OF OWNER'S EQUITY** The capital account for Autumn Chou, including an additional investment, and a partial work sheet are shown below.

REQUIRED

Prepare a statement of owner's equity.

GENERAL LEDGER

ACCOUNT: Autumn Chou, Capital   ACCOUNT NO. 311

DATE		ITEM	POST REF.	DEBIT	CREDIT	BALANCE DEBIT	BALANCE CREDIT
20— Jan.	1	Balance	✔				4 8 0 0 00
	18		J 1		1 2 0 0 00		6 0 0 0 00

Autumn's Home Designs
Work Sheet (Partial)
For Month Ended January 31, 20 - -

	ACCOUNT TITLE	INCOME STATEMENT DEBIT	INCOME STATEMENT CREDIT	BALANCE SHEET DEBIT	BALANCE SHEET CREDIT	
1	Cash			3 2 0 0 00		1
2	Accounts Receivable			1 6 0 0 00		2
3	Supplies			8 0 0 00		3
4	Prepaid Insurance			9 0 0 00		4
5	Office Equipment			2 5 0 0 00		5
6	Accum. Depr.—Office Equipment				5 0 00	6
7	Accounts Payable				1 9 5 0 00	7
8	Wages Payable				1 8 0 00	8
9	Autumn Chou, Capital				6 0 0 0 00	9
10	Autumn Chou, Drawing			1 0 0 0 00		10
11	Design Fees		4 8 6 6 00			11
12	Wages Expense	1 9 0 0 00				12
13	Advertising Expense	2 1 00				13
14	Rent Expense	6 0 0 00				14
15	Supplies Expense	2 0 0 00				15
16	Telephone Expense	8 5 00				16
17	Electricity Expense	4 8 00				17
18	Insurance Expense	6 0 00				18
19	Gas and Oil Expense	3 2 00				19
20	Depr. Expense—Office Equipment	5 0 00				20
21	Miscellaneous Expense	5 0 00				21
22		3 0 4 6 00	4 8 6 6 00	10 0 0 0 00	8 1 8 0 00	22
23	Net Income	1 8 2 0 00			1 8 2 0 00	23
24		4 8 6 6 00	4 8 6 6 00	10 0 0 0 00	10 0 0 0 00	24

Monte's Repairs
Work Sheet
For Month Ended January 31, 20 - -

	Account Title	Trial Balance Debit	Trial Balance Credit	Adjustments Debit	Adjustments Credit	Adjusted Trial Balance Debit	Adjusted Trial Balance Credit	Income Statement Debit	Income Statement Credit	Balance Sheet Debit	Balance Sheet Credit
1	Cash	3 0 8 0 00				3 0 8 0 00				3 0 8 0 00	
2	Accounts Receivable	1 2 0 0 00				1 2 0 0 00				1 2 0 0 00	
3	Supplies	8 0 0 00			(a) 2 0 0 00	6 0 0 00				6 0 0 00	
4	Prepaid Insurance	9 0 0 00			(b) 1 0 0 00	8 0 0 00				8 0 0 00	
5	Delivery Equipment	3 0 0 0 00				3 0 0 0 00				3 0 0 0 00	
6	Accum. Depr.—Delivery Equipment				(d) 3 0 00		3 0 00				3 0 00
7	Accounts Payable		1 1 0 0 00				1 1 0 0 00				1 1 0 0 00
8	Wages Payable				(c) 1 5 0 00		1 5 0 00				1 5 0 00
9	Monte Eli, Capital		7 0 0 0 00				7 0 0 0 00				7 0 0 0 00
10	Monte Eli, Drawing	1 0 0 0 00				1 0 0 0 00				1 0 0 0 00	
11	Repair Fees		4 2 3 0 00				4 2 3 0 00		4 2 3 0 00		
12	Wages Expense	1 6 5 0 00		(c) 1 5 0 00		1 8 0 0 00		1 8 0 0 00			
13	Advertising Expense	1 7 0 00				1 7 0 00		1 7 0 00			
14	Rent Expense	4 2 0 00				4 2 0 00		4 2 0 00			
15	Supplies Expense			(a) 2 0 0 00		2 0 0 00		2 0 0 00			
16	Telephone Expense	4 9 00				4 9 00		4 9 00			
17	Insurance Expense			(b) 1 0 0 00		1 0 0 00		1 0 0 00			
18	Gas and Oil Expense	3 3 00				3 3 00		3 3 00			
19	Depr. Expense—Delivery Equipment			(d) 3 0 00		3 0 00		3 0 00			
20	Miscellaneous Expense	2 8 00				2 8 00		2 8 00			
21		12 3 3 0 00	12 3 3 0 00	4 8 0 00	4 8 0 00	12 5 1 0 00	12 5 1 0 00	2 8 3 0 00	4 2 3 0 00	9 6 8 0 00	8 2 8 0 00
22	Net Income							1 4 0 0 00			1 4 0 0 00
23								4 2 3 0 00	4 2 3 0 00	9 6 8 0 00	9 6 8 0 00

(PROBLEM 6-1A)

PROBLEM 6-3A   (LO2/3)   **CLOSING ENTRIES AND POST-CLOSING TRIAL BALANCE** Refer to the work sheet in Problem 6-1A for Monte's Repairs. The trial balance amounts (before adjustments) have been entered in the ledger accounts provided in the working papers. If you are not using the working papers that accompany this book, set up ledger accounts and enter these balances as of January 31, 20--. A chart of accounts is provided below.

Monte's Repairs
Chart of Accounts

Assets		Revenues	
101	Cash	401	Repair Fees
122	Accounts Receivable		
141	Supplies	Expenses	
145	Prepaid Insurance	511	Wages Expense
185	Delivery Equipment	512	Advertising Expense
185.1	Accum. Depr.—Delivery Equip.	521	Rent Expense
		523	Supplies Expense
Liabilities		525	Telephone Expense
202	Accounts Payable	535	Insurance Expense
219	Wages Payable	538	Gas and Oil Expense
		541	Depr. Exp.—Delivery Equip.
Owner's Equity		549	Miscellaneous Expense
311	Monte Eli, Capital		
312	Monte Eli, Drawing		
313	Income Summary		

REQUIRED

1. Journalize (page 10) and post the adjusting entries

2. Journalize (page 11) and post the closing entries.

3. Prepare a post-closing trial balance.

SERIES B EXERCISES

EXERCISE 6-1B   (LO1)   **INCOME STATEMENT** From the partial work sheet for Adams' Shoe Shine on the next page, prepare an income statement.

EXERCISE 6-2B   (LO1)   **STATEMENT OF OWNER'S EQUITY** From the partial work sheet in Exercise 6-1B, prepare a statement of owner's equity, assuming no additional investment was made by the owner.

EXERCISE 6-3B   (LO1)   **BALANCE SHEET** From the partial work sheet in Exercise 6-1B, prepare a balance sheet for Adams' Shoe Shine.

(EXERCISE 6-1B)

Adams' Shoe Shine
Work Sheet (Partial)
For Month Ended June 30, 20 - -

	ACCOUNT TITLE	INCOME STATEMENT DEBIT	INCOME STATEMENT CREDIT	BALANCE SHEET DEBIT	BALANCE SHEET CREDIT	
1	Cash			3 2 6 2 00		1
2	Accounts Receivable			1 2 4 4 00		2
3	Supplies			8 0 0 00		3
4	Prepaid Insurance			6 4 0 00		4
5	Office Equipment			2 1 0 0 00		5
6	Accum. Depr.—Office Equipment				1 1 0 00	6
7	Accounts Payable				1 8 5 0 00	7
8	Wages Payable				2 6 0 00	8
9	Mary Adams, Capital				6 0 0 0 00	9
10	Mary Adams, Drawing			2 0 0 0 00		10
11	Service Fees		4 8 1 3 00			11
12	Wages Expense	1 0 8 0 00				12
13	Advertising Expense	3 4 00				13
14	Rent Expense	9 0 0 00				14
15	Supplies Expense	3 2 2 00				15
16	Telephone Expense	1 3 3 00				16
17	Utilities Expense	1 0 2 00				17
18	Insurance Expense	1 2 0 00				18
19	Gas and Oil Expense	8 8 00				19
20	Depr. Expense—Office Equipment	1 1 0 00				20
21	Miscellaneous Expense	9 8 00				21
22		2 9 8 7 00	4 8 1 3 00	10 0 4 6 00	8 2 2 0 00	22
23	Net Income	1 8 2 6 00			1 8 2 6 00	23
24		4 8 1 3 00	4 8 1 3 00	10 0 4 6 00	10 0 4 6 00	24

EXERCISE 6-4B   **(LO2)**   **CLOSING ENTRIES (NET INCOME)** Set up T accounts for Adams' Shoe Shine based on the work sheet in Exercise 6-1B and the chart of accounts provided below. Enter the existing balance for each account. Prepare closing entries in general journal form. Then, post the closing entries to the T accounts.

Chart of Accounts

Assets
101   Cash
122   Accounts Receivable
141   Supplies
145   Prepaid Insurance
181   Office Equipment
181.1 Accum. Depr.—Office Equip.

Liabilities
202   Accounts Payable
219   Wages Payable

Owner's Equity
311   Mary Adams, Capital
312   Mary Adams, Drawing
313   Income Summary

Revenues
401   Service Fees

Expenses
511   Wages Expense
512   Advertising Expense
521   Rent Expense
523   Supplies Expense
525   Telephone Expense
533   Utilities Expense
535   Insurance Expense
538   Gas and Oil Expense
542   Depr. Exp.—Office Equip.
549   Miscellaneous Expense

EXERCISE 6-5B   (LO2)   CLOSING ENTRIES (NET LOSS) Using the following T accounts, prepare closing entries in general journal form dated June 30, 20--. Then post the closing entries to the T accounts.

Accum. Depr.—Office Equip. 181.1		Wages Expense 511		Utilities Expense 533	
	Bal. 110	Bal. 1,080		Bal. 102	

Wages Payable 219		Advertising Expense 512		Insurance Expense 535	
	Bal. 260	Bal. 34		Bal. 120	

Raquel Zapata, Capital 311		Rent Expense 521		Gas and Oil Expense 538	
	Bal. 6,000	Bal. 900		Bal. 88	

Raquel Zapata, Drawing 312		Supplies Expense 523		Depr. Exp.—Office Equip. 541	
Bal. 2,000		Bal. 322		Bal. 110	

Income Summary 313		Telephone Expense 525		Miscellaneous Expense 549	
		Bal. 133		Bal. 98	

Referral Fees 401	
	Bal. 2,813

SERIES B PROBLEMS

PROBLEM 6-1B   (LO1)   FINANCIAL STATEMENTS A work sheet for Juanita's Consulting is shown on the following page. There were no additional investments made by the owner during the month.

REQUIRED

1. Prepare an income statement.

2. Prepare a statement of owner's equity.

3. Prepare a balance sheet.

Juanita's Consulting
Work Sheet
For Month Ended June 30, 20 - -

	ACCOUNT TITLE	TRIAL BALANCE DEBIT	TRIAL BALANCE CREDIT	ADJUSTMENTS DEBIT	ADJUSTMENTS CREDIT	ADJUSTED TRIAL BALANCE DEBIT	ADJUSTED TRIAL BALANCE CREDIT	INCOME STATEMENT DEBIT	INCOME STATEMENT CREDIT	BALANCE SHEET DEBIT	BALANCE SHEET CREDIT	
1	Cash	5 2 8 5 00				5 2 8 5 00				5 2 8 5 00		1
2	Accounts Receivable	1 0 7 5 00				1 0 7 5 00				1 0 7 5 00		2
3	Supplies	7 5 0 00			(a) 2 5 0 00	5 0 0 00				5 0 0 00		3
4	Prepaid Insurance	5 0 0 00			(b) 1 0 0 00	4 0 0 00				4 0 0 00		4
5	Office Equipment	2 2 0 0 00				2 2 0 0 00				2 2 0 0 00		5
6	Accum. Depr.—Office Equipment				(d) 1 1 0 00		1 1 0 00				1 1 0 00	6
7	Accounts Payable		1 5 0 0 00				1 5 0 0 00				1 5 0 0 00	7
8	Wages Payable				(c) 2 0 0 00		2 0 0 00				2 0 0 00	8
9	Juanita Alvarez, Capital		7 0 0 0 00				7 0 0 0 00				7 0 0 0 00	9
10	Juanita Alvarez, Drawing	8 0 0 00				8 0 0 00				8 0 0 00		10
11	Consulting Fees		4 2 0 4 00				4 2 0 4 00		4 2 0 4 00			11
12	Wages Expense	1 4 0 0 00		(c) 2 0 0 00		1 6 0 0 00		1 6 0 0 00				12
13	Advertising Expense	6 0 00				6 0 00		6 0 00				13
14	Rent Expense	5 0 0 00				5 0 0 00		5 0 0 00				14
15	Supplies Expense			(a) 2 5 0 00		2 5 0 00		2 5 0 00				15
16	Telephone Expense	4 6 00				4 6 00		4 6 00				16
17	Electricity Expense	3 9 00				3 9 00		3 9 00				17
18	Insurance Expense			(b) 1 0 0 00		1 0 0 00		1 0 0 00				18
19	Gas and Oil Expense	2 8 00				2 8 00		2 8 00				19
20	Depr. Expense—Office Equipment			(d) 1 1 0 00		1 1 0 00		1 1 0 00				20
21	Miscellaneous Expense	2 1 00				2 1 00		2 1 00				21
22		12 7 0 4 00	12 7 0 4 00	6 6 0 00	6 6 0 00	13 0 1 4 00	13 0 1 4 00	2 7 5 4 00	4 2 0 4 00	10 2 6 0 00	8 8 1 0 00	22
23	Net Income							1 4 5 0 00			1 4 5 0 00	23
24								4 2 0 4 00	4 2 0 4 00	10 2 6 0 00	10 2 6 0 00	24
25												25
26												26
27												27
28												28
29												29
30												30

(PROBLEM 6-1B)

PROBLEM 6-2B   **(LO1)**   **STATEMENT OF OWNER'S EQUITY** The capital account for Minta's Editorial Services, including an additional investment, and a partial work sheet are shown below.

GENERAL LEDGER

ACCOUNT: Minta Berry, Capital   ACCOUNT NO. 311

DATE		ITEM	POST REF.	DEBIT	CREDIT	BALANCE DEBIT	BALANCE CREDIT
20-- Jan.	1	Balance	✔				3 6 0 0 00
	22		J1		2 9 0 0 00		6 5 0 0 00

Minta's Editorial Services
Work Sheet (Partial)
For Month Ended January 31, 20 - -

	ACCOUNT TITLE	INCOME STATEMENT DEBIT	INCOME STATEMENT CREDIT	BALANCE SHEET DEBIT	BALANCE SHEET CREDIT	
1	Cash			3 8 0 0 00		1
2	Accounts Receivable			2 2 0 0 00		2
3	Supplies			1 0 0 0 00		3
4	Prepaid Insurance			9 5 0 00		4
5	Computer Equipment			4 5 0 0 00		5
6	Accum. Depr.—Computer Equipment				2 2 5 00	6
7	Accounts Payable				2 1 0 0 00	7
8	Wages Payable				1 5 0 00	8
9	Minta Berry, Capital				6 5 0 0 00	9
10	Minta Berry, Drawing			1 7 0 0 00		10
11	Editing Fees		7 0 1 2 00			11
12	Wages Expense	6 0 0 00				12
13	Advertising Expense	4 9 00				13
14	Rent Expense	4 5 0 00				14
15	Supplies Expense	2 8 8 00				15
16	Telephone Expense	4 4 00				16
17	Utilities Expense	3 8 00				17
18	Insurance Expense	1 2 5 00				18
19	Depr. Expense—Computer Equipment	2 2 5 00				19
20	Miscellaneous Expense	1 8 00				20
21		1 8 3 7 00	7 0 1 2 00	14 1 5 0 00	8 9 7 5 00	21
22	Net Income	5 1 7 5 00			5 1 7 5 00	22
23		7 0 1 2 00	7 0 1 2 00	14 1 5 0 00	14 1 5 0 00	23

REQUIRED

Prepare a statement of owner's equity.

PROBLEM 6-3B   (LO2/3)

CLOSING ENTRIES AND POST-CLOSING TRIAL BALANCE Refer to the work sheet for Juanita's Consulting in Problem 6-1B. The trial balance amounts (before adjustments) have been entered in the ledger accounts provided in the working papers. If you are not using the working papers that accompany this book, set up ledger accounts and enter these balances as of June 30, 20--. A chart of accounts is provided below.

Juanita's Consulting
Chart of Accounts

Assets
101   Cash
122   Accounts Receivable
141   Supplies
145   Prepaid Insurance
181   Office Equipment
181.1 Accum. Depr.—Office Equip.

Liabilities
202   Accounts Payable
219   Wages Payable

Owner's Equity
311   Juanita Alvarez, Capital
312   Juanita Alvarez, Drawing
313   Income Summary

Revenues
401   Consulting Fees

Expenses
511   Wages Expense
512   Advertising Expense
521   Rent Expense
523   Supplies Expense
525   Telephone Expense
533   Electricity Expense
535   Insurance Expense
538   Gas and Oil Expense
541   Depr. Exp.—Office Equip.
549   Miscellaneous Expense

REQUIRED

1. Journalize (page 10) and post the adjusting entries.

2. Journalize (page 11) and post the closing entries.

3. Prepare a post-closing trial balance.

CHALLENGE PROBLEM

Provided on the next page is a partial work sheet for Ardery Advising.

REQUIRED

During January, Ardery made an additional investment of $1,200. Prepare an income statement, statement of owner's equity, and balance sheet for Ardery Advising.

Ardery Advising
Work Sheet (Partial)
For Month Ended January 31, 20 - -

	ACCOUNT TITLE	INCOME STATEMENT DEBIT	INCOME STATEMENT CREDIT	BALANCE SHEET DEBIT	BALANCE SHEET CREDIT	
1	Cash			2 4 1 2 00		1
2	Accounts Receivable			8 9 6 00		2
3	Supplies			4 8 2 00		3
4	Prepaid Insurance			9 0 0 00		4
5	Office Equipment			3 0 0 0 00		5
6	Accum. Depr.—Office Equipment				2 0 0 0 00	6
7	Accounts Payable				2 1 9 0 00	7
8	Wages Payable				1 2 0 0 00	8
9	Notes Payable				3 0 0 0 00	9
10	Sam Ardery, Capital				2 2 0 0 00	10
11	Sam Ardery, Drawing			8 0 0 00		11
12	Advising Fees		3 8 0 2 00			12
13	Wages Expense	1 8 0 0 00				13
14	Advertising Expense	4 0 0 00				14
15	Rent Expense	1 5 0 0 00				15
16	Supplies Expense	1 2 0 00				16
17	Telephone Expense	3 0 0 00				17
18	Electricity Expense	4 4 00				18
19	Insurance Expense	2 0 0 00				19
20	Gas and Oil Expense	3 8 00				20
21	Depr. Expense—Office Equipment	1 0 0 0 00				21
22	Miscellaneous Expense	5 0 0 00				22
23		5 9 0 2 00	3 8 0 2 00	8 4 9 0 00	10 5 9 0 00	23
24	Net Income		2 1 0 0 00	2 1 0 0 00		24
25		5 9 0 2 00	5 9 0 2 00	10 5 9 0 00	10 5 9 0 00	25

MASTERY PROBLEM

Elizabeth Soltis owns and operates Aunt Ibby's Styling Salon. A year-end work sheet is provided on the next page. Using this information, prepare financial statements and closing entries. Soltis made no additional investments during the year.

Aunt Ibby's Styling Salon
Work Sheet
For Year Ended December 31, 20--

	ACCOUNT TITLE	TRIAL BALANCE Debit	TRIAL BALANCE Credit	ADJUSTMENTS Debit	ADJUSTMENTS Credit	ADJUSTED TRIAL BALANCE Debit	ADJUSTED TRIAL BALANCE Credit	INCOME STATEMENT Debit	INCOME STATEMENT Credit	BALANCE SHEET Debit	BALANCE SHEET Credit	
1	Cash	9 4 0 0 00				9 4 0 0 00				9 4 0 0 00		1
2	Styling Supplies	1 5 0 0 00			(a) 1 4 5 0 00	5 0 00				5 0 00		2
3	Prepaid Insurance	8 0 0 00			(b) 6 5 0 00	1 5 0 00				1 5 0 00		3
4	Salon Equipment	4 5 0 0 00				4 5 0 0 00				4 5 0 0 00		4
5	Accum. Depr.—Salon Equipment				(d) 9 0 0 00		9 0 0 00				9 0 0 00	5
6	Accounts Payable		2 2 5 00				2 2 5 00				2 2 5 00	6
7	Wages Payable				(c) 4 0 00		4 0 00				4 0 00	7
8	Elizabeth Soltis, Capital		2 7 6 5 00				2 7 6 5 00				2 7 6 5 00	8
9	Elizabeth Soltis, Drawing	3 5 4 0 00				3 5 4 0 00				3 5 4 0 00		9
10	Styling Fees		32 0 0 0 00				32 0 0 0 00		32 0 0 0 00			10
11	Wages Expense	8 0 0 0 00		(c) 4 0 00		8 0 4 0 00		8 0 4 0 00				11
12	Rent Expense	6 0 0 0 00				6 0 0 0 00		6 0 0 0 00				12
13	Styling Supplies Expense			(a) 1 4 5 0 00		1 4 5 0 00		1 4 5 0 00				13
14	Telephone Expense	4 5 0 00				4 5 0 00		4 5 0 00				14
15	Utilities Expense	8 0 0 00				8 0 0 00		8 0 0 00				15
16	Insurance Expense			(b) 6 5 0 00		6 5 0 00		6 5 0 00				16
17	Depr. Expense—Salon Equipment			(d) 9 0 0 00		9 0 0 00		9 0 0 00				17
18		34 9 9 0 00	34 9 9 0 00	3 0 4 0 00	3 0 4 0 00	35 9 3 0 00	35 9 3 0 00	18 2 9 0 00	32 0 0 0 00	17 6 4 0 00	3 9 3 0 00	18
19	Net Income							13 7 1 0 00			13 7 1 0 00	19
20								32 0 0 0 00	32 0 0 0 00	17 6 4 0 00	17 6 4 0 00	20
21												21
22												22
23												23
24												24
25												25
26												26
27												27
28												28
29												29
30												30

Self-Study Test Questions

True/False

1. Expenses are listed on the income statement as they appear in the chart of accounts or in descending order (by dollar amount). _____

2. Additional investments of capital during the month are not reported on the statement of owner's equity. _____

3. The income statement cannot be prepared using the work sheet alone. _____

4. A classified balance sheet groups similar items together such as current assets. _____

5. Temporary accounts are closed at the end of each accounting period. _____

Multiple Choice

1. Which of these types of accounts is considered a "permanent" account? _____

   (a) Revenue   (c) Drawing
   (b) Asset   (d) Expense

2. Which of these accounts is considered a "temporary" account? _____

   (a) Cash   (c) J. Jones, Capital
   (b) Accounts Payable   (d) J. Jones, Drawing

3. Which of these is the first step in the closing process? _____

   (a) Close revenue account(s).
   (b) Close expense accounts.
   (c) Close the income summary account.
   (d) Close the drawing account.

4. The _____ is prepared after closing entries are posted to prove the equality of debit and credit balances. _____

   (a) balance sheet   (c) post-closing trial balance
   (b) income statement   (d) statement of owner's equity

5. Steps that begin with analyzing source documents and conclude with the post-closing trial balance are called the _____ . _____

   (a) closing process   (c) adjusting entries
   (b) accounting cycle   (d) journalizing transactions

The answers to the Self-Study Test Questions are at the end of the text.

Careful study of this appendix should enable you to:

LO1 Classify business transactions as operating, investing, or financing.

LO2 Prepare a statement of cash flows by analyzing and categorizing a series of business transactions.

Chapter 6 Appendix
Statement of Cash Flows

Thus far, we have discussed three financial statements: the income statement, the statement of owner's equity, and the balance sheet. A fourth statement, the statement of cash flows, is also very important. It explains what the business did to generate cash and how the cash was used. This is done by categorizing all cash transactions into three types of activities: operating, investing, and financing.

TYPES OF BUSINESS ACTIVITIES

LO1 Classify business transactions as operating, investing, or financing.

Cash flows from **operating activities** are related to the revenues and expenses reported on the income statement. Examples include cash received for services performed and the payment of cash for expenses.

> **LEARNING KEY:** There are three types of business activities: operating, investing, and financing.

Investing activities are those transactions involving the purchase and sale of long-term assets, lending money, and collecting the principal on the related loans.

Financing activities are those transactions dealing with the exchange of cash between the business and its owners and creditors. Examples include cash received from the owner to finance the operations and cash paid to the owner as withdrawals. Financing activities also include borrowing cash and repaying the loan principal.

> **LEARNING KEY:** Lending money to another entity is an outflow of cash from investing activities. The collection of the principal when the loan is due is an inflow of cash from investing activities. Borrowing cash is an inflow from financing activities. Repayment of the loan principal is an outflow from financing activities.

Figure 6A-1 provides a review of the transactions for Jessie Jane's Campus Delivery for the month of June. The transactions are classified as operating, investing, or financing, and an explanation for the classification is provided.

SUMMARY OF TRANSACTIONS FOR JESSIE JANE'S CAMPUS DELIVERY	TYPE OF TRANSACTION	EXPLANATION
(a) Jessica Jane invested cash in her business, $2,000.	Financing	Cash received from the owner is an inflow from financing activities. Don't be fooled by the word "invested." From the company's point of view, this is a way to *finance* the business.
(b) Purchased delivery equipment for cash, $1,200.	Investing	Purchases of long-term assets are investments.
(c) Purchased delivery equipment on account from Big Red Scooters, $900. (Note: Big Red has loaned Jane $900.)	No cash involved	This transaction will not affect the main sections of the statement of cash flows. (This is a noncash investing and financing activity.)
(d) Paid first installment to Big Red Scooters, $300. (See transaction (c).)	Financing	Repayments of loans are financing activities.
(e) Received cash for delivery services rendered, $500.	Operating	Cash received as a result of providing services is classified as an operating activity.
(f) Paid cash for June office rent, $200.	Operating	Cash payments for expenses are classified as operating activities.
(g) Paid telephone bill, $50.	Operating	Cash payments for expenses are classified as operating activities.
(h) Made deliveries on account for a total of $600: $400 for the Accounting Department and $200 for the School of Music.	No cash involved	This transaction will not affect the statement of cash flows.
(i) Purchased supplies for cash, $80.	Operating	Cash payments for expenses are classified as operating activities. Most of these supplies were used up. Those that remain will be used in the near future. These are not long-term assets and, thus, do not qualify as investments.
(j) Paid cash for an eight-month liability insurance policy, $200. Coverage began on June 1.	Operating	Cash payments for expenses are classified as operating activities. Prepaid Insurance is not considered a long-term asset and, thus, does not qualify as an investment.
(k) Received $570 in cash for services performed in transaction (h): $400 from the Accounting Department and $170 from the School of Music.	Operating	Cash received as a result of providing services is classified as an operating activity.
(l) Purchased a third scooter from Big Red Scooters, $1,500. A down payment of $300 was made with the remaining payments expected over the next four months.	Investing	Purchases of long-term assets are investments. Only the $300 cash paid will be reported on the statement of cash flows.
(m) Paid wages of part-time employees, $650.	Operating	Cash payments for expenses are classified as operating activities.
(n) Earned delivery fees for the remainder of the month amounting to $1,050: $430 in cash and $620 on account. Deliveries on account: $250 for the Accounting Department and $370 for the Athletic Ticket Office.	Operating	Cash received ($430) as a result of providing services is classified as an operating activity.
(o) Jane withdrew cash for personal use, $150.	Financing	Cash payments to owners are classified as a financing activity.

FIGURE 6A-1 **Summary of Transactions for Jessie Jane's Campus Delivery**

PREPARING THE STATEMENT OF CASH FLOWS

LO2 Prepare a statement of cash flows by analyzing and categorizing a series of business transactions.

The classifications of the cash transactions for Jessie Jane's Campus Delivery are summarized in the expanded cash T account shown in Figure 6A-2. Using this information, we can prepare a statement of cash flows. As shown in Figure 6A-3 below, the heading is similar to that used for the income statement. Since the statement of cash flows reports on the flow of cash for a period of time, the statement is dated for the month ended June 30, 20--.

CASH

Event	Classification	Amount	Amount	Classification	Event	
(a) Investment by Jessie.	Financing	2,000	1,200	Investing	Purchased delivery equipment.	(b)
(e) Cash received for services.	Operating	500	300	Financing	Made payment on loan.	(d)
(k) Cash received for services.	Operating	570	200	Operating	Paid office rent.	(f)
(n) Cash received for services.	Operating	430	50	Operating	Paid telephone bill.	(g)
		3,500	80	Operating	Purchased supplies.	(i)
			200	Operating	Paid for insurance.	(j)
			300	Investing	Purchased delivery equipment.	(l)
			650	Operating	Paid wages.	(m)
			150	Financing	Withdrawal by owner.	(o)
			3,130			
	Bal.	370				

FIGURE 6A-2   Cash T Account for Jessie Jane's Campus Delivery with Classifications of Cash Transactions

Jessie Jane's Campus Delivery Statement of Cash Flows For Month Ended June 30, 20 - -															
Cash flows from operating activities:															
Cash received from customers for delivery services												$1	5	0	0	00
Cash paid for wages	$	(6	5	0	00)										
Cash paid for rent		(2	0	0	00)										
Cash paid for supplies			(8	0	00)										
Cash paid for telephone			(5	0	00)										
Cash paid for insurance		(2	0	0	00)										
Total cash paid for operations							(1	1	8	0	00)				
Net cash provided by operating activities							$	3	2	0	00				
Cash flows from investing activities:															
Cash paid for delivery equipment	$(1	5	0	0	00)										
Net cash used for investing activities							(1	5	0	0	00)				
Cash flows from financing activities:															
Cash investment by owner	$2	0	0	0	00										
Cash withdrawal by owner		(1	5	0	00)										
Payment made on loan		(3	0	0	00)										
Net cash provided by financing activities							1	5	5	0	00				
Net increase in cash							$	3	7	0	00				

FIGURE 6A-3   Statement of Cash Flows for Jessie Jane's Campus Delivery

The main body of the statement is arranged in three sections: operating, investing, and financing activities. First, cash received from customers is listed under operating activities. Then, cash payments for operating activities are listed and totaled. The net amount is reported as net cash provided by operating activities. Since this is the main purpose of the business, it is important to be able to generate positive cash flows from operating activities.

The next two sections list the inflows and outflows from investing and financing activities. Debits to the cash account are inflows and credits are outflows. Note that there was an outflow, or net use of cash, from investing activities resulting from the purchase of the motor scooters. In addition, cash was provided from financing activities because Jessie's initial investment more than covered her withdrawal and the payment on the loan. These investing and financing activities are typical for a new business.

The sum of the inflows and outflows from operating, investing, and financing activities equals the net increase (or decrease) in the cash account during the period. Since this is a new business, the cash account had a beginning balance of zero. The ending balance is $370. This agrees with the net increase in cash of $370 reported on the statement of cash flows.

LEARNING KEY: To prove the accuracy of the statement of cash flows, compare the net increase or decrease reported on the statement with the change in the balance of the cash account.

This appendix introduces you to the purpose and format of the statement of cash flows. Here, we classified entries made to the cash account as operating, investing, or financing. These classifications were then used to prepare the statement. Businesses have thousands of entries to the cash account. Thus, this approach to preparing the statement is not really practical. Other approaches to preparing the statement will be discussed in Chapter 25. However, the purpose and format of the statements are the same.

Learning Objectives	Key Points to Remember
1 **Classify business transactions as operating, investing, or financing.**	The purpose of the statement of cash flows is to report what the firm did to generate cash and how the cash was used. Business transactions are classified as operating, investing, and financing activities. *Operating activities* are those transactions related to the revenues and expenses reported on the income statement. *Investing activities* are those transactions involving the purchase and sale of long-term assets, lending money, and collecting the principal on the related loans. *Financing activities* are those transactions dealing with the exchange of cash between the business and its owners and creditors.
2 **Prepare a statement of cash flows by analyzing and categorizing a series of business transactions.**	The main body of the statement of cash flows consists of three sections: operating, investing, and financing activities.

Name of Business
Statement of Cash Flows
For Period Ended Date

Cash flows from operating activities:		
Cash received from customers		$x x x x xx
List cash paid for various expenses	$ (x x x xx)	
Total cash paid for operations		(x x x x xx)
Net cash provided by (used for) operating activities		$ x x x xx
Cash flows from investing activities:		
List cash received from the sale of long-term assets and other investing activities	$x x x x xx	
List cash paid for the purchase of long-term assets and other investing activities	(x x x x xx)	
Net cash provided by (used for) investing activities		x x x x xx
Cash flows from financing activities:		
List cash received from owners and creditors	$x x x x xx	
List cash paid to owners and creditors	(x x x xx)	
Net cash provided by (used for) financing activities		x x x x xx
Net increase (decrease) in cash		$ x x x xx

KEY TERMS

financing activities, (211)   Those transactions dealing with the exchange of cash between the business and its owners and creditors.

investing activities, (211)   Those transactions involving the purchase and sale of long-term assets, lending money, and collecting the principal on the related loans.

operating activities, (211)   Those transactions related to the revenues and expenses reported on the income statement.

REVIEW QUESTIONS

1. Explain the purpose of the statement of cash flows.

2. Define and provide examples of the three types of business activities.

SERIES A EXERCISE

EXERCISE 6Apx-1A (LO1) **CLASSIFYING BUSINESS TRANSACTIONS** Dolores Lopez opened a new consulting business. The following transactions occurred during January of the current year. Classify each transaction as an operating, investing, or financing activity.

(a) Invested cash in the business, $10,000.
(b) Paid office rent, $500.
(c) Purchased office equipment. Paid $1,500 cash and agreed to pay the balance of $2,000 in four monthly installments.
(d) Received cash for services rendered, $900.
(e) Paid telephone bill, $65.
(f) Made payment on loan in transaction (c), $500.
(g) Paid wages to part-time employee, $500.
(h) Received cash for services rendered, $800.
(i) Paid electricity bill, $85
(j) Withdrew cash for personal use, $100.
(k) Paid wages to part-time employee, $500.

SERIES A PROBLEM

PROBLEM 6Apx-1A (LO2) **PREPARING A STATEMENT OF CASH FLOWS** Prepare a statement of cash flows based on the transactions reported in Exercise 6Apx-1A.

SERIES B EXERCISE

EXERCISE 6Apx-1B (LO1) **CLASSIFYING BUSINESS TRANSACTIONS** Bob Jacobs opened an advertising agency. The following transactions occurred during January of the current year. Classify each transaction as an operating, investing, or financing activity.

(a) Invested cash in the business, $5,000.
(b) Purchased office equipment. Paid $2,500 cash and agreed to pay the balance of $2,000 in four monthly installments.
(c) Paid office rent, $400.
(d) Received cash for services rendered, $700.
(e) Paid telephone bill, $95.
(f) Received cash for services rendered, $600.
(g) Made payment on loan in transaction (b), $500.
(h) Paid wages to part-time employee, $800.
(i) Paid electricity bill, $100.
(j) Withdrew cash for personal use, $500.
(k) Paid wages to part-time employee, $600.

SERIES B PROBLEM

PROBLEM 6Apx-1B (LO2) **PREPARING A STATEMENT OF CASH FLOWS** Prepare a statement of cash flows based on the transactions reported in Exercise 6Apx-1B.

COMPREHENSIVE PROBLEM 1: THE ACCOUNTING CYCLE

Bob Night opened "The General's Favorite Fishing Hole." The fishing camp is open from April through September and attracts many famous college basketball coaches during the off-season. Guests typically register for one week, arriving on Sunday afternoon and returning home the following Saturday afternoon. The registration fee includes room and board, the use of fishing boats, and professional instruction in fishing techniques. The chart of accounts for the camping operations is provided below.

The General's Favorite Fishing Hole
Chart of Accounts

Assets		Revenues	
101	Cash	401	Registration Fees
142	Office Supplies		
144	Food Supplies	Expenses	
145	Prepaid Insurance	511	Wages Expense
181	Fishing Boats	521	Rent Expense
181.1	Accum. Depr.—Fishing Boats	523	Office Supplies Expense
		524	Food Supplies Expense
Liabilities		525	Telephone Expense
202	Accounts Payable	533	Utilities Expense
219	Wages Payable	535	Insurance Expense
		536	Postage Expense
Owner's Equity		542	Depr. Exp.—Fishing Boats
311	Bob Night, Capital		
312	Bob Night, Drawing		
313	Income Summary		

The following transactions took place during April 20--.

Apr. 1   Night invested cash in business, $90,000.

1   Paid insurance premium for camping season, $9,000.

2   Paid rent for lodge and campgrounds for the month of April, $40,000.

2   Deposited registration fees, $35,000.

2   Purchased ten fishing boats on account for $60,000. The boats have estimated useful lives of five years, at which time they will be donated to a local day camp. Arrangements were made to pay for the boats in July.

3   Purchased food supplies from Acme Super Market on account, $7,000.

5   Purchased office supplies from Gordon Office Supplies on account, $500.

7   Deposited registration fees, $38,600.

10   Purchased food supplies from Acme Super Market on account, $8,200.

10   Paid wages to fishing guides, $10,000.

14   Deposited registration fees, $30,500.

16   Purchased food supplies from Acme Super Market on account, $9,000.

17   Paid wages to fishing guides, $10,000.

18   Paid postage, $150.

21   Deposited registration fees, $35,600.

24   Purchased food supplies from Acme Super Market on account, $8,500.

24   Paid wages to fishing guides, $10,000.

28   Deposited registration fees, $32,000.

29   Paid wages to fishing guides, $10,000.

30   Purchased food supplies from Acme Super Market on account, $6,000.

30   Paid Acme Super Market on account, $32,700.

30   Paid utilities bill, $2,000.

30   Paid telephone bill, $1,200.

30   Bob Night withdrew cash for personal use, $6,000.

Adjustment information for the end of April is provided below.

(a) Office supplies remaining on hand, $100.

(b) Food supplies remaining on hand, $8,000.

(c) Insurance expired during the month of April, $1,500.

(d) Depreciation on the fishing boats for the month of April, $1,000.

(e) Wages earned, but not yet paid, at the end of April, $500.

REQUIRED

1. Enter the above transactions in a general journal. Enter transactions from April 1–5 on page 1, April 7–18 on page 2, April 21–29 and the first two entries for April 30 on page 3, and the remaining entries for April 30 on page 4.

2. Post the entries to the general ledger. (If you are not using the working papers that accompany this text, you will need to enter the account titles and account numbers in the general ledger accounts.)

3. Prepare a trial balance on a work sheet.

4. Complete the work sheet.

5. Prepare the income statement.

6. Prepare the statement of owner's equity.

7. Prepare the balance sheet.

8. Journalize the adjusting entries (page 5).

9. Post the adjusting entries to the general ledger.

10. Journalize the closing entries (pages 5 and 6).

11. Post the closing entries to the general ledger.

12. Prepare a post-closing trial balance.

Accounting for Cash, Payroll and Service Businesses

Accounting for Cash

John Zenith recently opened a sports equipment and clothing shop named Be A Sport in West Springfield, MA. To protect and properly manage cash, John uses a checking account. All cash and checks received from customers are deposited promptly. All bills are paid by check. In this way, John can use the deposit slips and monthly bank statement to verify his records of cash received. Similarly, canceled checks and the monthly bank statement can be used to verify John's records of cash payments. Complete and accurate records of cash receipts and cash payments help John control this important asset and plan for future cash needs.

At the end of the month, the balance in the cash account in John's books differs from the cash balance shown on the bank statement. In trying to reconcile the two amounts, how should John treat the checks he wrote during the month that have not yet been presented to the bank for payment?

OBJECTIVES

Careful study of this chapter should enable you to:

LO1 Describe how to open and use a checking account.

LO2 Prepare a bank reconciliation and related journal entries.

LO3 Establish and use a petty cash fund.

LO4 Establish a change fund and use the cash short and over account.

Cash is an asset that is quite familiar and important to all of us. We generally think of **cash** as the currency and coins in our pockets and the money we have in our checking accounts. To a business, cash also includes checks received from customers, money orders, and bank cashier's checks.

Because it plays such a central role in operating a business, cash must be carefully managed and controlled. A business should have a system of **internal control**—a set of procedures designed to ensure proper accounting for transactions. For good internal control of cash transactions, all cash received should be deposited daily in a bank. All disbursements, except for payments from petty cash, should be made by check.

CHECKING ACCOUNT

LO1 Describe how to open and use a checking account.

The key documents and forms required in opening and using a checking account are the signature card, deposit tickets, checks, and bank statements.

Opening a Checking Account

To open a checking account, each person authorized to sign checks must complete and sign a **signature card** (Figure 7-1). The bank uses this card to verify the depositor's signature on any banking transactions. The taxpayer identification number (TIN) is the depositor's social security number or employer identification number (EIN). This number is shown on the card to identify the depositor for income tax purposes. An EIN can be obtained from the Internal Revenue Service.

Making Deposits

A **deposit ticket** (Figure 7-2) is a form showing a detailed listing of items being deposited. Currency, coins, and checks are listed separately. Each check should be identified by its **ABA (American Bankers Association) Number**. This number is the small fraction printed in the upper right-hand corner of each check. The number also appears in **magnetic ink character recognition (MICR) code** on the lower left side of the front of each check. The code is used to sort and route checks throughout the U.S. banking system. Normally, only the numerator of the fraction is used in identifying checks on the deposit ticket.

The depositor delivers or mails the deposit ticket and all items being deposited to the bank. The bank then gives or mails a receipt to the depositor.

Endorsements. Each check being deposited must be endorsed by the depositor. The **endorsement** consists of stamping or writing the depositor's name and sometimes other information on the back of the check, in the space provided near the left end. There are two basic types of endorsements:

1. **Blank endorsement**—the depositor simply signs the back of the check. This makes the check payable to any bearer.

2. **Restrictive endorsement**—the depositor adds words such as "For deposit," "Pay to any bank," or "Pay to Daryl Beck only" to restrict the payment of the check.

ACCOUNT OWNER NAME & ADDRESS

ACCOUNT NUMBER

Number of signatures required for withdrawal _____ ☐ This is a temporary account agreement.

SIGNATURE(S) - THE UNDERSIGNED AGREE(S) TO THE TERMS STATED ON PAGES 1 AND 2 OF THIS FORM, AND ACKNOWLEDGE(S) RECEIPT OF A COMPLETED COPY ON TODAY'S DATE. THE UNDERSIGNED ALSO ACKNOWLEDGE(S) RECEIPT OF A COPY OF AND AGREE(S) TO THE TERMS OF THE FOLLOWING DISCLOSURE(S):

☐ Funds Availability Disclosure   ☐ Truth-In-Savings Disclosure
☐ Electronic Funds Transfer Disclosure   ☐ _____

Signature(s)   **Identifying Info.**

(1) _____

(2) _____

(3) _____

(4) _____

☐ **AUTHORIZED SIGNER (name)** _____
Individual Accounts Only

X _____

ADDITIONAL INFORMATION:

BACKUP WITHHOLDING CERTIFICATIONS

TIN: _____

☐ **TAXPAYER I.D. NUMBER -** The Taxpayer Identification Number shown above (TIN) is my correct taxpayer identification number.

☐ **BACKUP WITHHOLDING -** I am not subject to backup withholding either because I have not been notified that I am subject to backup withholding as a result of a failure to report all interest or dividends, or the Internal Revenue Service has notified me that I am no longer subject to backup withholding.

☐ **EXEMPT RECIPIENTS -** I am an exempt recipient under the Internal Revenue Service Regulations.

SIGNATURE - I certify under penalties of perjury the statements checked in this section.

X _____
(Date)

© 1983, 1988, 1990, 1991 Bankers Systems, Inc., St. Cloud, MN Form MPSC-KS 3/15/99   (page 1 of 2)

FIGURE 7-1   Signature Card

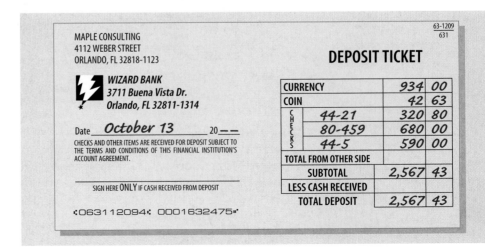

FIGURE 7-2   Deposit Ticket

Businesses commonly use a rubber stamp to endorse checks for deposit. The check shown in Figure 7-3 has been stamped with a restrictive endorsement.

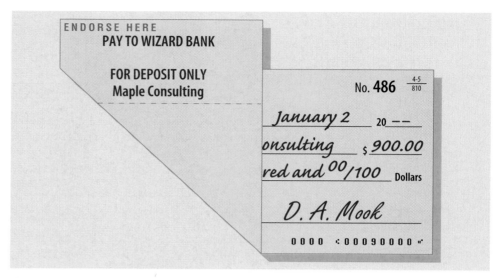

FIGURE 7-3 Restrictive Endorsement

Automated Teller Machines. Most banks now make **automated teller machines (ATMs)** available at all times to depositors for making deposits or withdrawals. Each depositor has a plastic card (Figure 7-4) and a personal identification number (PIN). The depositor inserts the card, keys in the PIN, indicates whether the transaction is a withdrawal or a deposit, and enters the amount. The machine has a drawer or door for the withdrawal or deposit.

FIGURE 7-4 Automated Teller Machine Card

Most ATMs are now on a system such as Cirrus that allows noncustomers to use other ATMs in both the United States and foreign countries. There are also "cash machines" that supply only cash and do not take deposits. These are often found at airports and convenience stores.

It is important for the depositor to keep an accounting record of ATM withdrawals and deposits. This is done on the check stub or register described in the following section, and with an appropriate journal entry.

Writing Checks

A **check** is a document ordering a bank to pay cash from a depositor's account. There are three parties to every check:

1. **Drawer**—the depositor who orders the bank to pay the cash.

2. **Drawee**—the bank on which the check is drawn.

3. **Payee**—the person being paid the cash.

Checks used by businesses are usually bound in the form of a book. In some checkbooks, each check is attached to a **check stub** (Figure 7-5) that contains space to record all relevant information about the check. Other checkbooks are accompanied by a small register book in which the relevant information is noted. If a financial computer software package is used, both the check and the register can be prepared electronically.

Use the following three steps in preparing a check.

STEP 1   Complete the check stub or register.

STEP 2   Enter the date, payee name, and amount on the check.

STEP 3   Sign the check.

The check stub is completed first so that the drawer retains a record of each check issued. This information is needed to determine the proper journal entry for the transaction.

The payee name is entered on the first long line on the check, followed by the amount in figures. The amount in words is then entered on the second long line. If the amount in figures does not agree with the amount in words, the bank usually contacts the drawer for the correct amount or returns the check unpaid.

The most critical point in preparing a check is signing it, and this should be done last. The signature authorizes the bank to pay cash from the drawer's account. The check signer should make sure that all other aspects of the check are correct before signing it.

Note that the check stubs in Figure 7-5 contain space to record amounts deposited. It generally is a good idea also to indicate the date of the deposit, as shown on check stub No. 108.

The payee and amount written in words should be followed by something, such as a line, to make it difficult to alter the payee or the amount.

LEARNING KEY: The check should not be signed until the check signer has verified that all aspects of the check are correct.

It is sometimes necessary to void a check. Proper procedures for doing so are to tear off or deface the signature box and to file the voided check numerically with the canceled checks.

PROFILES IN ACCOUNTING

Lisa Davis, Legal Coordinator

Lisa Davis began working as a part-time legal secretary with Zegarelli Associates. Lisa continued her career with this company after earning an Associate Degree in Legal Office Management.

After graduation, Lisa was hired as a legal assistant and later promoted to legal coordinator. Her duties include budgeting, accounts receivable, supervising two employees, coordinating schedules, researching, and dealing with clients on a daily basis.

According to Lisa, dependability, initiative, and loyalty lead to success. Lisa chose the legal field because she always had an interest in law and wanted to work in a fast-paced environment.

No. 107

DATE _April 3_ 20 _ _
TO _Linclay Corp._
FOR _April Rent_

ACCT. _Rent Expense_

	DOLLARS	CENTS
BAL BRO'T FOR'D	3,625	41
AMT. DEPOSITED		
TOTAL		
AMT. THIS CHECK	300	00
BAL CAR'D FOR'D	3,325	41

MAPLE CONSULTING
4112 WEBER STREET
ORLANDO, FL 32818-1123

No. 107 63-1209/631

April 3 20 _ _

PAY TO THE ORDER OF _Linclay Corporation_ — $ _300.00_

Three Hundred 00/100 —————————— Dollars

WIZARD BANK
3711 Buena Vista Dr.
Orlando, FL 32811-1314

FOR CLASSROOM USE ONLY

MEMO _____ BY _James Maple_

⑆063112094⑆ 0001632475⑈

No. 108

DATE _April 4_ 20 _ _
TO _Continental Mfg. Co._
FOR _Inv. March 31_

ACCT. _Accounts Payable_

	DOLLARS	CENTS
BAL BRO'T FOR'D	3,325	41
AMT. DEPOSITED	1,694	20
4/4 TOTAL	5,019	61
AMT. THIS CHECK	1,478	18
BAL CAR'D FOR'D	3,541	43

MAPLE CONSULTING
4112 WEBER STREET
ORLANDO, FL 32818-1123

No. 108 63-1209/631

April 4 20 _ _

PAY TO THE ORDER OF _Continental Mfg. Co._ — $ _1,478.18_

One Thousand Four Hundred Seventy-Eight 18/100 Dollars

WIZARD BANK
3711 Buena Vista Dr.
Orlando, FL 32811-1314

FOR CLASSROOM USE ONLY

MEMO _____ BY _James Maple_

⑆063112094⑆ 0001632475⑈

FIGURE 7-5 Checks and Check Stubs

Bank Statement

A statement of account issued by a bank to each depositor once a month is called a **bank statement**. Figure 7-6 is a bank statement for a checking account. The statement shows:

1. The balance at the beginning of the period.

2. Deposits and other amounts added during the period.

3. Checks and other amounts subtracted during the period.

4. The balance at the end of the period.

With the bank statement, the bank normally sends to the depositor:

1. **Canceled checks**—the depositor's checks paid by the bank during the period. The bank may send the checks themselves, "imaged" sheets showing only the faces of the checks, or simply a listing of the checks on the bank statement.

2. Any other forms representing items added to or subtracted from the account.

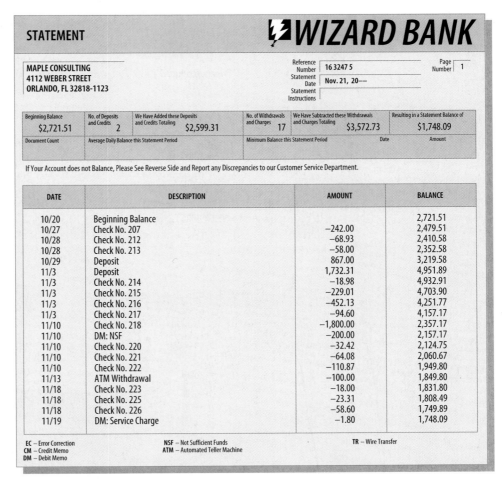

STATEMENT   **WIZARD BANK**

MAPLE CONSULTING
4112 WEBER STREET
ORLANDO, FL 32818-1123

Reference Number 16 3247 5   Page Number 1
Statement Date Nov. 21, 20—
Statement Instructions

Beginning Balance	No. of Deposits and Credits	We Have Added these Deposits and Credits Totaling	No. of Withdrawals and Charges	We Have Subtracted these Withdrawals and Charges Totaling	Resulting in a Statement Balance of
$2,721.51	2	$2,599.31	17	$3,572.73	$1,748.09
Document Count	Average Daily Balance this Statement Period		Minimum Balance this Statement Period	Date	Amount

If Your Account does not Balance, Please See Reverse Side and Report any Discrepancies to our Customer Service Department.

DATE	DESCRIPTION	AMOUNT	BALANCE
10/20	Beginning Balance		2,721.51
10/27	Check No. 207	−242.00	2,479.51
10/28	Check No. 212	−68.93	2,410.58
10/28	Check No. 213	−58.00	2,352.58
10/29	Deposit	867.00	3,219.58
11/3	Deposit	1,732.31	4,951.89
11/3	Check No. 214	−18.98	4,932.91
11/3	Check No. 215	−229.01	4,703.90
11/3	Check No. 216	−452.13	4,251.77
11/3	Check No. 217	−94.60	4,157.17
11/10	Check No. 218	−1,800.00	2,357.17
11/10	DM: NSF	−200.00	2,157.17
11/10	Check No. 220	−32.42	2,124.75
11/10	Check No. 221	−64.08	2,060.67
11/10	Check No. 222	−110.87	1,949.80
11/13	ATM Withdrawal	−100.00	1,849.80
11/18	Check No. 223	−18.00	1,831.80
11/18	Check No. 225	−23.31	1,808.49
11/18	Check No. 226	−58.60	1,749.89
11/19	DM: Service Charge	−1.80	1,748.09

EC – Error Correction   NSF – Not Sufficient Funds   TR – Wire Transfer
CM – Credit Memo   ATM – Automated Teller Machine
DM – Debit Memo

FIGURE 7-6   Bank Statement

RECONCILING THE BANK STATEMENT

LO2 **Prepare a bank reconciliation and related journal entries.**

On any given day, the balance in the cash account on the depositor's books (the book balance) is unlikely to be the same as that on the bank's books (the bank balance). This difference can be due to errors, but it usually is caused by timing. Transactions generally are recorded by the business at a time that is different from when the bank records them.

Deposits

Suppose there are cash receipts of $600.00 on April 30. These cash receipts would be recorded on the depositor's books on April 30 and a deposit of $600.00 would be sent to the bank. The deposit would not reach the bank, however, until at least the following day, May 1. This timing difference in recording the $600.00 of cash receipts is illustrated in Figure 7-7. Notice that on April 30, the balances in the depositor's books and in the bank's books would be different.

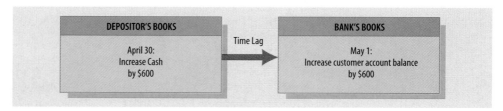

FIGURE 7-7   Depositor and Bank Records—Deposits

Cash Payments

Similar timing differences occur with cash payments. Suppose a check for $350.00 is written on April 30. This cash payment would be recorded on the depositor's books on April 30 and the check mailed to the payee. The check probably would not be received by the payee until May 3. If the payee deposited the check promptly, it still would not clear the bank until May 4. This timing difference in recording the $350.00 cash payment is illustrated in Figure 7-8. Notice once again that on April 30, the balances in the depositor's books and in the bank's books would be different.

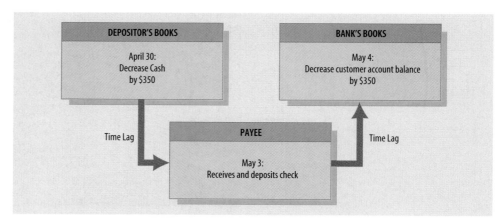

FIGURE 7-8   Depositor and Bank Records—Cash Payments

Reasons for Differences Between Bank and Book Balances

When the bank statement is received, the depositor examines the records to identify the items that explain the difference between the book and bank balances. This process of bringing the book and bank balances into agreement is called preparing a **bank reconciliation**.

The most common reasons for differences between the book and bank balances are the following:

1. **Outstanding checks.** Checks issued during the period that have not been presented to the bank for payment before the statement is prepared.

2. **Deposits in transit.** Deposits that have not reached or been recorded by the bank before the statement is prepared.

3. **Service charges.** Bank charges for services such as check printing and processing.

4. **Collections.** Collections of promissory notes or charge accounts made by the bank on behalf of the depositor.

5. **Not sufficient funds (NSF) checks.** Checks deposited by the depositor that are not paid because the drawer did not have sufficient funds.

6. **Errors.** Errors made by the bank or the depositor in recording cash transactions.

Steps in Preparing the Bank Reconciliation

Use the following three steps in preparing the bank reconciliation:

STEP 1   Identify deposits in transit and any related errors.

STEP 2   Identify outstanding checks and any related errors.

STEP 3   Identify additional reconciling items.

Deposits in Transit and Related Errors. Follow these steps:

STEP 1   Compare deposits listed on the bank statement with deposits in transit on last month's bank reconciliation. All of last month's deposits in transit should appear on the current month's bank statement.

STEP 2   Compare the remaining deposits on the bank statement with deposits listed in the accounting records. Any deposits listed in the accounting records but not on the bank statement are deposits in transit on the current bank reconciliation.

STEP 3   Compare the individual deposit amounts on the bank statement and in the accounting records. If they differ, the error needs to be corrected.

Outstanding Checks and Related Errors. Follow these steps:

STEP 1   Compare canceled checks with the bank statement and the accounting records. If the amounts differ, the error needs to be corrected.

STEP 2   As each canceled check is compared with the accounting records, place a check mark on the check stub or other accounting record to indicate that the check has cleared.

STEP 3   Any checks written that have not been checked off represent outstanding checks on the bank reconciliation.

Additional Reconciling Items. Compare any additions and deductions on the bank statement that are not deposits or checks with the accounting records. Items that the bank adds to the account are called **credit memos**. Items that the bank deducts from the account are called **debit memos**. Remember that a depositor's account is a liability to the bank. Thus, a credit memo increases this liability; a debit memo reduces the liability. Any of these items not appearing in the accounting records represent additional items on the bank reconciliation.

Illustration of a Bank Reconciliation

A general format for the bank reconciliation is shown in Figure 7-9. Not every item shown in this illustration would be in every bank reconciliation, but this format is helpful in determining where to put items. A bank reconciliation form also can be found on the back of most bank statements.

BANK RECONCILIATION

Bank statement balance		$xxxx
Add: Deposits in transit	$xxxx	
Bank errors	xxxx	xxxx
		$xxxx
Deduct: Outstanding checks	$xxxx	
Bank errors	xxxx	xxxx
Adjusted bank balance		$xxxx
Book balance		$xxxx
Add: Bank credit memos	$xxxx	
Book errors	xxxx	xxxx
		$xxxx
Deduct: Bank debit memos	$xxxx	
Book errors	xxxx	xxxx
Adjusted book balance		$xxxx

FIGURE 7-9 **Bank Reconciliation Format**

To illustrate the preparation of a bank reconciliation, we will use the Maple Consulting bank statement shown in Figure 7-6. That statement shows a balance of $1,748.09 as of November 21. The balance in Maple's check stubs and general ledger cash account is $2,393.23. The three steps described on page 229 were used to identify the following items, and the reconciliation in Figure 7-10 was prepared.

1. A deposit of $637.02 recorded on November 21 had not been received by the bank. Maple has received the funds but the amount has not yet been counted by the bank. This deposit in transit is added to the bank statement balance.

2. Check numbers 219, 224, and 227 are outstanding. The funds have been disbursed by Maple but have not yet been paid out by the bank. The amount of these outstanding checks is subtracted from the bank statement balance.

3. Check number 214 was written for $18.98, but was entered on the check stub and on the books as $19.88. This $.90 error is added to the book balance because $.90 too much had been deducted from the book balance.

4. Maple made an ATM withdrawal of $100.00 on November 13 for personal use but did not record the withdrawal on the books. The bank has reduced Maple's balance by this amount. Thus, this amount is deducted from the book balance.

5. The bank returned an NSF check of $200.00. This was a check received by Maple from a customer. The bank has reduced Maple's balance by $200.00 but Maple has not yet recorded it. This amount is deducted from the book balance.

6. The bank service charge was $1.80. The bank has reduced Maple's balance by this amount but Maple has not yet recorded it. This amount is deducted from the book balance.

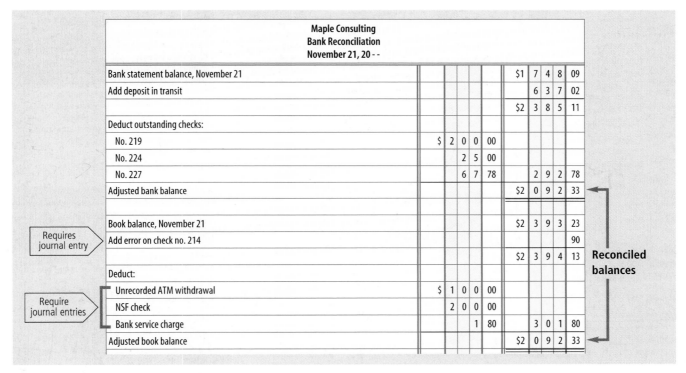

Maple Consulting
Bank Reconciliation
November 21, 20 - -

Bank statement balance, November 21			$1 7 4 8 09
Add deposit in transit			6 3 7 02
			$2 3 8 5 11
Deduct outstanding checks:			
No. 219	$ 2 0 0 00		
No. 224	2 5 00		
No. 227	6 7 78	2 9 2 78	
Adjusted bank balance			$2 0 9 2 33
Book balance, November 21			$2 3 9 3 23
Add error on check no. 214			90
			$2 3 9 4 13
Deduct:			
Unrecorded ATM withdrawal	$ 1 0 0 00		
NSF check	2 0 0 00		
Bank service charge	1 80	3 0 1 80	
Adjusted book balance			$2 0 9 2 33

Requires journal entry → Add error on check no. 214

Require journal entries → Unrecorded ATM withdrawal / NSF check / Bank service charge

Reconciled balances

FIGURE 7-10   **Bank Reconciliation**

Journal Entries

Only two kinds of items appearing on a bank reconciliation require journal entries:

1. Errors in the books.

2. Bank additions and deductions that do not already appear in the accounting records.

LEARNING KEY: Journal entries are needed to correct errors in the books and to record bank additions and deductions that are not in the accounting records.

A BROADER VIEW

Fraud—A Real Threat to Small Business

The bookkeeper for Kramer Iron, Inc., in Hamden, CT, embezzled $213,539 from the company over a four-year period. She used two schemes. One was to alter the number of the dollar amount printed on checks payable to her. The other technique involved putting her own name on the "pay to" line on checks intended for other parties.

This fraud shows the importance of two procedures described in this chapter: (1) Make sure that all aspects of a check are correct before signing it. (2) In preparing the bank reconciliation, compare canceled checks with the accounting records.

Figure 7-11 contains a detailed list of items that require journal entries.

ADDITIONS TO CASH BALANCE	DEDUCTIONS FROM CASH BALANCE
* Unrecorded deposits (including ATM)	* Unrecorded ATM withdrawals
* Note collected by bank	* NSF checks
* Interest earned	* Bank service charges
* Errors:	* Deposits recorded twice
1. Added too little as a deposit	* Unrecorded checks
2. Deducted too much as a check	* Loan payments
	* Interest payments
	* Errors:
	1. Added too much as a deposit
	2. Deducted too little as a check

FIGURE 7-11   Bank Reconciliation Items that Require Journal Entries

Note the four items in the lower portion of the bank reconciliation in Figure 7-10. A journal entry always is required for each item in this portion of the bank reconciliation.

The $.90 item is an error in the accounting records that occurred when the check amount was incorrectly entered. Assume the $18.98 was in payment of an account payable which had been incorrectly debited for $19.88. The entry to correct this error is:

4	Cash				90			4
5	Accounts Payable						90	5
6	Error in recording check							6

The $100.00 ATM withdrawal has been deducted from Maple's account by the bank. Maple has not yet recorded the withdrawal. Maple withdrew the funds for personal use, so the following journal entry is required:

8		James Maple, Drawing		1	0	0	00							8
9		Cash							1	0	0	00			9
10		Unrecorded ATM withdrawal													10

The $200.00 NSF check is a deduction by the bank for a check deposited by Maple that proved to be worthless. This amount must be deducted from the book balance. Assuming the $200.00 was received from a customer on account, the following journal entry is required:

12		Accounts Receivable		2	0	0	00							12
13		Cash							2	0	0	00			13
14		Unrecorded NSF check													14

The $1.80 bank service charge is a fee for bank services received by Maple. The bank has deducted this amount from Maple's account. Bank service charges are usually small and are charged to Miscellaneous Expense.

16		Miscellaneous Expense			1	80							16
17		Cash							1	80			17
18		Bank service charge											18

Electronic Funds Transfer

Electronic funds transfer (EFT) uses a computer rather than paper checks to complete transactions with the bank. This technique is being used increasingly today. Applications of EFT include payrolls, social security payments, retail purchases, mortgage payments, and the ATM transactions described earlier in the chapter.

Heavy use of EFT can present a challenge in preparing bank reconciliations. Many of the documents handled in a purely manual environment disappear when EFT is used. Bank accounts are just one of many areas where computers require accountants to think in new ways. Regardless of what system is used, the key point to remember is that the accounting records must be correctly updated.

THE PETTY CASH FUND

LO3 Establish and use a petty cash fund.

For good control over cash, payments generally should be made by check. Unfortunately, payments of very small amounts by check can be both inconvenient and inefficient. For example, the time and cost required to write a check for $.70 to mail a letter might be greater than the cost of the postage. Therefore, businesses customarily establish a **petty cash fund** to pay for small items with cash. "Petty" means small, and both the amount of the fund and the maximum amount of any bill that can be paid from the fund are small.

Establishing a Petty Cash Fund

To establish a petty cash fund, a check is written to the petty cash custodian for the amount to be set aside in the fund. The amount may be $50.00, $100.00, $200.00, or any amount considered necessary. The journal entry to establish a petty cash fund of $100.00 would be as follows:

4		Petty Cash		1	0	0	00							4
5		Cash							1	0	0	00			5
6		Establish petty cash fund													6

Petty Cash is an asset that is listed immediately below Cash on the balance sheet.

The custodian cashes the check and places the money in a petty cash box. For good control, the custodian should be the only person authorized to make payments from the fund. The custodian should be able to account for the full amount of the fund at any time.

Making Payments from a Petty Cash Fund

A receipt called a **petty cash voucher** (Figure 7-12) should be prepared for every payment from the fund. The voucher shows the name of the payee, the purpose of the payment, and the account to be charged for the payment. Each voucher should be signed by the custodian and by the person receiving the cash. The vouchers should be numbered consecutively so that all vouchers can be accounted for.

PETTY CASH VOUCHER

NO. _2_
DATE _December 8,_ 20 _--_

PAID TO _James Maple_
FOR _Client Luncheon_
CHARGE TO _Travel & Entertainment Expense_ | $ | ¢ |
| 15 | 75 |

REMITTANCE RECEIVED APPROVED BY
James Maple _Tina Blank_

FIGURE 7-12   Petty Cash Voucher

Petty Cash Payments Record

When a petty cash fund is maintained, a formal record is often kept of all payments from the fund. The **petty cash payments record** (Figure 7-13) is a special multi-column record that supplements the regular accounting records. It is not a journal. The headings of the Distribution of Payments columns may vary, depending upon the types of expenditures.

The petty cash payments record of Maple Consulting is shown in Figure 7-13 on page 236. A narrative of the petty cash transactions shown in Figure 7-13 is as follows:

Dec. 1   Maple issued a check for $200.00 payable to Tina Blank, Petty Cash Custodian. Blank cashed the check and placed the money in a secure cash box.

A notation of the amount received is made in the Description column of the petty cash payments record. In addition, this transaction is entered in the journal as follows:

8	Dec. 1	Petty Cash			2	0	0	00						8
9		Cash							2	0	0	00	9
10		Establish petty cash fund											10

During the month of December, the following payments were made from the petty cash fund:

Dec. 5   Paid $32.80 to Jerry's Auto for servicing the company automobile. Voucher No. 1.

8   Reimbursed Maple $15.75 for the amount spent for lunch with a client. Voucher No. 2.

9   Gave Maple $30.00 for personal use. Voucher No. 3.

There is no special Distribution column for entering amounts withdrawn by the owner for personal use. Therefore this payment is entered by writing the account name in the Account column and $30.00 in the Amount column at the extreme right of the petty cash payments record.

15   Paid $28.25 for typewriter repairs. Voucher No. 4.

17   Reimbursed Maple $14.50 for travel expenses. Voucher No. 5.

19   Paid $8.00 to Big Red Car Care for washing the company automobile. Voucher No. 6.

22   Paid $9.50 for mailing a package. Voucher No. 7.

29   Paid $30.00 for postage stamps. Voucher No. 8.

Replenishing the Petty Cash Fund

The petty cash fund should be replenished whenever the fund runs low and at the end of each accounting period, so that the accounts are brought up to date. The amount columns of the petty cash payments record are totaled to verify that the total of the Total Amount column equals the total of the Distribution columns. The amount columns are then ruled as shown in Figure 7-13.

The information in the petty cash payments record is then used to replenish the petty cash fund. On December 31, a check for $168.80 is issued to the petty cash custodian. The journal entry to record the replenishment of the fund is as follows:

18	Dec.	31	Automobile Expense			4	0	80							18
19			Postage Expense			3	9	50							19
20			Travel and Entertainment Expense			3	0	25							20
21			Miscellaneous Expense			2	8	25							21
22			James Maple, Drawing			3	0	00							22
23			Cash							1	6	8	80		23
24			Replenishment of petty cash fund												24

Note two important aspects of the functioning of a petty cash fund:

1. Once the fund is established by debiting Petty Cash and crediting Cash, no further entries are made to Petty Cash. Notice in the journal entry to replenish the fund that the debits are to appropriate expense accounts and the credit is to Cash. Only if the amount of the fund itself is being changed would there be a debit or credit to Petty Cash.

2. The petty cash payments record is strictly a supplement to the regular accounting records. Because it is not a journal, no posting is done from this record. A separate entry must be made in the journal to replenish the fund and update the expense accounts.

FIGURE 7-13   Maple Consulting's Petty Cash Payments Record

PETTY CASH PAYMENTS FOR THE MONTH OF December 20—   PAGE 1

	DAY	DESCRIPTION		VOU. NO.	TOTAL AMOUNT	DISTRIBUTION OF PAYMENTS					
						AUTO EXP.	POST. EXP.	TRAVEL/ ENTERT. EXP.	MISC. EXP.	ACCOUNT	AMOUNT
1	1	Received in fund	200.00								
2	5	Automobile repairs		1	32 80	32 80					
3	8	Client luncheon		2	15 75			15 75			
4	9	James Maple, personal use		3	30 00					James Maple, Drawing	30 00
5	15	Typewriter repairs		4	28 25				28 25		
6	17	Traveling expenses		5	14 50			14 50			
7	19	Washing automobile		6	8 00	8 00					
8	22	Postage expense		7	9 50		9 50				
9	29	Postage stamps		8	30 00		30 00				
10					168 80	40 80	39 50	30 25	28 25		30 00
11	31	Balance	31.20								
12	31	Replenished fund	168.80								
13		Total	200.00								

Credit to replenish petty cash fund

Debits to replenish petty cash fund

> **LEARNING KEY:** Once the petty cash fund is established, an entry is made to Petty Cash only if the amount of the fund is being changed.

THE CHANGE FUND AND CASH SHORT AND OVER

LO4 Establish a change fund and use the cash short and over account.

Businesses generally must be able to make change when customers use cash to pay for goods or services received. To do so, generally it is a good idea to establish a **change fund**. A change fund is a supply of currency and coins kept in a cash register or cash drawer for use in handling cash sales.

Establishing and Operating the Change Fund

The journal entries for establishing and maintaining a change fund are very similar to the ones just used for petty cash. To establish a change fund of $200.00 on June 1, the following entry would be made:

8	June 1	Change Fund		2 0 0 00		8
9		Cash			2 0 0 00	9
10		Establish change fund				10

At the end of the day, cash received during the day is deposited, but the change fund is held back for use the following business day. For example, if cash sales of $1,250.00 were made on June 3, the cash drawer would contain $1,450.00, as follows:

Change fund	$ 200.00
Cash sales	1,250.00
Total cash on hand	$1,450.00

The $1,250 would be deposited in the bank and the following journal entry would be made:

12	June 3	Cash		1 2 5 0 00		12
13		Sales			1 2 5 0 00	13
14		Cash Sales				14

Notice the additional similarity between the change fund and the petty cash fund. Once the change fund is established by a debit to Change Fund and a credit to Cash, no further entries are made to the change fund. Only if the amount of the change fund itself is being changed would there be a debit or credit to Change Fund.

> **LEARNING KEY:** Once the change fund is established, an entry is made to Change Fund only if the amount of the fund is being changed.

Cash Short and Over

An unavoidable part of the change-making process is that errors can occur. It is important to know whether such errors have occurred and how to account for them.

Businesses commonly use cash registers with tapes that accumulate a record of the day's receipts. The amount of cash according to the tapes plus the amount of the change fund can be compared with the amount of cash in the register to determine any error. For example, assume a cash shortage is identified for June 19.

Change fund	$ 200.00
Receipts per register tapes	963.00
Cash count	1,161.00
Cash shortage	$ 2.00

Similarly, assume a cash overage is identified for June 20.

Change fund	$ 200.00
Receipts per register tapes	814.00
Cash count	1,015.00
Cash overage	$ 1.00

We account for such errors by using an account called Cash Short and Over. In T account form, Cash Short and Over appears as follows:

Cash Short and Over	
Shortage (Expense)	Overage (Revenue)

The register tapes on June 19 showed receipts of $963.00 and the change fund was $200.00, but only $1,161.00 in cash was counted. The journal entry on June 19 to record the revenues and cash shortage (remember that we hold back the change fund) would be:

18	June	19	Cash				9	6	1	00							18
19			Cash Short and Over						2	00							19
20			Service Fees									9	6	3	00	20
21			Record cash shortage													21

The entry on June 20 to record the revenues and cash overage (holding back the change fund) would be:

23	June	20	Cash				8	1	5	00							23
24			Service Fees									8	1	4	00	24
25			Cash Short and Over											1	00	25
26			Record cash overage													26

The cash short and over account is used to accumulate cash shortages and overages throughout the accounting period. At the end of the period, a debit balance in the account (a net shortage) is treated as an expense. A credit balance in the account (a net overage) is treated as revenue.

Learning Objectives	Key Points to Remember
1 **Describe how to open and use a checking account.**	Three steps to follow in preparing a check are: 1. Complete the check stub or register. 2. Enter the date, payee name, and amount on the check. 3. Sign the check.
2 **Prepare a bank reconciliation and related journal entries.**	The most common reasons for differences between the book and bank cash balances are: 1. Outstanding checks 2. Deposits in transit 3. Bank service charges 4. Bank collections for the depositor 5. NSF checks 6. Errors by the bank or the depositor Three steps to follow in preparing a bank reconciliation are: 1. Identify deposits in transit and any related errors. 2. Identify outstanding checks and any related errors. 3. Identify additional reconciling items. Only two kinds of items on a bank reconciliation require journal entries: 1. Errors on the depositor's books. 2. Bank additions and deductions that do not already appear in the accounting records.
3 **Establish and use a petty cash fund.**	Two important aspects of the functioning of a petty cash fund are: 1. Once the fund is established, subsequent entries do not affect the petty cash account balance, unless the size of the fund itself is being changed. 2. The petty cash payments record is supplemental to the regular accounting records. No posting is done from this record.
4 **Establish a change fund and use the cash short and over account.**	A change fund is established by debiting Change Fund and crediting Cash. Cash shortages and overages are accounted for using the cash short and over account. A debit balance in this account represents expense; a credit balance represents revenue.

Reflection: Answering the Opening Question

Checks John wrote that have not been presented to the bank for payment are considered outstanding checks. In reconciling the book and bank balances, outstanding checks are subtracted from the bank statement balance to determine the adjusted bank balance. If the outstanding checks are not subtracted correctly on the bank reconciliation, John could overstate his cash balance and risk writing a check for funds he does not have in the bank. This would harm John's credibility with both the bank and his creditors.

KEY TERMS

ABA (American Bankers Association) Number, (222)   The small fraction printed in the upper right-hand corner of each check.

automated teller machines (ATMs), (224)   Machines used by depositors to make withdrawals or deposits at any time.

bank reconciliation, (229)   A report used to bring the book and bank balances into agreement.

bank statement, (227)   A statement of account issued by a bank to each depositor once a month.

blank endorsement, (222)   An endorsement where the depositor simply signs the back of the check, making the check payable to any bearer.

canceled checks, (227)   The depositor's checks paid by the bank during the bank statement period.

cash, (222)   To a business, cash includes currency, coins, checks received from customers, money orders, and bank cashier's checks.

change fund, (237)   A supply of currency and coins kept in a cash register or cash drawer for use in handling cash sales.

check, (225)   A document ordering a bank to pay cash from a depositor's account.

check stub, (225)   In some checkbooks, a document attached to a check that contains space for relevant information about the check.

credit memos, (230)   Items that the bank adds to the account.

debit memos, (230)   Items that the bank deducts from the account.

deposit ticket, (222)   A form showing a detailed listing of items being deposited.

deposits in transit, (229)   Deposits that have not reached or been recorded by the bank before the bank statement is prepared.

drawee, (225)   The bank on which the check is drawn.

drawer, (225)   The depositor who orders the bank to pay the cash.

electronic funds transfer (EFT), (233)   A process using a computer rather than paper checks to complete transactions with the bank.

endorsement, (222)   Stamping or writing the depositor's name and sometimes other information on the back of the check.

internal control, (222)   A set of procedures designed to ensure proper accounting for transactions.

magnetic ink character recognition (MICR) code, (222)   The character code used to print identifying information on the lower left front side of each check.

not sufficient funds (NSF) checks, (229)   Checks deposited by the depositor that are not paid because the drawer did not have sufficient funds.

outstanding checks, (229)   Checks issued during the bank statement period that have not been presented to the bank for payment before the statement is prepared.

payee, (225)   The person being paid the cash.

petty cash fund, (233)   A fund established to pay for small items with cash.

petty cash payments record, (234)   A special multi-column record that supplements the regular accounting records.

petty cash voucher, (234)   A receipt that is prepared for every payment from the petty cash fund.

restrictive endorsement, (222)   An endorsement where the depositor adds words such as "For deposit" to restrict the payment of the check.

service charges, (229)   Bank charges for services such as check printing and processing.

signature card, (222)   A card that is completed and signed by each person authorized to sign checks.

DEMONSTRATION PROBLEM

Jason Kuhn's check stubs indicated a balance of $4,673.12 for Kuhn's Wilderness Outfitters on March 31. This included a record of a deposit of $926.10 mailed to the bank on March 30, but not credited to Kuhn's account until April 1. In addition, the following checks were outstanding on March 31:

No. 462,	$524.26
No. 465,	$213.41
No. 473,	$543.58
No. 476,	$351.38
No. 477,	$197.45

The bank statement showed a balance of $5,419.00 as of March 31. The bank statement included a service charge of $4.10 with the date of March 29. In matching the canceled checks and record of deposits with the stubs, it was discovered that check no. 456, to Office Suppliers, Inc., for $93.00 was erroneously recorded on the stub for $39.00. This caused the bank balance on that stub and those following to be $54.00 too large. It was also discovered that an ATM withdrawal of $100.00 for personal use was not recorded on the books.

Kuhn maintains a $200.00 petty cash fund. His petty cash payments record showed the following totals at the end of March of the current year.

Automobile expense	$ 32.40
Postage expense	27.50
Charitable contributions expense	35.00
Telephone expense	6.20
Travel and entertainment expense	38.60
Miscellaneous expense	17.75
Jason Kuhn, Drawing	40.00
Total	$197.45

This left a balance of $2.55 in the petty cash fund.

REQUIRED

1. Prepare a bank reconciliation for Jason Kuhn as of March 31, 20--.

2. Journalize the entries that should be made by Kuhn on his books as of March 31, 20--: (a) as a result of the bank reconciliation and (b) to replenish the petty cash fund.

3. Show proof that, after these entries, the total of the cash and petty cash account balances equals $4,715.02.

(continued)

Solution

1.

Kuhn's Wilderness Outfitters Bank Reconciliation March 31, 20 - -					
Bank statement balance, March 31				$5 4 1 9 00
Add deposit in transit				9 2 6 10
				$6 3 4 5 10
Deduct outstanding checks:				
No. 462	$ 5 2 4 26			
No. 465	2 1 3 41			
No. 473	5 4 3 58			
No. 476	3 5 1 38			
No. 477	1 9 7 45	1 8 3 0 08		
Adjusted bank balance		$4 5 1 5 02		
Book balance, March 31		$4 6 7 3 12		
Deduct: Bank service charge	$ 4 10			
Error on check no. 456	5 4 00			
Unrecorded ATM withdrawal	1 0 0 00	1 5 8 10		
Adjusted book balance		$4 5 1 5 02		

2a.

				Debit	Credit	
3						3
4	20-- Mar.	31	Miscellaneous Expense	4 10		4
5			Accounts Payable—Office Supp., Inc	5 4 00		5
6			Jason Kuhn, Drawing	1 0 0 00		6
7			Cash		1 5 8 10	7
8			Bank transactions for March			8
9						9
b. 10		31	Automobile Expense	3 2 40		10
11			Postage Expense	2 7 50		11
12			Charitable Contributions Expense	3 5 00		12
13			Telephone Expense	6 20		13
14			Travel and Entertainment Expense	3 8 60		14
15			Miscellaneous Expense	1 7 75		15
16			Jason Kuhn, Drawing	4 0 00		16
17			Cash		1 9 7 45	17
18			Replenishment of petty cash			18
19			fund			19
20						20
21						21

3. Cash in bank:

Check stub balance, March 31	$4,673.12
Less bank charges	158.10
Adjusted cash in bank	$4,515.02

Cash on hand:

Petty cash fund	$ 2.55
Add replenishment	197.45
Adjusted cash on hand	$ 200.00
Total cash in bank and petty cash on hand	$4,715.02

REVIEW QUESTIONS

1. Why must a signature card be filled out and signed to open a checking account?

2. Explain the difference between a blank endorsement and a restrictive endorsement.

3. Who are the three parties to every check?

4. What are the three steps to follow in preparing a check?

5. What are the most common reasons for differences between the book and bank cash balances?

6. What are the three steps to follow in preparing a bank reconciliation?

7. What two kinds of items on a bank reconciliation require journal entries?

8. Name four applications of electronic funds transfer in current use.

9. What is the purpose of a petty cash fund?

10. What should be prepared every time a petty cash payment is made?

11. At what two times should the petty cash fund be replenished?

12. From what source is the information obtained for issuing a check to replenish the petty cash fund?

13. At what two times would an entry be made affecting the change fund?

14. What does a debit balance in the cash short and over account represent? What does a credit balance in this account represent?

MANAGING YOUR WRITING

The current month's bank statement for your account arrives in the mail. In reviewing the statement, you notice a deposit listed for $400.00 that you did not make. It has been credited in error to your account.

Discuss whether you have an ethical or legal obligation to inform the bank of the error. What action should you take?

ETHICS CASE

Ben Thomas works as a teller for First National Bank. When he arrived at work on Friday, the branch manager, Frank Mills, asked him to get his cash drawer out early because the head teller, Naomi Ray, was conducting a surprise cash count for all the tellers. Surprise cash counts are usually done four or five times a year by the branch manager or the head teller and once or twice a year by internal auditors. Ben's drawer was $100.00 short and his reconciliation tape showed that he was in balance on Thursday night. Naomi asked Ben for an explanation, and Ben immediately took $100.00 out of his pocket and handed it to her. He went on to explain he needed the cash to buy prescriptions for his son and pay for groceries and intended to put the $100.00 back in his cash drawer on Monday, which was pay day. He also told Naomi that this was the first time he had ever "borrowed" money from his cash drawer and that he would never do it again.

(continued)

1. What are the ethical considerations in this case from both Ben's and Naomi's perspectives?

2. What options does Naomi have to address this problem?

3. Assume Naomi chooses to inform the branch manager. Write a short incident report describing the findings.

4. In small groups come up with as many ideas as possible on how to safeguard cash on hand in a bank (petty cash, teller drawer cash, and vault cash) from employee theft and mismanagement.

WEB WORK

Your business will, at some point in time, need to write a check to pay a vendor or an employee, or to cover an unforeseen expense. What do you need to do to open an account? What are some of the costs and restrictions a business owner needs to be aware of? Check out these sites for information on checking accounts:
http://www.bankofamerica.com/businesscenter/
http://www.banking.us.hsbc.com/businessbanking/
(http://heintz.swcollege.com)

SERIES A EXERCISES

EXERCISE 7-1A **(LO1)** **CHECKING ACCOUNT TERMS** Match the following words with their definitions.

1. An endorsement where the depositor simply signs on the back of the check

2. An endorsement that contains words like "For Deposit Only" together with the signature

3. A card filled out and signed by each person authorized to sign checks on an account

4. The depositor who orders the bank to pay cash from the depositor's account

5. The bank on which the check is drawn

6. The person being paid the cash

7. A check that has been paid by the bank and is being returned to the depositor

a. signature card

b. canceled check

c. blank endorsement

d. drawer

e. restrictive endorsement

f. drawee

g. payee

EXERCISE 7-2A **(LO1)** **PREPARE DEPOSIT TICKET** Based on the following information, prepare a deposit ticket.

Date:		January 15, 20--
Currency:		$334.00
Coin:		26.00
Checks:	No. 4-11	311.00
	No. 80-322	108.00
	No. 3-9	38.00

EXERCISE 7-3A (LO1) **PREPARE CHECK AND STUB** Based on the following information, prepare a check and stub.

Date:	January 15, 20--
Balance brought forward:	$2.841.50
Deposit:	(from Exercise 7-2A)
Check to:	J.M. Suppliers
Amount:	$150.00
For:	Office Supplies
Signature:	Sign your name

EXERCISE 7-4A (LO2) **BANK RECONCILIATION TERMINOLOGY** In a format similar to the following, indicate whether the action at the left will result in an addition to (+) or subtraction from (–) the ending bank balance or the ending checkbook balance.

	Ending Bank Balance	Ending Checkbook Balance
1. Deposits in transit to the bank	_____	_____
2. Error in checkbook: check recorded as $32.00 but was actually for $23.00	_____	_____
3. Service fee charged by bank	_____	_____
4. Outstanding checks	_____	_____
5. NSF check deposited earlier	_____	_____
6. Error in checkbook: check recorded as $22.00 but was actually for $220.00	_____	_____
7. Bank credit memo advising they collected a note for us	_____	_____

EXERCISE 7-5A (LO2) **PREPARE JOURNAL ENTRIES FOR BANK RECONCILIATION** Based on bank reconciliation information shown below, prepare the journal entries.

Lisa Choy Associates Bank Reconciliation July 31, 20 - -			
Bank statement balance, July 31			$2 7 6 4 40
Add deposits in transit	$ 2 5 0 00		
	9 8 00	3 4 8 00	
		$3 1 1 2 40	
Deduct outstanding checks:			
No. 387	$ 3 5 3 50		
No. 393	1 7 80		
No. 398	3 3 20	4 0 4 50	
Adjusted bank balance		$2 7 0 7 90	
Book balance, July 31			$3 1 3 0 90
Deduct: Error on check no. 394*	$ 2 3 00		
NSF check	3 9 0 00		
Bank service charge	1 0 00	4 2 3 00	
Adjusted book balance		$2 7 0 7 90	
*Accounts Payable was debited in original entry.			

EXERCISE 7-6A   (LO3)   PETTY CASH JOURNAL ENTRIES Based on the following petty cash information, prepare (a) the journal entry to establish a petty cash fund, and (b) the journal entry to replenish the petty cash fund.

On January 1, 20--, a check was written in the amount of $200.00 to establish a petty cash fund. During January, the following vouchers were written for cash removed from the petty cash drawer:

Voucher No.	Account Debited	Amount
1	Telephone Expense	$17.50
2	Automobile Expense	33.00
3	Joseph Levine, Drawing	70.00
4	Postage Expense	12.50
5	Charitable Contributions Expense	15.00
6	Miscellaneous Expense	49.00

EXERCISE 7-7A   (LO4)   CASH SHORT AND OVER ENTRIES Based on the following information, prepare the weekly entries for cash receipts from service fees and cash short and over. A change fund of $100.00 is maintained.

Date	Change Fund	Cash Register Receipt Amount	Actual Cash Counted
April 2	$100.00	$268.50	$366.50
9	100.00	237.75	333.50
16	100.00	309.25	411.00
23	100.00	226.50	324.00
30	100.00	318.00	422.00

SERIES A PROBLEMS

PROBLEM 7-1A   (LO2)   BANK RECONCILIATION AND RELATED JOURNAL ENTRIES The balance in the checking account of Violette Enterprises as of October 31 is $4,765.00. The bank statement shows an ending balance of $4,235.00. The following information is discovered by (1) tracing last month's deposits in transit to this month's bank statement, (2) comparing checks deposited and written per books and per bank in the current month, and (3) noting service charges and other debit and credit memos shown on the bank statement.

Deposits in transit:	10/26	$175.00
	10/28	334.00
Outstanding checks:	No. 1764	$ 47.00
	No. 1767	146.00
	No. 1781	369.00
Unrecorded ATM withdrawal*:		180.00
Bank service charge:		43.00
NSF check:		370.00
Error on check no. 1754	Checkbook shows it was for $72.00, but was actually written for $62.00. Accounts Payable was debited.	

*Funds were withdrawn by Guy Violette for personal use.

1. Prepare a bank reconciliation as of October 31, 20--.

2. Prepare the required journal entries.

PROBLEM 7-2A   (LO2)

BANK RECONCILIATION AND RELATED JOURNAL ENTRIES The balance in the checking account of Lyle's Salon as of November 30 is $3,282.95. The bank statement shows an ending balance of $2,127.00. By examining last month's bank reconciliation, comparing the checks deposited and written per books and per bank in November, and noting the service charges and other debit and credit memos shown on the bank statement, the following were found:

a. An ATM withdrawal of $150.00 on November 18 by Lyle for personal use was not recorded on the books.

b. A bank debit memo issued for an NSF check from a customer of $19.50.

c. A bank credit memo issued for interest of $19.00 earned during the month.

d. On November 30, a deposit of $1,177.00 was made, which is not shown on the bank statement.

e. A bank debit memo issued for $17.50 for bank service charges.

f. Checks for the amounts of $185.00, $21.00, and $9.40 were written during November but have not yet been received by the bank.

g. The reconciliation from the previous month showed outstanding checks of $271.95. One of those checks for $18.65 has not yet been received by the bank.

h. Check No. 523 written to a creditor in the amount of $372.90 was recorded in the books as $327.90.

REQUIRED

1. Prepare a bank reconciliation as of November 30.

2. Prepare the required journal entries.

PROBLEM 7-3A   (LO3)   **PETTY CASH RECORD AND JOURNAL ENTRIES** On May 1, a petty cash fund was established for $150.00. The following vouchers were issued during May:

Date	Voucher No.	Purpose	Amount
May 1	1	postage due	$ 3.50
3	2	office supplies	11.00
5	3	auto repair (miscellaneous)	22.00
7	4	drawing (Joy Adams)	25.00
11	5	donation (Red Cross)	10.00
15	6	travel expenses	28.00
22	7	postage stamps	3.50
26	8	telephone call	5.00
30	9	donation (Boy Scouts)	30.00

REQUIRED

1. Prepare the journal entry to establish the petty cash fund.

2. Record the vouchers in the petty cash record. Total and rule the petty cash record.

3. Prepare the journal entry to replenish the petty cash fund. Make the appropriate entry in the petty cash record.

PROBLEM 7-4A   **(LO4)**   **CASH SHORT AND OVER ENTRIES** Listed below are the weekly cash register tape amounts for service fees and the related cash counts during the month of July. A change fund of $100.00 is maintained.

Date	Change Fund	Cash Register Receipt Amount	Actual Cash Counted
July 2	$100.00	$289.50	$387.00
9	100.00	311.50	411.50
16	100.00	306.00	408.50
23	100.00	317.50	415.00
30	100.00	296.00	399.50

REQUIRED

1. Prepare the journal entries to record the cash service fees and cash short and over for each of the five weeks.

2. Post to the cash short and over account (use account no. 573).

3. Determine the ending balance of the cash short and over account. Does it represent an expense or revenue?

SERIES B EXERCISES

EXERCISE 7-1B   **(LO1)**   **CHECKING ACCOUNT TERMS** Match the following words with their definitions.

1. Banking number used to identify checks for deposit tickets

2. A card filled out to open a checking account

3. A machine from which withdrawals can be taken or deposits made to accounts

4. A place where relevant information is recorded about a check

5. A set of procedures designed to ensure proper accounting for transactions

6. A statement of account issued to each depositor once a month

7. A detailed listing of items being deposited to an account

a. bank statement
b. deposit ticket
c. signature card
d. internal control
e. check stub
f. ATM
g. ABA number

EXERCISE 7-2B   **(LO1)**   **PREPARE DEPOSIT TICKET** Based on the following information, prepare a deposit ticket.

Date:		November 15, 20--
Currency:		$283.00
Coin:		19.00
Checks:	No. 3-22	201.00
	No. 19-366	114.00
	No. 3-2	28.00

EXERCISE 7-3B   (LO1)   **PREPARE CHECK AND STUB** Based on the following information, prepare a check and stub.

Date:	November 15, 20--
Balance brought forward:	$3,181.00
Deposit:	(from Exercise 7-2B)
Check to:	R.J. Smith Co.
Amount:	$120.00
For:	Payment on account
Signature:	Sign your name

EXERCISE 7-4B   (LO2)   **BANK RECONCILIATION TERMINOLOGY** In a format similar to the following, indicate whether the action at the left will result in an addition to (+) or subtraction from (–) the ending bank balance or the ending checkbook balance.

	Ending Bank Balance	Ending Checkbook Balance
1. Service fee of $12 charged by bank	_____	_____
2. Outstanding checks	_____	_____
3. Error in checkbook: check recorded as $36.00 was actually for $28.00	_____	_____
4. NSF check deposited earlier	_____	_____
5. Bank credit memo advising they collected a note for us	_____	_____
6. Deposits in transit to the bank	_____	_____
7. Error in checkbook: check recorded as $182.00 was actually for $218.00	_____	_____

EXERCISE 7-5B   (LO2)   **PREPARE JOURNAL ENTRIES FOR BANK RECONCILIATION** Based on the bank reconciliation information that appears below, prepare the journal entries.

Regina D'Alfonso Associates Bank Reconciliation July 31, 20 - -			
Bank statement balance, July 31			$1,784.00
Add deposits in transit	$418.50		
	100.50	519.00	
			$2,303.00
Deduct outstanding checks:			
No. 185	$206.50		
No. 203	317.40		
No. 210	56.10	580.00	
Adjusted bank balance			$1,723.00
Book balance, July 31			$1,794.00
Add error on check no. 191*			10.00
			$1,804.00
Deduct: NSF check	$66.00		
Bank service charge	15.00	81.00	
Adjusted book balance			$1,723.00
*Accounts Payable was debited in original entry.			

EXERCISE 7-6B   **(LO3)**   **PETTY CASH JOURNAL ENTRIES** Based on the following petty cash information, prepare (a) the journal entry to establish a petty cash fund, and (b) the journal entry to replenish the petty cash fund.

On October 1, 20--, a check was written in the amount of $200.00 to establish a petty cash fund. During October, the following vouchers were written for cash taken from the petty cash drawer:

Voucher No.	Account Debited	Amount
1	Postage Expense	$13.00
2	Miscellaneous Expense	17.00
3	John Flanagan, Drawing	45.00
4	Telephone Expense	36.00
5	Charitable Contributions Expense	50.00
6	Automobile Expense	29.00

EXERCISE 7-7B   **(LO4)**   **CASH SHORT AND OVER ENTRIES** Based on the following information, prepare the weekly entries for cash receipts from service fees and cash short and over. A change fund of $100.00 is maintained

Date	Change Fund	Cash Register Receipt Amount	Actual Cash Counted
June 1	$100.00	$330.00	$433.00
8	100.00	297.00	400.00
15	100.00	233.00	331.00
22	100.00	302.00	396.50
29	100.00	316.00	412.00

SERIES B PROBLEMS

PROBLEM 7-1B   **(LO2)**   **BANK RECONCILIATION AND RELATED JOURNAL ENTRIES** The balance in the checking account of Kyros Enterprises as of November 30 is $3,004.00. The bank statement shows an ending balance of $2,525.00. The following information is discovered by (1) tracing last month's deposits in transit to this month's bank statement, (2) comparing checks deposited and written per books and per bank in the current month, and (3) noting service charges and other debit and credit memos shown on the bank statement.

Deposits in transit:	11/21	$125.00
	11/26	200.00
Outstanding checks:	No. 322	17.00
	No. 324	105.00
	No. 327	54.00
Unrecorded ATM withdrawal*:		100.00
Bank service charge:		25.00
NSF check:		185.00
Error on check no. 321	Checkbook shows it was for $44.00, but was actually written for $64.00. Accounts Payable was debited.	

*Funds were withdrawn by Steve Kyros for personal use.

REQUIRED

1. Prepare a bank reconciliation as of November 30, 20--.

2. Prepare the required journal entries.

PROBLEM 7-2B   (LO2)

BANK RECONCILIATION AND RELATED JOURNAL ENTRIES The balance in the checking account of Tori's Health Center as of April 30 is $4,690.30. The bank statement shows an ending balance of $3,275.60. By examining last month's bank reconciliation, comparing the checks deposited and written per books and per bank in April, and noting the service charges and other debit and credit memos shown on the bank statement, the following were found:

a. An ATM withdrawal of $200.00 on April 20 by Tori for personal use was not recorded on the books.

b. A bank debit memo issued for an NSF check from a customer of $29.10.

c. A bank credit memo issued for interest of $28.00 earned during the month.

d. On April 30, a deposit of $1,592.00 was made, which is not shown on the bank statement.

e. A bank debit memo issued for $24.50 for bank service charges.

f. Checks for the amounts of $215.00, $71.00, and $24.30 were written during April but have not yet been received by the bank.

g. The reconciliation from the previous month showed outstanding checks of $418.25. One of these checks for $38.60 has not yet been received by the bank.

h. Check No. 422 written to a creditor in the amount of $217.90 was recorded in the books as $271.90.

REQUIRED

1. Prepare a bank reconciliation as of April 30.

2. Prepare the required journal entries.

PROBLEM 7-3B   (LO3)

PETTY CASH RECORD AND JOURNAL ENTRIES On July 1, a petty cash fund was established for $100.00. The following vouchers were issued during July:

Date	Voucher No.	Purpose	Amount
July 1	1	office supplies	$ 3.00
3	2	donation (Goodwill)	15.00
5	3	travel expenses	5.00
7	4	postage due	2.00
8	5	office supplies	4.00
11	6	postage due	3.50
15	7	telephone call	5.00
21	8	travel expenses	11.00
25	9	withdrawal by owner (L. Ortiz)	20.00
26	10	copier repair (miscellaneous)	18.50

REQUIRED

1. Prepare the journal entry to establish the petty cash fund.

(continued)

2. Record the vouchers in the petty cash record. Total and rule the petty cash record.

3. Prepare the journal entry to replenish the petty cash fund. Make the appropriate entry in the petty cash record.

PROBLEM 7-4B   **(LO4)**   **CASH SHORT AND OVER ENTRIES**   Listed below are the weekly cash register tape amounts for service fees and the related cash counts during the month of July. A change fund of $200.00 is maintained.

Date	Change Fund	Cash Register Receipt Amount	Actual Cash Counted
Aug. 1	$200.00	$292.50	$495.00
8	200.00	305.00	501.50
15	200.00	286.00	486.00
22	200.00	330.25	532.75
29	200.00	298.50	495.00

REQUIRED

1. Prepare the journal entries to record the cash service fees and cash short and over for each of the five weeks.

2. Post to the cash short and over account. (Use account no. 573.)

3. Determine the ending balance of the cash short and over account. Does it represent an expense or revenue?

CHALLENGE PROBLEM

Susan Panera is preparing the June 30 bank reconciliation for Panera Bakery. She discovers the following items that explain the difference between the cash balance on her books and the balance as reported by Lawrence Bank.

1. An ATM withdrawal of $200.00 for personal use was not recorded by Susan.

2. A deposit of $850.00 was recorded by Susan but has not been received by Lawrence Bank as of June 30.

3. A check written in payment on account to Jayhawk Supply for $340.00 was recorded by Susan as $430.00 and by Lawrence Bank as $530.00

4. An ATM deposit of $350.00 was recorded twice by Lawrence Bank.

5. An electronic funds transfer of $260.00 to Sunflower Mills as a payment on account was not recorded by Susan.

6. Check No. 103 for $235.00 and No. 110 for $127.00 had not cleared Lawrence Bank as of June 30.

REQUIRED

1. Prepare the journal entries required to correct Panera Bakery's books as of June 30.

2. Prepare the journal entries required to correct Lawrence Bank's books as of June 30.

MASTERY PROBLEM

Turner Excavation maintains a checking account and has decided to open a petty cash fund. The following petty cash fund transactions occurred during July.

July 2   Established a petty cash fund by issuing Check No. 301 for $100.00.

5   Paid $25.00 from the petty cash fund for postage. Voucher No. 1.

7   Paid $30.00 from the petty cash fund for delivery of flowers for the secretaries (Miscellaneous Expense). Voucher No. 2.

8   Paid $20.00 from the petty cash fund to repair a tire on the company truck. Voucher No. 3.

12   Paid $22.00 from the petty cash fund for a newspaper advertisement. Voucher No. 4.

13   Issued Check No. 303 to replenish the petty cash fund. (Total and rule the petty cash payments record. Record the balance and the amount needed to replenish the fund in the Description column of the petty cash payments record.)

20   Paid $26.00 from the petty cash fund to reimburse an employee for expenses incurred to repair the company truck. Voucher No. 5.

24   Paid $12.50 from the petty cash fund for telephone calls made from a phone booth. Voucher No. 6.

28   Paid $25.00 from the petty cash fund as a contribution to the YMCA. Voucher No. 7.

31   Issued Check No. 308 to replenish the petty cash fund. (Total and rule the petty cash payments record. Record the balance and the amount needed to replenish the fund in the Description column of the petty cash payments record.)

The following additional transactions occurred during July.

July 5   Issued Check No. 302 to pay office rent, $650.00.

15   Issued Check No. 304 for office equipment, $525.00.

17   Issued Check No. 305 for the purchase of supplies, $133.00.

18   Issued Check No. 306 to pay attorney fees, $1,000.00.

30   Issued Check No. 307 to pay newspaper for an advertisement, $200.20.

REQUIRED

1.   Record the petty cash transactions in a petty cash payments record.

2.   Make all required general journal entries for the cash transactions. (Note: The petty cash fund was established and replenished twice during July.)

3.   The following bank statement (Figure 7-14) was received in the mail. Deposits were made on July 6 for $3,500.00 and on July 29 for $2,350.00. The checkbook balance on July 31 is $4,331.55. Notice the discrepancy in Check No. 302 that cleared the bank for $655.00. This check was written on July 5 for rent expense, but was incorrectly entered on the check stub and in the journal as $650.00. Prepare a bank reconciliation and make any necessary journal entries as of July 31.

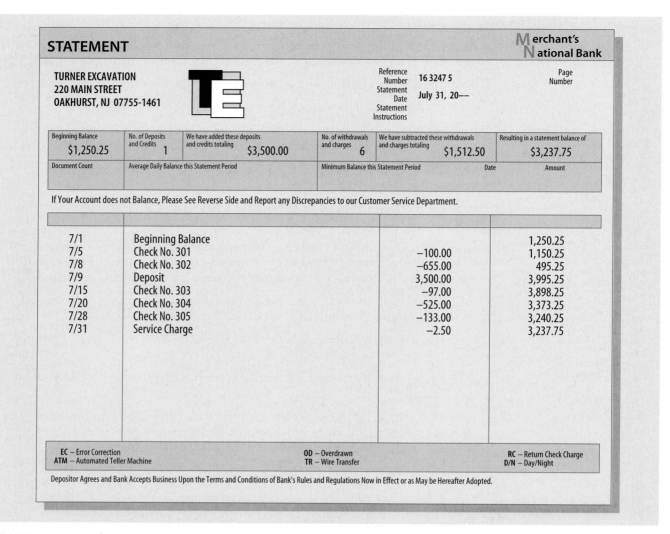

STATEMENT

Merchant's **N**ational Bank

TURNER EXCAVATION
220 MAIN STREET
OAKHURST, NJ 07755-1461

Reference Number	16 3247 5
Statement Date	July 31, 20––
Statement Instructions	

Page Number

Beginning Balance	No. of Deposits and Credits	We have added these deposits and credits totaling	No. of withdrawals and charges	We have subtracted these withdrawals and charges totaling	Resulting in a statement balance of
$1,250.25	1	$3,500.00	6	$1,512.50	$3,237.75

Document Count	Average Daily Balance this Statement Period	Minimum Balance this Statement Period	Date	Amount

If Your Account does not Balance, Please See Reverse Side and Report any Discrepancies to our Customer Service Department.

7/1	Beginning Balance		1,250.25
7/5	Check No. 301	−100.00	1,150.25
7/8	Check No. 302	−655.00	495.25
7/9	Deposit	3,500.00	3,995.25
7/15	Check No. 303	−97.00	3,898.25
7/20	Check No. 304	−525.00	3,373.25
7/28	Check No. 305	−133.00	3,240.25
7/31	Service Charge	−2.50	3,237.75

EC – Error Correction	**OD** – Overdrawn	**RC** – Return Check Charge
ATM – Automated Teller Machine	**TR** – Wire Transfer	**D/N** – Day/Night

Depositor Agrees and Bank Accepts Business Upon the Terms and Conditions of Bank's Rules and Regulations Now in Effect or as May be Hereafter Adopted.

FIGURE 7-14   Bank Statement

Self-Study Test Questions

True/False

1. The primary purpose of a bank reconciliation is to detect and correct errors made by the bank in its records. _____

2. NSF checks are subtracted from the bank's ending balance on the bank reconciliation. _____

3. The bank service charge requires a journal entry to record its effects on the cash account. _____

4. Unrecorded ATM withdrawals are added to the checkbook balance on the bank reconciliation. _____

5. The petty cash record is a journal of original entry (entries are posted from it to the general ledger accounts). _____

Multiple Choice

1. To establish a petty cash fund, which account is debited? _____

   (a) Cash   (c) Miscellaneous Expense
   (b) Petty Cash   (d) Revenue

2. When the cash short and over account has a debit balance at the end of the month, it is considered _____

   (a) an expense.   (c) revenue.
   (b) an asset.   (d) a liability.

3. Which of these could be *added* to the ending checkbook balance? _____

   (a) service charges   (c) checkbook errors
   (b) NSF check   (d) outstanding checks

4. Which of these is *subtracted* from the ending checkbook balance? _____

   (a) deposits in transit   (c) note collection
   (b) service charges   (d) bank errors

5. Which of these is *added* to the ending bank statement balance? _____

   (a) outstanding checks   (c) checkbook errors
   (b) service charges   (d) deposits in transit

The answers to the Self-Study Test Questions are at the end of the text.

8

Payroll Accounting: Employee Earnings and Deductions

Six months after opening the Be A Sport shop described at the beginning of Chapter 7, John Zenith is pleased to find that the business is doing very well. John has hired a student who is studying accounting at the local college as a part-time bookkeeper. He also has added an employee to help in the shop during peak periods and to keep the inventory organized. He knows he needs to keep a record of the hours worked so that he can compute the employees' earnings. His new bookkeeper says he also needs to withhold certain taxes from the employees' wages. What taxes must John withhold from his employees' wages? How does he determine the correct amounts to withhold?

Careful study of this chapter should enable you to:

LO1 Distinguish between employees and independent contractors.

LO2 Calculate employee earnings and deductions.

LO3 Describe and prepare payroll records.

LO4 Account for employee earnings and deductions.

LO5 Describe various payroll record-keeping methods.

The only contact most of us have with payroll is receiving a paycheck. Few of us have seen the large amount of record keeping needed to produce that paycheck.

Employers maintain complete payroll accounting records for two reasons. First, payroll costs are major expenditures for most companies. Payroll accounting records provide data useful in analyzing and controlling these expenditures. Second, federal, state, and local laws require employers to keep payroll records. Companies must accumulate payroll data both for the business as a whole and for each employee.

There are two major types of payroll taxes: those paid by the employee and those paid by the employer. In this chapter we discuss employee taxes. In Chapter 9 we address payroll taxes paid by the employer.

EMPLOYEES AND INDEPENDENT CONTRACTORS

LO1 Distinguish between employees and independent contractors.

Not every person who performs services for a business is considered an employee. An **employee** works under the control and direction of an employer. Examples include secretaries, maintenance workers, salesclerks, and plant supervisors. In contrast, an **independent contractor** performs a service for a fee and does not work under the control and direction of the company paying for the service. Examples of independent contractors include public accountants, real estate agents, and lawyers.

The distinction between an employee and an independent contractor is important for payroll purposes. Government laws and regulations regarding payroll are much more complex for employees than for independent contractors. Employers must deduct certain taxes, maintain payroll records, and file numerous reports for all employees. Only one form (Form 1099) must be filed for independent contractors. The payroll accounting procedures described in this chapter apply only to employer/employee relationships.

EMPLOYEE EARNINGS AND DEDUCTIONS

LO2 Calculate employee earnings and deductions.

Three steps are required to determine how much to pay an employee for a pay period:

1. Calculate total earnings.
2. Determine the amounts of deductions.
3. Subtract deductions from total earnings to compute net pay.

Salaries and Wages

Compensation for managerial or administrative services usually is called **salary**. A salary normally is expressed in biweekly (every two weeks), monthly, or annual terms. Compensation for skilled or unskilled labor usually is referred to as **wages**. Wages ordinarily are expressed in terms of hours, weeks, or units produced. The terms "salaries" and "wages" often are used interchangeably in practice.

The **Fair Labor Standards Act (FLSA)** requires employers to pay overtime at 1½ times the regular rate to any hourly employee who works over 40 hours in a week. Some companies pay a higher rate for hours worked on Saturday or Sunday, but this is not required by the FLSA. Some salaried employees are exempt from the FLSA rules and are not paid overtime.

Computing Total Earnings

Compensation usually is based on the time worked during the payroll period. Sometimes earnings are based on sales or units of output during the period. When compensation is based on time, a record must be kept of the time worked by each employee. Time cards (Figure 8-1) are helpful for this purpose. In large businesses with computer-based timekeeping systems, plastic cards or badges with special barcodes (Figure 8-2) can be used.

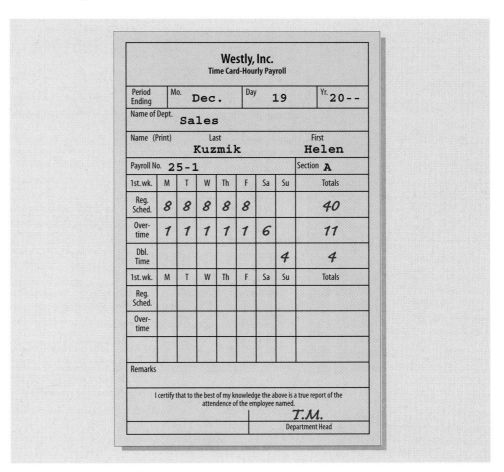

FIGURE 8-1   Time Card

FIGURE 8-2 **Barcode Time Card**

To illustrate the computation of total earnings, look at the time card of Helen Kuzmik in Figure 8-1. The card shows that Kuzmik worked 55 hours for the week:

Regular hours	40 hours
Overtime	11
Double time	4
Total hours worked	55 hours

Kuzmik's regular rate of pay is $12 per hour. She is paid 1½ times the regular rate for hours in excess of 8 on Monday through Friday and any hours worked on Saturday, and twice the regular rate for hours on Sunday. Kuzmik's total earnings for the week ended December 19 are computed as follows:

40 hours × $12	$480
11 hours × $18 (1½ × $12 = $18)	198
4 hours (on Sunday) × $24 (2 × $12 = $24)	96
Total earnings for the week	$774

An employee who is paid a salary may also be entitled to premium pay for overtime. If this is the case, it is necessary to compute the regular hourly rate of pay before computing the overtime rate. To illustrate, assume that Linda Swaney has a salary of $2,288 a month plus 1½ times the regular hourly rate for hours in excess of 40 per week. Swaney's overtime rate of pay is computed as follows:

$2,288 × 12 months	$27,456 annual pay
$27,456 ÷ 52 weeks	$528.00 pay per week
$528.00 ÷ 40 hours	$13.20 pay per regular hour
$13.20 × 1½	$19.80 overtime pay per hour

There are 52 weeks in each year but not 4 weeks in each month. That is why monthly salaries must be annualized in order to determine the hourly rate.

If Swaney worked 50 hours during the week ended December 19, her total earnings for the week would be computed as follows:

40 hours × $13.20	$528.00
10 hours × $19.80	198.00
Total earnings for the week	$726.00

Deductions from Total Earnings

An employee's total earnings are called **gross pay**. Various deductions are made from gross pay to yield take-home or **net pay**. Deductions from gross pay fall into three major categories:

1. Federal (and possibly state and city) income tax withholding

2. Employee FICA tax withholding

3. Voluntary deductions

Income Tax Withholding. Federal law requires employers to withhold certain amounts from the total earnings of each employee. These withholdings are applied toward the payment of the employee's federal income tax. Four factors determine the amount to be withheld from an employee's gross pay each pay period:

1. Total earnings

2. Marital status

3. Number of withholding allowances claimed

4. Length of the pay period

Withholding Allowances. Each employee is required to furnish the employer an Employee's Withholding Allowance Certificate, Form W-4 (Figure 8-3). The marital status of the employee and the number of allowances claimed on Form W-4 determine the dollar amount of earnings subject to withholding. A **withholding allowance** exempts a specific dollar amount of an employee's gross pay from federal income tax withholding. In general, each employee is permitted one personal withholding allowance, one for a spouse who does not also claim an allowance, and one for each dependent.

A withholding certificate completed by Ken Istone is shown in Figure 8-3. Istone is married, has a spouse who does not claim an allowance, and has four dependent children. On line 5 of the W-4 form, Istone claims 6 allowances, calculated as follows:

Personal allowance	1
Spouse allowance	1
Allowances for dependents	4
Total withholding allowances	6

Form **W-4**	**Employee's Withholding Allowance Certificate**	OMB No. 1545-0010
Department of the Treasury Internal Revenue Service	▶ For Privacy Act and Paperwork Reduction Act Notice, see page 2.	**20--**

1	Type or print your first name and middle initial *Ken M.*	Last name *Istone*	2	Your social security number *393 58 8194*

Home address (number and street or rural route)
1546 Swallow Drive

3	☐ Single ☒ Married ☐ Married, but withhold at higher Single rate.

Note: *If married, but legally separated, or spouse is a nonresident alien, check the Single box.*

City or town, state, and Zip code
St. Louis, MO 63144-4752

4   If your last name differs from that on your social security card, check here and call 1-800-772-1213 for a new card . . . . . ▶ ☐

5	Total number of allowances you are claiming (from line H above or from the worksheets on page 2 if they apply) . .	5	*6*
6	Additional amount, if any, you want withheld from each paycheck	6	$

7   I claim exemption from withholding for 1998, and I certify that I meet **BOTH** of the following conditions for exemption:

• Last year I had a right to a refund of **ALL** Federal income tax withheld because I had **NO** tax liability **AND**

• This year I expect a refund of **ALL** Federal income tax withheld because I expect to have **NO** tax liability.

If you meet both conditions, enter "EXEMPT" here   . . . . ▶ | *7* |

Under penalties of perjury, I certify that I am entitled to the number of withholding allowances claimed on this certificate or entitled to claim exempt status.

Employee's signature ▶ *Ken M. Istone*   Date ▶ *January 3*   , 20--

8	Employer's name and address (Employer: Complete 8 and 10 only if sending to IRS)	9	Office code (optional)	10	Employer identification number

Cat. No. 10220Q

FIGURE 8-3   Employee's Withholding Allowance Certificate (Form W-4)

Wage-Bracket Method. Employers generally use the **wage-bracket method** to determine the amount of tax to be withheld from an employee's pay. The employee's gross pay for a specific time period is traced into the appropriate wage-bracket table provided by the Internal Revenue Service (IRS). These tables cover various time periods, and there are separate tables for single and married taxpayers. Copies are provided in *Circular E—Employer's Tax Guide*, which may be obtained from any local IRS office or at the IRS Internet Site.

Portions of weekly income tax wage-bracket withholding tables for single and married persons are illustrated in Figure 8-4. Assume that Ken Istone (who claims 6 allowances) had gross earnings of $545 for the week ending December 19, 20--. The table for married persons is used as follows:

1. Find the row for wages of "at least $540, but less than $550."

2. Find the column headed "6 withholding allowances."

3. Where the row and column cross, $15.00 is given as the amount to be withheld.

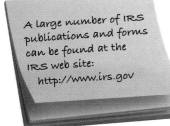

A large number of IRS publications and forms can be found at the IRS web site: http://www.irs.gov

LEARNING KEY: 1. Find the row for wages.
2. Find the column for withholding allowances.
3. Find the amount where they cross.

For state or city income taxes, withholding generally is handled in one of two ways: (1) forms and tables similar to those provided by the IRS are used or (2) an amount equal to a percentage of the federal withholding amount is withheld.

SINGLE Persons   WEEKLY Payroll Period
(For Wages Paid in 20--)

If the wages are		And the number of withholding allowances claimed is										
At least	But less than	0	1	2	3	4	5	6	7	8	9	10
		The amount of income tax to be withheld is										
$300	$310	38	30	22	14	6	0	0	0	0	0	0
310	320	40	32	23	15	7	0	0	0	0	0	0
320	330	41	33	25	17	9	1	0	0	0	0	0
330	340	43	35	26	18	10	2	0	0	0	0	0
340	350	44	36	28	20	12	4	0	0	0	0	0
350	360	46	38	29	21	13	5	0	0	0	0	0
360	370	47	39	31	23	15	7	0	0	0	0	0
370	380	49	41	32	24	16	8	0	0	0	0	0
380	390	50	42	34	26	18	10	2	0	0	0	0
390	400	52	44	35	27	19	11	3	0	0	0	0
400	410	53	45	37	29	21	13	5	0	0	0	0
410	420	55	47	38	30	22	14	6	0	0	0	0
420	430	56	48	40	32	24	16	8	0	0	0	0
430	440	58	50	41	33	25	17	9	1	0	0	0
440	450	59	51	43	35	27	19	11	3	0	0	0
450	460	61	53	44	36	28	20	12	4	0	0	0
460	470	62	54	46	38	30	22	14	6	0	0	0
470	480	64	56	47	39	31	23	15	7	0	0	0
480	490	65	57	49	41	33	25	17	9	0	0	0
490	500	67	59	50	42	34	26	18	10	2	0	0
500	510	68	60	52	44	36	28	20	12	3	0	0
510	520	70	62	53	45	37	29	21	13	5	0	0
520	530	71	63	55	47	39	31	23	15	6	0	0
530	540	73	65	56	48	40	32	24	16	8	0	0
540	550	75	66	58	50	42	34	26	18	9	1	0
550	560	78	68	59	51	43	35	27	19	11	3	0
560	570	81	69	61	53	45	37	29	21	12	4	0
570	580	84	71	62	54	46	38	30	22	14	6	0
580	590	87	72	64	56	48	40	32	24	15	7	0
590	600	89	74	65	57	49	41	33	25	17	9	1
600	610	92	77	67	59	51	43	35	27	18	10	2
610	620	95	80	68	60	52	44	36	28	20	12	4
620	630	98	83	70	62	54	46	38	30	21	13	5
630	640	101	85	71	63	55	47	39	31	23	15	7
640	650	103	88	73	65	57	49	41	33	24	16	8
650	660	106	91	76	66	58	50	42	34	26	18	10
660	670	109	94	79	68	60	52	44	36	27	19	11
670	680	112	97	82	69	61	53	45	37	29	21	13
680	690	115	99	84	71	63	55	47	39	30	22	14
690	700	117	102	87	72	64	56	48	40	32	24	16
700	710	120	105	90	75	66	58	50	42	33	25	17
710	720	123	108	93	78	67	59	51	43	35	27	19
720	730	126	111	96	81	69	61	53	45	36	28	20
730	740	129	113	98	83	70	62	54	46	38	30	22
740	750	131	116	101	86	72	64	56	48	39	31	23
750	760	134	119	104	89	74	65	57	49	41	33	25
760	770	137	122	107	92	77	67	59	51	42	34	26
770	780	140	125	110	95	79	68	60	52	44	36	28
780	790	143	127	112	97	82	70	62	54	45	37	29
790	800	145	130	115	100	85	71	63	55	47	39	31
800	810	148	133	118	103	88	73	65	57	48	40	32
810	820	151	136	121	106	91	76	66	58	50	42	34
820	830	154	139	124	109	93	78	68	60	51	43	35
830	840	157	141	126	111	96	81	69	61	53	45	37
840	850	159	144	129	114	99	84	71	63	54	46	38
850	860	162	147	132	117	102	87	72	64	56	48	40
860	870	165	150	135	120	105	90	74	66	57	49	41
870	880	168	153	138	123	107	92	77	67	59	51	43
880	890	171	155	140	125	110	95	80	69	60	52	44
890	900	173	158	143	128	113	98	83	70	62	54	46
900	910	176	161	146	131	116	101	86	72	63	55	47
910	920	179	164	149	134	119	104	88	73	65	57	49
920	930	182	167	152	137	121	106	91	76	66	58	50
930	940	185	169	154	139	124	109	94	79	68	60	52
940	950	187	172	157	142	127	112	97	82	69	61	53
950	960	190	175	160	145	130	115	100	85	71	63	55
960	970	193	178	163	148	133	118	102	87	72	64	56
970	980	196	181	166	151	135	120	105	90	75	66	58
980	990	199	183	168	153	138	123	108	93	78	67	59
990	1,000	201	186	171	156	141	126	111	96	81	69	61
1,000	1,010	204	189	174	159	144	129	114	99	84	70	62
1,010	1,020	207	192	177	162	147	132	116	101	86	72	64
1,020	1,030	210	195	180	165	149	134	119	104	89	74	65
1,030	1,040	213	197	182	167	152	137	122	107	92	77	67
1,040	1,050	215	200	185	170	155	140	125	110	95	80	68
1,050	1,060	218	203	188	173	158	143	128	113	98	82	70
1,060	1,070	221	206	191	176	161	146	130	115	100	85	71
1,070	1,080	224	209	194	179	163	148	133	118	103	88	73
1,080	1,090	227	211	196	181	166	151	136	121	106	91	76
1,090	1,100	229	214	199	184	169	154	139	124	109	94	79
1,100	1,110	232	217	202	187	172	157	142	127	112	96	81
1,110	1,120	235	220	205	190	175	160	144	129	114	99	84
1,120	1,130	238	223	208	193	177	162	147	132	117	102	87
1,130	1,140	241	225	210	195	180	165	150	135	120	105	90
1,140	1,150	243	228	213	198	183	168	153	138	123	108	93
1,150	1,160	246	231	216	201	186	171	156	141	126	110	95
1,160	1,170	249	234	219	204	189	174	158	143	128	113	98
1,170	1,180	252	237	222	207	191	176	161	146	131	116	101
1,180	1,190	256	239	224	209	194	179	164	149	134	119	104
1,190	1,200	259	242	227	212	197	182	167	152	137	122	107
1,200	1,210	262	245	230	215	200	185	170	155	140	124	109
1,210	1,220	265	248	233	218	203	188	172	157	142	127	112
1,220	1,230	268	251	236	221	205	190	175	160	145	130	115
1,230	1,240	271	254	238	223	208	193	178	163	148	133	118
1,240	1,250	274	257	241	226	211	196	181	166	151	136	121

FIGURE 8-4   Federal Withholding Tax Table: Single Persons

MARRIED Persons   WEEKLY Payroll Period
(For Wages Paid in 20‑‑)

If the wages are		And the number of withholding allowances claimed is										
At least	But less than	0	1	2	3	4	5	6	7	8	9	10
		The amount of income tax to be withheld is										
$390	400	41	33	24	16	8	0	0	0	0	0	0
400	410	42	34	26	18	10	2	0	0	0	0	0
410	420	44	36	27	19	11	3	0	0	0	0	0
420	430	45	37	29	21	13	5	0	0	0	0	0
430	440	47	39	30	22	14	6	0	0	0	0	0
440	450	48	40	32	24	16	8	0	0	0	0	0
450	460	50	42	33	25	17	9	1	0	0	0	0
460	470	51	43	35	27	19	11	3	0	0	0	0
470	480	53	45	36	28	20	12	4	0	0	0	0
480	490	54	46	38	30	22	14	6	0	0	0	0
490	500	56	48	39	31	23	15	7	0	0	0	0
500	510	57	49	41	33	25	17	9	1	0	0	0
510	520	59	51	42	34	26	18	10	2	0	0	0
520	530	60	52	44	36	28	20	12	4	0	0	0
530	540	62	54	45	37	29	21	13	5	0	0	0
540	550	63	55	47	39	31	23	15	7	0	0	0
550	560	65	57	48	40	32	24	16	8	0	0	0
560	570	66	58	50	42	34	26	18	10	2	0	0
570	580	68	60	51	43	35	27	19	11	3	0	0
580	590	69	61	53	45	37	29	21	13	5	0	0
590	600	71	63	54	46	38	30	22	14	6	0	0
600	610	72	64	56	48	40	32	24	16	8	0	0
610	620	74	66	57	49	41	33	25	17	9	1	0
620	630	75	67	59	51	43	35	27	19	11	2	0
630	640	77	69	60	52	44	36	28	20	12	4	0
640	650	78	70	62	54	46	38	30	22	14	5	0
650	660	80	72	63	55	47	39	31	23	15	7	0
660	670	81	73	65	57	49	41	33	25	17	8	0
670	680	83	75	66	58	50	42	34	26	18	10	2
680	690	84	76	68	60	52	44	36	28	20	11	3
690	700	86	78	69	61	53	45	37	29	21	13	5
700	710	87	79	71	63	55	47	39	31	23	14	6
710	720	89	81	72	64	56	48	40	32	24	16	8
720	730	90	82	74	66	58	50	42	34	26	17	9
730	740	92	84	75	67	59	51	43	35	27	19	11
740	750	93	85	77	69	61	53	45	37	29	20	12
750	760	95	87	78	70	62	54	46	38	30	22	14
760	770	96	88	80	72	64	56	48	40	32	23	15
770	780	98	90	81	73	65	57	49	41	33	25	17
780	790	99	91	83	75	67	59	51	43	35	26	18
790	800	101	93	84	76	68	60	52	44	36	28	20
800	810	102	94	86	78	70	62	54	46	38	29	21
810	820	104	96	87	79	71	63	55	47	39	31	23
820	830	105	97	89	81	73	65	57	49	41	32	24
830	840	107	99	90	82	74	66	58	50	42	34	26
840	850	108	100	92	84	76	68	60	52	44	35	27
850	860	110	102	93	85	77	69	61	53	45	37	29
860	870	111	103	95	87	79	71	63	55	47	38	30
870	880	113	105	96	88	80	72	64	56	48	40	32
880	890	114	106	98	90	82	74	66	58	50	41	33
890	900	116	108	99	91	83	75	67	59	51	43	35
900	910	117	109	101	93	85	77	69	61	53	44	36
910	920	119	111	102	94	86	78	70	62	54	46	38
920	930	120	112	104	96	88	80	72	64	56	47	39
930	940	122	114	105	97	89	81	73	65	57	49	41
940	950	125	115	107	99	91	83	75	67	59	50	42
950	960	128	117	108	100	92	84	76	68	60	52	44
960	970	131	118	110	102	94	86	78	70	62	53	45
970	980	133	120	111	103	95	87	79	71	63	55	47
980	990	136	121	113	105	97	89	81	73	65	56	48
990	1,000	139	124	114	106	98	90	82	74	66	58	50
1,000	1,010	142	127	116	108	100	92	84	76	68	59	51
1,010	1,020	145	130	117	109	101	93	85	77	69	61	53
1,020	1,030	147	132	119	111	103	95	87	79	71	62	54
1,030	1,040	150	135	120	112	104	96	88	80	72	64	56
1,040	1,050	153	138	123	114	106	98	90	82	74	65	57
1,050	1,060	156	141	126	115	107	99	91	83	75	67	59
1,060	1,070	159	144	128	117	109	101	93	85	77	68	60
1,070	1,080	161	146	131	118	110	102	94	86	78	70	62
1,080	1,090	164	149	134	120	112	104	96	88	80	71	63
1,090	1,100	167	152	137	122	113	105	97	89	81	73	65
1,100	1,110	170	155	140	125	115	107	99	91	83	74	66
1,110	1,120	173	158	142	127	116	108	100	92	84	76	68
1,120	1,130	175	160	145	130	118	110	102	94	86	77	69
1,130	1,140	178	163	148	133	119	111	103	95	87	79	71
1,140	1,150	181	166	151	136	121	113	105	97	89	80	72
1,150	1,160	184	169	154	139	123	114	106	98	90	82	74
1,160	1,170	187	172	156	141	126	116	108	100	92	83	75
1,170	1,180	189	174	159	144	129	117	109	101	93	85	77
1,180	1,190	192	177	162	147	132	119	111	103	95	86	78
1,190	1,200	195	180	165	150	135	120	112	104	96	88	80
1,200	1,210	198	183	168	153	137	122	114	106	98	89	81
1,210	1,220	201	186	170	155	140	125	115	107	99	91	83
1,220	1,230	203	188	173	158	143	128	117	109	101	92	84
1,230	1,240	206	191	176	161	146	131	118	110	102	94	86
1,240	1,250	209	194	179	164	149	134	120	112	104	95	87
1,250	1,260	212	197	182	167	151	136	121	113	105	97	89
1,260	1,270	215	200	184	169	154	139	124	115	107	98	90
1,270	1,280	217	202	187	172	157	142	127	116	108	100	92
1,280	1,290	220	205	190	175	160	145	130	118	110	101	93
1,290	1,300	223	208	193	178	163	148	133	119	111	103	95
1,300	1,310	226	211	196	181	165	150	135	121	113	104	96
1,310	1,320	229	214	198	183	168	153	138	123	114	106	98
1,320	1,330	231	216	201	186	171	156	141	126	116	107	99
1,330	1,340	234	219	204	189	174	159	144	129	117	109	101
1,340	1,350	237	222	207	192	177	162	147	131	119	110	102
1,350	1,360	240	225	210	195	179	164	149	134	120	112	104
1,360	1,370	243	228	212	197	182	167	152	137	122	113	105
1,370	1,380	245	230	215	200	185	170	155	140	125	115	107
1,380	1,390	248	233	218	203	188	173	158	143	128	116	108

FIGURE 8-4   Federal Withholding Tax Table: (continued) Married Persons

Employee FICA Tax Withholding. The Federal Insurance Contributions Act requires employers to withhold **FICA taxes** from employees' earnings. FICA taxes include amounts for both Social Security and Medicare programs. Social Security provides pensions and disability benefits. Medicare provides health insurance.

Congress has frequently changed the tax rates and the maximum amounts of earnings subject to FICA taxes. For this text, we assume the Social Security rate is 6.2% on maximum earnings of $76,200. The Medicare rate is 1.45% on all earnings; there is no maximum.

To illustrate the calculation of FICA taxes, assume the following earnings for Sarah Cadrain:

	Earnings	
Pay Period	Week	Year-to-Date
Dec. 6–12	$1,500	$75,540
Dec. 13–19	$1,260	$76,800

For the week of December 6–12, FICA taxes on Cadrain's earnings would be:

Gross Pay	×	Tax Rate		=	Tax
$1,500		Social Security	6.2%		$93.00
		Medicare	1.45%		21.75
					$114.75

During the week of December 13–19, Cadrain's earnings for the calendar year went over the $76,200 Social Security maximum by $600 ($76,800 – $76,200). Therefore, $600 of her $1,260 earnings for the week would not be subject to the Social Security tax.

Year-to-date earnings	$76,800
Social Security maximum	76,200
Amount not subject to Social Security tax	$ 600

The Social Security tax on Cadrain's December 13–19 earnings would be:

Gross pay	$1,260.00
Amount not subject to Social Security tax	600.00
Amount subject to Social Security tax	660.00
Tax rate	6.2%
Social Security tax	$ 40.92

Since there is no Medicare maximum, all of Cadrain's December 13–19 earnings would be subject to the Medicare tax.

Gross pay	$1,260.00
Tax rate	1.45%
Medicare tax	$ 18.27

The total FICA tax would be:

Social Security tax	$40.92
Medicare tax	18.27
Total FICA tax	$59.19

For the rest of the calendar year through December 31, Cadrain's earnings would be subject only to Medicare taxes.

When the Social Security program was established in 1937, the tax was 1% on earnings up to $3,000 per year!

Voluntary Deductions. In addition to the mandatory deductions from employee earnings for income and FICA taxes, many other deductions are possible. These deductions are usually voluntary and depend on specific agreements between the employee and employer. Examples of voluntary deductions are:

1. United States savings bond purchases

2. Health insurance premiums

3. Credit union deposits

4. Pension plan payments

5. Charitable contributions

Computing Net Pay

To compute an employee's net pay for the period, subtract all tax withholdings and voluntary deductions from the gross pay. Ken Istone's net pay for the week ended December 19 would be calculated as follows:

Gross pay		$545.00
Deductions:		
Federal income tax withholding	$15.00	
Social Security tax withholding	33.79	
Medicare tax withholding	7.90	
Health insurance premiums	10.00	
Total deductions		66.69
Net pay		$478.31

PAYROLL

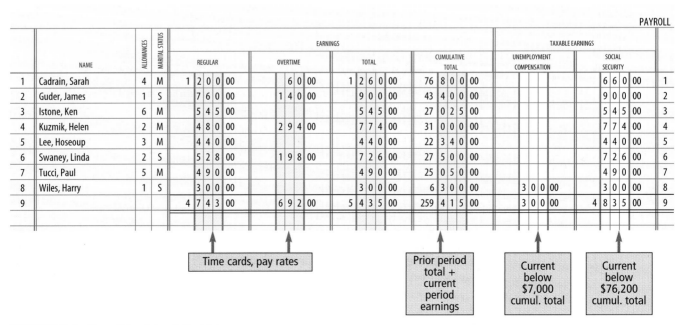

	NAME	ALLOWANCES	MARITAL STATUS	EARNINGS						TAXABLE EARNINGS			
				REGULAR	OVERTIME	TOTAL	CUMULATIVE TOTAL	UNEMPLOYMENT COMPENSATION	SOCIAL SECURITY	
1	Cadrain, Sarah	4	M	1 2 0 0 00	6 0 00	1 2 6 0 00	76 8 0 0 00		6 6 0 00	1
2	Guder, James	1	S	7 6 0 00	1 4 0 00	9 0 0 00	43 4 0 0 00		9 0 0 00	2
3	Istone, Ken	6	M	5 4 5 00		5 4 5 00	27 0 2 5 00		5 4 5 00	3
4	Kuzmik, Helen	2	M	4 8 0 00	2 9 4 00	7 7 4 00	31 0 0 0 00		7 7 4 00	4
5	Lee, Hoseoup	3	M	4 4 0 00		4 4 0 00	22 3 4 0 00		4 4 0 00	5
6	Swaney, Linda	2	S	5 2 8 00	1 9 8 00	7 2 6 00	27 5 0 0 00		7 2 6 00	6
7	Tucci, Paul	5	M	4 9 0 00		4 9 0 00	25 0 5 0 00		4 9 0 00	7
8	Wiles, Harry	1	S	3 0 0 00		3 0 0 00	6 3 0 0 00	3 0 0 00	3 0 0 00	8
9				4 7 4 3 00	6 9 2 00	5 4 3 5 00	259 4 1 5 00	3 0 0 00	4 8 3 5 00	9

Time cards, pay rates

Prior period total + current period earnings

Current below $7,000 cumul. total

Current below $76,200 cumul. total

FIGURE 8-5 **Payroll Register (left side)**

PAYROLL RECORDS

LO3 Describe and prepare payroll records.

Payroll records should provide the following information for each employee:

1. Name, address, occupation, social security number, marital status, and number of withholding allowances

2. Gross amount of earnings, date of payment, and period covered by each payroll

3. Gross amount of earnings accumulated for the year

4. Amounts of taxes and other items withheld

Three types of payroll records are used to accumulate this information:

1. The payroll register

2. The payroll check with earnings statement attached

3. The employee earnings record

These records can be prepared by either manual or automated methods. The illustrations in this chapter are based on a manual system. The forms and procedures illustrated are equally applicable to both manual and automated systems.

Payroll Register

A **payroll register** is a form used to assemble the data required at the end of each payroll period. Figure 8-5 illustrates Westly, Inc.'s payroll register for the payroll period ended December 19, 20--. Detailed information on earnings, taxable earnings, deductions, and net pay is provided for each employee. Column headings for deductions may vary, depending on which deductions are commonly used by a particular business. The sources of key information in the register are indicated in Figure 8-5 below.

REGISTER—WEEK ENDED 12/19/--

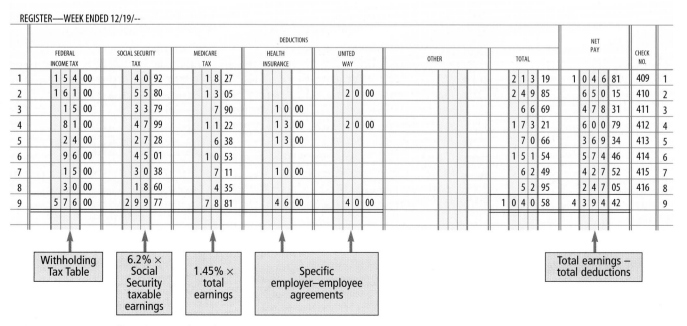

	FEDERAL INCOME TAX	SOCIAL SECURITY TAX	MEDICARE TAX	HEALTH INSURANCE	UNITED WAY	OTHER	TOTAL	NET PAY	CHECK NO.	
1	1 5 4 00	4 0 92	1 8 27				2 1 3 19	1 0 4 6 81	409	1
2	1 6 1 00	5 5 80	1 3 05		2 0 00		2 4 9 85	6 5 0 15	410	2
3	1 5 00	3 3 79	7 90	1 0 00			6 6 69	4 7 8 31	411	3
4	8 1 00	4 7 99	1 1 22	1 3 00	2 0 00		1 7 3 21	6 0 0 79	412	4
5	2 4 00	2 7 28	6 38	1 3 00			7 0 66	3 6 9 34	413	5
6	9 6 00	4 5 01	1 0 53				1 5 1 54	5 7 4 46	414	6
7	1 5 00	3 0 38	7 11	1 0 00			6 2 49	4 2 7 52	415	7
8	3 0 00	1 8 60	4 35				5 2 95	2 4 7 05	416	8
9	5 7 6 00	2 9 9 77	7 8 81	4 6 00	4 0 00		1 0 4 0 58	4 3 9 4 42		9

| Withholding Tax Table | 6.2% × Social Security taxable earnings | 1.45% × total earnings | Specific employer–employee agreements | | Total earnings – total deductions |

FIGURE 8-5 Payroll Register (right side)

Westly, Inc., has eight employees. The first $76,200 of earnings of each employee is subject to Social Security tax. The Cumulative Total column, under the Earnings category, shows that Sarah Cadrain has exceeded this limit during the period. Thus only $660 of her earnings for this pay period is subject to Social Security tax, as shown in the Taxable Earnings columns. The Taxable Earnings columns are needed for determining the Social Security tax and the employer's payroll taxes. Employers must pay unemployment tax on the first $7,000 of employee earnings and Social Security tax on the first $76,200. Employer payroll taxes are discussed in Chapter 9.

Regular deductions are made from employee earnings for federal income tax and Social Security and Medicare taxes. In addition, voluntary deductions are made for health insurance and United Way contributions, based on agreements with individual employees.

After the data for each employee have been entered, the amount columns in the payroll register should be totaled and the totals verified as follows:

Regular earnings		$4,743.00
Overtime earnings		692.00
Gross earnings		$5,435.00
Deductions:		
Federal income tax	$576.00	
Social Security tax	299.77	
Medicare tax	78.81	
Health insurance premiums	46.00	
United Way	40.00	1,040.58
Net amount of payroll		$4,394.42

In a computerized accounting system, the payroll software performs this proof. An error in the payroll register could cause the payment of an incorrect amount to an employee. It also could result in sending an incorrect amount to the government or other agencies for whom funds are withheld.

Payroll Check

Employees may be paid in cash or by check. In many cases, the employee does not even handle the paycheck. Rather, payment is made by **direct deposit** or electronic funds transfer (EFT) by the employer to the employee's bank. The employee receives the earnings statement from the check and a nonnegotiable copy of the check indicating the deposit has been made. Payment by check or direct deposit provides better internal accounting control than payment by cash.

Data needed to prepare a paycheck for each employee are contained in the payroll register. In a computer-based system, the paychecks and payroll register normally are prepared at the same time. The employer furnishes a statement of payroll deductions to each employee along with each paycheck. Paychecks with detachable earnings statements, like the one for Ken Istone illustrated in Figure 8-6, are widely used for this purpose. Before the check is deposited or cashed, the employee should detach the stub and keep it.

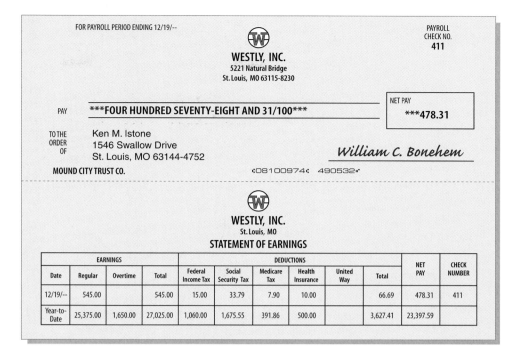

FOR PAYROLL PERIOD ENDING 12/19/--

WESTLY, INC.
5221 Natural Bridge
St. Louis, MO 63115-8230

PAYROLL
CHECK NO.
411

PAY   ***FOUR HUNDRED SEVENTY-EIGHT AND 31/100***

NET PAY
***478.31

TO THE
ORDER
OF
Ken M. Istone
1546 Swallow Drive
St. Louis, MO 63144-4752

William C. Bonehem

MOUND CITY TRUST CO.   ⑆08100974⑆ 490532⑈

WESTLY, INC.
St. Louis, MO
STATEMENT OF EARNINGS

	EARNINGS			DEDUCTIONS						NET PAY	CHECK NUMBER
Date	Regular	Overtime	Total	Federal Income Tax	Social Security Tax	Medicare Tax	Health Insurance	United Way	Total		
12/19/--	545.00		545.00	15.00	33.79	7.90	10.00		66.69	478.31	411
Year-to-Date	25,375.00	1,650.00	27,025.00	1,060.00	1,675.55	391.86	500.00		3,627.41	23,397.59	

FIGURE 8-6   Paycheck and Earnings Statement

A BROADER VIEW

Payroll Fraud—Paying for Ghosts

A supervisor at Haas Transfer Warehouse embezzled $12,000 from the company by collecting paychecks for former employees. When an employee left the company, the supervisor continued to submit a department time report for the employee. This caused a paycheck to be generated for the "ghost" employee. The supervisor then simply kept this paycheck when others were distributed to actual employees.

This fraud shows the importance of two procedures that appear in this chapter: (1) a time card, plastic card,

or badge should be used for each employee to keep an accurate record of time worked and (2) payment by direct deposit or electronic funds transfer to the employee's bank is a good internal control.

EMPLOYEE EARNINGS RECORD

PERIOD ENDED	REGULAR	OVERTIME	TOTAL	CUMULATIVE TOTAL	UNEMPLOYMENT COMPENSATION	SOCIAL SECURITY
		EARNINGS			TAXABLE EARNINGS	
11/28	5 4 5 00	7 5 00	6 2 0 00	25 2 4 0 00		6 2 0 00
12/5	5 4 5 00	7 5 00	6 2 0 00	25 8 6 0 00		6 2 0 00
12/12	5 4 5 00	7 5 00	6 2 0 00	26 4 8 0 00		6 2 0 00
12/19	5 4 5 00		5 4 5 00	27 0 2 5 00		5 4 5 00

GENDER	DEPARTMENT	OCCUPATION	SOCIAL SECURITY NUMBER	MARITAL STATUS	ALLOWANCES
M ✔ F	Maintenance	Service	393-58-8194	M	6

FIGURE 8-7   Employee Earnings Record (left side)

Employee Earnings Record

A separate record of each employee's earnings is called an **employee earnings record**. An employee earnings record for Ken M. Istone for a portion of the last quarter of the calendar year is illustrated in Figure 8-7.

The information in this record is obtained from the payroll register. In a computer-based system, the employee earnings record can be updated at the same time the payroll register is prepared.

Istone's earnings for four weeks of the last quarter of the year are shown on this form. Note that the entry for the pay period ended December 19 is the same as that in the payroll register illustrated in Figure 8-5. This linkage between the payroll register and the employee earnings record always exists. The payroll register provides a summary of the earnings of all employees for each pay period. The earnings record provides a summary of the annual earnings of an individual employee.

The earnings record illustrated in Figure 8-7 is designed to accumulate both quarterly and annual totals. The employer needs this information to prepare several reports. These reports will be discussed in Chapter 9.

ACCOUNTING FOR EMPLOYEE EARNINGS AND DEDUCTIONS

LO4   Account for employee earnings and deductions.

The payroll register described in the previous section provides complete payroll data for each pay period. But the payroll register is not a journal. We still need to make a journal entry for payroll.

Journalizing Payroll Transactions

The totals at the bottom of the columns of the payroll register in Figure 8-5 show the following information.

Regular earnings		$4,743.00
Overtime earnings		692.00
Gross earnings		$5,435.00
Deductions:		
Federal income tax	$576.00	
Social Security tax	299.77	
Medicare tax	78.81	
Health insurance premiums	46.00	
United Way contributions	40.00	1,040.58
Net amount of payroll		$4,394.42

FOR PERIOD ENDED 20--

DEDUCTIONS								
FEDERAL INCOME TAX	SOCIAL SECURITY TAX	MEDICARE TAX	HEALTH INSURANCE	UNITED WAY	OTHER	TOTAL	CHECK NO.	AMOUNT
27 00	38 44	8 99	10 00			84 43	387	535 57
27 00	38 44	8 99	10 00			84 43	395	535 57
27 00	38 44	8 99	10 00			84 43	403	535 57
15 00	33 79	7 90	10 00			66 69	411	478 31

PAY RATE	DATE OF BIRTH	DATE HIRED	NAME/ADDRESS	EMPLOYEE NUMBER
$545/wk	8/17/64	1/3/87	Ken M. Istone 1546 Swallow Drive St. Louis, MO 63144-4752	3

FIGURE 8-7 Employee Earnings Record (right side)

The payroll register column totals thus provide the basis for recording the payroll. If the employee paychecks are written from the regular bank account, the following journal entry is made:

5	Dec.	19	Wages and Salaries Expense		5 4 3 5 00		5
6			Employee Income Tax Payable			5 7 6 00	6
7			Social Security Tax Payable			2 9 9 77	7
8			Medicare Tax Payable			7 8 81	8
9			Health Insurance Premiums Payable			4 6 00	9
10			United Way Contributions Payable			4 0 00	10
11			Cash			4 3 9 4 42	11
12			Payroll for week ended Dec. 19				12

Employee paychecks also can be written from a special payroll bank account. Large businesses with many employees commonly use a payroll bank account. If Westly used a payroll bank account, it first would have made the following entry on December 19 to transfer funds from the regular bank account to the payroll bank account:

5	Dec.	19	Payroll Cash		4 3 9 4 42		5
6			Cash			4 3 9 4 42	6
7			Cash for Dec. 19 payroll				7

Then, the payroll entry shown above would be made, except that the credit of $4,394.42 would be to Payroll Cash rather than Cash.

If a payroll bank account is used, individual checks totaling $4,394.42 are written to the employees from that account. Otherwise, individual checks totaling that amount are written to the employees from the regular bank account.

Notice two important facts about the payroll entry. First, Wages and Salaries Expense is debited for the gross pay of the employees. The expense to the employer is the gross pay, not the employees' net pay after deductions. Second, a separate account is kept for each deduction.

LEARNING KEY: Wages and Salaries Expense is debited for the gross pay. A separate account is kept for each earnings deduction. Cash is credited for the net pay.

The accounts needed in entering deductions depend upon the deductions involved. To understand the accounting for these deductions, consider what the employer is doing. By deducting amounts from employees' earnings, the employer is simply serving as an agent for the government and other groups. Amounts that are deducted from an employee's gross earnings must be paid by the employer to these groups. Therefore, a separate account should be kept for the liability for each type of deduction.

To help us understand the journal entry for payroll, let's use the accounting equation to examine the accounts involved. The seven accounts affected by the payroll entry on page 271 are shown in the accounting equation in Figure 8-8.

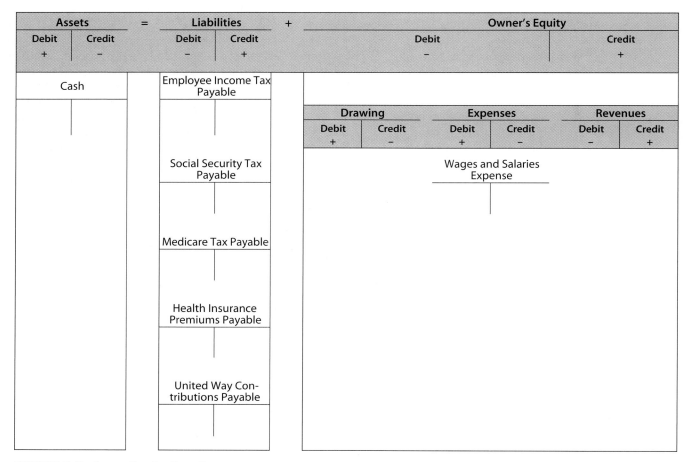

FIGURE 8-8 **Accounting for Payroll**

Wages and Salaries Expense

This account is debited for the gross pay of all employees for each pay period. Sometimes separate expense accounts are kept for the employees of different departments. Thus separate accounts may be kept for Office Salaries Expense, Sales Salaries Expense, and Factory Wages Expense.

Wages and Salaries Expense

Debit	Credit
gross pay of employees for each pay period	

Employee Income Tax Payable

This account is credited for the total federal income tax withheld from employees' earnings. The account is debited for amounts paid to the IRS. When all of the income taxes withheld have been paid, the account will have a zero balance. A state or city income tax payable account is used in a similar manner.

Employee Income Tax Payable

Debit	Credit
payment of income tax previously withheld	federal income tax withheld from employees' earnings

Social Security and Medicare Taxes Payable

These accounts are credited for (1) the Social Security and Medicare tax withheld from employees' earnings and (2) the Social Security and Medicare taxes imposed on the employer. Social Security and Medicare taxes imposed on the employer are discussed in Chapter 9. The accounts are debited for amounts paid to the IRS. When all of the Social Security and Medicare taxes have been paid, the accounts will have zero balances.

Social Security Tax Payable

Debit	Credit
payment of Social Security tax previously withheld or imposed	Social Security taxes (1) withheld from employees' earnings and (2) imposed on the employer

Medicare Tax Payable

Debit	Credit
payment of Medicare tax previously withheld or imposed	Medicare taxes (1) withheld from employees' earnings and (2) imposed on the employer

Other Deductions

Health Insurance Premiums Payable is credited for health insurance contributions deducted from an employee's pay. The account is debited for the subsequent payment of these amounts to the health insurer. United Way Contributions Payable is handled in a similar manner.

PAYROLL RECORD-KEEPING METHODS

LO5 Describe various payroll record-keeping methods.

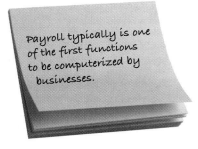

Payroll typically is one of the first functions to be computerized by businesses.

You probably noticed that the same information appears in several places in the payroll records—in the payroll register, paycheck and stub, and employee earnings records. If all records are prepared by hand (a **manual system**), the same information would be recorded several times. Unless an employer has only a few employees, this can be very inefficient. Various approaches are available to make payroll accounting more efficient and accurate.

Both medium- and large-size businesses commonly use two approaches for payroll record keeping: payroll processing centers and electronic systems. A **payroll processing center** is a business that sells payroll record-keeping services. The employer provides the center with all basic employee data and each period's report of hours worked. The processing center maintains all payroll records and prepares each period's payroll checks. Payroll processing center fees tend to be much less than the cost to an employer of handling payroll internally.

An **electronic system** is a computer system based on a software package that performs all payroll record keeping and prepares payroll checks. In this system, only the employee number and hours worked need to be entered into a computer each pay period, as shown in Figure 8-9. All other payroll data needed to prepare the payroll records can be stored in the computer. The computer uses the employee number and hours worked to determine the gross pay, deductions, and net pay. The payroll register, checks, and employee earnings records are provided as outputs.

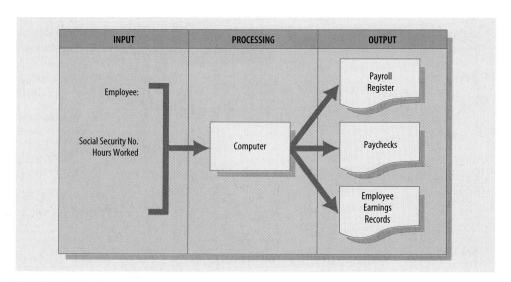

FIGURE 8-9 **Electronic Payroll System**

The same inputs and outputs are required in all payroll systems. Even with a computer, the data required for payroll processing have to be entered into the system at some point. The outputs—the payroll register, paychecks, and employee earnings records—are basically the same under each system.

Learning Objectives	Key Points to Remember
1 **Distinguish between employees and independent contractors.**	Employees work under the control and direction of an employer. Independent contractors perform a service for a fee and do not work under the control and direction of the company paying for the service. Payroll accounting procedures apply only to employees, not to independent contractors.

2 **Calculate employee earnings and deductions.**	Three steps are required to determine how much to pay an employee for a pay period:
	
	  1. Calculate total earnings.
	
	  2. Determine the amounts of deductions.
	
	  3. Subtract deductions from total earnings to compute net pay.
	
	Deductions from gross pay fall into three categories:
	
	  1. Income tax withholding.
	
	  2. Employee Social Security and Medicare taxes withholding.
	
	  3. Voluntary deductions.
	
	Four factors determine the amount to be withheld from an employee's gross pay each pay period:
	
	  1. Total earnings
	
	  2. Marital status
	
	  3. Number of withholding allowances claimed
	
	  4. Length of the pay period

3 **Describe and prepare payroll records.**	The payroll register and the employee earnings record are linked. The payroll register provides a summary of earnings of all employees for each pay period. The earnings record provides a summary of the annual earnings of an individual employee.
4 **Account for employee earnings and deductions.**	The totals at the bottom of the columns of the payroll register provide the basis for the journal entry for payroll. Amounts withheld or deducted by the employer from employee earnings are credited to liability accounts. The employer must pay these amounts to the proper government groups and other appropriate groups.
5 **Describe various payroll record-keeping methods.**	In a manual payroll system, the same information needs to be recorded several times. An electronic payroll system is much more efficient.

Reflection: Answering the Opening Question

John must withhold amounts for federal (and possibly city and state) income taxes and for FICA taxes (Social Security and Medicare). To determine the correct amount of income tax withholding, the employee must complete Form W-4. Based on the number of withholding allowances claimed, John can use the withholding tables to determine the amount to withhold. These tables are provided in *Circular E—Employer's Tax Guide*. FICA tax should be withheld at a rate of 6.2% for Social Security and 1.45% for Medicare. *Circular E* also provides guidance regarding FICA taxes. John's bookkeeper should be able to handle all of these payroll matters.

KEY TERMS

direct deposit, (268)   The employee does not handle the paycheck; payment is made by the employer directly to the employee's bank.

electronic system, (274)   A computer system based on a software package that performs all payroll record keeping and prepares payroll checks.

employee, (258)   Someone who works under the control and direction of an employer.

employee earnings record, (270)   A separate record of each employee's earnings.

Fair Labor Standards Act (FLSA), (259)   Requires employers to pay overtime at 1½ times the regular rate to any hourly employee who works over 40 hours in a week.

FICA taxes, (265)   Payroll taxes withheld to provide Social Security and Medicare benefits.

gross pay, (261)   An employee's total earnings.

independent contractor, (258)   Someone who performs a service for a fee and does not work under the control and direction of the company paying for the service.

manual system, (274)   Payroll system in which all records are prepared by hand.

net pay, (261)   Gross pay less mandatory and voluntary deductions.

payroll processing center, (274)   A business that sells payroll record-keeping services.

payroll register, (267)   A form used to assemble the data required at the end of each payroll period.

salary, (259)   Compensation for managerial or administrative services.

wage-bracket method, (262)   Employers determine the amount to withhold from an employee's gross pay for a specific time period from the appropriate wage-bracket table provided by the Internal Revenue Service.

wages, (259)   Compensation for skilled or unskilled labor.

withholding allowance, (261)   Exempts a specific dollar amount of an employee's gross pay from federal income tax withholding.

DEMONSTRATION PROBLEM

Carole Vohsen operates a pet grooming salon called Canine Coiffures. She has five employees, all of whom are paid on a weekly basis. Canine Coiffures uses a payroll register, individual employee earnings records, a journal, and a general ledger.

The payroll data for each employee for the week ended January 21, 20--, are given below. Employees are paid 1½ times the regular rate for work over 40 hours a week and double time for work on Sunday.

Name	Employee No.	No. of Allowances	Marital Status	Total Hours Worked Jan. 15–21	Rate	Total Earnings Jan. 1–14
DeNourie, Katie	1	2	S	44	$11.50	$1,058.00
Garriott, Pete	2	1	M	40	12.00	1,032.00
Martinez, Sheila	3	3	M	39	12.50	987.50
Parker, Nancy	4	4	M	42	11.00	957.00
Shapiro, John	5	2	S	40	11.50	931.50

Sheila Martinez is the manager of the Shampooing Department. Her Social Security number is 500-88-4189, and she was born April 12, 1969. She lives at 46 Darling Crossing, Norwich, CT 06360. Martinez was hired September 1 of last year.

Canine Coiffures uses a federal income tax withholding table. A portion of this weekly table is provided in Figure 8-4 on pages 263 and 264. Social Security tax is withheld at the rate of 6.2% of the first $76,200 earned. Medicare tax is withheld at the rate of 1.45%, and city earnings tax at the rate of 1%, both applied to gross pay. Garriott and Parker each have $14.00 and Denourie and Martinez each have $4.00 withheld for health insurance. DeNourie, Martinez, and Shapiro each have $15.00 withheld to be invested in the groomers' credit union. Garriott and Shapiro each have $18.75 withheld under a savings bond purchase plan.

Canine Coiffures' payroll is met by drawing checks on its regular bank account. This week, the checks were issued in sequence, beginning with no. 811.

REQUIRED

1. Prepare a payroll register for Canine Coiffures for the week ended January 21, 20--. (In the Taxable Earnings/Unemployment Compensation column, enter the same amounts as in the Social Security column.) Total the amount columns, verify the totals, and rule with single and double lines.

2. Prepare an employee earnings record for Sheila Martinez for the week ended January 21, 20--.

3. Assuming that the wages for the week ended January 21 were paid on January 23, prepare the journal entry for the payment of this payroll.

4. Post the entry in requirement 3 to the affected accounts in the ledger of Canine Coiffures. Do not enter any amounts in the Balance columns. Use account numbers as follows: Cash—101; Employee Income Tax Payable—211; Social Security Tax Payable—212; Medicare Tax Payable—213; City Earnings Tax Payable—215; Health Insurance Premiums Payable—216; Credit Union Payable—217; Savings Bond Deductions Payable—218; Wages and Salaries Expense—511.

(continued)

Solution

1.

PAYROLL

	NAME	EMPLOYEE NO.	ALLOWANCES	MARITAL STATUS	EARNINGS REGULAR	EARNINGS OVERTIME	TOTAL	CUMULATIVE TOTAL	TAXABLE EARNINGS UNEMPLOYMENT COMPENSATION	TAXABLE EARNINGS SOCIAL SECURITY	
1	DeNourie, Katie	1	2	S	460 00	69 00	529 00	1587 00	529 00	529 00	1
2	Garriott, Pete	2	1	M	480 00		480 00	1512 00	480 00	480 00	2
3	Martinez, Sheila	3	3	M	487 50		487 50	1475 00	487 50	487 50	3
4	Parker, Nancy	4	4	M	440 00	33 00	473 00	1430 00	473 00	473 00	4
5	Shapiro, John	5	2	S	460 00		460 00	1391 50	460 00	460 00	5
6					2327 50	102 00	2429 50	7395 50	2429 50	2429 50	6
7											7

REGISTER—WEEK ENDED January 21, 20--

	FEDERAL INCOME TAX	SOCIAL SECURITY TAX	MEDICARE TAX	CITY TAX	HEALTH INSURANCE	CREDIT UNION	OTHER		TOTAL	NET PAY	CHECK NO.	
1	55 00	32 80	7 67	5 29	4 00	15 00			119 76	409 24	811	1
2	46 00	29 76	6 96	4 80	14 00		U.S. Savings Bond	18 75	120 27	359 73	812	2
3	30 00	30 23	7 07	4 88	4 00	15 00			91 18	396 32	813	3
4	20 00	29 33	6 86	4 73	14 00				74 92	398 08	814	4
5	46 00	28 52	6 67	4 60		15 00	U.S. Savings Bond	18 75	119 54	340 46	815	5
6	197 00	150 64	35 23	24 30	36 00	45 00		37 50	525 67	1903 83		6
7												7

2.

EMPLOYEE EARNINGS RECORD

20-- PERIOD ENDED	EARNINGS REGULAR	EARNINGS OVERTIME	TOTAL	CUMULATIVE TOTAL	TAXABLE EARNINGS UNEMPLOYMENT COMPENSATION	TAXABLE EARNINGS SOCIAL SECURITY
1/7						
1/14						
1/21	487 50		487 50	1475 00	487 50	487 50
1/28						

GENDER	DEPARTMENT	OCCUPATION	SOCIAL SECURITY NUMBER	MARITAL STATUS	ALLOWANCES
M / F ✔	Shampooing	Manager	500-88-4189	M	3

FOR PERIOD ENDED   20--

FEDERAL INCOME TAX	SOCIAL SECURITY TAX	MEDICARE TAX	CITY TAX	HEALTH INSURANCE	CREDIT UNION	OTHER	TOTAL	CHECK NO.	AMOUNT
30 00	30 23	7 07	4 88	4 00	15 00		91 18	813	396 32

PAY RATE	DATE OF BIRTH	DATE HIRED	NAME/ADDRESS	EMPLOYEE NUMBER
$12.50	4/12/69	9/1/--	Sheila Martinez 46 Darling Crossing Norwich, CT 06360	3

3.

GENERAL JOURNAL   PAGE 1

	DATE		DESCRIPTION	POST REF.	DEBIT	CREDIT	
1	20-- Jan.	23	Wages and Salaries Expense	511	2 4 2 9 50		1
2			Employee Income Tax Payable	211		1 9 7 00	2
3			Social Security Tax Payable	212		1 5 0 64	3
4			Medicare Tax Payable	213		3 5 23	4
5			City Earnings Tax Payable	215		2 4 30	5
6			Health Insurance Premiums Payable	216		3 6 00	6
7			Credit Union Payable	217		4 5 00	7
8			Savings Bond Deductions Payable	218		3 7 50	8
9			Cash	101		1 9 0 3 83	9
10			Payroll for week ended Jan. 21				10

4.

GENERAL LEDGER

ACCOUNT: Cash   ACCOUNT NO. 101

DATE	ITEM	POST REF.	DEBIT	CREDIT	BALANCE DEBIT	BALANCE CREDIT
20-- Jan. 23		J 1		1 9 0 3 83		

ACCOUNT: Employee Income Tax Payable   ACCOUNT NO. 211

DATE	ITEM	POST REF.	DEBIT	CREDIT	BALANCE DEBIT	BALANCE CREDIT
20-- Jan. 23		J 1		1 9 7 00		

ACCOUNT: Social Security Tax Payable   ACCOUNT NO. 212

DATE	ITEM	POST REF.	DEBIT	CREDIT	BALANCE DEBIT	BALANCE CREDIT
20-- Jan. 23		J 1		1 5 0 64		

ACCOUNT: Medicare Tax Payable   ACCOUNT NO. 213

DATE	ITEM	POST REF.	DEBIT	CREDIT	BALANCE DEBIT	BALANCE CREDIT
20-- Jan. 23		J 1		3 5 23		

ACCOUNT: City Earnings Tax Payable   ACCOUNT NO. 215

DATE	ITEM	POST REF.	DEBIT	CREDIT	BALANCE DEBIT	BALANCE CREDIT
20-- Jan. 23		J 1		2 4 30		

ACCOUNT: Health Insurance Premiums Payable   ACCOUNT NO. 216

DATE	ITEM	POST REF.	DEBIT	CREDIT	BALANCE DEBIT	BALANCE CREDIT
20-- Jan. 23		J 1		3 6 00		

(continued)

ACCOUNT: Credit Union Payable							ACCOUNT NO. 217
DATE	ITEM	POST REF.	DEBIT	CREDIT	BALANCE DEBIT	BALANCE CREDIT	
20-- Jan. 23		J 1		4 5 00			

ACCOUNT: Savings Bond Deductions Payable							ACCOUNT NO. 218
DATE	ITEM	POST REF.	DEBIT	CREDIT	BALANCE DEBIT	BALANCE CREDIT	
20-- Jan. 23		J 1		3 7 50			

ACCOUNT: Wages and Salaries Expense							ACCOUNT NO. 511
DATE	ITEM	POST REF.	DEBIT	CREDIT	BALANCE DEBIT	BALANCE CREDIT	
20-- Jan. 23		J 1	2 4 2 9 50				

REVIEW QUESTIONS

1. Why is it important for payroll accounting purposes to distinguish between an employee and an independent contractor?

2. Name three major categories of deductions from an employee's gross pay.

3. Identify the four factors that determine the amount of federal income tax that is withheld from an employee's pay each pay period.

4. In general, an employee is entitled to withholding allowances for what purposes?

5. Identify the three payroll records usually needed by an employer.

6. Describe the information contained in the payroll register.

7. Why is it important to total and verify the totals of the payroll register after the data for each employee have been entered?

8. Distinguish between the payroll register and the employee earnings record.

9. Explain what an employer does with the amounts withheld from an employee's pay.

10. Explain why payroll processing centers and electronic systems are commonly used in payroll accounting.

MANAGING YOUR WRITING

The minimum wage originally was only 25 cents an hour. Today it is $5.15 an hour. Assume that Congress is considering raising the minimum wage again and your United States representative is asking for public opinion on this issue. Write a letter to your representative with arguments for and against a higher minimum wage.

ETHICS CASE

Maura Lowe is a payroll accountant for N & L Company. She prepares and processes the company's payroll on a weekly basis and has been at N & L for only three months. All employees are paid on Friday. On Wednesday afternoon, Simon Lentz, one of the company's top sales associates, asks Maura to not take out any payroll deductions from his pay this week. He explains that he is short of cash and needs the full amount of his gross salary just to put food on the table and make his past-due car payment. He promises Maura that she can catch up on the deductions over the next month. The deductions include employee income tax, Social Security tax, Medicare tax, and health insurance premiums.

1. Is Simon's request of Maura ethical? Why or why not?

2. If this were the first pay period of the year and Maura agreed not to take out deductions from Simon's pay, what effect would this have on the liabilities section of the balance sheet?

3. Write a short paragraph from Maura to Simon explaining how omitting deductions from a pay period will cause errors in the company's financial statements.

4. In small groups, discuss what action Maura should take regarding Simon's request.

WEB WORK

Most people receive paychecks; they don't issue them. The bottom line and the benefits are noted and grumbled about, but what really goes into a person's paycheck? What are various benefits and compensation strategies?
For general compensation reviews across the nation, look here:

http://jobsmart.org/tools/salary/surv-gen.htm

For an explanation of some benefits, check out

http://www.bestjobsusa.com/erframe.htm
(http://heintz/swcollege.com)

SERIES A EXERCISES

EXERCISE 8-1A   (LO2)   **COMPUTING NET PAY** Mary Sue Guild works for a company that pays its employees 1½ times the regular rate for all hours worked in excess of 40 per week. Guild's pay rate is $10.00 per hour. Her wages are subject to deductions for federal income tax, Social Security tax, and Medicare tax. She is married and claims 4 withholding allowances. Guild has a ½-hour lunch break during an 8½-hour day. Her time card is shown on the next page.

Name	Mary Sue Guild					
Week Ending	March 30, 20--					
Day	In	Out	In	Out	Hours Worked	
					Regular	Overtime
M	7:57	12:05	12:35	4:33	8	
T	7:52	12:09	12:39	5:05	8	½
W	7:59	12:15	12:45	5:30	8	1
T	8:00	12:01	12:30	6:31	8	2
F	7:56	12:05	12:34	4:30	8	
S	8:00	10:31				2½

Complete the following:

a) _____ regular hours × $10.00 per hour $_____

b) _____ overtime hours × $15.00 per hour $_____

c) Total gross wages $_____

d) Federal income tax withholding (from tax tables in Figure 8-4, pages 263 and 264) $_____

e) Social Security withholding at 6.2% $_____

f) Medicare withholding at 1.45% $_____

g) Total withholding $_____

h) Net pay $_____

EXERCISE 8-2A (LO2) **COMPUTING WEEKLY GROSS PAY** Ryan Lawrence's regular hourly rate is $15.00. He receives 1½ times the regular rate for any hours worked over 40 a week and double the rate for work on Sunday. During the past week, Lawrence worked 8 hours each day Monday through Thursday, 10 hours on Friday, and 5 hours on Sunday. Compute Lawrence's gross pay for the past week.

EXERCISE 8-3A (LO2) **COMPUTING OVERTIME RATE OF PAY AND GROSS WEEKLY PAY** Rebecca Huang receives a regular salary of $2,600 a month and is paid 1½ times the regular hourly rate for hours worked in excess of 40 per week.

a) Calculate Huang's overtime rate of pay.

b) Calculate Huang's total gross weekly pay if she works 45 hours during the week.

EXERCISE 8-4A (LO2) **COMPUTING FEDERAL INCOME TAX** Using the table in Figure 8-4 on pages 263 and 264, determine the amount of federal income tax an employer should withhold weekly for employees with the following marital status, earnings, and withholding allowances.

	Marital Status	Total Weekly Earnings	Number of Allowances	Amount of Withholding
a)	S	$327.90	2	_____
b)	S	$410.00	1	_____
c)	M	$438.16	5	_____
d)	S	$518.25	0	_____
e)	M	$603.98	6	_____

EXERCISE 8-5A   (LO2)   **CALCULATING SOCIAL SECURITY AND MEDICARE TAXES** Assume a Social Security tax rate of 6.2% is applied to maximum earnings of $76,200 and a Medicare tax rate of 1.45% is applied to all earnings. Calculate the Social Security and Medicare tax for the following situations.

Cumul. Pay Before Current Weekly Payroll	Current Gross Pay	Year-to-Date Earnings	Soc. Sec. Maximum	Amount Over Max. Soc. Sec.	Amount Subject to Soc. Sec.	Soc. Sec. Tax Withheld	Medicare Tax Withheld
$22,000	$1,200	_____	$76,200	_____	_____	_____	_____
$54,000	$4,200	_____	$76,200	_____	_____	_____	_____
$73,600	$3,925	_____	$76,200	_____	_____	_____	_____
$75,600	$4,600	_____	$76,200	_____	_____	_____	_____

EXERCISE 8-6A   (LO4)   **JOURNALIZING PAYROLL TRANSACTIONS** On December 31, the payroll register of Hamstreet Associates indicated the following information:

Wages and Salaries Expense $8,700.00
Employee Income Tax Payable 920.00
United Way Contributions Payable 200.00
Earnings subject to Social Security tax 8,000.00

Determine the amount of Social Security and Medicare taxes to be withheld and record the journal entry for the payroll, crediting Cash for the net pay.

EXERCISE 8-7A   (LO4)   **PAYROLL JOURNAL ENTRY** Journalize the following data taken from the payroll register of University Printing as of April 15, 20--.

Regular earnings $5,418.00
Overtime earnings 824.00
Deductions:
Federal income tax 593.00
Social Security tax 387.00
Medicare tax 90.51
Pension plan 90.00
Health insurance premiums 225.00
United Way contributions 100.00

SERIES A PROBLEMS

PROBLEM 8-1A (LO2/4) **GROSS PAY, DEDUCTIONS, AND NET PAY** Donald Chin works for Northwest Supplies. His rate of pay is $8.50 per hour, and he is paid 1½ times the regular rate for all hours worked in excess of 40 per week. During the last week of January of the current year he worked 48 hours. Chin is married and claims 4 withholding allowances on his W-4 form. His weekly wages are subject to the following deductions:

a) Employee income tax (use Figure 8-4 on pages 263 and 264)

b) Social Security tax at 6.2%

c) Medicare tax at 1.45%

d) Health insurance premium, $85.00

e) Credit union, $125.00

f) United Way contribution, $10.00

REQUIRED

1. Compute Chin's regular pay, overtime pay, gross pay, and net pay.

2. Journalize the payment of his wages for the week ended January 31, crediting Cash for the net amount.

PROBLEM 8-2A (LO2/3/4) **PAYROLL REGISTER AND PAYROLL JOURNAL ENTRY** Don McCullum operates a travel agency called Don's Luxury Travel. He has five employees, all of whom are paid on a weekly basis. The travel agency uses a payroll register, individual employee earnings records, and a general journal.

Don's Luxury Travel uses a weekly federal income tax withholding table. The payroll data for each employee for the week ended March 22, 20--, are given below. Employees are paid 1½ times the regular rate for working over 40 hours a week.

Name	No. of Allowances	Marital Status	Total Hours Worked Mar. 16–22	Rate	Total Earnings Jan. 1–Mar. 15
Ali, Loren	4	M	45	$11.00	$5,280.00
Carson, Judy	1	S	40	12.00	5,760.00
Hernandez, Maria	3	M	43	9.50	4,560.00
Knox, Wayne	1	S	39	11.00	5,125.50
Paglione, Jim	2	M	40	10.50	4,720.50

Social Security tax is withheld from the first $76,200 of earnings at the rate of 6.2%. Medicare tax is withheld at the rate of 1.45%, and city earnings tax at the rate of 1%, both applied to gross pay. Ali and Knox have $15.00 withheld and Carson and Hernandez have $5.00 withheld for health insurance. Ali and Knox have $20.00 withheld to be invested in the travel agencies' credit union. Carson has $38.75 withheld and Hernandez $18.75 withheld under a savings bond purchase plan.

Don's Luxury Travel's payroll is met by drawing checks on its regular bank account. The checks were issued in sequence, beginning with check no. 423.

REQUIRED

1. Prepare a payroll register for Don's Luxury Travel for the week ended March 22, 20--. (In the Taxable Earnings/Unemployment Compensation column,

enter the same amounts as in the Social Security column.) Total the amount columns, verify the totals, and rule with single and double lines.

2. Assuming that the wages for the week ended March 22 were paid on March 24, prepare the journal entry for the payment of the payroll.

PROBLEM 8-3A   **(LO3)**   **EMPLOYEE EARNINGS RECORD** Don's Luxury Travel in Problem 8-2A keeps employee earnings records. Judy Carson, employee number 62, is employed as a manager in the ticket sales department. She was born on May 8, 1959, and was hired on June 1 of last year. Her Social Security number is 544-67-1283. She lives at 28 Quarry Drive, Vernon, CT 06066.

REQUIRED

For the week ended March 22, complete an employee earnings record for Judy Carson. (Insert earnings data only for the week of March 22.)

SERIES B EXERCISES

EXERCISE 8-1B   **(LO2)**   **COMPUTING NET PAY** Tom Hallinan works for a company that pays its employees 1½ times the regular rate for all hours worked in excess of 40 per week. Hallinan's pay rate is $12.00 per hour. His wages are subject to deductions for federal income tax, Social Security tax, and Medicare tax. He is married and claims 5 withholding allowances. Hallinan has a ½-hour lunch break during an 8½-hour day. His time card is shown below.

Name	Tom Hallinan					
Week Ending	March 30, 20--					
Day	In	Out	In	Out	Hours Worked	
					Regular	Overtime
M	7:55	12:02	12:32	5:33	8	1
T	7:59	12:04	12:34	6:05	8	1½
W	7:59	12:05	12:35	4:30	8	
T	8:00	12:01	12:30	5:01	8	½
F	7:58	12:02	12:31	5:33	8	1
S	7:59	9:33				1½

Complete the following:

a) _____ regular hours × $12.00 per hour $_____

b) _____ overtime hours × $18.00 per hour $_____

c) Total gross wages $_____

d) Federal income tax withholding (from tax tables in Figure 8-4, pages 263 and 264) $_____

e) Social Security withholding at 6.2% $_____

f) Medicare withholding at 1.45% $_____

g) Total withholding $_____

h) Net pay $_____

EXERCISE 8-2B   **(LO2)**   **COMPUTING WEEKLY GROSS PAY** Manuel Soto's regular hourly rate is $12.00. He receives 1½ times the regular rate for hours worked in excess of 40 a week and double the rate for work on Sunday. During the past week, Soto worked 8 hours each day Monday through Thursday, 11 hours on Friday, and 6 hours on Sunday. Compute Soto's gross pay for the past week.

EXERCISE 8-3B   **(LO2)**   **COMPUTING OVERTIME RATE OF PAY AND GROSS WEEKLY PAY** Mike Fritz receives a regular salary of $3,250 a month and is paid 1½ times the regular hourly rate for hours worked in excess of 40 per week.

a) Calculate Fritz's overtime rate of pay. (Compute to the nearest half cent.)

b) Calculate Fritz's total gross weekly pay if he works 46 hours during the week.

EXERCISE 8-4B   **(LO2)**   **COMPUTING FEDERAL INCOME TAX** Using the table in Figure 8-4 on pages 263 and 264, determine the amount of federal income tax an employer should withhold weekly for employees with the following marital status, earnings, and withholding allowances.

	Marital Status	Total Weekly Earnings	Number of Allowances	Amount of Withholding
a)	M	$546.00	4	_____
b)	M	$390.00	3	_____
c)	S	$461.39	2	_____
d)	M	$522.88	6	_____
e)	S	$612.00	0	_____

EXERCISE 8-5B   **(LO2)**   **CALCULATING SOCIAL SECURITY AND MEDICARE TAXES** Assume a Social Security tax rate of 6.2% is applied to maximum earnings of $76,200 and a Medicare tax rate of 1.45% is applied to all earnings. Calculate the Social Security and Medicare tax for the following situations.

Cumul. Pay Before Current Weekly Payroll	Current Gross Pay	Year-to-Date Earnings	Soc. Sec. Maximum	Amount Over Max. Soc. Sec.	Amount Subject to Soc. Sec.	Soc. Sec. Tax Withheld	Medicare Tax Withheld
$31,000	$1,500	_____	$76,200	_____	_____	_____	_____
$53,000	$2,860	_____	$76,200	_____	_____	_____	_____
$73,300	$3,140	_____	$76,200	_____	_____	_____	_____
$75,600	$2,920	_____	$76,200	_____	_____	_____	_____

EXERCISE 8-6B   **(LO4)**   **JOURNALIZING PAYROLL TRANSACTIONS**   On November 30, the payroll register of Webster & Smith indicated the following information:

Wages and Salaries Expense	$9,400.00
Employee Income Tax Payable	985.00
United Way Contributions Payable	200.00
Earnings subject to Social Security tax	9,400.00

Determine the amount of Social Security and Medicare taxes to be withheld and record the journal entry for the payroll, crediting Cash for the net pay.

EXERCISE 8-7B   (LO4)   **PAYROLL JOURNAL ENTRY** Journalize the following data taken from the payroll register of Himes Bakery as of June 12, 20--.

Regular earnings	$6,520.00
Overtime earnings	950.00
Deductions:	
Federal income tax	782.00
Social Security tax	463.14
Medicare tax	108.32
Pension plan	80.00
Health insurance premiums	190.00
United Way contributions	150.00

SERIES B PROBLEMS

PROBLEM 8-1B   (LO2/4)   **GROSS PAY, DEDUCTIONS, AND NET PAY** Elyse Lin works for Columbia Industries. Her rate of pay is $9.00 per hour, and she is paid 1½ times the regular rate for all hours worked in excess of 40 per week. During the last week of January of the current year she worked 46 hours. Lin is married and claims 5 withholding allowances on her W-4 form. Her weekly wages are subject to the following deductions:

a)   Employee income tax (use Figure 8-4 on pages 263 and 264)

b)   Social Security tax at 6.2%

c)   Medicare tax at 1.45%

d)   Health insurance premium, $92.00

e)   Credit union, $110.00

f)   United Way contribution, $5.00

REQUIRED

1.   Compute Lin's regular pay, overtime pay, gross pay, and net pay.

2.   Journalize the payment of her wages for the week ended January 31, crediting Cash for the net amount.

PROBLEM 8-2B   (LO2/3/4)   **PAYROLL REGISTER AND PAYROLL JOURNAL ENTRY** Karen Jolly operates a bakery called Karen's Cupcakes. She has five employees, all of whom are paid on a weekly basis. Karen's Cupcakes uses a payroll register, individual employee earnings records, and a general journal.

    Karen's Cupcakes uses a weekly federal income tax withholding table. The payroll data for each employee for the week ended February 15, 20--, are given below. Employees are paid 1½ times the regular rate for working over 40 hours a week.

Name	No. of Allowances	Marital Status	Total Hours Worked Feb. 9–15	Rate	Total Earnings Jan. 1–Feb. 8
Barone, William	1	S	40	$10.00	$2,400.00
Hastings, Gene	4	M	45	12.00	3,360.00
Nitobe, Isako	3	M	46	8.75	2,935.00
Smith, Judy	4	M	42	11.00	2,745.00
Tarshis, Dolores	1	S	39	10.50	2,650.75

(continued)

Social Security tax is withheld from the first $76,200 of earnings at the rate of 6.2%. Medicare tax is withheld at the rate of 1.45%, and city earnings tax at the rate of 1%, both applied to gross pay. Hastings and Smith have $35.00 withheld and Nitobe and Tarshis have $15.00 withheld for health insurance. Nitobe and Tarshis have $25.00 withheld to be invested in the bakers' credit union. Hastings has $18.75 withheld and Smith $43.75 withheld under a savings bond purchase plan.

Karen's Cupcakes payroll is met by drawing checks on its regular bank account. The checks were issued in sequence, beginning with no. 365.

REQUIRED

1. Prepare a payroll register for Karen's Cupcakes for the week ended February 15, 20--. (In the Taxable Earnings/Unemployment Compensation column, enter the same amounts as in the Social Security column.) Total the amount columns, verify the totals, and rule with single and double lines.

2. Assuming that the wages for the week ended February 15 were paid on February 17, prepare the journal entry for the payment of this payroll.

PROBLEM 8-3B   **(LO3)**   **EMPLOYEE EARNINGS RECORD** Karen's Cupcakes in Problem 8-2B keeps employee earnings records. William Barone, employee number 19, is employed as a baker in the desserts department. He was born on August 26, 1959, and was hired on October 1 of last year. His Social Security number is 342-73-4681. He lives at 30 Timber Lane, Willington, CT 06279.

REQUIRED

For the week ended February 15, complete an employee earnings record for William Barone. (Insert earnings data only for the week of February 15.)

CHALLENGE PROBLEM

Irina Company pays its employees weekly. The last pay period for 20-1 was on December 28. From December 28 through December 31, the employees earned $1,754.00, so the following adjusting entry was made:

	20-1								
5	Dec.	31	Wages and Salaries Expense		1 7 5 4 00				5
6			Wages and Salaries Payable			1 7 5 4 00			6
7			To record accrued wages and salaries						7

The first pay period in 20-2 was on January 4. The totals line from Irina Company's payroll register for the week ended January 4, 20-2 was as follows:

PAYROLL

			EARNINGS				TAXABLE EARNINGS		
			REGULAR	OVERTIME	TOTAL	CUMULATIVE TOTAL	UNEMPLOYMENT COMPENSATION	SOCIAL SECURITY	
1	Totals		3 3 5 0 00		3 3 5 0 00	3 3 5 0 00	3 3 5 0 00	3 3 5 0 00	1

REGISTER—WEEK ENDED January 4, 20-2

		DEDUCTIONS						NET PAY	
	FEDERAL INCOME TAX	SOCIAL SECURITY TAX	MEDICARE TAX	HEALTH INSURANCE	UNITED WAY	OTHER	TOTAL		
1	3 4 2 00	2 0 7 70	4 8 58	5 0 00	8 0 00		7 2 8 28	2 6 2 1 72	1

REQUIRED

1. Prepare the journal entry for the payment of the payroll on January 4, 20-2.

2. Prepare T accounts for Wages and Salaries Expense and Wages and Salaries Payable showing the beginning balance, January 4, 20-2 entry, and ending balance as of January 4, 20-2.

MASTERY PROBLEM

Abigail Trenkamp owns and operates the Trenkamp Collection Agency. Listed below are the name, number of allowances claimed, marital status, information from time cards on hours worked each day, and the hourly rate of each employee. All hours worked in excess of 40 hours for Monday through Friday are paid at 1½ times the regular rate. All weekend hours are paid at double the regular rate.

Trenkamp uses a weekly federal income tax withholding table (see Figure 8-4 on pages 263 and 264). Social Security tax is withheld at the rate of 6.2% for the first $76,200 earned. Medicare tax is withheld at 1.45% and state income tax at 3.5%. Each employee has $5.00 withheld for health insurance. All employees use payroll deduction to the credit union for varying amounts as listed below.

Trenkamp Collection Agency
Payroll Information for the Week Ended November 18, 20--

Name	Employee No.	No. of Allow.	Marital Status	Regular Hours Worked S	S	M	T	W	T	F	Hourly Rate	Credit Union Deposit	Total Earnings 1/1–11/11
Berling, James	1	3	M	2	2	9	8	8	9	10	$12.00	$149.60	$24,525.00
Merz, Linda	2	4	M	4	3	8	8	8	8	11	10.00	117.00	20,480.00
Goetz, Ken	3	5	M	0	0	6	7	8	9	10	11.00	91.30	21,500.00
Menick, Judd	4	2	M	8	8	0	0	8	8	9	11.00	126.50	22,625.00
Morales, Eva	5	3	M	0	0	8	8	8	6	8	13.00	117.05	24,730.00
Heimbrock, Jacob	6	2	S	0	0	8	8	8	8	8	34.00	154.25	75,240.00
Townsley, Sarah	7	2	M	4	0	6	6	6	6	4	9.00	83.05	21,425.00
Salzman, Ben	8	4	M	6	2	8	8	6	6	6	11.00	130.00	6,635.00
Layton, Esther	9	4	M	0	0	8	8	8	8	8	11.00	88.00	5,635.00
Thompson, David	10	5	M	0	2	10	9	7	7	10	11.00	128.90	21,635.00
Vadillo, Carmen	11	2	S	8	0	4	8	8	8	9	13.00	139.11	24,115.00

The Trenkamp Collection Agency follows the practice of drawing a single check for the net amount of the payroll and depositing the check in a special payroll account at the bank. Individual checks issued were numbered consecutively, beginning with no. 331.

REQUIRED

1. Prepare a payroll register for Trenkamp Collection Agency for the week ended November 18, 20--. (In the Taxable Earnings/Unemployment Compensation column, enter $365 for Salzman and $440 for Layton. Leave this column blank for all other employees.) Total the amount columns, verify the totals, and rule with single and double lines.

2. Assuming that the wages for the week ended November 18 were paid on November 21, prepare the journal entry for the payment of this payroll.

(continued)

3. The current employee earnings record for Ben Salzman is provided in the working papers. Update Salzman's earnings record to reflect the November 18 payroll. Although this information should have been entered earlier, complete the required information on the earnings record. The necessary information is provided below.

Name	Ben F. Salzman
Address	12 Windmill Lane
	Trumbull, CT 06611
Employee No.	8
Gender	Male
Department	Administration
Occupation	Office Manager
Social Security No.	446-46-6321
Marital Status	Married
Allowances	4
Pay Rate	$11.00 per hour
Date of Birth	4/5/64
Date Hired	7/22/--

Self-Study Test Questions

True/False

1. An independent contractor is one who works under the control and direction of an employer. _____

2. Government laws and regulations regarding payroll are more complex for employees than for independent contractors. _____

3. Compensation for skilled or unskilled labor expressed in terms of hours, weeks, or units is called salary. _____

4. An employee's total earnings is called gross pay. _____

5. A payroll register is a multi-column form used to assemble the data required at the end of each payroll period. _____

Multiple Choice

1. Jack Smith is married, has a spouse who is not employed, has five dependent children, and does not anticipate large itemized deductions. How many withholding allowances is Smith entitled to? _____

   (a) 5   (c) 7
   (b) 6   (d) 8

2. A separate record of each employee's earnings is called a(n) _____

   (a) payroll register.   (c) W-4.
   (b) employee earnings record.   (d) earnings statement.

3. Nancy Summers worked 44 hours during the past week. She is entitled to 1½ times her regular pay for all hours worked in excess of 40 during the week. Her regular rate of pay is $12.00. Social Security tax is withheld at the rate of 6.2% and Medicare tax is withheld at the rate of 1.45%; federal income tax withheld is $68; and $5 of union dues are withheld. Her net pay for the week is _____

   (a) $440.89.   (c) $552.00.
   (b) $472.00.   (d) $436.78.

4. Social Security Tax Payable and Medicare Tax Payable are classified as _____

   (a) liabilities.   (c) owner's equity.
   (b) assets.   (d) expenses.

5. Which of the following is *not* a factor that determines the amount of federal income tax to be withheld from an employee's gross pay? _____

   (a) marital status   (c) total earnings
   (b) number of withholding allowances claimed (d) age of employee

The answers to the Self-Study Test Questions are at the end of the text.

9

Payroll Accounting: Employer Taxes and Reports

John Zenith's new shop assistant has worked out extremely well. Be A Sport is better organized and customers receive more direct attention. Having worked in a similar store in Connecticut, the new hire also was able to help John obtain accounts with two new vendors. The only negative feature of having the new employee has been the cost. Based on 25 hours per week at $8 an hour, John had budgeted a cost of $200 per week for the help. In fact, as John's bookkeeper had warned him, the cost is substantially higher. In simple terms, John has discovered that he must pay numerous payroll taxes, in addition to the basic wages of the employee. What payroll taxes must John pay as an employer? Assuming the employee works a full year and is paid $10,400

(52 weeks × $200), what is the total payroll cost to John of having this employee?

Careful study of this chapter should enable you to:

LO1 Describe and calculate employer payroll taxes.

LO2 Account for employer payroll taxes expense.

LO3 Describe employer reporting and payment responsibilities.

LO4 Describe and account for workers' compensation insurance.

The taxes we discussed in Chapter 8 had one thing in common—they all were levied on the employee. The employer withheld them from employees' earnings and paid them to the government. They did not add anything to the employer's payroll expenses.

In this chapter, we will examine several taxes that are imposed directly on the employer. All of these taxes represent additional payroll expenses.

EMPLOYER PAYROLL TAXES

LO1 Describe and calculate employer payroll taxes.

Most employers must pay FICA taxes, FUTA (Federal Unemployment Tax Act) taxes, and SUTA (state unemployment tax) taxes.

Employer's FICA Taxes

Both the employer and employee must pay Social Security and Medicare taxes. The employer FICA tax equals the employee FICA tax and the employer Medicare tax equals the employee Medicare tax.

Employer FICA taxes are levied on employers at the same rates and on the same earnings bases as the employee FICA taxes. As explained in Chapter 8, we are assuming the Social Security component is 6.2% on maximum earnings of $76,200 for each employee. Since there is no maximum on the Medicare component, this tax is 1.45% on all earnings.

The payroll register we saw in Chapter 8 is a key source of information for computing employer payroll taxes. That payroll register is reproduced in Figure 9-1. The Taxable Earnings Social Security column shows that $4,835 of employee earnings were subject to Social Security tax for the pay period. The employer's Social Security tax on these earnings is computed as follows:

PAYROLL

	NAME	ALLOWANCES	MARITAL STATUS	EARNINGS REGULAR	EARNINGS OVERTIME	EARNINGS TOTAL	CUMULATIVE TOTAL	TAXABLE EARNINGS UNEMPLOYMENT COMPENSATION	TAXABLE EARNINGS SOCIAL SECURITY	
1	Cadrain, Sarah	4	M	1 2 0 0 00	6 0 00	1 2 6 0 00	76 8 0 0 00		6 6 0 00	1
2	Guder, James	1	S	7 6 0 00	1 4 0 00	9 0 0 00	43 4 0 0 00		9 0 0 00	2
3	Istone, Ken	6	M	5 4 5 00		5 4 5 00	27 0 2 5 00		5 4 5 00	3
4	Kuzmik, Helen	2	M	4 8 0 00	2 9 4 00	7 7 4 00	31 0 0 0 00		7 7 4 00	4
5	Lee, Hoseoup	3	M	4 4 0 00		4 4 0 00	22 3 4 0 00		4 4 0 00	5
6	Swaney, Linda	2	S	5 2 8 00	1 9 8 00	7 2 6 00	27 5 0 0 00		7 2 6 00	6
7	Tucci, Paul	5	M	4 9 0 00		4 9 0 00	25 0 5 0 00		4 9 0 00	7
8	Wiles, Harry	1	S	3 0 0 00		3 0 0 00	6 3 0 0 00	3 0 0 00	3 0 0 00	8
9				4 7 4 3 00	6 9 2 00	5 4 3 5 00	259 4 1 5 00	3 0 0 00	4 8 3 5 00	9

Time cards, pay rates

Prior period total + current period earnings

Current below $7,000 cumul. total

Current below $76,200 cumul. total

FIGURE 9-1   Payroll Register (left side)

Social Security Taxable Earnings	×	Tax Rate	=	Tax
$4,835		.062		$299.77

 LEARNING KEY: Use the information in the payroll register to compute employer payroll taxes.

The Medicare tax applies to the total earnings of $5,435. The employer's Medicare tax on these earnings is computed as follows:

Total Earnings	×	Tax Rate	=	Tax
$5,435		.0145		$78.81

These amounts plus the employees' Social Security and Medicare taxes withheld must be paid by the employer to the Internal Revenue Service (IRS).

Self-Employment Tax

The self-employment tax rate is double the employee and employer Social Security and Medicare rates because the self-employed person is considered both the employer and employee.

Individuals who own and run their own business are considered self-employed. These individuals can be viewed as both employer and employee. They do not receive salary or wages from the business, but they do have earnings in the form of the business net income. **Self-employment income** is the net income of a trade or business run by an individual. Currently, persons earning self-employment income of $400 or more must pay a **self-employment tax**. Self-employment tax is a contribution to the FICA program. The tax rates are double the Social Security and Medicare rates. They are applied to the same income bases as those used for the Social Security and Medicare taxes.

One half of the self-employment tax is a personal expense of the owner of the business. The other half is similar to the employer Social Security and Medicare taxes paid for each employee. This portion of the tax is considered a business expense and is debited to Self-Employment Tax.

REGISTER—WEEK ENDED 12/19/--

	FEDERAL INCOME TAX	SOCIAL SECURITY TAX	MEDICARE TAX	HEALTH INSURANCE	UNITED WAY	OTHER	TOTAL	NET PAY	CHECK NO.	
1	154 00	40 92	18 27				213 19	1046 81	409	1
2	161 00	55 80	13 05		20 00		249 85	650 15	410	2
3	15 00	33 79	7 90	10 00			66 69	478 31	411	3
4	81 00	47 99	11 22	13 00	20 00		173 21	600 79	412	4
5	24 00	27 28	6 38	13 00			70 66	369 34	413	5
6	96 00	45 01	10 53				151 54	574 46	414	6
7	15 00	30 38	7 11	10 00			62 49	427 52	415	7
8	30 00	18 60	4 35				52 95	247 05	416	8
9	576 00	299 77	78 81	46 00	40 00		1040 58	4394 42		9

Withholding Tax Table — 6.2% × Social Security taxable earnings — 1.45% × total earnings — Specific employer–employee agreements — Total earnings − total deductions

FIGURE 9-1   Payroll Register (right side)

Employer's FUTA Tax

The **FUTA (Federal Unemployment Tax Act) tax** is levied only on employers. It is not deducted from employees' earnings. The purpose of this tax is to raise funds to administer the combined federal/state unemployment compensation program. The maximum amount of earnings subject to the FUTA tax and the tax rate can be changed by Congress. The current rate is 6.2% applied to maximum earnings of $7,000 for each employee. But employers are allowed a credit of up to 5.4% for participation in state unemployment programs. Thus, the effective federal rate is commonly 0.8%.

Gross FUTA rate	6.2%
Credit for state unemployment taxes	5.4%
Net FUTA rate	0.8%

To illustrate the computation of the FUTA tax, refer to Figure 9-1. The Taxable Earnings Unemployment Compensation column shows that only $300 of employee earnings were subject to the FUTA tax. This amount is so low because the payroll period is late in the calendar year (December 19, 20--). It is common for most employees to exceed the $7,000 earnings limit by this time. The FUTA tax is computed as shown in Figure 9-2.

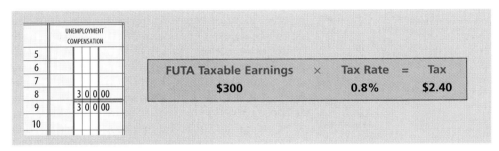

FUTA Taxable Earnings × Tax Rate = Tax
$300   0.8% $2.40

FIGURE 9-2   Computation of FUTA Tax

Employer's SUTA Tax

The **SUTA (state unemployment tax) tax** is also levied only on employers in most states. The purpose of this tax is to raise funds to pay unemployment benefits. Tax rates and unemployment benefits vary among the states. The most common rate is 5.4% applied to maximum earnings of $7,000 for each employee. Most states have a **merit-rating system** to encourage employers to provide regular employment to workers. If an employer has very few former employees receiving unemployment compensation, the employer qualifies for a lower state unemployment tax rate. If an employer qualifies for a lower state rate, the full credit of 5.4% would still be allowed in computing the federal unemployment tax due.

Refer to the payroll register in Figure 9-1. As we saw with the FUTA tax, only $300 of employee earnings for this pay period are subject to the state unemployment tax. The tax is computed as shown in Figure 9-3.

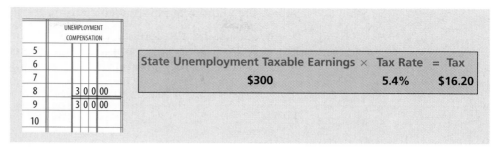

FIGURE 9-3   Computation of SUTA Tax

ACCOUNTING FOR EMPLOYER PAYROLL TAXES

LO2 Account for employer payroll taxes expense.

Now that we have computed the employer payroll taxes, we need to journalize them. It is common to debit all employer payroll taxes to a single account—Payroll Taxes Expense. However, we usually credit separate liability accounts for Social Security, Medicare, FUTA, and SUTA taxes payable.

Journalizing Employer Payroll Taxes

The employer payroll taxes computed in the previous section can be summarized as follows:

Employer's Social Security tax	$299.77
Employer's Medicare tax	78.81
FUTA tax	2.40
SUTA tax	16.20
Total employer payroll taxes	$397.18

These amounts provide the basis for the following journal entry:

5	Dec.	19	Payroll Taxes Expense		3 9 7 18					5
6			Social Security Tax Payable			2 9 9 77		6
7			Medicare Tax Payable			7 8 81		7
8			FUTA Tax Payable			2 40		8
9			SUTA Tax Payable			1 6 20		9
10			Employer payroll taxes for week ended Dec. 19					10

The steps needed to prepare this journal entry for employer payroll taxes are:

STEP 1   Obtain the taxable earnings amounts from the Taxable Earnings columns of the payroll register. In this case, Social Security taxable earnings were $4,835; Unemployment Compensation taxable earnings were $300.

STEP 2   Compute the amount of employer Social Security tax by multiplying the Social Security taxable earnings by 6.2%.

STEP 3   Compute the amount of employer Medicare tax by multiplying total earnings by 1.45%.

STEP 4   Compute the amount of FUTA tax by multiplying the Unemployment Taxable earnings by 0.8%.

STEP 5   Compute the amount of SUTA tax by multiplying the Unemployment Taxable earnings by 5.4%.

STEP 6   Prepare the appropriate journal entry using the amounts computed in steps 2–5.

To understand the journal entry for employer payroll taxes, let's use the accounting equation to examine the accounts involved. The five accounts affected by the payroll taxes entry above are shown in the accounting equation in Figure 9-4.

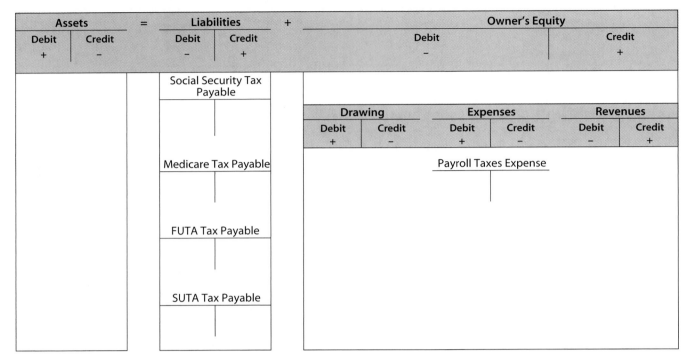

FIGURE 9-4   Accounting for Payroll Taxes

Payroll Taxes Expense

The Social Security, Medicare, FUTA, and SUTA taxes imposed on the employer are expenses of doing business. Each of the employer taxes is debited to Payroll Taxes Expense.

Payroll Taxes Expense

Debit	Credit
Social Security, Medicare, FUTA, and SUTA taxes imposed on the employer	

Social Security and Medicare Taxes Payable

These are the same liability accounts used in Chapter 8 to record the Social Security and Medicare taxes withheld from employees' earnings. The accounts are credited to enter the Social Security and Medicare taxes imposed on the employer. They are debited when the taxes are paid to the IRS. When all of the Social Security and Medicare taxes have been paid, the accounts will have zero balances.

Social Security Tax Payable

Debit	Credit
payment of Social Security tax	Social Security taxes (1) withheld from employees' earnings and (2) imposed on the employer

Medicare Tax Payable

Debit	Credit
payment of Medicare tax	Medicare taxes (1) withheld from employees' earnings and (2) imposed on the employer

LEARNING KEY: Employer and employee Social Security and Medicare taxes are credited to the same liability accounts because both of these taxes are due and will be paid to the IRS.

FUTA Tax Payable

A separate liability account entitled FUTA Tax Payable is kept for the employer's FUTA tax. This account is credited for the tax imposed on employers under the Federal Unemployment Tax Act. The account is debited when this tax is paid. When all of the FUTA taxes have been paid, the account will have a zero balance.

FUTA Tax Payable

Debit	Credit
payment of FUTA tax	FUTA tax imposed on the employer

SUTA Tax Payable

A separate liability account entitled SUTA Tax Payable is kept for the state unemployment tax. This account is credited for the tax imposed on employers under the state unemployment compensation laws. The account is debited when this tax is paid. When all of the state unemployment taxes have been paid, the account will have a zero balance.

SUTA Tax Payable

Debit	Credit
payment of SUTA tax	SUTA tax imposed on the employer

Total Payroll Cost of an Employee

It is interesting to note what it really costs to employ a person. The employer must, of course, pay the gross wages of an employee. In addition, the employer must pay payroll taxes on employee earnings up to certain dollar limits.

To illustrate, assume that an employee earns $26,000 a year. The total cost of this employee to the employer is calculated as follows:

Gross wages	$26,000
Employer Social Security tax, 6.2% of $26,000	1,612
Employer Medicare tax, 1.45% of $26,000	377
State unemployment tax, 5.4% of $7,000	378
FUTA tax, 0.8% of $7,000	56
	$28,423

Thus, the total payroll cost of employing a person whose stated compensation is $26,000 is $28,423. Employer payroll taxes clearly are a significant cost of doing business. Employer-paid medical insurance and pension plans can further increase total payroll costs.

REPORTING AND PAYMENT RESPONSIBILITIES

LO3 Describe employer reporting and payment responsibilities.

Employer payroll reporting and payment responsibilities fall into five areas:

1. Federal income tax withholding and Social Security and Medicare taxes

2. FUTA taxes

3. SUTA taxes

4. Employee Wage and Tax Statement (Form W-2)

5. Summary of employee wages and taxes

Federal Income Tax Withholding and Social Security and Medicare Taxes

Three important aspects of employer reporting and payment responsibilities for federal income tax withholding and Social Security and Medicare taxes are:

1. Determining when payments are due

2. Use of Form 8109, Federal Tax Deposit Coupon

3. Use of Form 941, Employer's Quarterly Federal Tax Return

When Payments are Due. The date by which federal income tax withholding and Social Security and Medicare taxes must be paid depends on the amount of these taxes. Figure 9-5 summarizes the deposit rules stated in *Circular E—Employer's Tax Guide*. In general, the larger the amount that needs to be deposited, the more frequently payments must be made. For simplicity, we will assume that deposits must be made 15 days after the end of each month.

DEPOSIT AMOUNT	DEPOSIT DUE
1. Less than $1,000 at the end of the current quarter	1. Pay with Form 941 at end of the month following end of the quarter
2. $1,000 or more at the end of the current quarter and $50,000 or less in total during the lookback period*	2. Deposit 15 days after end of the month
3. $500 or more at the end of the current quarter and more than $50,000 in total during the lookback period*	3. Deposit every other Wednesday or Friday, depending on day of the week payroll payments are made
4. $100,000 or more on any day during the current quarter	4. Deposit by the end of the next banking day

*Lookback period is the four quarters beginning July 1, two years ago, and ending June 30, one year ago.

FIGURE 9-5   **Summary of Deposit Rules**

> Taxpayers who are not required to make electronic deposits may voluntarily participate in EFTPS.

Form 8109. Deposits may be made using either the **Electronic Federal Tax Payment System (EFTPS)** or Form 8109. The EFTPS is an electronic funds transfer system for making federal tax deposits. Any taxpayer whose deposits in the prior year exceeded $200,000 is required to use this system. Deposits other than EFTPS are made at a Federal Reserve Bank or other authorized commercial bank using Form 8109, Federal Tax Deposit Coupon (Figure 9-6). The **Employer Identification Number (EIN)** shown on this form is obtained by the employer from the IRS. This number identifies the employer and must be shown on all payroll forms and reports filed with the IRS.

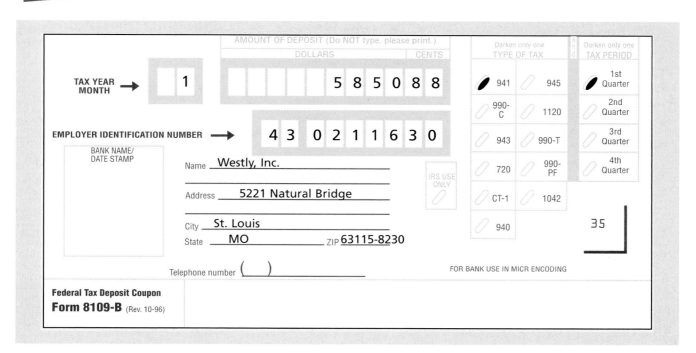

FIGURE 9-6   **Federal Tax Deposit Coupon (Form 8109)**

The $5,850.88 deposit shown in Figure 9-6 for Westly, Inc. was for the following taxes:

Employees' income tax withheld from wages		$2,526.80
Social Security tax:		
Withheld from employees' wages	$1,346.24	
Imposed on employer	1,346.24	2,692.48
Medicare tax:		
Withheld from employees' wages	$ 315.80	
Imposed on employer	315.80	631.60
Amount of check		$5,850.88

The journal entry for this deposit would be:

5	Feb.	15	Employee Income Tax Payable		2 5 2 6 80		5
6			Social Security Tax Payable		2 6 9 2 48		6
7			Medicare Tax Payable		6 3 1 60		7
8			Cash			5 8 5 0 88	8
9			Deposit of employee federal income tax and				9
10			Social Security and Medicare taxes				10

Form 941. Form 941, Employer's Quarterly Federal Tax Return, must be filed with the IRS at the end of the month following each calendar quarter. This form reports the following taxes for the quarter:

1. Employee federal income tax withheld

2. Employee Social Security and Medicare taxes withheld

3. Employer Social Security and Medicare taxes

A completed form for Westly, Inc. for the first quarter of the calendar year is shown in Figure 9-7. Instructions for completing the form are provided with the form and in *Circular E.*

FUTA Taxes

Federal unemployment taxes must be calculated on a quarterly basis. If the accumulated liability exceeds $100, the total must be paid to a Federal Reserve Bank or other authorized commercial bank. The total is due by the end of the month following the close of the quarter. If the liability is $100 or less, no deposit is necessary. The amount is simply added to the amount to be deposited for the next quarter. FUTA taxes are deposited using either EFTPS or Form 8109 (Figure 9-6).

Assume that Westly, Inc.'s accumulated FUTA tax liability for the first quarter of the calendar year is $408. Westly would use Form 8109 to deposit this amount on April 30. The journal entry for this transaction would be as follows:

15	Apr.	30	FUTA Tax Payable		4 0 8 00		15
16			Cash			4 0 8 00	16
17			Paid federal unemployment tax				17

Form **941**
(Rev. January 2000)
Department of the Treasury
Internal Revenue Service

Employer's Quarterly Federal Tax Return
▶ See separate instructions for information on completing this return.
Please type or print.

Enter state code for state in which deposits were made ONLY if different from state in address to the right ▶ M:O (see page 2 of instructions).

Name (as distinguished from trade name)	Date quarter ended	OMB No. 1545-0029
	March 30, 20--	
Trade name, if any	Employer identification number	T
Westly, Inc	43-0211630	FF
Address (number and street)	City, state, and ZIP code	FD
5221 Natural Bridge	St. Louis, Mo 63115-8230	FP
		I
		T

If address is different from prior return, check here ▶ ☐

IRS Use

1 1 1 1 1 1 1 1 1 1 1   2   3 3 3 3 3 3 3 3   4 4 4   5 5 5
6   7   8 8 8 8 8 8 8   9 9 9 9 9   10 10 10 10 10 10 10 10 10 10

If you do not have to file returns in the future, check here ▶ ☐ and enter date final wages paid ▶
If you are a seasonal employer, see **Seasonal employers** on page 1 of the instructions and check here ▶ ☐

1	Number of employees in the pay period that includes March 12th . ▶	1		
2	Total wages and tips, plus other compensation	**2**	65,160	8
3	Total income tax withheld from wages, tips, and sick pay	**3**	65,160	00
4	Adjustment of withheld income tax for preceding quarters of calendar year	**4**	7,595	80
5	Adjusted total of income tax withheld (line 3 as adjusted by line 4—see instructions) . . .	**5**		0
6	Taxable social security wages . . . . . **6a** 65,160 00 × 12.4% (.124) =	**6b**	7,595	80
	Taxable social security tips . . . . . **6c** 0 × 12.4% (.124) =	**6d**	8,079	84
7	Taxable Medicare wages and tips . . . **7a** 65,160 00 × 2.9% (.029) =	**7b**		0
8	Total social security and Medicare taxes (add lines 6b, 6d, and 7b). Check here if wages are not subject to social security and/or Medicare tax . . . . ▶ ☐	**8**	1,889	64
9	Adjustment of social security and Medicare taxes (see instructions for required explanation) Sick Pay $ _____ ± Fractions of Cents $ _____ ± Other $ _____ =	**9**	9,969	48
10	Adjusted total of social security and Medicare taxes (line 8 as adjusted by line 9—see instructions)	**10**		0
11	**Total taxes** (add lines 5 and 10)	**11**	9,969	48
12	Advance earned income credit (EIC) payments made to employees	**12**	17,565	28
13	Net taxes (subtract line 12 from line 11). **If $1,000 or more, this must equal line 17, column (d) below (or line D of Schedule B (Form 941))**	**13**		
14	Total deposits for quarter, including overpayment applied from a prior quarter	**14**	17, 565	28
15	**Balance due** (subtract line 14 from line 13). See instructions	**15**	17,565	28
16	**Overpayment.** If line 14 is more than line 13, enter excess here ▶ $ _____ and check if to be: ☐ Applied to next return **OR** ☐ Refunded.			

● **All filers:** If line 13 is less than $1,000, you need not complete line 17 or Schedule B (Form 941).
● **Semiweekly schedule depositors:** Complete Schedule B (Form 941) and check here . . . . ▶ ☐
● **Monthly schedule depositors:** Complete line 17, columns (a) through (d), and check here. . . . . ▶ ☒

17	Monthly Summary of Federal Tax Liability. Do not complete if you were a semiweekly schedule depositor.		
(a) First month liability	**(b)** Second month liability	**(c)** Third month liability	**(d)** Total liability for quarter
5,850.88	5,690.77	6,023.63	17,565.28

Sign Here
Under penalties of perjury, I declare that I have examined this return, including accompanying schedules and statements, and to the best of my knowledge and belief, it is true, correct, and complete.

Signature ▶ *William P. Jones*   Print Your Name and Title ▶ *Treasurer*   Date ▶ *4/30/--*

For Privacy Act and Paperwork Reduction Act Notice, see back of Payment Voucher.   Cat. No. 17001Z   Form **941** (Rev. 1-2000)

FIGURE 9-7 **Employer's Quarterly Federal Tax Return (Form 941)**

Form **940**	**Employer's Annual Federal Unemployment (FUTA) Tax Return**	OMB No. 1545-0028
Department of the Treasury Internal Revenue Service (99)	▶ See separate Instructions for Form 940 for information on completing this form.	**20--**

⌐ Name (as distinguished from trade name)	Calendar year ⌐
Trade name, if any	
Westly, Inc	
Address and ZIP code	Employer identification number
⌐ 5221 Natural Bridge	⌐ 43:0211630 ⌐
St. Louis, Mo 63115-8230	

	T	
	FF	
	FD	
	FP	
	I	
	T	

A Are you required to pay unemployment contributions to only one state? (If "No," skip questions B and C.) . . ☒ Yes ☐ No

B Did you pay all state unemployment contributions by January 31, 2000? ((1) If you deposited your total FUTA tax when due, check "Yes" if you paid all state unemployment contributions by February 10. (2) If a 0% experience rate is granted, check "Yes." (3) If "No," skip question C.) . . . . ☒ Yes ☐ No

C Were all wages that were taxable for FUTA tax also taxable for your state's unemployment tax? . . . . . ☒ Yes ☐ No

If you answered "No" to any of these questions, you must file Form 940. If you answered "Yes" to all the questions, you may file Form 940-EZ, which is a simplified version of Form 940. (Successor employers see **Special credit for successor employers** on page 3 of the instructions.) You can get Form 940-EZ by calling 1-800-TAX-FORM (1-800-829-3676) or from the IRS's Internet Web Site at **www.irs.gov.**

If you will not have to file returns in the future, check here (see **Who Must File** in separate instructions), **and** complete and sign the return . . . . ▶ ☐

If this is an Amended Return, check here. . . . . ▶ ☐

Part I **Computation of Taxable Wages**

1	Total payments (including payments shown on lines 2 and 3) during the calendar year for services of employees	**1**		258,954 00
2	Exempt payments. (Explain all exempt payments, attaching additional sheets if necessary.) ▶	**2**		
3	Payments of more than $7,000 for services. Enter only amounts over the first $7,000 paid to each employee. Do not include any exempt payments from line 2. The $7,000 amount is the Federal wage base. Your state wage base may be different. **Do not use your state wage limitation** .	**3**	203,254 00	
4	Total exempt payments (add lines 2 and 3)	**4**		203,254 00
5	**Total taxable wages** (subtract line 4 from line 1) . . . . ▶	**5**		55,700 00

Be sure to complete both sides of this form, and sign in the space provided on the back.

For Privacy Act and Paperwork Reduction Act Notice, see separate instructions.   Cat. No. 11234O   Form **940** (1999)

Form 940 (1999)   Page **2**

Part II **Tax Due or Refund**

1	Gross FUTA tax. Multiply the wages from Part I, line 5, by .062	**1**	3,453 40
2	Maximum credit. Multiply the wages from Part I, line 5, by .054 . . | **2** | 3,007 80		
3	Computation of tentative credit (**Note:** All taxpayers must complete the applicable columns.)		

(a) Name of state	(b) State reporting number(s) as shown on employer's state contribution returns	(c) Taxable payroll (as defined in state act)	(d) State experience rate period From	(d) To	(e) State experience rate	(f) Contributions if rate had been 5.4% (col. (c) x .054)	(g) Contributions payable at experience rate (col. (c) x col. (e))	(h) Additional credit (col. (f) minus col.(g)). If 0 or less, enter -0-.	(i) Contributions paid to state by 940 due date
MO	36112	55,700.00	1/1/--	12/31/--	.054	3,007.80	3,007.80	-0-	3,007.80

3a	Totals . . . ▶	55,700.00			
3b	**Total tentative credit** (add line 3a, columns (h) and (i) only—for late payments also see the instructions for Part II, line 6 . . . . ▶		**3b**	3,007 80
4				
5				
6	**Credit:** Enter the smaller of the amount from Part II, line 2 or line 3b; or the amount from the worksheet in the Part II, line 6 instructions	**6**	3,007 80
7	**Total FUTA tax** (subtract line 6 from line 1). If the result is over $100, also complete Part III . .	**7**	445 60
8	Total FUTA tax deposited for the year, including any overpayment applied from a prior year . .	**8**	427 60
9	**Balance due** (subtract line 8 from line 7). Pay to the "United States Treasury". If you owe more than $100, see **Depositing FUTA Tax** on page 3 of the separate instructions . . . . ▶	**9**	18 00
10	**Overpayment** (subtract line 7 from line 8). Check if it is to be: ☐ **Applied to next return** or ☐ **Refunded** . . . . ▶	**10**	

Part III **Record of Quarterly Federal Unemployment Tax Liability** (Do not include state liability.) **Complete only if** line 7 is over $100. See page 6 of the separate instructions.

Quarter	First (Jan. 1–Mar. 31)	Second (Apr. 1–June 30)	Third (July 1–Sept. 30)	Fourth (Oct. 1–Dec. 31)	Total for year
Liability for quarter	408.00	26.00	5.60	6.00	445.60

Under penalties of perjury, I declare that I have examined this return, including accompanying schedules and statements, and, to the best of my knowledge and belief, it is true, correct, and complete, and that no part of any payment made to a state unemployment fund claimed as a credit was, or is to be, deducted from the payments to employees.

Signature ▶ *William P. Jones*	Title (Owner, etc.) ▶ *Treasurer*	Date ▶ 1/31/--

Form **940** (1999)

FIGURE 9-8 Employer's Annual Federal Unemployment (FUTA) Tax Return (Form 940)

Form 940. In addition to making quarterly deposits, employers are required to file an annual report of federal unemployment tax using Form 940. This form must be filed with the IRS by January 31 following the end of the calendar year. Figure 9-8 shows a completed Form 940 for Westly, Inc. Instructions for completing the form are provided with the form and in *Circular E*.

SUTA Taxes

Deposit rules and forms for state unemployment taxes vary among the states. Deposits usually are required on a quarterly basis. Assume that Westly's accumulated state unemployment liability for the first quarter of the calendar year is $2,754. The journal entry for the deposit of this amount with the state on April 30 would be:

19	Apr.	30	SUTA Tax Payable	2 7 5 4 00		19
20			Cash		2 7 5 4 00	20
21			Paid state unemployment tax			21

Employee Wage and Tax Statement

By January 31 of each year, employers must furnish each employee with a Wage and Tax Statement, Form W-2 (Figure 9-9). This form shows the total amount of wages paid to the employee and the amounts of taxes withheld during the preceding taxable year. The employee earnings record contains the information needed to complete this form.

a Control number		Void ☐	For Official Use Only ▶ OMB No. 1545-0008	
b Employer identification number 43-0211630			1 Wages, tips, other compensation 27,645.00	2 Federal income tax withheld 1,088.00
c Employer's name, address, and ZIP code Westly, Inc. 5221 Natural Bridge St. Louis, MO 63115-8230			3 Social security wages 27,645.00	4 Social security tax withheld 1,713.99
			5 Medicare wages and tips 27,645.00	6 Medicare tax withheld 400.85
			7 Social security tips	8 Allocated tips
d Employee's social security number			9 Advance EIC payment	10 Dependent care benefits
e Employee's name (first, middle initial, last) 393-58-8194			11 Nonqualified plans	12 Benefits included in box 1
Ken M. Istone 1546 Swallow Dr. St. Louis, MO 63144-4752			13 See Instrs. for box 13	14 Other
			15 Statutory employee ☐ Deceased ☐ Pension plan ☐ Legal rep. ☐ Deferred compensation ☐	
f Employee's address and ZIP code				
16 State Employer's state I.D. no.	17 State wages, tips, etc.	18 State income tax	19 Locality name 20 Local wages, tips, etc.	21 Local income tax

Form **W-2** Wage and Tax Statement 20--

Copy A For Social Security Administration—Send this entire page with Form W-3 to the Social Security Administration; photocopies are not acceptable.

Cat. No. 10134D

Department of the Treasury—Internal Revenue Service

For Privacy Act and Paperwork Reduction Act Notice, see separate instructions.

FIGURE 9-9   Wage and Tax Statement (Form W-2)

Multiple copies of Form W-2 are needed for the following purposes:

- Copy A—Employer sends to Social Security Administration
- Copy B—Employee attaches to federal income tax return
- Copy C—Employee retains for his or her own records
- Copy D—Employer retains for business records
- Copy 1—Employer sends to state or local tax department
- Copy 2—Employee attaches to state or local income tax return

Summary of Employee Wages and Taxes

Employers send Form W-3, Transmittal of Wage and Tax Statements (Figure 9-10), with Copy A of Forms W-2 to the Social Security Administration. Form W-3 must be filed by the last day of February following the end of each taxable year. This form summarizes the employee earnings and tax information presented on Forms W-2 for the year. Information needed to complete Form W-3 is contained in the employee earnings records.

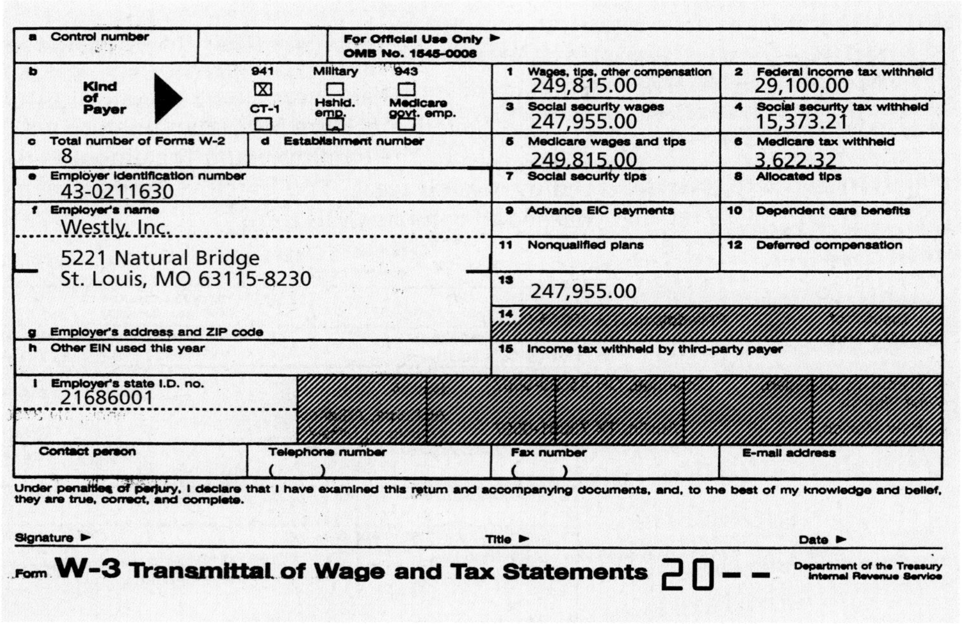

FIGURE 9-10   Transmittal of Wage and Tax Statements (Form W-3)

Summary of Reports and Payments

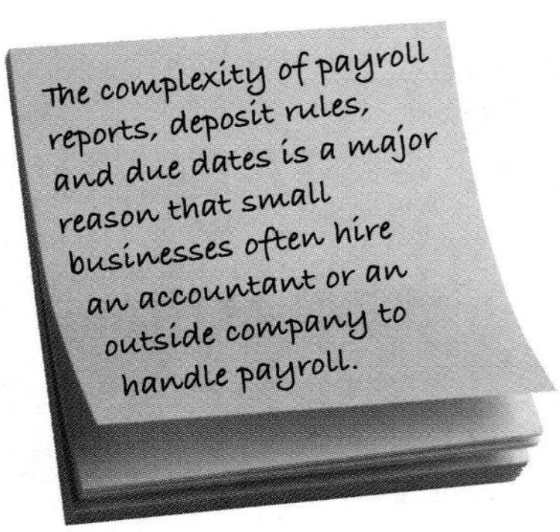

The complexity of payroll reports, deposit rules, and due dates is a major reason that small businesses often hire an accountant or an outside company to handle payroll.

Keeping track of the many payroll reports, deposits, and due dates can be a challenge for an employer. Figure 9-11 shows a calendar that highlights the due dates for the various reports and deposits. The calendar assumes the following for an employer:

1. Undeposited FIT (federal income tax) and Social Security and Medicare taxes of $1,000 at the end of each quarter and less than $50,000 during the lookback period.

2. Undeposited FUTA taxes of more than $100 at the end of each quarter.

3. SUTA taxes deposited quarterly.

Color Key

File Forms 940, 941, state unemployment tax report, and send W-2 to employees.	File form W-3 with Copy A of W-2s.	File Form 941 and state unemployment tax report.	Deposit FIT and Social Security and Medicare taxes from previous month.

January

S	M	T	W	T	F	S
			1	2	3	4
5	6	7	8	9	10	11
12	13	14	15	16	17	18
19	20	21	22	23	24	25
26	27	28	29	30	31	

February

S	M	T	W	T	F	S
						1
2	3	4	5	6	7	8
9	10	11	12	13	14	15
16	17	18	19	20	21	22
23	24	25	26	27	28	29

March

S	M	T	W	T	F	S
1	2	3	4	5	6	7
8	9	10	11	12	13	14
15	16	17	18	19	20	21
22	23	24	25	26	27	28
29	30	31				

April

S	M	T	W	T	F	S
			1	2	3	4
5	6	7	8	9	10	11
12	13	14	15	16	17	18
19	20	21	22	23	24	25
26	27	28	29	30		

May

S	M	T	W	T	F	S
					1	2
3	4	5	6	7	8	9
10	11	12	13	14	15	16
17	18	19	20	21	22	23
24	25	26	27	28	29	30
31						

June

S	M	T	W	T	F	S
	1	2	3	4	5	6
7	8	9	10	11	12	13
14	15	16	17	18	19	20
21	22	23	24	25	26	27
28	29	30				

July

S	M	T	W	T	F	S
			1	2	3	4
5	6	7	8	9	10	11
12	13	14	15	16	17	18
19	20	21	22	23	24	25
26	27	28	29	30	31	

August

S	M	T	W	T	F	S
						1
2	3	4	5	6	7	8
9	10	11	12	13	14	15
16	17	18	19	20	21	22
23	24	25	26	27	28	29
30	31					

September

S	M	T	W	T	F	S
		1	2	3	4	5
6	7	8	9	10	11	12
13	14	15	16	17	18	19
20	21	22	23	24	25	26
27	28	29	30			

October

S	M	T	W	T	F	S
				1	2	3
4	5	6	7	8	9	10
11	12	13	14	15	16	17
18	19	20	21	22	23	24
25	26	27	28	29	30	31

November

S	M	T	W	T	F	S
1	2	3	4	5	6	7
8	9	10	11	12	13	14
15	16	17	18	19	20	21
22	23	24	25	26	27	28
29	30					

December

S	M	T	W	T	F	S
		1	2	3	4	5
6	7	8	9	10	11	12
13	14	15	16	17	18	19
20	21	22	23	24	25	26
27	28	29	30	31		

FIGURE 9-11   **Payroll Calendar**

A BROADER VIEW

Dealing with Payroll Complexity—Let Someone Else Do It

A common way for both small and large businesses to deal with the complexity of payroll reports, deposit rules, and due dates is to hire an outside company to handle the payroll. Payroll processing companies have combined payroll expertise with the power of computers to create a major business enterprise based on the efficient and effective provision of payroll services.

To give you some idea of the extent to which businesses have turned to outside companies to handle payroll, consider Automatic Data Processing, Inc. (ADP), the world's largest provider of payroll services. ADP currently processes payrolls for more than 450,000 employers, with over 20 million employees in North America plus several million in Europe. ADP prepares employee paychecks, journals, and summary reports; collects and remits funds for federal, state, and local payroll taxes; and files all required forms with government taxing authorities.

WORKERS' COMPENSATION INSURANCE

LO4 Describe and account for workers' compensation insurance.

Most states require employers to carry workers' compensation insurance. **Workers' compensation insurance** provides insurance for employees who suffer a job-related illness or injury.

The employer usually pays the entire cost of workers' compensation insurance. The cost of the insurance depends on the number of employees, riskiness of the job, and the company's accident history. For example, the insurance premium for workers in a chemical plant could be higher than for office workers. Employers generally obtain the insurance either from the state in which they operate or from a private insurance company.

The employer usually pays the premium at the beginning of the year, based on the estimated payroll for the year. At the end of the year, after the actual amount of payroll is known, an adjustment is made. If the employer has overpaid, a credit is received from the state or insurance company. If the employer has underpaid, an additional premium is paid.

To illustrate the accounting for workers' compensation insurance, assume that Lockwood Co. expects its payroll for the year to be $210,000. If Lockwood's insurance premium rate is 0.2%, its payment for workers' compensation insurance at the beginning of the year would be $420:

Estimated Payroll	×	Rate	=	Estimated Insurance Premium
$210,000		.002		$420.00

The journal entry for the payment of this $420 premium would be:

7			Workers' Compensation Insurance Expense		4 2 0 00			7
8			Cash			4 2 0 00		8
9			Paid insurance premium					9

If Lockwood's actual payroll for the year is $220,000, Lockwood would owe an additional premium of $20 at year end:

Actual Payroll	×	Rate	=	Insurance Premium
$220,000		.002		$440.00
Less premium paid				420.00
Additional premium due				$ 20.00

The adjusting entry at year end for this additional expense would be:

11	Dec.	31	Workers' Compensation Insurance Expense		2 0 00			11
12			Workers' Compensation Insurance Payable			2 0 00		12
13			Adjustment for insurance premium					13

In T account form, the total Workers' Compensation Insurance Expense of $440.00 would look like this:

Workers' Compensation Insurance Expense

Debit	Credit
420.00	
20.00	
440.00	

If Lockwood's actual payroll for the year is only $205,000, Lockwood would be due a refund of $10:

Payroll	×	Rate	=	Insurance Premium
$205,000		**.002**		**$410.00**
Less premium paid				**420.00**
Refund due				**$ (10.00)**

The adjusting entry at year end for this refund due would be:

16	Dec.	31	Insurance Refund Receivable			1 0 00			16
17			Workers' Compensation Insurance Expense				1 0 00		17
18			Adjustment for insurance premium						18

In T account form, the total Workers' Compensation Insurance Expense of $410 would look like this:

Workers' Compensation Insurance Expense

Debit	Credit
420.00	10.00
410.00	

Computers and Accounting

Computerized Payroll Systems—Gary P. Schneider

Payroll, as you have learned in this and the previous chapter, is one of the most detailed and computation-laden parts of accounting. For this reason, payroll was one of the first accounting activities that companies computerized. All payroll systems, no matter how large or small, divide the work into four main parts: (1) maintaining basic records about employees and tax rates, (2) recording employee activities such as time worked or commissions earned, (3) calculating the net pay and payroll taxes, and (4) reporting the results of those calculations in a variety of formats. You can see parts (1), (2), and (4) illustrated in Figure A (in a computerized payroll system, the calculations are done by the computer behind the scenes). The figure on the following page shows the main payroll module screen for Peachtree®, one of the popular accounting software packages for small and medium sized businesses.

As you can see in the figure, Peachtree's payroll module is organized into three sections, Maintain, Tasks, and Reports. The program performs the payroll calculations based on information that accountants enter in the Maintain section and the Tasks section. The results of those calculations are made available in the Reports section.

The Maintain section allows accountants to enter information about employees and tax rates. Employee information includes names, addresses, social security numbers, pay rates, marital status and number of tax exemptions claimed. The Edit Company Tax Tables part lets accountants keep the payroll module updated to reflect changes in federal and state tax laws. Payroll Setup Wizard helps accountants specify the general ledger accounts in which payroll information will be recorded. It also sets up the payroll module so the

Computers and Accounting *(continued)*

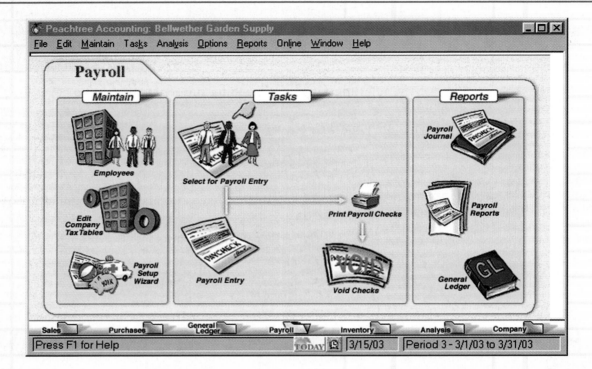

company's rules about such things as vacation pay and sick leave are properly applied.

The Tasks section gives accountants a place to enter time worked, commissions earned, and other information that the computer uses to calculate regular and overtime pay. Also, this section is where accountants can print paychecks (selecting all or just some employees) and record voided checks as necessary.

The Reports section provides a choice of many different reports, including all of the reports you learned about in this and the previous chapter. These include the payroll register, the payroll journal, and federal employment tax reports, such as the Forms 940 and 941.

In smaller companies, the payroll module can provide all of the information that managers need to track the people they hire, promote, and fire. It also can do a very good job of recording raises. However, as the business gets larger, hires more employees, and introduces more complex benefit plans, the company's information needs can exceed the capabilities of accounting software payroll modules.

When they grow to this point, many companies buy or create separate human resource management (HRM) information systems to keep track of hirings, firings, promotions, and benefit plan participation. Ideally, these HRM systems can share information with the payroll module of the accounting software. Virtually all of the information stored in the employee records section of a payroll module (for example, employee names, addresses, social security numbers, pay rates) is the same information a company will want to have in its HRM. It is more efficient to keep that information stored in one format and in one place. The employee information can then be shared effectively by the payroll department and the human resources department.

Learning Objectives	Key Points to Remember
1 Describe and calculate employer payroll taxes. **2 Account for employer payroll taxes expense.**	Employer payroll taxes include FICA, FUTA, and SUTA taxes. These taxes represent additional payroll expenses of the employer. The journal entry for payroll taxes is | 8		Payroll Taxes Expense	x x x xx		8
9		Social Security Tax Payable		x x x xx	9
10		Medicare Tax Payable		x x x xx	10
11		FUTA Tax Payable		x x x xx	11
12		SUTA Tax Payable		x x x xx	12	 The steps to be followed in preparing this journal entry are: 1. Obtain the taxable earnings amounts from the Taxable Earnings columns of the payroll register. 2. Compute the amount of employer Social Security tax by multiplying the Social Security taxable earnings by 6.2%. 3. Compute the amount of Medicare tax by multiplying total earnings by 1.45%. 4. Compute the amount of FUTA tax by multiplying the Unemployment Taxable earnings by 0.8%. 5. Compute the amount of SUTA tax by multiplying the Unemployment Taxable earnings by 5.4%. 6. Prepare the appropriate journal entry using the amounts computed in steps 2–5.
3 Describe employer reporting and payment responsibilities.	Employer payroll reporting and payment responsibilities fall into five areas: 1. Federal income tax withholding and Social Security and Medicare taxes 2. FUTA taxes 3. SUTA taxes 4. Employee Wage and Tax Statement (Form W-2) 5. Summary of employee wages and taxes Key forms needed in reporting and paying employer payroll taxes are: 1. Form 8109, Federal Tax Deposit Coupon 2. Form 941, Employer's Quarterly Federal Tax Return 3. Form 940, Employer's Annual Federal Unemployment Tax Return By January 31 of each year, employers must provide each employee with a Wage and Tax Statement, Form W-2. By February 28 of each year, employers must file Form W-3 and Copy A of Forms W-2 with the Social Security Administration.
4 Describe and account for workers' compensation insurance.	Workers' compensation insurance provides insurance for employees who suffer a job-related illness or injury. Employers generally are required to carry and pay the entire cost of this insurance.

Reflection: Answering the Opening Question

John must pay employer Social Security and Medicare taxes, SUTA tax, and FUTA tax. The total payroll cost of this employee is:

Gross wages	$10,400.00
Social Security tax (6.2% of $10,400)	644.80
Medicare tax (1.45% of $10,400)	150.80
SUTA tax (5.4% of $7,000)	378.00
FUTA tax (0.8% of $7,000)	56.00
Total cost	$11,629.60

KEY TERMS

Electronic Federal Tax Payment System (EFTPS), (301)   An electronic funds transfer system for making federal tax deposits.

employer FICA taxes, (294)   Taxes levied on employers at the same rates and on the same earnings bases as the employee FICA taxes.

Employer Identification Number (EIN), (301)   A number that identifies the employer on all payroll forms and reports filed with the IRS.

FUTA (Federal Unemployment Tax Act) tax, (296)   A tax levied on employers to raise funds to administer the federal/state unemployment compensation program.

merit-rating system, (296)   A system to encourage employers to provide regular employment to workers.

self-employment income, (295)   The net income of a trade or business run by an individual.

self-employment tax, (295)   A contribution to the FICA program.

SUTA (state unemployment tax) tax, (296)   A tax levied on employers to raise funds to pay unemployment benefits.

workers' compensation insurance, (308)   Provides insurance for employees who suffer a job-related illness or injury.

DEMONSTRATION PROBLEM

The totals line from Hart Company's payroll register for the week ended December 31, 20--, is as follows:

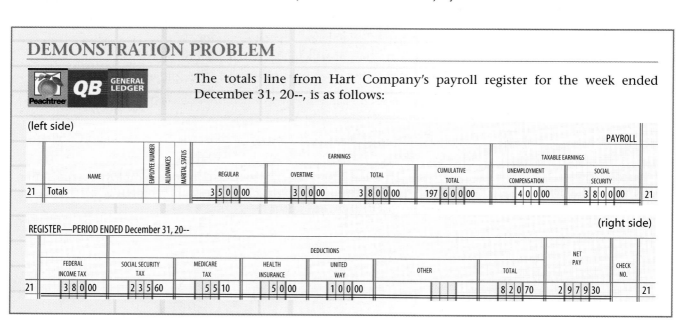

Payroll taxes are imposed as follows: Social Security, 6.2%; Medicare, 1.45%; FUTA, 0.8%; and SUTA, 5.4%.

REQUIRED

1. a. Prepare the journal entry for payment of this payroll on December 31, 20--.

    b. Prepare the journal entry for the employer's payroll taxes for the period ended December 31, 20--.

2. Hart Company had the following balances in its general ledger *after* the entries for requirement (1) were made:

Employee Income Tax Payable	$1,520.00
Social Security Tax Payable	1,847.00
Medicare Tax Payable	433.00
FUTA Tax Payable	27.20
SUTA Tax Payable	183.60

    a. Prepare the journal entry for payment of the liabilities for employee federal income taxes and Social Security and Medicare taxes on January 15, 20--.

    b. Prepare the journal entry for payment of the liability for FUTA tax on January 31, 20--.

    c. Prepare the journal entry for payment of the liability for SUTA tax on January 31, 20--.

3. Hart Company paid a premium of $280 for workers' compensation insurance based on estimated payroll as of the beginning of the year. Based on actual payroll as of the end of the year, the premium is $298. Prepare the adjusting entry to reflect the underpayment of the insurance premium.

Solution

1.

GENERAL JOURNAL   PAGE 1

	DATE		DESCRIPTION	POST REF.	DEBIT	CREDIT	
1	20-- Dec.	31	Wages and Salaries Expense		3 8 0 0 00		1
2			Employee Income Tax Payable			3 8 0 00	2
3			Social Security Tax Payable			2 3 5 60	3
4			Medicare Tax Payable			5 5 10	4
5			Health Insurance Premiums Payable			5 0 00	5
6			United Way Contributions Payable			1 0 0 00	6
7			Cash			2 9 7 9 30	7
8			To record Dec. 31 payroll				8
9							9
10	Dec.	31	Payroll Taxes Expense		3 1 5 50		10
11			Social Security Tax Payable			2 3 5 60	11
12			Medicare Tax Payable			5 5 10	12
13			FUTA Tax Payable			3 20	13
14			SUTA Tax Payable			2 1 60	14
15			Employer payroll taxes for week ended Dec. 31				15

(continued)

2, 3.

18	Jan.	15	Employee Income Tax Payable				1	5	2	0	00							
19			Social Security Tax Payable				1	8	4	7	00							
20			Medicare Tax Payable					4	3	3	00							
21			Cash										3	8	0	0	00	
22			Deposit of employee federal income tax and															
23			Social Security and Medicare taxes															
24																		
25	Jan.	31	FUTA Tax Payable						2	7	20						
26			Cash												2	7	20
27			Paid FUTA tax															
28																		
29	Jan.	31	SUTA Tax Payable					1	8	3	60						
30			Cash											1	8	3	60
31			Paid SUTA tax															
32																		
33	Dec.	31	Workers' Compensation Insurance Expense						1	8	00						
34			Workers' Compensation Insurance Payable												1	8	00
35			Adjustment for insurance premium															

REVIEW QUESTIONS

1. Why do employer payroll taxes represent an additional expense to the employer, whereas the various employee payroll taxes do not?

2. At what rate and on what earnings base is the employer's Social Security tax levied?

3. What is the purpose of the FUTA tax and who must pay it?

4. What is the purpose of the state unemployment tax and who must pay it?

5. What accounts are affected when employer payroll tax expenses are properly recorded?

6. Identify all items that are debited or credited to Social Security Tax Payable and to Medicare Tax Payable.

7. Explain why an employee whose gross salary is $20,000 costs an employer more than $20,000 to employ.

8. What is the purpose of Form 8109, Federal Tax Deposit Coupon?

9. What is the purpose of Form 941, Employer's Quarterly Federal Tax Return?

10. What is the purpose of Form 940, Employer's Annual Federal Unemployment Tax Return?

11. What information appears on Form W-2, the employee's Wage and Tax Statement?

12. What is the purpose of workers' compensation insurance and who must pay for it?

MANAGING YOUR WRITING

The Director of the Art Department, Wilson Watson, wants to hire new office staff. His boss tells him that to do so he must find in his budget not only the base salary for this position but an additional 30% for "fringe benefits." Wilson explodes: "How in the world can there be 30% in fringe benefits?" Write a memo to Wilson Watson explaining the costs that probably make up these fringe benefits.

ETHICS CASE

Bob Estes works at Cliffrock Company in the central receiving department. He unpacks incoming shipments and verifies quantities of goods received. Over the weekend, Bob pulled a muscle in his back while playing basketball. When he came to work on Monday and started unpacking shipments, his back started to hurt again. Bob called the Human Resources Department and told them he hurt his back lifting a package at work. He was told to fill out an accident report and sent to an orthopedic clinic with a workers' compensation form. The doctor at the clinic told Bob not to lift anything heavy for two weeks and to stay home from work for at least one week.

1. Is Bob entitled to workers' compensation? Why or why not?

2. What effect will Bob's claim have on Cliffrock Company's workers' compensation insurance premium?

3. Write a short memo from the Human Resources Department to Cliffrock Company's employees explaining the purpose of worker's compensation.

4. In small groups discuss the job-related illness or injury risks of a computer input operator and measures an employer might take to minimize these risks.

WEB WORK

How long are employers required to keep employment tax records? For this and other tax advice, go to the IRS business resource page at

http://www.irs.ustreas.gov/prod/bus_info/index.html
(http://heintz.swcollege.com)

Choose Tax Topics for Business, then Recordkeeping.

SERIES A EXERCISES

EXERCISE 9-1A   (LO1/2)   **JOURNAL ENTRY FOR EMPLOYER PAYROLL TAXES** Portions of the payroll register for Barney's Bagels for the week ended July 15 are shown below. The SUTA tax rate is 5.4% and the FUTA tax rate is 0.8%, both of which are levied on the first $7,000 of earnings. The Social Security tax rate is 6.2% on the first $76,200 of earnings. The Medicare rate is 1.45% on gross earnings.

(continued)

Barney's Bagels
Payroll Register
Total Taxable Earnings of All Employees

Total Earnings	Unemployment Compensation	Social Security
$12,200	$10,500	$12,200

Calculate the employer's payroll taxes expense and prepare the journal entry to record the employer's payroll taxes expense for the week ended July 15 of the current year.

EXERCISE 9-2A   (LO1/2)   EMPLOYER PAYROLL TAXES Earnings for several employees for the week ended March 12, 20--, are as follows:

		Taxable Earnings	
		Unemployment	Social
Employee Name	Total Earnings	Compensation	Security
Aus, Glenn E.	$ 700	$200	$ 700
Diaz, Charles K.	350	350	350
Knapp, Carol S.	1,200	—	1,200
Mueller, Deborah F.	830	125	830
Yeager, Jackie R.	920	35	920

Calculate the employer's payroll taxes expense and prepare the journal entry as of March 12, 20--, assuming that FUTA tax is 0.8%, SUTA tax is 5.4%, Social Security tax is 6.2%, and Medicare tax is 1.45%.

EXERCISE 9-3A   (LO1/2)   TAXABLE EARNINGS AND EMPLOYER'S PAYROLL TAXES JOURNAL ENTRY
Selected information from the payroll register of Raynette's Boutique for the week ended September 14, 20--, is as follows. Social Security tax is 6.2% on the first $76,200 of earnings for each employee. Medicare tax is 1.45% of gross earnings. FUTA tax is 0.8% and SUTA tax is 5.4% on the first $7,000 of earnings.

			Taxable Earnings	
	Cumulative Pay Before Current	Current Gross	Unemployment	Social
Employee Name	Earnings	Pay	Compensation	Security
Burgos, Juan	$ 6,800	$1,250		
Ellis, Judy A.	6,300	1,100		
Lewis, Arlene S.	54,200	2,320		
Mason, Jason W.	53,900	2,270		
Yates, Ruby L.	27,650	1,900		
Zielke, Ronald M.	74,330	2,680		

Calculate the amount of taxable earnings for unemployment, Social Security, and Medicare taxes, and prepare the journal entry to record the employer's payroll taxes as of September 14, 20--.

EXERCISE 9-4A   (LO1/2)   TOTAL COST OF EMPLOYEE J. B. Kenton employs Sharla Knox at a salary of $32,000 a year. Kenton is subject to employer Social Security taxes at a rate of 6.2% and Medicare taxes at a rate of 1.45% on Knox's salary. In addition, Kenton must pay SUTA tax at a rate of 5.4% and FUTA tax at a rate of 0.8% on the first $7,000 of Knox's salary.

Compute the total cost to Kenton of employing Knox for the year.

EXERCISE 9-5A (LO3) **JOURNAL ENTRY FOR PAYMENT OF EMPLOYER'S PAYROLL TAXES** Angel Ruiz owns a business called Ruiz Construction Co. He does his banking at Citizens National Bank in Portland, Oregon. The amounts in his general ledger for payroll taxes and the employees' withholding of Social Security, Medicare, and federal income tax payable as of April 15 of the current year are as follows:

Social Security tax payable (includes both employer and employee)	$3,750
Medicare tax payable (includes both employer and employee)	875
FUTA tax payable	200
SUTA tax payable	1,350
Employee income tax payable	2,275

Journalize the payment of the Form 941 deposit (i.e., Social Security, Medicare, and federal income tax) to Citizens National Bank and the payment of the SUTA tax to the state of Oregon as of April 15, 20--.

EXERCISE 9-6A (LO4) **WORKERS' COMPENSATION INSURANCE AND ADJUSTMENT** General Manufacturing estimated that its total payroll for the coming year would be $425,000. The workers' compensation insurance premium rate is 0.2%.

REQUIRED

1. Calculate the estimated workers' compensation insurance premium and prepare the journal entry for the payment as of January 2, 20--.

2. Assume that General Manufacturing's actual payroll for the year is $432,000. Calculate the total insurance premium owed and prepare a journal entry as of December 31, 20--, to record the adjustment for the underpayment. The actual payment of the additional premium will take place in January of the next year.

SERIES A PROBLEMS

PROBLEM 9-1A (LO1/2) **CALCULATING PAYROLL TAXES EXPENSE AND PREPARING JOURNAL ENTRY** Selected information from the payroll register of Anderson's Dairy for the week ended May 7, 20--, is shown below. The SUTA tax rate is 5.4% and the FUTA tax rate is 0.8%, both on the first $7,000 of earnings. Social Security tax on the employer is 6.2% on the first $76,200 of earnings and Medicare tax is 1.45% on gross earnings.

			Taxable Earnings	
Employee Name	Cumulative Pay Before Current Earnings	Current Weekly Earnings	Unemployment Compensation	Social Security
Barnum, Alex	$ 6,750	$ 820		
Duel, Richard	6,340	725		
Hunt, J. B.	23,460	1,235		
Larson, Susan	6,950	910		
Mercado, Denise	74,850	2,520		
Swan, Judy	15,470	1,125		
Yates, Keith	28,675	1,300		

REQUIRED

1. Calculate the total employer payroll taxes for these employees.

2. Prepare the journal entry to record the employer payroll taxes as of May 7, 20--.

PROBLEM 9-2A (LO2)

JOURNALIZING AND POSTING PAYROLL ENTRIES The Cascade Company has four employees. All are paid on a monthly basis. The fiscal year of the business is July 1 to June 30. Payroll taxes are imposed as follows:

1. Social Security tax of 6.2% withheld from employees' wages on the first $76,200 of earnings and Medicare tax withheld at 1.45% of gross earnings.
2. Social Security tax of 6.2% imposed on the employer on the first $76,200 of earnings and Medicare tax of 1.45% on gross earnings.
3. SUTA tax of 5.4% imposed on the employer on the first $7,000 of earnings.
4. FUTA tax of 0.8% imposed on the employer on the first $7,000 of earnings.

The accounts kept by Cascade include the following:

Account Number	Title	Balance on July 1
101	Cash	$50,200
211	Employee Income Tax Payable	1,015
212	Social Security Tax Payable	1,458
213	Medicare Tax Payable	342
218	Savings Bond Deductions Payable	350
221	FUTA Tax Payable	164
222	SUTA Tax Payable	810
511	Wages and Salaries Expense	0
530	Payroll Taxes Expense	0

The following transactions relating to payrolls and payroll taxes occurred during July and August.

July 15	Paid $2,815 covering the following June taxes:			
	Social Security tax			$ 1,458
	Medicare tax			342
	Employee income tax withheld			1,015
	Total			$ 2,815
31	July payroll:			
	Total wages and salaries expense			$12,000
	Less amounts withheld:			
	Social Security tax		$ 744	
	Medicare tax		174	
	Employee income tax		1,020	
	Savings bond deductions		350	2,288
	Net amount paid			$ 9,712
31	Purchased savings bonds for employees, $700			
31	Data for completing employer's payroll taxes expense for July:			
	Social Security taxable wages			$12,000
	Unemployment taxable wages			3,000
Aug. 15	Paid $2,856 covering the following July taxes:			
	Social Security tax			$ 1,488
	Medicare tax			348
	Employee income tax withheld			1,020
	Total			$ 2,856
15	Paid SUTA tax for the quarter, $972			
15	Paid FUTA tax, $188			

REQUIRED

1. Journalize the preceding transactions using a general journal.
2. Open T accounts for the payroll expenses and liabilities. Enter the beginning balances and post the transactions recorded in the journal.

PROBLEM 9-3A   **(LO4)**   **WORKERS' COMPENSATION INSURANCE AND ADJUSTMENT** Willamette Manufacturing estimated that its total payroll for the coming year would be $650,000. The workers' compensation insurance premium rate is 0.3%.

REQUIRED

1. Calculate the estimated workers' compensation insurance premium and prepare the journal entry for the payment as of January 2, 20--.

2. Assume that Willamette Manufacturing's actual payroll for the year was $672,000. Calculate the total insurance premium owed and prepare a journal entry as of December 31, 20--, to record the adjustment for the underpayment. The actual payment of the additional premium will take place in January of the next year.

3. Assume instead that Willamette Manufacturing's actual payroll for the year was $634,000. Prepare a journal entry as of December 31, 20--, for the total amount that should be refunded. The refund will not be received until the next year.

SERIES B EXERCISES

EXERCISE 9-1B   **(LO1/2)**   **JOURNAL ENTRY FOR EMPLOYER PAYROLL TAXES** Portions of the payroll register for Kathy's Cupcakes for the week ended June 21 are shown below. The SUTA tax rate is 5.4% and the FUTA tax rate is 0.8%, both on the first $7,000 of earnings. The Social Security tax rate is 6.2% on the first $76,200 of earnings. The Medicare rate is 1.45% on gross earnings.

Kathy's Cupcakes
Payroll Register
Total Taxable Earnings of All Employees

Total Earnings	Unemployment Compensation	Social Security
$15,680	$12,310	$15,680

Calculate the employer's payroll taxes expense and prepare the journal entry to record the employer's payroll taxes expense for the week ended June 21 of the current year.

EXERCISE 9-2B   **(LO1/2)**   **EMPLOYER PAYROLL TAXES** Earnings for several employees for the week ended April 7, 20--, are as follows:

| | | Taxable Earnings | |
| | | Unemployment | Social |
Employee Name	Total Earnings	Compensation	Security
Boyd, Glenda L.	$ 850	$300	$ 850
Evans, Sheryl N.	970	225	970
Fox, Howard J.	830	830	830
Jacobs, Phyllis J.	1,825	—	1,825
Roh, William R.	990	25	990

Calculate the employer's payroll taxes expense and prepare the journal entry as of April 7, 20--, assuming that FUTA tax is 0.8%, SUTA tax is 5.4%, Social Security tax is 6.2%, and Medicare tax is 1.45%.

EXERCISE 9-3B   **(LO1/2)**   **TAXABLE EARNINGS AND EMPLOYER'S PAYROLL TAXES JOURNAL ENTRY** Selected information from the payroll register of Howard's Cutlery for the week ended October 7, 20--, is presented below. Social Security tax is 6.2% on the first $76,200 of earnings for each employee. Medicare tax is 1.45% on gross earnings. FUTA tax is 0.8% and SUTA tax is 5.4% on the first $7,000 of earnings.

(continued)

	Cumulative Pay Before Current	Current Gross	Taxable Earnings	
Employee Name	Earnings	Pay	Unemployment Compensation	Social Security
Carlson, David J.	$ 6,635	$ 950		
Delgado, Luisa	6,150	1,215		
Lewis, Arlene S.	54,375	2,415		
Nixon, Robert R.	53,870	1,750		
Shippe, Lance W.	24,830	1,450		
Watts, Brandon Q.	74,800	2,120		

Calculate the amount of taxable earnings for unemployment, Social Security, and Medicare taxes, and prepare the journal entry to record the employer's payroll taxes as of October 7, 20--.

EXERCISE 9-4B   (LO1/2)   **TOTAL COST OF EMPLOYEE** B. F. Goodson employs Eduardo Gonzales at a salary of $46,000 a year. Goodson is subject to employer Social Security taxes at a rate of 6.2% and Medicare taxes at a rate of 1.45% on Gonzales' salary. In addition, Goodson must pay SUTA tax at a rate of 5.4% and FUTA tax at a rate of 0.8% on the first $7,000 of Gonzales' salary.

Compute the total cost to Goodson of employing Gonzales for the year.

EXERCISE 9-5B   (LO3)   **JOURNAL ENTRY FOR PAYMENT OF EMPLOYER'S PAYROLL TAXES** Francis Baker owns a business called Baker Construction Co. She does her banking at the American National Bank in Seattle, Washington. The amounts in her general ledger for payroll taxes and employees' withholding of Social Security, Medicare, and federal income tax payable as of July 15 of the current year are as follows:

Social Security tax payable (includes both employer and employee)	$6,375
Medicare tax payable (includes both employer and employee)	1,500
FUTA tax payable	336
SUTA tax payable	2,268
Employee federal income tax payable	4,830

Journalize the payment of the Form 941 deposit (i.e., Social Security, Medicare, and federal income tax) to the American National Bank and the payment of the state unemployment tax to the state of Washington as of July 15, 20--.

EXERCISE 9-6B   (LO4)   **WORKERS' COMPENSATION INSURANCE AND ADJUSTMENT** Columbia Industries estimated that its total payroll for the coming year would be $385,000. The workers' compensation insurance premium rate is 0.2%.

REQUIRED

1. Calculate the estimated workers' compensation insurance premium and prepare the journal entry for the payment as of January 2, 20--.

2. Assume that Columbia Industries' actual payroll for the year is $396,000. Calculate the total insurance premium owed and prepare a journal entry as of December 31, 20--, to record the adjustment for the underpayment. The actual payment of the additional premium will take place in January of the next year.

SERIES B PROBLEMS

PROBLEM 9-1B   (LO1/2)   **CALCULATING PAYROLL TAXES EXPENSE AND PREPARING JOURNAL ENTRY** Selected information from the payroll register of Wray's Drug Store for the week ended July 7, 20--, is shown below. The SUTA tax rate is 5.4% and the FUTA tax rate is 0.8%, both on the first $7,000 of earnings. Social Security tax on the employer is 6.2% on the first $76,200 of earnings and Medicare tax is 1.45% on gross earnings.

| Employee Name | Cumulative Pay Before Current Earnings | Current Weekly Earnings | Taxable Earnings | |
			Unemployment Compensation	Social Security
Ackers, Alice	$ 6,460	$ 645		
Conley, Dorothy	27,560	1,025		
Davis, James	6,850	565		
Lawrence, Kevin	52,850	2,875		
Rawlings, Judy	16,350	985		
Tanaka, Sumio	22,320	835		
Vadillo, Raynette	74,360	2,540		

REQUIRED

1. Calculate the total employer payroll taxes for these employees.

2. Prepare the journal entry to record the employer payroll taxes as of July 7, 20--.

PROBLEM 9-2B   (LO2)

JOURNALIZING AND POSTING PAYROLL ENTRIES The Oxford Company has five employees. All are paid on a monthly basis. The fiscal year of the business is June 1 to May 31. Payroll taxes are imposed as follows:

1. Social Security tax of 6.2% to be withheld from employees' wages on the first $76,200 of earnings and Medicare tax of 1.45% on gross earnings.

2. Social Security tax of 6.2% imposed on the employer on the first $76,200 of earnings and Medicare tax of 1.45% on gross earnings.

3. SUTA tax of 5.4% imposed on the employer on the first $7,000 of earnings.

4. FUTA tax of 0.8% imposed on the employer on the first $7,000 of earnings.

The accounts kept by the Oxford Company include the following:

Account Number	Title	Balance on June 1
101	Cash	$48,650
211	Employee Income Tax Payable	1,345
212	Social Security Tax Payable	1,823
213	Medicare Tax Payable	427
218	Savings Bond Deductions Payable	525
221	FUTA Tax Payable	360
222	SUTA Tax Payable	920
511	Wages and Salaries Expense	0
530	Payroll Taxes Expense	0

The following transactions relating to payrolls and payroll taxes occurred during June and July.

June 15   Paid $3,595.00 covering the following May taxes:

Social Security tax	$ 1,823.00
Medicare tax	427.00
Employee income tax withheld	1,345.00
Total	$ 3,595.00

(continued)

<table>
<tr><td>30</td><td colspan="2">June payroll:</td><td></td><td></td></tr>
<tr><td></td><td colspan="2">Total wages and salaries expense</td><td></td><td>$14,700.00</td></tr>
<tr><td></td><td colspan="2">Less amounts withheld:</td><td></td><td></td></tr>
<tr><td></td><td>Social Security tax</td><td></td><td>$ 911.40</td><td></td></tr>
<tr><td></td><td>Medicare tax</td><td></td><td>213.15</td><td></td></tr>
<tr><td></td><td>Employee income tax</td><td></td><td>1,280.00</td><td></td></tr>
<tr><td></td><td>Savings bond deductions</td><td></td><td>525.00</td><td>2,929.55</td></tr>
<tr><td></td><td colspan="2">Net amount paid</td><td></td><td>$11,770.45</td></tr>
</table>

30   Purchased savings bonds for employees, $1,050.00

30   Data for completing employer's payroll taxes expense
for June:

Social Security taxable wages	$14,700.00
Unemployment taxable wages	4,500.00

July 15   Paid $3,529.10 covering the following June taxes:

Social Security tax	$ 1,822.80
Medicare tax	426.30
Employee income tax withheld	1,280.00
Total	$ 3,529.10

15   Paid SUTA tax for the quarter, $1,163.00

15   Paid FUTA tax, $396.00

REQUIRED

1.   Journalize the preceding transactions using a general journal.

2.   Open T accounts for the payroll expenses and liabilities. Enter the beginning balances and post the transactions recorded in the journal.

PROBLEM 9-3B   **(LO4)**   **WORKERS' COMPENSATION INSURANCE AND ADJUSTMENT** Multnomah Manufacturing estimated that its total payroll for the coming year would be $540,000. The workers' compensation insurance premium rate is 0.2%.

REQUIRED

1.   Calculate the estimated workers' compensation insurance premium and prepare the journal entry for the payment as of January 2, 20--.

2.   Assume that Multnomah Manufacturing's actual payroll for the year was $562,000. Calculate the total insurance premium owed and prepare a journal entry as of December 31, 20--, to record the adjustment for the underpayment. The actual payment of the additional premium will take place in January of the next year.

3.   Assume instead that Multnomah Manufacturing's actual payroll for the year was $532,000. Prepare a journal entry as of December 31, 20--, for the total amount that should be refunded. The refund will not be received until the next year.

CHALLENGE PROBLEM

Payrex Co. has six employees. All are paid on a weekly basis. For the payroll period ending January 7, total employee earnings were $12,500, all of which were subject to SUTA, FUTA, Social Security, and Medicare taxes. The SUTA tax rate in Payrex's state is 5.4%, but Payrex qualifies for a rate of 2.0% because of its good record of providing regular employment to its employees. Other employer payroll taxes are at the rates described in the chapter.

REQUIRED

1. Calculate Payrex's FUTA, SUTA, Social Security, and Medicare taxes for the week ended January 7.

2. Prepare the journal entry for Payrex's payroll taxes for the week ended January 7.

3. What amount of payroll taxes did Payrex save because of its good employment record?

MASTERY PROBLEM

The totals line from Nix Company's payroll register for the week ended March 31, 20--, is as follows:

(left side)

	NAME	EMPLOYEE NUMBER	ALLOWANCES	MARITAL STATUS	EARNINGS				PAYROLL TAXABLE EARNINGS		
					REGULAR	OVERTIME	TOTAL	CUMULATIVE TOTAL	UNEMPLOYMENT COMPENSATION	SOCIAL SECURITY	
21	Totals				5 4 0 0 00	1 0 0 00	5 5 0 0 00	71 5 0 0 00	5 0 0 0 00	5 5 0 0 00	21

REGISTER—PERIOD ENDED March 31, 20--

(right side)

	DEDUCTIONS							NET PAY	CHECK NO.	
	FEDERAL INCOME TAX	SOCIAL SECURITY TAX	MEDICARE TAX	HEALTH INSURANCE	LIFE INSURANCE	OTHER	TOTAL			
21	5 0 0 00	3 4 1 00	7 9 75	1 6 5 00	2 0 0 00		1 2 8 5 75	4 2 1 4 25		21

Payroll taxes are imposed as follows: Social Security tax, 6.2%; Medicare tax, 1.45%; FUTA tax 0.8%, and SUTA tax, 5.4%.

REQUIRED

1. a. Prepare the journal entry for payment of this payroll on March 31, 20--.

   b. Prepare the journal entry for the employer's payroll taxes for the period ended March 31, 20--.

2. Nix Company had the following balances in its general ledger before the entries for requirement (1) were made:

Employee income tax payable	$2,500
Social Security tax payable	2,008
Medicare tax payable	470
FUTA tax payable	520
SUTA tax payable	3,510

   a. Prepare the journal entry for payment of the liabilities for federal income taxes and Social Security and Medicare taxes on April 15, 20--.

   b. Prepare the journal entry for payment of the liability for FUTA tax on April 30, 20--.

   c. Prepare the journal entry for payment of the liability for SUTA tax on April 30, 20--.

3. Nix Company paid a premium of $420 for workers' compensation insurance based on the estimated payroll as of the beginning of the year. Based on actual payroll as of the end of the year, the premium is only $400. Prepare the adjusting entry to reflect the overpayment of the insurance premium at the end of the year (December 31, 20--).

Self-Study Test Questions

True/False

1. Employer payroll taxes are deducted from the employee's pay. _____

2. The payroll register is a key source of information for computing employer payroll taxes. _____

3. Self-employment income is the net income of a trade or business owned and run by an individual. _____

4. The FUTA tax is levied only on the employees. _____

5. The W-4, which shows total annual earnings and deductions for federal and state income taxes, must be completed by the employer and given to the employee by January 31. _____

Multiple Choice

1. The general ledger accounts commonly used to record the employer's Social Security, Medicare, FUTA, and SUTA taxes are classified as _____

   (a) assets.
   (b) liabilities.
   (c) expenses.
   (d) owner's equity.

2. Joyce Lee earns $30,000 a year. Her employer pays a matching Social Security tax of 6.2% on the first $76,200 in earnings, a Medicare tax of 1.45% on gross earnings, and a FUTA tax of 0.8% and a SUTA tax of 5.4%, both on the first $7,000 in earnings. What is the total cost of Joyce Lee to her employer? _____

   (a) $32,250
   (b) $30,000
   (c) $30,434
   (d) $32,729

3. The Form 941 tax deposit includes which of the following types of taxes withheld from the employee and paid by the employer? _____

   (a) Federal income tax and FUTA tax
   (b) Federal income tax and Social Security and Medicare taxes
   (c) Social Security and Medicare taxes and SUTA tax
   (d) FUTA tax and SUTA tax

4. Workers' compensation provides insurance for employees who _____

   (a) are unemployed due to a layoff.
   (b) are unemployed due to a plant closing.
   (c) are underemployed and need additional compensation.
   (d) suffer a job-related illness or injury.

5. The journal entry at the end of the year that recognizes an additional premium owed under workers' compensation insurance will include a _____

   (a) debit to Workers' Compensation Insurance Expense.
   (b) debit to Cash.
   (c) debit to Workers' Compensation Insurance Payable.
   (d) credit to Workers' Compensation Insurance Expense.

The answers to the Self-Study Test Questions are at the end of the text.

10

Accounting for a
Professional Service Business:
The Combination Journal

Betty Jenkins, John's bookkeeper, was comparing notes with a college classmate who recently accepted a bookkeeping position in a doctor's office. The classmate has been observing general office procedures and is a bit confused about the accounting methods employed. Recording revenues is a good example. Some patients pay cash as they leave the office. Others submit forms that are filed with insurance companies. Sometimes the insurance companies pay the entire amount. Other times, insurance companies pay only a portion of the bill, and the balance is billed to the patient. Generally, the patients pay the balance, but occasionally they don't. Finally, there are some patients that never seem to pay. It appears that the doctor's office simply waits until cash is collected before recognizing any revenue. This seems contrary to the accrual method of accounting. Is this an acceptable procedure, or should Betty's friend seek employment elsewhere?

Careful study of this chapter should enable you to:

LO1 Explain the cash, modified cash, and accrual bases of accounting.

LO2 Describe special records for a professional service business using the modified cash basis.

LO3 Describe and use a combination journal to record transactions of a professional service business.

LO4 Post from the combination journal to the general ledger.

LO5 Prepare a work sheet, financial statements, and adjusting and closing entries for a professional service business.

The accrual basis of accounting offers the best matching of revenues and expenses and is required under generally accepted accounting principles. Throughout the first nine chapters, the accrual basis was demonstrated for a service business. For simplicity, we used a general journal as the book of original entry.

GAAP financial statements prepared using the accrual method are particularly important when major businesses want to raise large amounts of money. Investors and creditors expect GAAP financial statements and generally will not invest or make loans without them.

However, many small professional service organizations are not concerned with raising large amounts of money from investors and creditors. These organizations include CPAs, doctors, dentists, lawyers, engineers, and architects. Since these organizations do not need to prepare GAAP financial statements, they often use the cash or modified cash basis. Further, instead of using a general journal, a manual or computerized specialized journal is employed. These methods simplify the accounting process and provide results similar to GAAP if receivables and payables are minimal. Further, if one of these organizations needs to borrow money from a bank that requires GAAP financial statements, an accountant can convert the financial statements to the accrual basis.

In this chapter we explain the cash basis and modified cash basis of accounting. In addition, we demonstrate the advantages of using a combination journal as the book of original entry.

ACCRUAL BASIS VERSUS CASH BASIS

LO1 Explain the cash, modified cash, and accrual bases of accounting.

Under the **accrual basis of accounting**, revenues are recorded when earned. Revenues are considered earned when a service is provided or a product sold, regardless of whether cash is received. If cash is not received, a receivable is set up. The accrual basis also assumes that expenses are recorded when incurred. Expenses are incurred when a service is received or an asset consumed, regardless of when cash is paid. If cash is not paid when a service is received, a payable is set up. When assets are consumed, prepaid assets are decreased or long-term assets are depreciated. Since the accrual basis accounts for long-term assets, prepaid assets, receivables, and payables, it is the most comprehensive system and best method of measuring income for the vast majority of businesses.

LEARNING KEY:

Accrual Basis

Accounting for:

Revenues and Expenses	Assets and Liabilities	
Record revenue when earned.	Accounts receivable:	Yes
Record expenses when incurred.	Accounts payable:	Yes
	Prepaid assets:	Yes
	Long-term assets:	Yes

Under the **cash basis of accounting**, revenues are recorded when cash is received and expenses are recorded when cash is paid. This method will provide results that are similar to the accrual basis if there are few receivables, payables, and assets. However, as shown in Figure 10-1, the cash and accrual bases can result in very different measures of net income if a business has significant amounts of receivables, payables, and assets.

LEARNING KEY:

Cash Basis

Accounting for:

Revenues and Expenses
    Record revenue when cash is received.
    Record expenses when cash is paid.

Assets and Liabilities
Accounts receivable: No
Accounts payable: No
Prepaid assets: No
Long-term assets: No

LEARNING KEY:
Accrual Basis:
Revenues recorded when earned.
Expenses recorded when incurred.

Cash Basis:
Revenues recorded when cash is received.
Expenses recorded when cash is paid.

RECOGNITION OF REVENUES AND EXPENSES: ACCRUAL BASIS VS. CASH BASIS

		Method of Accounting			
		Accrual Basis		Cash Basis	
	Transaction	Expense	Revenue	Expense	Revenue
(a)	Provided services on account, $600.		$600		
(b)	Paid wages, $300.	$300		$300	
(c)	Received cash for services performed on account last month, $200.				$200
(d)	Received cleaning bill for month, $250.	250			
(e)	Paid on account for last month's advertising, $100.			100	
(f)	Purchase of supplies, $50.			50	
(g)	Supplies used during month, $40.	40			
		$590	$600	$450	$200

	Accrual	Cash
Revenue	$600	$200
Expense	590	450
Net Income (Loss)	$ 10	($250)

	Accrual	Cash
Revenues are recognized when:	earned	cash is received
Expenses are recognized when:	incurred	cash is paid

FIGURE 10-1   Cash Versus Accrual Accounting

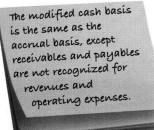

The modified cash basis is the same as the accrual basis, except receivables and payables are not recognized for revenues and operating expenses.

    A third method of accounting combines aspects of the cash and accrual methods. With the **modified cash basis**, a business uses the cash basis for recording revenues and most expenses. Exceptions are made when cash is paid for assets with useful lives greater than one accounting period. For example, under a strict cash basis, if cash is paid for equipment, buildings, supplies, or insurance, the amount is immediately recorded as an expense. This approach would cause

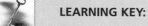

LEARNING KEY:

Modified Cash Basis

Accounting for:

Revenues and Expenses
    Record revenue when cash is received.
    Record expenses when cash is paid, except for assets with useful lives greater than one accounting period. Accrual accounting is used for prepaid assets (insurance and supplies) and long-term assets.

Assets and Liabilities
Accounts receivable: No
Accounts payable
   for purchase of assets: Yes
   for services received: No
Prepaid assets: Yes
Long-term assets: Yes

major distortions when measuring net income. Under the modified cash basis, cash payments like these are recorded as assets, and adjustments are made each period as under the accrual basis. Liabilities associated with the acquisition of these assets are also recognized.

Although similar to the accrual basis, the modified cash basis does not account for receivables or for payables for services received. Thus, the modified cash basis is a combination of the cash and accrual methods of accounting. The differences and similarities among the cash, modified cash, and accrual methods of accounting are demonstrated in Figure 10-2.

If all businesses were the same, only one method of accounting would be needed. However, businesses vary in their need for major assets like buildings and

ENTRIES MADE UNDER EACH ACCOUNTING METHOD

Event	Cash	Modified Cash	Accrual
Revenues: Perform services for cash	Cash Professional Fees	Cash Professional Fees	Cash Professional Fees
Perform services on account	No entry	No entry	Accounts Receivable Professional Fees
Expenses: Pay cash for operating expenses: wages, advertising, rent, telephone, etc.	Expense Cash	Expense Cash	Expense Cash
Pay cash for prepaid items: insurance, supplies, etc.	Expense Cash	Prepaid Asset Cash	Prepaid Asset Cash
Pay cash for property, plant, and equipment (PP&E)	Expense Cash	PP&E Asset Cash	PP&E Asset Cash
Receive bill for services received	No entry	No entry	Expense Accounts Payable
End-of-period adjustments: Wages earned by employees but not paid	No entry	No entry	Wages Expense Wages Payable
Prepaid items used	No entry	Expense Prepaid Asset	Expense Prepaid Asset
Depreciation on property, plant, and equipment	No entry	Depreciation Expense Accumulated Depreciation	Depreciation Expense Accumulated Depreciation
Other: Purchase of assets on account	No entry	Asset Accounts Payable	Asset Accounts Payable
Payments for assets purchased on account	Expense Cash	Accounts Payable Cash	Accounts Payable Cash

FIGURE 10-2   Comparison of Cash, Modified Cash, and Accrual Methods

LEARNING KEY: Shaded area shows that sometimes the modified cash basis is the same as the cash basis and sometimes it is the same as the accrual basis. For some transactions, all methods are the same.

A BROADER VIEW
The Modified Cash Basis

Many professional and small service businesses use the modified cash basis of accounting. Doctors do this because it permits the recognition of medical equipment as assets that are depreciated as services are provided. Further, it simplifies accounting for revenues. Doctors are somewhat uncertain about the actual amount of revenue earned at the time a visit with a

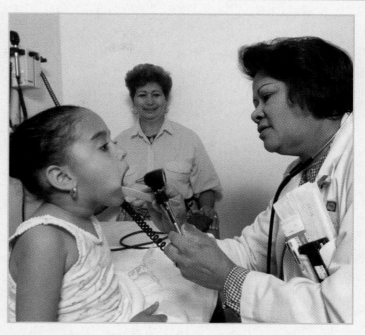

patient has been completed. Insurance companies pay different amounts for various procedures. Sometimes this is the same as the amount charged by the doctor, but not always. Some doctors simply accept what the insurance company pays. Others bill the patient for the difference. And, of course, not all patients pay their bills. Thus, it is easier to wait until cash is received to recognize revenue.

equipment, the amount of customer receivables, and payables to suppliers. For example, if a business were rather small with no major assets, receivables, or payables, it would be simpler to use the cash basis of accounting. In addition, under these circumstances, the difference in net income under the accrual and cash bases of accounting would be small. Most individuals fit this description and use the cash basis on their tax returns.

Businesses with buildings and equipment, but few receivables and payables, might use the modified cash basis. Again, the accounting would be a little simpler and differences between net income computed under the modified cash and accrual bases would be small.

Finally, businesses with buildings and equipment, and receivables and payables, should use the accrual basis of accounting to achieve the best matching of revenues and expenses. The following sections will focus primarily on the modified cash basis of accounting.

ACCOUNTING FOR A PROFESSIONAL SERVICE BUSINESS

LO2 **Describe special records for a professional service business using the modified cash basis.**

Many small professional service businesses use the modified cash basis of accounting. Professional service businesses include law, dentistry, medicine, optometry, architecture, engineering, and accounting.

Look again at Figure 10-2. There are two primary differences between the accrual basis and the modified cash basis. First, under the modified cash basis, no adjusting entries are made for accrued wages expense. Second, under the modified cash basis, revenues from services performed on account are not

Date: 6/4/--

Time	Patient	Medical Service	Fees	Payments
8:00	Dennis Rogan	OV	40.00	40.00
15				
30	Rick Cosier	OV;EKG	120.00	
45				
9:00	George Hettenhouse	OV;MISC	50.00	
15				
30	Sam Frumer	OV;LAB	75.00	75.00
45				
10:00	Dan Dalton	OV	40.00	
15				
30	Louis Biagioni	OV;X	65.00	
45				
11:00	Mike Groomer	X	40.00	40.00
15				
30				
45				
12:00				
15				
30				
45				
1:00	Mike Tiller	OV;LAB	80.00	
15				
30	Peggy Hite	OV;PHYS	190.00	
45				
2:00				
15				
30				
45				
3:00	Vivian Winston	OV;MISC	40.00	
15				
30				
45				
4:00	Hank Davis	OV	40.00	40.00
15				
30				
45				
	Bill Sharp			150.00
	Phil Jones			80.00
	Diane Gallagher			200.00
			780.00	625.00

FIGURE 10-3 Appointment Record

recorded until cash is received. Thus, no accounts receivable are entered in the accounting system. This means that other records must be maintained to keep track of amounts owed by clients and patients. These records generally include an appointment record and a client or patient ledger record. These records are illustrated in Figures 10-3 and 10-4.

The appointment record is used to schedule appointments and to maintain a record of the services rendered, fees charged, and payments received. It also serves as a source document for the patient ledger records, which show the amount owed by each client or patient for services performed. A copy of this record may also be used for billing purposes.

Patient Name	Dennis Rogan				
Address	1542 Hamilton Avenue Cincinnati OH 45240-5524				
Phone Number	555-1683				
Date	**Service Rendered**	**Time**	**Debit**	**Credit**	**Balance**
20-- June 4	Office Visit	8:00	40.00		40.00
4				40.00	—

FIGURE 10-4   Client or Patient Ledger Account

THE COMBINATION JOURNAL

LO3 Describe and use a combination journal to record transactions of a professional service business.

The two-column general journal illustrated in Chapter 4 can be used to enter every transaction of a business. However, in most businesses, there are many similar transactions that involve the same account or accounts. Cash receipts and payments are good examples. Suppose that in a typical month there are 30 transactions that result in an increase in cash and 40 transactions that cause a decrease in cash. In a two-column general journal, this would require entering the account Cash 70 times, using a journal line each time.

A considerable amount of time and space is saved if a journal contains **special columns** for cash debits and cash credits. At the end of the month, the special columns for cash debits and credits are totaled. The total of the Cash Debit column is posted as one amount to the debit side of the cash account and the total of the Cash Credit column is posted as one amount to the credit side of the cash account. Thus, instead of receiving 70 postings, Cash receives only two: one debit and one credit. This method requires much less time and reduces the risk of making posting errors.

LEARNING KEY: The totals of special journal columns are posted as one amount to the account. This saves time and reduces the possibility of posting errors.

If other accounts are used frequently, special columns can be added for these accounts. **General Debit** and **General Credit columns** are used for accounts not affected by many transactions. A journal with such special and general columns is called a **combination journal**.

Many small professional enterprises use a combination journal to record business transactions. To demonstrate the use of a combination journal, let's consider the medical practice of Dr. Ray Bonita. Bonita uses the modified cash basis of accounting. The chart of accounts for his medical practice is shown in Figure 10-5. The transactions for the month of June, his first month in practice, are provided in Figure 10-6.

A combination journal for Bonita's medical practice is illustrated in Figure 10-7 on page 334. Note that special columns were set up for Cash (Debit and Credit), Medical Fees (Credit), Wages Expense (Debit), Laboratory Expense (Debit), Medical Supplies (Debit), and Office Supplies (Debit). Special columns were set up for these accounts because they will be used frequently in this business. Other businesses might set up special columns for different accounts depending on the frequency of their use. Of course, General Debit and Credit columns for transactions affecting other accounts are also needed.

LEARNING KEY: Set up special columns for the most frequently used accounts.

RAY BONITA, M.D. CHART OF ACCOUNTS

Assets			Revenue	
101	Cash		401	Medical Fees
141	Medical Supplies			
142	Office Supplies		**Expenses**	
145	Prepaid Insurance		511	Wages Expense
182	Office Furniture		521	Rent Expense
182.1	Accum. Depr. —Office Furn.		523	Office Supplies Expense
185	Medical Equipment		524	Medical Supplies Expense
185.1	Accum. Depr.—Med. Equip.		525	Telephone Expense
			526	Laboratory Expense
Liabilities			535	Insurance Expense
202	Accounts Payable		541	Depr. Exp.—Office Furn.
			542	Depr. Exp.—Med. Equip.
Owner's Equity				
311	Ray Bonita, Capital			
312	Ray Bonita, Drawing			
313	Income Summary			

FIGURE 10-5 Chart of Accounts

June 1	Ray Bonita invested cash to start a medical practice, $50,000.
2	Paid for a one-year liability insurance policy, $6,000. Coverage began on June 1.
3	Purchased medical equipment for cash, $22,000.
4	Paid bill for laboratory work, $300.
5	Purchased office furniture on credit from Bittle's Furniture, $9,000.
6	Received cash from patients and insurance companies for medical services rendered, $5,000.
7	Paid June office rent, $2,000.
8	Paid part-time wages, $3,000.
9	Purchased medical supplies for cash, $250.
15	Paid telephone bill, $150.
15	Received cash from patients and insurance companies for medical services rendered, $10,000.
16	Paid bill for laboratory work, $280.
17	Paid part-time wages, $3,000.
19	Purchased office supplies for cash, $150.
20	Received cash from patients and insurance companies for medical services rendered, $3,200.
22	Paid the first installment to Bittle's Furniture, $3,300.
23	Purchased medical supplies for cash, $200.
24	Paid bill for laboratory work, $400.
25	Purchased additional furniture from Bittle's Furniture, $4,000. A down payment of $500 was made, with the remaining payments expected over the next four months.
27	Paid part-time wages, $2,500.
30	Received cash from patients and insurance companies for medical services rendered, $7,000.
30	Bonita withdrew cash for personal use, $10,000.

FIGURE 10-6 Summary of Transactions for Ray Bonita's Medical Practice

Journalizing in a Combination Journal

The following procedures were used to enter the transactions for Bonita for June.

General Columns. Enter transactions in the *general columns* in a manner similar to that used for the *general journal*. Look at the entry for June 5 in Figure 10-7.

a. Enter the name of the debited account (Office Furniture) first at the extreme left of the Description column.

b. Enter the amount in the General Debit column.

c. Enter the name of the account credited (Accounts Payable—Bittle's Furniture) on the next line, indented.

d. Enter the amount in the General Credit column.

General and Special Accounts. Some transactions affect both a *general account and a special account*. Look at the entry for June 1 in Figure 10-7.

a. Enter the name of the general account in the Description column.

b. Enter the amount in the General Debit or Credit column.

c. Enter the amount of the debit or credit for the special account in the appropriate special column.

Enter all of this information on the same line.

Special Accounts. Many transactions affect only *special accounts*. Look at the entry for June 6 in Figure 10-7.

a. Enter the amounts in the appropriate special debit and credit columns.

b. Do not enter anything in the Description column.

c. Place a dash in the Posting Reference column to indicate that this amount is not posted individually. It will be posted as part of the total of the special column at the end of the month. (The posting process is described later in this chapter.)

Description Column. In general, the **Description column** is used for the following:

a. To enter the account titles for the General Debit and General Credit columns.

b. To identify specific creditors when assets are purchased on account (see entry for June 5).

   NOTE: For firms using the accrual basis of accounting, this column also would be used to identify specific customers receiving services on account (accounts receivable) and specific businesses that provided services on account (accounts payable).

c. To identify specific creditors when payments are made on account (see entry for June 22).

d. To identify adjusting and closing entries.

COMBINATION JOURNAL

PAGE 1

Date	Description	Post Ref.	Cash Debit	Cash Credit	General Debit	General Credit	Medical Fees Credit	Wages Expense Debit	Laboratory Expense Debit	Medical Supplies Debit	Office Supplies Debit
20– June 1	Ray Bonita, Capital	311	50 000 00			50 000 00					
2	Prepaid Insurance	145		6 000 00	6 000 00						
3	Medical Equipment	185		22 000 00	22 000 00						
4	—			300 00					300 00		
5	Office Furniture	182			9 000 00						
5	Accounts Payable—Bittle's Furn.	202				9 000 00					
6			5 000 00				5 000 00				
7	Rent Expense	521		2 000 00	2 000 00						
8	—			300 00				300 00			
9	—			250 00						250 00	
15	Telephone Expense	525		150 00	150 00						
15			10 000 00				10 000 00				
16				280 00					280 00		
17	—			300 00				300 00			
19	—			150 00							150 00
20			3 200 00				3 200 00				
22	Accounts Payable—Bittle's Furniture	202		3 300 00	3 300 00						
23	—			200 00						200 00	
24	—			400 00					400 00		
25	Office Furniture	182			4 000 00						
25	Accounts Payable—Bittle's Furn.	202		500 00		3 500 00					
27			7 000 00				7 000 00				
30	—			2 500 00				2 500 00			
30	Ray Bonita, Drawing	312		10 000 00	10 000 00						
			75 200 00	54 030 00	56 450 00	62 500 00	25 200 00	8 500 00	980 00	450 00	150 00
			(101)	(101)	(✓)	(✓)	(401)	(511)	(526)	(141)	(142)

Proving the Combination Journal

Debit Columns		Credit Columns	
Cash	75,200	Cash	54,030
General	56,450	General	62,500
Wages Expense	8,500	Medical Fees	25,200
Laboratory Expense	980		141,730
Medical Supplies	450		
Office Supplies	150		
	141,730		

Note: The account numbers in the Posting Reference Column and at the bottom of the Special Columns are inserted as posting is completed. The same is true for the (✓) at the bottom of the General Debit and Credit Columns.

FIGURE 10-7   Combination Journal: Modified Cash Basis

e. To identify amounts forwarded. When more than one page is required during an accounting period, amounts from the previous page are brought forward. In this situation, "Amounts Forwarded" is entered in the Description column on the first line.

Proving the Combination Journal

At the end of the accounting period, all columns of the combination journal should be totaled and ruled. The sum of the debit columns should be compared with the sum of the credit columns to verify that they are equal. The proving of Bonita's combination journal for the month of June is shown at the bottom of Figure 10-7 on page 334.

POSTING FROM THE COMBINATION JOURNAL

LO4 Post from the combination journal to the general ledger.

The procedures for posting a special column are different from the procedures used when posting a general column. Accounts debited or credited in the general columns are posted individually throughout the month in the same manner followed for the general journal. A different procedure is used for special columns. Figure 10-8 describes the procedures to follow in posting from the combination journal.

GENERAL COLUMNS	Since a combination journal is being used, enter "CJ" and the page number in each general ledger account's **Posting Reference column**. Once the amount has been posted to the general ledger account, the account number is entered in the Posting Reference column of the combination journal. Accounts in the general column should be posted daily. The check marks at the bottom of the General Debit and Credit columns are entered at the end of the month and serve as a reminder that these totals should not be posted.
SPECIAL COLUMNS	1. Post the totals of the special columns to the appropriate general ledger accounts.
	2. Once posted, enter the account number (in parentheses) beneath the column and "CJ" and the page number in each general ledger account's Posting Reference column.

FIGURE 10-8   Posting from a Combination Journal

LEARNING KEY: Amounts in the General column are posted individually. Only the totals of the special columns are posted.

Portions of the combination journal in Figure 10-7 and general ledger accounts for Cash, Office Furniture, Accounts Payable, and Medical Fees are shown in Figure 10-9 to illustrate the effects of this posting process. Note that the individual debits and credits in the General Columns are posted individually throughout the month. Only the totals of the Special Columns are posted at the end of the month.

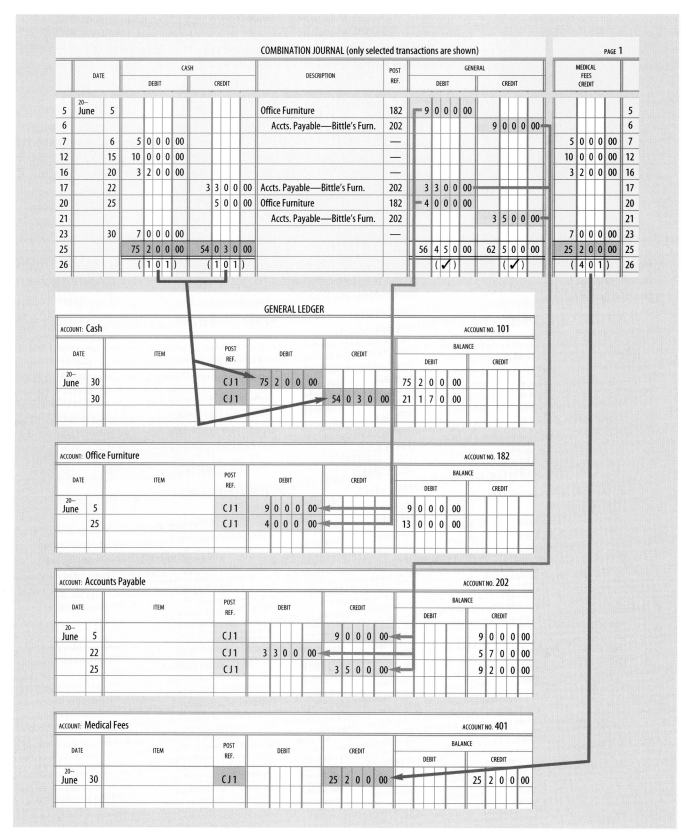

FIGURE 10-9 **Posting the Combination Journal**

To see the advantages of posting a combination journal compared with the general journal, simply compare the accounts in Figure 10-9 with the same accounts in Chapter 4, Figure 4-12. Note the number of postings required for the general journal and combination journal.

Number of Postings

	General Journal	Combination Journal	
Cash	13	2	(Special columns for cash)
Delivery Equip./Office Furniture	3	3	(No special column)
Accounts Payable	3	3	(No special column)
Delivery/Medical Fees	3	1	(Special column for Medical Fees)

Clearly, using the combination journal can be quite efficient.

Determining the Cash Balance

The debits and credits to Cash are not posted until the end of the accounting period. Therefore, the cash balance must be computed when this information is needed. The cash balance may be computed at any time during the month by taking the beginning balance, adding total cash debits and subtracting total cash credits to date. Figure 10-10 shows the calculation of Bonita's cash balance on June 15.

LEARNING KEY:

Beginning cash balance
+ Cash debits to date
− Cash credits to date
Current cash balance

PERFORMING END-OF-PERIOD WORK FOR A PROFESSIONAL SERVICE BUSINESS

LO5 Prepare a work sheet, financial statements, and adjusting and closing entries for a professional service business.

Once the combination journal has been posted to the general ledger, the end-of-period work sheet is prepared in the same way as described in Chapter 5. Recall that financial statements are prepared and end-of-period work is normally performed at the end of the fiscal year. For illustration purposes, we will perform these activities at the end of Bonita's first month of operations.

Preparing the Work Sheet

Bonita's work sheet is illustrated in Figure 10-11 on page 339. Adjustments were made for the following items:

(a) Medical supplies remaining on June 30, $350.

(b) Office supplies remaining on June 30, $100.

(c) Prepaid insurance expired during June, $500.

(d) Depreciation on office furniture for June, $200.

(e) Depreciation on medical equipment for June, $300.

COMBINATION JOURNAL   PAGE 1

Line	DATE 20—	CASH DEBIT	CASH CREDIT	DESCRIPTION	POST REF.	GENERAL DEBIT	GENERAL CREDIT	MEDICAL FEES CREDIT	WAGES EXPENSE DEBIT	LABORATORY EXPENSE DEBIT	MEDICAL SUPPLIES DEBIT	OFFICE SUPPLIES DEBIT
1	June 1	50 0 0 0 00		Ray Bonita, Capital	311		50 0 0 0 00					
2	2		6 0 0 0 00	Prepaid Insurance	145	6 0 0 0 00						
3	3		22 0 0 0 00	Medical Equipment	185	22 0 0 0 00						
4	4		3 0 0 00		—					3 0 0 00		
5	5			Office Furniture	182	9 0 0 0 00						
6				Accounts Payable—Bittle's Furn.	202		9 0 0 0 00					
7	6	5 0 0 0 00			—			5 0 0 0 00				
8	7		2 0 0 0 00	Rent Expense	521	2 0 0 0 00						
9	8		3 0 0 0 00		—				3 0 0 0 00			
10	9		2 5 0 00		—						2 5 0 00	
11	15	10 0 0 0 00			—			10 0 0 0 00				
12	15		1 5 0 00	Telephone Expense	525	1 5 0 00						
13		65 0 0 0 00	33 7 0 0 00		—							

Beginning balance	$ 0
Add cash debits	65,000
Total	$65,000
Less cash credits	33,700
Cash balance, June 15	$31,300

FIGURE 10-10   Determining the Cash Balance

Ray Bonita, M.D.
Worksheet
For Month Ended June 30, 20 - -

	TRIAL BALANCE		ADJUSTMENTS		ADJUSTED TRIAL BALANCE		INCOME STATEMENT		BALANCE SHEET	
ACCOUNT TITLE	DEBIT	CREDIT	DEBIT	CREDIT	DEBIT	CREDIT	DEBIT	CREDIT	DEBIT	CREDIT
1 Cash	21 1 7 0 00				21 1 7 0 00				21 1 7 0 00	
2 Medical Supplies	4 5 0 00			(a) 1 0 0 00	3 5 0 00				3 5 0 00	
3 Office Supplies	1 5 0 00			(b) 5 0 00	1 0 0 00				1 0 0 00	
4 Prepaid Insurance	6 0 0 0 00			(c) 5 0 0 00	5 5 0 0 00				5 5 0 0 00	
5 Office Furniture	13 0 0 0 00				13 0 0 0 00				13 0 0 0 00	
6 Accum. Depr.—Office Furniture				(d) 2 0 0 00		2 0 0 00				2 0 0 00
7 Medical Equipment	22 0 0 0 00				22 0 0 0 00				22 0 0 0 00	
8 Accum. Depr.—Medical Equipment				(e) 3 0 0 00		3 0 0 00				3 0 0 00
9 Accounts Payable		9 2 0 0 00				9 2 0 0 00				9 2 0 0 00
10 Ray Bonita, Capital		50 0 0 0 00				50 0 0 0 00				50 0 0 0 00
11 Ray Bonita, Drawing	10 0 0 0 00				10 0 0 0 00				10 0 0 0 00	
12 Medical Fees		25 2 0 0 00				25 2 0 0 00		25 2 0 0 00		
13 Wages Expense	8 5 0 0 00				8 5 0 0 00		8 5 0 0 00			
14 Rent Expense	2 0 0 0 00				2 0 0 0 00		2 0 0 0 00			
15 Office Supplies Expense			(b) 5 0 00		5 0 00		5 0 00			
16 Medical Supplies Expense			(a) 1 0 0 00		1 0 0 00		1 0 0 00			
17 Telephone Expense	1 5 0 00				1 5 0 00		1 5 0 00			
18 Laboratory Expense	9 8 0 00				9 8 0 00		9 8 0 00			
19 Insurance Expense			(c) 5 0 0 00		5 0 0 00		5 0 0 00			
20 Depr. Expense—Office Furniture			(d) 2 0 0 00		2 0 0 00		2 0 0 00			
21 Depr. Expense—Medical Equipment			(e) 3 0 0 00		3 0 0 00		3 0 0 00			
22	84 4 0 0 00	84 4 0 0 00	1 1 5 0 00	1 1 5 0 00	84 9 0 0 00	84 9 0 0 00	12 7 8 0 00	25 2 0 0 00	72 1 2 0 00	59 7 0 0 00
23 Net Income							12 4 2 0 00			12 4 2 0 00
24							25 2 0 0 00	25 2 0 0 00	72 1 2 0 00	72 1 2 0 00
25										
26										
27										
28										
29										
30										

FIGURE 10-11   Work Sheet for Ray Bonita, M.D.

Preparing Financial Statements

Dr. Bonita made no additional investment during June. Thus, as we saw in Chapter 6, the financial statements can be prepared directly from the work sheet. Recall that if Bonita had made an additional investment, this amount would be identified by reviewing Bonita's capital account and would need to be reported in the statement of owner's equity. Bonita's financial statements are illustrated in Figure 10-12.

Ray Bonita, M.D.
Income Statement
For Month Ended June 30, 20 - -

Revenue:		
Medical fees		$25 2 0 0 00
Expenses:		
Wages expense	$8 5 0 0 00	
Rent expense	2 0 0 0 00	
Office supplies expense	5 0 00	
Medical supplies expense	1 0 0 00	
Telephone expense	1 5 0 00	
Laboratory expense	9 8 0 00	
Insurance expense	5 0 0 00	
Depreciation expense—office furniture	2 0 0 00	
Depreciation expense—medical equipment	3 0 0 00	
Total expenses		12 7 8 0 00
Net income		$12 4 2 0 00

Ray Bonita, M.D.
Statement of Owner's Equity
For Month Ended June 30, 20 - -

Ray Bonita, capital, June 1, 20 - -		$50 0 0 0 00
Net income for June	$12 4 2 0 00	
Less withdrawals for June	10 0 0 0 00	
Increase in capital		2 4 2 0 00
Ray Bonita, capital, June 30, 20 - -		$52 4 2 0 00

Ray Bonita, M.D.
Balance Sheet
June 30, 20 - -

Assets			
Current assets:			
Cash	$21 1 7 0 00		
Medical supplies	3 5 0 00		
Office supplies	1 0 0 00		
Prepaid insurance	5 5 0 0 00		
Total current assets		$27 1 2 0 00	
Property, plant, and equipment:			
Office furniture	$13 0 0 0 00		
Less accumulated depreciation	2 0 0 00	12 8 0 0 00	
Medical equipment	$22 0 0 0 00		
Less accumulated depreciation	3 0 0 00	21 7 0 0 00	
Total assets		$61 6 2 0 00	
Liabilities			
Current liabilities:			
Accounts payable		$ 9 2 0 0 00	
Owner's Equity			
Ray Bonita, capital		52 4 2 0 00	
Total liabilities and owner's equity		$61 6 2 0 00	

FIGURE 10-12   Financial Statements for Ray Bonita, M.D.

PROFILES IN ACCOUNTING
Amy Butler, Office Manager

Amy Butler earned an Associate Degree in Travel/Hospitality Management. After completing her externship with the Clubhouse Inn, Amy worked for Design Coatings as a receptionist. After eight months, she accepted an office manager's position with EMI, a database consulting firm.

Amy's duties include accounts payable and receivable, payroll, word processing, filing, and supervising and training eight employees.

She considers being professional at all times the key to success.

Preparing Adjusting and Closing Entries

Adjusting and closing entries are made in the combination journal in the same manner demonstrated for the general journal in Chapter 6. We simply use the Description and General Debit and Credit columns. These posted entries are illustrated in Figures 10-13 and 10-14.

COMBINATION JOURNAL

	DATE		CASH DEBIT	CASH CREDIT	DESCRIPTION	POST REF.	GENERAL DEBIT	GENERAL CREDIT	
1					Adjusting Entries				1
2	20-- June	30			Medical Supplies Expense	524	1 0 0 00		2
3					Medical Supplies	141		1 0 0 00	3
4		30			Office Supplies Expense	523	5 0 00		4
5					Office Supplies	142		5 0 00	5
6		30			Insurance Expense	535	5 0 0 00		6
7					Prepaid Insurance	145		5 0 0 00	7
8		30			Depr. Expense—Office Furniture	541	2 0 0 00		8
9					Accum. Depr.—Office Furn.	182.1		2 0 0 00	9
10		30			Depr. Expense—Medical Equip.	542	3 0 0 00		10
11					Accum. Depr.—Medical Equip.	185.1		3 0 0 00	11

FIGURE 10-13   Adjusting Entries

COMBINATION JOURNAL

	DATE		CASH DEBIT	CASH CREDIT	DESCRIPTION	POST REF.	GENERAL DEBIT	GENERAL CREDIT	
12									12
13					Closing Entries				13
14	20-- June	30			Medical Fees	401	25 2 0 0 00		14
15					Income Summary	313		25 2 0 0 00	15
16		30			Income Summary	313	12 7 8 0 00		16
17					Wages Expense	511		8 5 0 0 00	17
18					Rent Expense	521		2 0 0 0 00	18
19					Office Supplies Expense	523		5 0 00	19
20					Medical Supplies Expense	524		1 0 0 00	20
21					Telephone Expense	525		1 5 0 00	21
22					Laboratory Expense	526		9 8 0 00	22
23					Insurance Expense	535		5 0 0 00	23
24					Depr. Expense—Office Furn.	541		2 0 0 00	24
25					Depr. Expense—Med. Equip.	542		3 0 0 00	25
26		30			Income Summary	313	12 4 2 0 00		26
27					Ray Bonita, Capital	311		12 4 2 0 00	27
28		30			Ray Bonita, Capital	311	10 0 0 0 00		28
29					Ray Bonita, Drawing	312		10 0 0 0 00	29

FIGURE 10-14   Closing Entries

Learning Objectives	Key Points to Remember
1 **Explain the cash, modified cash, and accrual bases of accounting.**	There are three bases of accounting: cash, modified cash, and accrual. Differences in the recording of revenues, expenses, assets, and liabilities are listed below.

Recording revenues

Cash: when cash is received
Modified cash: when cash is received
Accrual: when earned

Recording expenses

Cash: when cash is paid
Modified cash: when cash is paid, except for property, plant, and equipment and prepaid items
Accrual: when incurred

Recording assets and liabilities

	Cash Basis	Modified Cash Basis	Accrual Basis
Accounts receivable	No	No	Yes
Payables			
for purchase of assets	No	Yes	Yes
for services received (wages payable)	No	No	Yes
Prepaid assets	No	Yes	Yes
Long-term assets	No	Yes	Yes

Learning Objectives	Key Points to Remember
2 **Describe special records for a professional service business using the modified cash basis.**	Special records are required for a professional service business using the modified cash basis. Since accounts receivable are not entered in the accounting system, other records must be maintained to keep track of amounts owed by clients and patients. These records generally include an appointment record and a client or patient ledger record.
3 **Describe and use a combination journal to record transactions of a professional service business.**	A combination journal is used by some businesses to improve the efficiency of recording and posting transactions. It includes general and special columns. The headings for a typical combination journal for a doctor's office are shown below.

COMBINATION JOURNAL   PAGE 1

DATE	CASH		DESCRIPTION	POST REF.	GENERAL		MEDICAL FEES CREDIT	WAGES EXPENSE DEBIT	LABORATORY EXPENSE DEBIT	MEDICAL SUPPLIES DEBIT	OFFICE SUPPLIES DEBIT
	DEBIT	CREDIT			DEBIT	CREDIT					

Learning Objectives	Key Points to Remember
4 **Post from the combination journal to the general ledger.**	Rules for posting a combination journal: 1. Amounts entered in the general columns are posted individually to the general ledger on a daily basis. 2. The totals of the special columns are posted to the general ledger at the end of the month.
5 **Prepare a work sheet, financial statements, and adjusting and closing entries for a professional service business.**	The work sheet, financial statements, adjusting entries, and closing entries are prepared in the same manner as discussed in Chapters 5 and 6. Remember, however, that under the modified cash basis, adjustments are made only for prepaid items and depreciation of plant and equipment.

Reflection: Answering the Opening Question

To comply with generally accepted accounting principles (GAAP), all firms should use the accrual basis. As you recall, this means that revenues should be recognized when earned, regardless of when cash is received, and expenses should be recognized when incurred, regardless of when cash is paid. Investors and creditors expect GAAP financial statements when major companies seek to raise funds. Thus, if the doctor wants GAAP financial statements, revenues should be recorded when the doctor provides the service. (Later, in Chapter 17, we will discuss what should be done about differences between the amount charged by the doctor and the amount finally paid by the patient, or insurance company.)

Many small professional service businesses are not concerned with raising large amounts of money from investors and creditors. These firms include CPAs, doctors, dentists, lawyers, engineers, and architects. Since these firms do not need to prepare GAAP financial statements, they often use the cash or modified cash basis. This simplifies the accounting process and provides results similar to GAAP if receivables and payables are minimal. Further, if one of these organizations needs to borrow money from a bank that requires GAAP financial statements, an accountant can convert the financial statements to the accrual basis.

KEY TERMS

accrual basis of accounting, (326)   A method of accounting under which revenues are recorded when earned and expenses are recorded when incurred.

cash basis of accounting, (326)   A method of accounting under which revenues are recorded when cash is received and expenses are recorded when cash is paid.

combination journal, (331)   A journal with special and general columns.

Description column, (333)   The column in the combination journal used to enter the account titles for the General Debit and General Credit columns, to identify specific creditors when assets are purchased on account, and to identify amounts forwarded.

General Credit column, (331)   The column in the combination journal used to credit accounts that are used infrequently.

General Debit column, (331)   The column in the combination journal used to debit accounts that are used infrequently.

modified cash basis, (327)   A method of accounting that combines aspects of the cash and accrual methods. It uses the cash basis for recording revenues and most expenses. Exceptions are made when cash is paid for assets with useful lives greater than one accounting period.

Posting Reference column, (335)   The column in the combination journal where the account number is entered after posting.

special columns, (331)   Columns in journals for frequently used accounts.

DEMONSTRATION PROBLEM

Maria Vietor is a financial planning consultant. She developed the following chart of accounts for her business.

Vietor Financial Planning
Chart of Accounts

Assets	Revenues
101 Cash	401 Professional Fees
142 Office Supplies	
	Expenses
Liabilities	511 Wages Expense
202 Accounts Payable	521 Rent Expense
	523 Office Supplies Expense
Owner's Equity	525 Telephone Expense
311 Maria Vietor, Capital	526 Automobile Expense
312 Maria Vietor, Drawing	533 Utilities Expense
313 Income Summary	534 Charitable Contributions Expense

Vietor completed the following transactions during the month of December of the current year:

Dec. 1 Vietor invested cash to start a consulting business, $20,000.

3 Paid December office rent, $1,000.

4 Received a check from Aaron Bisno, a client, for services, $2,500.

6 Paid Union Electric for December heating and light, $75.

7 Received a check from Will Carter, a client, for services, $2,000.

12 Paid Smith's Super Service for gasoline and oil purchases, $60.

14 Paid Comphelp for temporary secretarial services obtained through them during the past two weeks, $600.

17 Purchased office supplies on account from Cleat Office Supply, $280.

20 Paid Cress Telephone Co. for local and long-distance business calls during the past month, $100.

21 Vietor withdrew cash for personal use, $1,100.

24 Made donation to the National Multiple Sclerosis Society, $100.

27 Received a check from Ellen Thaler, a client, for services, $2,000.

28 Paid Comphelp for temporary secretarial services obtained through them during the past two weeks, $600.

29 Made payment on account to Cleat Office Supply, $100.

REQUIRED

1. Enter the transactions in a combination journal. Establish special columns for Professional Fees, Wages Expense, and Automobile Expense. Vietor uses the modified cash basis of accounting. (Refer to the Chapter 4 Demonstration Problem to see how similar transactions were recorded in a general journal. Notice that the combination journal is much more efficient.)

2. Prove the combination journal.

3. Post these transactions to a general ledger.

4. Prepare a trial balance.

Solution
1, 2.

COMBINATION JOURNAL   PAGE 1

	DATE	DESCRIPTION	POST REF.	CASH DEBIT	CASH CREDIT	GENERAL DEBIT	GENERAL CREDIT	PROFESSIONAL FEES CREDIT	WAGES EXPENSE DEBIT	AUTOMOBILE EXPENSE DEBIT
1	20– Dec. 1	Maria Vietor, Capital	311	20 0 0 0 00			20 0 0 0 00			
2	3	Rent Expense	521		1 0 0 0 00	1 0 0 0 00				
3	4		—	2 5 0 0 00				2 5 0 0 00		
4	6	Utilities Expense	533		7 5 00	7 5 00				
5	7		—	2 0 0 0 00				2 0 0 0 00		
6	12		—		6 0 0 00				6 0 0 00	
7	14		—		6 0 00					6 0 00
8	17	Office Supplies	142			2 8 0 00				
9		Accounts Payable—Cleat Office Supply	202				2 8 0 00			
10	20	Telephone Expense	525		1 0 0 00	1 0 0 00				
11	21	Maria Vietor, Drawing	312		1 1 0 0 00	1 1 0 0 00				
12	24	Charitable Contributions Expense	534		1 0 0 00	1 0 0 00				
13	27		—	2 0 0 0 00				2 0 0 0 00		
14	28		—		6 0 0 00				6 0 0 00	
15	29	Accounts Payable—Cleat Office Supply	202		1 0 0 00	1 0 0 00				
16				26 5 0 0 00	3 7 3 5 00	2 7 5 5 00	20 2 8 0 00	6 5 0 0 00	1 2 0 0 00	6 0 00
17				(1 0 1)	(1 0 1)	(✓)	(✓)	(4 0 1)	(5 1 1)	(5 2 6)
18										

Proving the Combination Journal

Debit Columns		Credit Columns	
Cash	26,500	Cash	3,735
General	2,755	General	20,280
Wages Expense	1,200	Professional Fees	6,500
Auto. Expense	60		30,515
	30,515		

(continued)

3.

GENERAL LEDGER

ACCOUNT: Cash   ACCOUNT NO. 101

DATE	ITEM	POST REF.	DEBIT	CREDIT	BALANCE DEBIT	BALANCE CREDIT
20-- Dec. 31		CJ1	26 500 00		26 500 00	
31		CJ1		3 735 00	22 765 00	

ACCOUNT: Office Supplies   ACCOUNT NO. 142

DATE	ITEM	POST REF.	DEBIT	CREDIT	BALANCE DEBIT	BALANCE CREDIT
20-- Dec. 17		CJ1	280 00		280 00	

ACCOUNT: Accounts Payable   ACCOUNT NO. 202

DATE	ITEM	POST REF.	DEBIT	CREDIT	BALANCE DEBIT	BALANCE CREDIT
20-- Dec. 17		CJ1		280 00		280 00
29		CJ1	100 00			180 00

ACCOUNT: Maria Vietor, Capital   ACCOUNT NO. 311

DATE	ITEM	POST REF.	DEBIT	CREDIT	BALANCE DEBIT	BALANCE CREDIT
20-- Dec. 1		CJ1		20 000 00		20 000 00

ACCOUNT: Maria Vietor, Drawing   ACCOUNT NO. 312

DATE	ITEM	POST REF.	DEBIT	CREDIT	BALANCE DEBIT	BALANCE CREDIT
20-- Dec. 21		CJ1	1 100 00		1 100 00	

ACCOUNT: Income Summary   ACCOUNT NO. 313

DATE	ITEM	POST REF.	DEBIT	CREDIT	BALANCE DEBIT	BALANCE CREDIT
20--						

ACCOUNT: Professional Fees   ACCOUNT NO. 401

DATE	ITEM	POST REF.	DEBIT	CREDIT	BALANCE DEBIT	BALANCE CREDIT
20-- Dec. 31		CJ1		6 500 00		6 500 00

ACCOUNT: Wages Expense   ACCOUNT NO. 511

DATE	ITEM	POST REF.	DEBIT	CREDIT	BALANCE DEBIT	BALANCE CREDIT
20-- Dec. 31		CJ1	1 200 00		1 200 00	

3.

ACCOUNT: Rent Expense   ACCOUNT NO. 521

DATE	ITEM	POST REF.	DEBIT	CREDIT	BALANCE DEBIT	BALANCE CREDIT
20-- Dec. 3		CJ1	1 0 0 0 00		1 0 0 0 00	

ACCOUNT: Office Supplies Expense   ACCOUNT NO. 523

DATE	ITEM	POST REF.	DEBIT	CREDIT	BALANCE DEBIT	BALANCE CREDIT
20--						

ACCOUNT: Telephone Expense   ACCOUNT NO. 525

DATE	ITEM	POST REF.	DEBIT	CREDIT	BALANCE DEBIT	BALANCE CREDIT
20-- Dec. 20		CJ1	1 0 0 00		1 0 0 00	

ACCOUNT: Automobile Expense   ACCOUNT NO. 526

DATE	ITEM	POST REF.	DEBIT	CREDIT	BALANCE DEBIT	BALANCE CREDIT
20-- Dec. 31		CJ1	6 0 00		6 0 00	

ACCOUNT: Utilities Expense   ACCOUNT NO. 533

DATE	ITEM	POST REF.	DEBIT	CREDIT	BALANCE DEBIT	BALANCE CREDIT
20-- Dec. 6		CJ1	7 5 00		7 5 00	

ACCOUNT: Charitable Contributions Expense   ACCOUNT NO. 534

DATE	ITEM	POST REF.	DEBIT	CREDIT	BALANCE DEBIT	BALANCE CREDIT
20-- Dec. 24		CJ1	1 0 0 00		1 0 0 00	

4.

Vietor Financial Planning
Trial Balance
December 31, 20 - -

ACCOUNT TITLE	ACCOUNT NO.	DEBIT BALANCE	CREDIT BALANCE
Cash	101	22 7 6 5 00	
Office Supplies	142	2 8 0 00	
Accounts Payable	202		1 8 0 00
Maria Vietor, Capital	311		20 0 0 0 00
Maria Vietor, Drawing	312	1 1 0 0 00	
Professional Fees	401		6 5 0 0 00
Wages Expense	511	1 2 0 0 00	
Rent Expense	521	1 0 0 0 00	
Telephone Expense	525	1 0 0 00	
Automobile Expense	526	6 0 00	
Utilities Expense	533	7 5 00	
Charitable Contributions Expense	534	1 0 0 00	
		26 6 8 0 00	26 6 8 0 00

REVIEW QUESTIONS

1. Explain when revenues are recorded under the cash basis, modified cash basis, and accrual basis of accounting.

2. Explain when expenses are recorded under the cash basis, modified cash basis, and accrual basis of accounting.

3. Explain the purpose of an appointment record.

4. Explain the purpose of a patient ledger account.

5. Explain the purpose of a special column in the combination journal.

6. Explain the purpose of the General columns in the combination journal.

7. How does the use of the combination journal save time and space in entering cash transactions?

8. Explain the purpose of the Description column in the combination journal.

9. What is the purpose of proving the totals in the combination journal?

10. When an entry is posted from the combination journal to a ledger account, what information is entered in the Posting Reference column of the combination journal? in the Posting Reference column of the ledger account?

MANAGING YOUR WRITING

Your friend is planning to start her own business and has asked you for advice. In particular, she is concerned about which method of accounting she should use. She has heard about the cash, modified cash, and accrual methods of accounting. However, she does not really understand the differences. Write a memo that explains each method and the type of business for which each method is most appropriate.

ETHICS CASE

Nancy Bowles, the owner of Bowles Services, a sole proprietorship, rushed into the office late Monday morning carrying a deposit receipt from the bank. Upon handing the receipt to Sarah, the accountant, she instructed her to debit Cash and credit Professional Fees for the full $10,000. When Sarah examined the source document she saw that the cash had come from the account of Richard Bowles, Nancy's father. Nancy explained to Sarah that she was applying for a bank loan and needed to "show that her company earned more year-to-date income than it actually had." Nancy used the rationale that the company would earn at least $10,000 in revenue during the next few months but the financial statements the bank required were as of the end of this month.

1. Does Nancy's explanation make sense? Is it ethical?

2. How should this transaction be entered in Bowles Services' books? Does it matter whether the cash basis or accrual basis of accounting is used?

3. Make a written list of all the consequences Nancy might face as a result of recording this transaction as a debit to Cash and a credit to Professional Fees.

4. Break up into groups of two and role play Nancy and Sarah's points of view in this situation.

WEB WORK

For some other views on accrual and cash accounting, check out these Web pages. What are some differences between cash and accrual accounting? Can businesses use one method for internal record keeping and another method for tax reporting?

American Express offers a small business services page at

http://www.americanexpress.com/smallbusiness

Choose Business Planning and Resources, and then Managing Your Business. Small Office/Home Office has information in which you can search for accrual and cash accounting at

http://www.toolkit.cch.com

(http://heintz.swcollege.com)

SERIES A EXERCISES

EXERCISE 10-1A   (LO1)   **CASH, MODIFIED CASH, AND ACCRUAL BASES OF ACCOUNTING** Prepare the entry for each of the following transactions, using the (a) cash basis, (b) modified cash basis, and (c) accrual basis of accounting.

1. Purchase supplies on account.

2. Make payment on asset previously purchased.

3. Purchase supplies for cash.

4. Purchase insurance for cash.

5. Pay cash for wages.

6. Pay cash for telephone expense.

7. Pay cash for new equipment.

End-of-Period Adjusting Entries:

8. Wages earned but not paid.

9. Prepaid item purchased, partly used.

10. Depreciation on long-term assets.

EXERCISE 10-2A (LO1/3) **JOURNAL ENTRIES** Jean Akins opened a consulting business. Journalize the following transactions that occurred during the month of January of the current year using the modified cash basis and a combination journal. Set up special columns for Consulting Fees (credit) and Wages Expense (debit).

Jan. 1 Invested cash in the business, $10,000.

2 Paid office rent, $500.

3 Purchased office equipment on account from Business Machines, Inc., $1,500.

5 Received cash for services rendered, $750.

8 Paid telephone bill, $65.

10 Paid for a magazine subscription (miscellaneous expense), $15.

11 Purchased office supplies on account from Leo's Office Supplies, $300.

15 Paid for one-year liability insurance policy, $150.

18 Paid part-time help, $500.

21 Received cash for services rendered, $350.

25 Paid electricity bill, $85.

27 Withdrew cash for personal use, $100.

29 Paid part-time help, $500.

EXERCISE 10-3A (LO1/3) **JOURNAL ENTRIES** Bill Rackes opened a bicycle repair shop. Journalize the following transactions that occurred during the month of October of the current year. Use the modified cash basis and a combination journal with special columns for Repair Fees (credit) and Wages Expense (debit). Prove the combination journal.

Oct. 1 Invested cash in the business, $15,000.

2 Paid shop rental for the month, $300.

3 Purchased bicycle parts on account from Tracker's Bicycle Parts, $2,000.

5 Purchased office supplies on account from Downtown Office Supplies, $250.

8 Paid telephone bill, $38.

9 Received cash for services, $140.

11 Paid for a sports magazine subscription (miscellaneous expense), $15.

12 Made payment on account for parts previously purchased, $100.

14 Paid part-time help, $300.

15 Received cash for services, $350.

16 Paid electricity bill, $48.

19 Received cash for services, $250.

23 Withdrew cash for personal use, $50.

25 Made payment on account for office supplies previously purchased, $50.

29 Paid part-time help, $300.

SERIES A PROBLEMS

PROBLEM 10-1A (LO3/4/5)   **JOURNALIZING AND POSTING TRANSACTIONS AND PREPARING A TRIAL BALANCE** Angela McWharton opened an on-call nursing services business. She rented a small office space and pays a part-time worker to answer the telephone. Her chart of accounts is shown below.

Angela McWharton Nursing Services
Chart of Accounts

Assets	Revenues
101 Cash	401 Nursing Care Fees
142 Office Supplies	
181 Office Equipment	Expenses
	511 Wages Expense
Liabilities	512 Advertising Expense
202 Accounts Payable	521 Rent Expense
	525 Telephone Expense
Owner's Equity	526 Transportation Expense
311 Angela McWharton, Capital	533 Electricity Expense
312 Angela McWharton, Drawing	549 Miscellaneous Expense
313 Income Summary	

McWharton's transactions for the first month of business are as follows:

Jan. 1   Invested cash in the business, $10,000.

1   Paid January rent, $500.

2   Purchased office supplies on account from Crestline Office Supplies, $300.

4   Purchased office equipment on account from Office Technology, Inc., $1,500.

6   Received cash for nursing services rendered, $580.

7   Paid telephone bill, $42.

8   Paid electricity bill, $38.

10   Received cash for nursing services rendered, $360.

12   Made payment on account for office supplies previously purchased, $50.

13   Reimbursed part-time worker for use of personal automobile (transportation expense), $150.

15   Paid part-time worker, $360.

17   Received cash for nursing services rendered, $420.

18   Withdrew cash for personal use, $100.

20   Paid for newspaper advertising, $26.

22   Paid for gas and oil, $35.

24   Paid subscription for journal on nursing care practices (miscellaneous expense), $28.

25   Received cash for nursing services rendered, $320.

27   Made payment on account for office equipment previously purchased, $150.

29   Paid part-time worker, $360.

30   Received cash for nursing services rendered, $180.

(continued)

REQUIRED

1. Journalize the transactions for January using the modified cash basis and page 1 of a combination journal. Set up special columns for Nursing Care Fees (credit), Wages Expense (debit), and Transportation Expense (debit).

2. Determine the cash balance as of January 12 (using the combination journal).

3. Prove the combination journal.

4. Set up four-column general ledger accounts from the chart of accounts and post the transactions from the combination journal.

5. Prepare a trial balance.

PROBLEM 10-2A (LO3/4/5)

JOURNALIZING AND POSTING TRANSACTIONS AND PREPARING FINANCIAL STATEMENTS Sue Reyton owns a suit tailoring shop. She opened her business in September. She rents a small work space and has an assistant to receive job orders and process claim tickets. Her trial balance shows her account balances for the first two months of business (September and October). No adjustments were made in September or October.

Sue Reyton Tailors
Trial Balance
October 31, 20 - -

ACCOUNT TITLE	ACCOUNT NO.	DEBIT BALANCE	CREDIT BALANCE
Cash	101	5 7 1 1 00	
Tailoring Supplies	141	1 0 0 0 00	
Office Supplies	142	4 8 5 00	
Prepaid Insurance	145	1 0 0 00	
Tailoring Equipment	188	3 8 0 0 00	
Accumulated Depreciation—Tailoring Equipment	188.1		
Accounts Payable	202		4 1 2 5 00
Sue Reyton, Capital	311		5 4 3 0 00
Sue Reyton, Drawing	312	5 0 0 00	
Tailoring Fees	401		3 6 0 0 00
Wages Expense	511	8 0 0 00	
Advertising Expense	512	3 3 00	
Rent Expense	521	6 0 0 00	
Telephone Expense	525	6 0 00	
Electricity Expense	533	4 4 00	
Miscellaneous Expense	549	2 2 00	
		13 1 5 5 00	13 1 5 5 00

Reyton's transactions for November are as follows:

Nov. 1   Paid November rent, $300.

2   Purchased tailoring supplies on account from Sew Easy Supplies, $150.

3   Purchased a new button hole machine on account from Seam's Sewing Machines, $3,000.

5   Earned first week's revenue: $400 in cash.

8   Paid for newspaper advertising, $13.

9   Paid telephone bill, $28.

10   Paid electricity bill, $21.

12   Earned second week's revenue: $200 in cash, $300 on account.

15   Paid part-time worker, $400.

16   Made payment on account for tailoring supplies, $100.

17   Paid for magazine subscription (miscellaneous expense), $12.

19   Earned third week's revenue: $450 in cash.

21   Paid for prepaid insurance for the year, $500.

23   Received cash from customers (previously owed), $300.

24   Paid for newspaper advertising, $13.

26   Paid for special delivery fee (miscellaneous expense), $12.

29   Earned fourth week's revenue: $600 in cash.

Additional accounts needed are as follows:

313   Income Summary
523   Office Supplies Expense
524   Tailoring Supplies Expense
535   Insurance Expense
542   Depreciation Expense—Tailoring Equipment

Nov. 30 Adjustments:

(a) Tailoring supplies on hand, $450.

(b) Office supplies on hand, $285.

(c) Prepaid insurance expired over past three months, $150.

(d) Depreciation on tailoring equipment for the last three months, $300.

REQUIRED

1. Journalize the transactions for November using the modified cash basis and page 5 of a combination journal. Set up special columns for Tailoring Fees (credit), Wages Expense (debit), and Advertising Expense (debit).

2. Determine the cash balance as of November 12.

3. Prove the combination journal.

4. Set up four-column general ledger accounts, including the additional accounts listed above, entering the balances as of November 1, 20--. Post the entries from the combination journal.

5. Prepare a work sheet for the three months ended November 30, 20--.

6. Prepare an income statement and statement of owner's equity for the three months ended November 30, and a balance sheet as of November 30, 20--. (Assume that Reyton made an investment of $5,430 on September 1, 20--.)

7. Record the adjusting and closing entries on page 6 of the combination journal and post to the general ledger accounts.

SERIES B EXERCISES

EXERCISE 10-1B   **(LO1)**   **CASH, MODIFIED CASH, AND ACCRUAL BASES OF ACCOUNTING** For each journal entry shown below, indicate the accounting method(s) for which the entry would be appropriate. If the journal entry is not appropriate for a particular accounting method, explain the proper accounting treatment for that method.

1. Office Equipment
   Cash
      Purchased equipment for cash

2. Office Equipment
   Accounts Payable
      Purchased equipment on account

3. Cash
   Revenue
      Cash receipts for week

4. Accounts Receivable
   Revenue
      Services performed on account

5. Prepaid Insurance
   Cash
      Purchased prepaid asset

6. Supplies
   Accounts Payable
      Purchased prepaid asset

7. Telephone Expense
   Cash
      Paid telephone bill

8. Wages Expense
   Cash
      Paid wages for month

9. Accounts Payable
   Cash
      Payment on account

   Adjusting Entries:

10. Supplies Expense
    Supplies

11. Wages Expense
    Wages Payable

12. Depreciation Expense—Office Equipment
    Accumulated Depreciation—Office Equipment

EXERCISE 10-2B   **(LO1/3)**   **JOURNAL ENTRIES** Bill Miller opened a bookkeeping service business. Journalize the following transactions that occurred during the month of March of the current year. Use the modified cash basis and a combination journal with special columns for Bookkeeping Fees (credit) and Wages Expense (debit).

Mar. 1   Invested cash in the business, $7,500.

3   Paid March office rent, $500.

5   Purchased office equipment on account from Desk Top Office Equipment, $800.

6   Received cash for services rendered, $400.

8   Paid telephone bill, $48.

10   Paid for a magazine subscription (miscellaneous expense), $25.

11   Purchased office supplies, $200.

14   Received cash for services rendered, $520.

16   Paid for a one-year insurance policy, $200.

18   Paid part-time worker, $400.

21   Received cash for services rendered, $380.

22   Made payment on account for office equipment previously purchased, $100.

24   Paid electricity bill, $56.

27   Withdrew cash for personal use, $200.

29   Paid part-time worker, $400.

30   Received cash for services rendered, $600.

EXERCISE 10-3B   **(LO1/3)**   **JOURNAL ENTRIES** Amy Anjelo opened a delivery service. Journalize the following transactions that occurred in January of the current year. Use the modified cash basis and a combination journal with special columns for Delivery Fees (credit) and Wages Expense (debit). Prove the combination journal.

Jan. 1   Invested cash in the business, $10,000.

2   Paid shop rental for the month, $400.

3   Purchased a delivery cart on account from Walt's Wheels, $1,000.

5   Purchased office supplies, $250.

6   Paid telephone bill, $51.

8   Received cash for delivery services, $428.

11   Paid electricity bill, $37.

12   Paid part-time employee, $480.

13   Paid for postage stamps (miscellaneous expense), $29.

15   Received cash for delivery services, $382.

18   Made payment on account for delivery cart previously purchased, $90.

21   Withdrew cash for personal use, $250.

24   Paid for a one-year liability insurance policy, $180.

26   Received cash for delivery services, $292.

29   Paid part-time employee, $480.

SERIES B PROBLEMS

PROBLEM 10-1B (LO3/4/5)   **JOURNALIZING AND POSTING TRANSACTIONS AND PREPARING A TRIAL BALANCE** J. B. Hoyt opened a training center at the marina where he provides private water-skiing lessons. He rented a small building at the marina and has a part-time worker to assist him. His chart of accounts is shown below.

Water Walking by Hoyt
Chart of Accounts

Assets	Revenues
101 Cash	401 Training Fees
142 Office Supplies	
183 Skiing Equipment	Expenses
	511 Wages Expense
Liabilities	521 Rent Expense
202 Accounts Payable	525 Telephone Expense
	526 Transportation Expense
Owner's Equity	533 Electricity Expense
311 J. B. Hoyt, Capital	537 Repair Expense
312 J. B. Hoyt, Drawing	549 Miscellaneous Expense
313 Income Summary	

Transactions for the first month of business are as follows:

July 1	Invested cash in the business, $5,000.
2	Paid rent for the month, $250.
3	Purchased office supplies, $150.
4	Purchased skiing equipment on account from Water Fun, Inc., $2,000.
6	Paid telephone bill, $36.
7	Received cash for skiing lessons, $200.
10	Paid electricity bill, $28.
12	Paid part-time worker, $250.
14	Received cash for skiing lessons, $300.
16	Paid for gas and oil (transportation expense), $60.
17	Received cash for skiing lessons, $250.
20	Paid for repair to ski rope, $20.
21	Made payment on account for skiing equipment previously purchased, $100.
24	Received cash for skiing lessons, $310.
26	Paid for award certificates (miscellaneous expense), $18.
28	Paid part-time worker, $250.
30	Received cash for skiing lessons, $230.
31	Paid for repair to life jacket, $20.

REQUIRED

1. Journalize the transactions for July using the modified cash basis and page 1 of a combination journal. Set up special columns for Training Fees (credit), Wages Expense (debit), and Repair Expense (debit).

2. Determine the cash balance as of July 14, 20--.

3. Prove the combination journal.

4. Set up four-column general ledger accounts from the chart of accounts and post the transactions from the combination journal.

5. Prepare a trial balance.

PROBLEM 10-2B (LO3/4/5)

JOURNALIZING AND POSTING TRANSACTIONS AND PREPARING FINANCIAL STATEMENTS Molly Claussen owns a lawn care business. She opened her business in April. She rents a small shop area where she stores her equipment and has an assistant to receive orders and process accounts. Her trial balance shows her account balances for the first two months of business (April and May). No adjustments were made at the end of April or May.

Molly Claussen's Green Thumb
Trial Balance
May 31, 20 - -

ACCOUNT TITLE	ACCOUNT NO.	DEBIT BALANCE	CREDIT BALANCE
Cash	101	4 6 0 4 00	
Lawn Care Supplies	141	5 8 8 00	
Office Supplies	142	2 4 3 00	
Prepaid Insurance	145	1 5 0 00	
Lawn Care Equipment	189	2 4 0 8 00	
Accumulated Depreciation—Lawn Care Equipment	189.1		
Accounts Payable	202		1 0 8 0 00
Molly Claussen, Capital	311		5 0 0 0 00
Molly Claussen, Drawing	312	8 0 0 00	
Lawn Care Fees	401		4 0 3 3 00
Wages Expense	511	6 0 0 00	
Rent Expense	521	4 0 0 00	
Telephone Expense	525	8 8 00	
Electricity Expense	533	6 2 00	
Repair Expense	537	5 0 00	
Gas and Oil Expense	538	1 2 0 00	
		10 1 1 3 00	10 1 1 3 00

Transactions for June are as follows:

June 1   Paid shop rent, $200.

2   Purchased office supplies, $230.

3   Purchased new landscaping equipment on account from Earth Care, Inc., $1,000.

5   Paid telephone bill, $31.

6   Received cash for lawn care fees, $640.

8   Paid electricity bill, $31.

(continued)

10   Paid part-time worker, $300.

11   Received cash for lawn care fees, $580.

12   Paid for a one-year insurance policy, $200.

14   Made payment on account for landscaping equipment previously purchased, $100.

15   Paid for gas and oil, $40.

19   Paid for mower repairs, $25.

21   Received $310 cash for lawn care fees and earned $480 on account.

24   Withdrew cash for personal use, $100.

26   Paid for edging equipment repairs, $20.

28   Received cash from customers (previously owed), $480.

29   Paid part-time worker, $300.

Additional accounts needed are as follows:

313   Income Summary
523   Office Supplies Expense
524   Lawn Care Supplies Expense
535   Insurance Expense
542   Depreciation Expense—Lawn Care Equipment

June 30 Adjustments:

(a) Office supplies on hand, $273.

(b) Lawn care supplies on hand, $300.

(c) Prepaid insurance expired over past three months, $100.

(d) Depreciation on lawn care equipment for past three months, $260.

REQUIRED

1. Journalize the transactions for June using the modified cash basis and page 5 of a combination journal. Set up special columns for Lawn Care Fees (credit), Repair Expense (debit), and Wages Expense (debit).

2. Determine the cash balance as of June 12.

3. Prove the combination journal.

4. Set up four-column general ledger accounts including the additional accounts listed above, entering balances as of June 1, 20--. Post the entries from the combination journal.

5. Prepare a work sheet for the three months ended June 30, 20--.

6. Prepare an income statement and statement of owner's equity for the three months ended June 30, and a balance sheet as of June 30, 20--. Assume that Claussen invested $5,000 on April 1, 20--.

7. Record the adjusting and closing entries on page 6 of the combination journal and post to the general ledger accounts.

CHALLENGE PROBLEM

Gerald Resler recently opened a financial consulting business. Summary transactions for the month of June, his second month of operation, are provided below.

1. Cash collected from clients for consulting fees, $10,000. $1,500 of the $10,000 was for consulting fees earned in May, but received in June.

2. Consulting fees earned in June, but to be received in July, $2,000.

3. Supplies on hand at the beginning of June amounted to $500. All purchases of supplies are made on account. Supplies purchased during June, $1,000. At the end of June, $600 worth of supplies remained unused.

4. Paid cash on account to suppliers during June, $800. $200 of the $800 was for purchases of supplies made in May.

5. Wages paid to an assistant, $2,000. Of this $2,000, $300 had been earned in May. In addition, the assistant earned $500 in June, which will be paid next month.

6. Purchased a laptop. Paid $1,200 cash in June and will pay the balance of $1,200 in July. Gerald expects to use the laptop for two years at which time he expects that it will be obsolete and have a zero salvage value.

REQUIRED

Prepare income statements for the month of June using the cash, modified cash, and accrual bases.

MASTERY PROBLEM

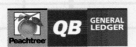

John McRoe opened a tennis resort in June 20--. Most guests register for one week, arriving on Sunday afternoon and returning home the following Saturday afternoon. Guests stay at an adjacent hotel. The tennis resort provides lunch and dinner. Dining and exercise facilities are provided in a building rented by McRoe. A dietitian, masseuse, physical therapist, and athletic trainers are on call to assure the proper combination of diet and exercise. The chart of accounts and transactions for the month of June are provided below. McRoe uses the modified cash basis of accounting.

McRoe Tennis Resort
Chart of Accounts

Assets
101   Cash
142   Office Supplies
144   Food Supplies
184   Tennis Facilities
184.1 Accum. Depr.—Tennis Facilities
186   Exercise Equipment
186.1 Accum. Depr.—Exercise Equip.

Liabilities
202   Accounts Payable

Revenue
401   Registration Fees

Expenses
511   Wages Expense
521   Rent Expense
523   Office Supplies Expense
524   Food Supplies Expense
525   Telephone Expense
533   Utilities Expense
535   Insurance Expense
536   Postage Expense
541   Depr. Exp.—Tennis Facilities
542   Depr. Exp.—Exercise Equip.

(continued)

Owner's Equity
311   John McRoe, Capital
312   John McRoe, Drawing
313   Income Summary

June 1   McRoe invested cash in the business, $90,000.

1   Paid for new exercise equipment, $9,000.

2   Deposited registration fees in the bank, $15,000.

2   Paid rent for month of June on building and land, $2,500.

2   Rogers Construction completed work on new tennis courts that cost $70,000. The estimated useful life of the facility is five years, at which time the courts will have to be resurfaced. Arrangements were made to pay the bill in July.

3   Purchased food supplies on account from Au Naturel Foods, $5,000.

5   Purchased office supplies on account from Gordon Office Supplies, $300.

7   Deposited registration fees in the bank, $16,200.

10   Purchased food supplies on account from Au Naturel Foods, $6,200.

10   Paid wages to staff, $500.

14   Deposited registration fees in the bank, $13,500.

16   Purchased food supplies on account from Au Naturel Foods, $4,000.

17   Paid wages to staff, $500.

18   Paid postage, $85.

21   Deposited registration fees in the bank, $15,200.

24   Purchased food supplies on account from Au Naturel Foods, $5,500.

24   Paid wages to staff, $500.

28   Deposited registration fees in the bank, $14,000.

30   Purchased food supplies on account from Au Naturel Foods, $6,000.

30   Paid wages to staff, $500.

30   Paid Au Naturel Foods on account, $28,700.

30   Paid utility bill, $500.

30   Paid telephone bill, $120.

30   McRoe withdrew cash for personal use, $1,500.

REQUIRED

1.   Enter the transactions in a combination journal (page 1). Establish special columns for Registration Fees (credit), Wages Expense (debit), and Food Supplies (debit).

2.   Prove the combination journal.

3.   Post these transactions to a general ledger.

4.   Prepare a trial balance as of June 30.

Self-Study Test Questions

True/False

1. Under the accrual basis of accounting, revenues are recorded when earned. _____

2. The cash basis of accounting is used by most large businesses. _____

3. The modified cash basis uses the accrual basis when recording revenues and expenses. _____

4. The modified cash basis is a combination of the cash and accrual methods of accounting. _____

5. Many small professional service businesses use the modified cash basis. _____

Multiple Choice

1. Which of these would make the best "special column" in a combination journal? _____

   (a) Office Equipment   (c) Revenue
   (b) Prepaid Insurance   (d) Telephone Expense

2. Verifying that debit column totals equal credit column totals is the process of _____

   (a) debiting.   (c) closing.
   (b) proving.   (d) adjusting.

3. Posting from the combination journal is accomplished by placing a " _____ " and page number in the Posting Reference column of the general ledger account. _____

   (a) G   (c) J
   (b) DJ   (d) CJ

4. Using the modified cash basis, when a business provides services on account, _____ is debited. _____

   (a) no entry   (c) Cash
   (b) Accounts Receivable   (d) Owner's Equity

5. Using the modified cash basis, when wages are earned but not paid, _____ is debited. _____

   (a) Wages Expense   (c) Wages Payable
   (b) no entry   (d) Accrued Wages

The answers to the Self-Study Test Questions are at the end of the text.

CHAPTER 2

True/False

1. T
2. F (A/P is a liability)
3. T
4. T
5. F (other changes could occur: capital could increase, revenue could increase, etc.)
6. F (net income)   7. T

Multiple Choice

1. c   2. a   3. b   4. d   5. b

CHAPTER 3

True/False

1. T
2. F (liability accounts normally have credit balances)
3. T   4. F (credit balances)
5. T   6. F (increase)

Multiple Choice

1. c   2. c   3. b   4. d   5. a

CHAPTER 4

True/False

1. T   2. T   3. T
4. F (A, L, OE, R, E)   5. T

Multiple Choice

1. b   2. c   3. b   4. a   5. d

CHAPTER 5

True/False

1. F (match revenues and expenses)
2. F (to bring accounts up-to-date)
3. T
4. F (depreciable cost = cost − salvage value)
5. F (to match cost of asset against revenues it will help generate)

Multiple Choice

1. a   2. c   3. d   4. c   5. a

CHAPTER 6

True/False

1. T
2. F (additional investments are added to the beginning balance)
3. F   4. T   5. T

Multiple Choice

1. b   2. d   3. a   4. c   5. b

CHAPTER 7

True/False

1. F (primary purpose is to reconcile book balance with bank balance)
2. F (deducted from book balance)   3. T
4. F (deducted from book balance)
5. F (entries are not posted from petty cash record to general ledger)

Multiple Choice

1. b   2. a   3. c   4. b   5. d

CHAPTER 8

True/False

1. F (does *not* work under control and direction)
2. T   3. F (is called wages)
4. T   5. T

Multiple Choice

1. c   2. b   3. d   4. a   5. d

CHAPTER 9

True/False

1. F (these taxes are paid by the employer)
2. T   3. T
4. F (FUTA tax is levied on employers)
5. F (this form is W-2)

Multiple Choice

1. b   2. d   3. b   4. d   5. a

CHAPTER 10

True/False

1. T
2. F (large businesses use the accrual basis)
3. F (see Figure 7-2)   4. T   5. T

Multiple Choice

1. c   2. b   3. d   4. a   5. b

*Page references in bold indicate defined terms.

NOTES

NOTES

NOTES

NOTES

NOTES

THE ACCOUNTING EQUATION

Assets = Liabilities + Owner's Equity

FINANCIAL STATEMENTS

Income Statement	Revenues – Expenses = Net Income or Loss
Statement of Owner's Equity	Beginning Capital + Investments + Net Income – Withdrawals = Ending Capital
Balance Sheet	Assets = Liabilities + Owner's Equity

T ACCOUNT

Title

Debit = Left	Credit = Right

EXPANDED ACCOUNTING EQUATION SHOWING RULES OF DEBIT AND CREDIT

Assets

Dr.	Cr.
+	–

=

Liabilities

Dr.	Cr.
–	+

+

Owner's Equity

Dr.	Cr.
–	+

Drawing

Dr.	Cr.
+	–

Expenses

Dr.	Cr.
+	–

Revenue

Dr.	Cr.
–	+

STEPS IN MAJOR ACCOUNTING PROCESSES

Steps in Journalizing a Transaction
1. Enter the date.
2. Enter the account title and debit amount.
3. Enter the account title and credit amount.
4. Enter the explanation.

Steps in Posting from the Journal to the Ledger
In the ledger:
1. Enter the date in the Date column.
2. Enter the amount of each transaction in the Debit or Credit column and enter the new balance in the Balance column under Debit or Credit.
3. Enter the page number of the journal from which each transaction is posted in the Posting Reference column.

In the journal:
4. Enter the account number in the Posting Reference column in the journal.

Steps in Preparing the Work Sheet
1. Prepare the trial balance.
2. Prepare the adjustments.
3. Prepare the adjusted trial balance.
4. Extend adjusted balances to the Income Statement and Balance Sheet columns.
5. Complete the work sheet.

Steps in the Closing Process
1. Close revenue accounts to Income Summary.
2. Close expense accounts to Income Summary.
3. Close Income Summary to Capital.
4. Close the drawing account to the owner's capital account.

STEPS IN THE ACCOUNTING CYCLE

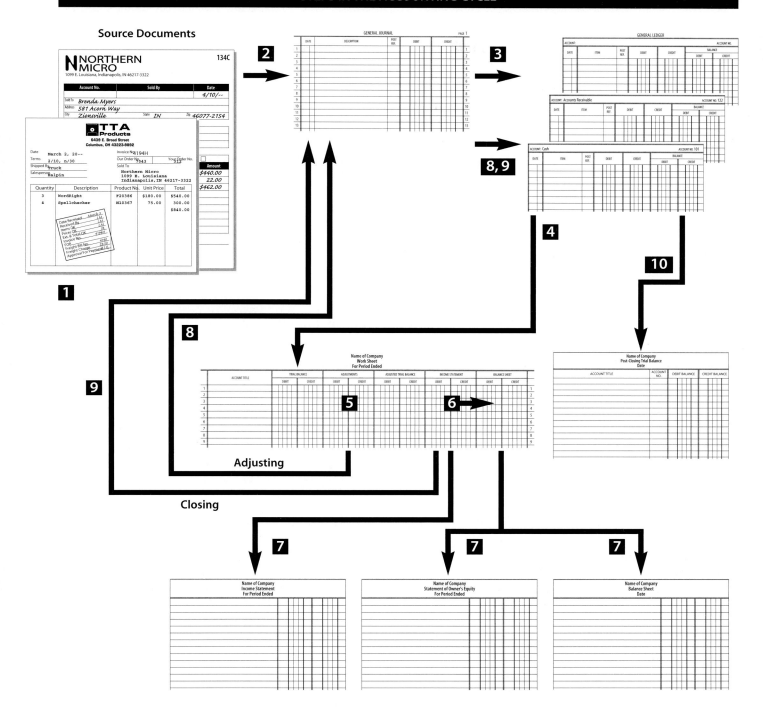

Steps in the Accounting Cycle

During Accounting Period:
1. Analyze source documents.
2. Journalize the transactions.
3. Post to the ledger accounts.

End of Accounting Period:
4. Prepare a trial balance.
5. Determine and prepare the needed adjustments on the work sheet.
6. Complete an end-of-period work sheet.
7. Prepare an income statement, statement of owner's equity, and balance sheet.
8. Journalize and post the adjusting entries.
9. Journalize and post the closing entries.
10. Prepare a post-closing trial balance.

Note: While for a specific company each account number used would have only one title, titles vary from company to company as needed.

Assets (100–199)

100s—Cash Related Accounts
- 101 Cash
- 105 Petty Cash

120s—Receivables
- 121 Notes Receivable
- 122 Accounts Receivable
- 122.1 Allowance for Bad Debts
- 123 Interest Receivable (Also Accrued Interest Receivable)
- 125 Common Stock Subscriptions Receivable
- 126 Preferred Stock Subscriptions Receivable

130s—Inventories
- 131 Merchandise Inventory
- 132 Raw Materials
- 133 Work in Process
- 134 Finished Goods

140s—Prepaid Items
- 141 Supplies (Specialty items like Medical, Bicycle, Tailoring, etc.)
- 142 Office Supplies
- 144 Food Supplies
- 145 Prepaid Insurance

150s—Long-Term Investments
- 153 Bond Sinking Fund

160s—Land
- 161 Land
- 162 Natural Resources
- 162.1 Accumulated Depletion

170s—Buildings
- 171 Buildings
- 171.1 Accumulated Depreciation—Buildings

180s—Equipment
- 181 Office Equipment (Also Store Equipment)
- 181.1 Accumulated Depreciation—Office Equipment (Also Store Equipment)
- 182 Office Furniture
- 182.1 Accumulated Depreciation—Office Furniture
- 183 Athletic Equipment (Also Tailoring, Lawn, Cleaning)
- 183.1 Accumulated Depreciation—Athletic Equipment (Also Tailoring, Lawn, Cleaning)
- 184 Tennis Facilities (Also Basketball Facilities)
- 184.1 Accumulated Depreciation—Tennis Facilities (Also Basketball Facilities)
- 185 Delivery Equipment (Also Medical, Van)
- 185.1 Accumulated Depreciation—Delivery Equipment (Also Medical, Van)
- 186 Exercise Equipment
- 186.1 Accumulated Depreciation—Exercise Equipment
- 187 Computer Equipment
- 187.1 Accumulated Depreciation—Computer Equipment

190s—Intangibles
- 191 Patents
- 192 Copyrights
- 193 Organization Costs

Liabilities (200–299)

200s—Short-Term Payables
- 201 Notes Payable
- 201.1 Discount on Notes Payable
- 202 Accounts Payable (Also Vouchers Payable)
- 203 United Way Contribution Payable
- 204 Income Tax Payable
- 205 Common Dividends Payable
- 206 Preferred Dividends Payable
- 207 Interest Payable (Also Bond Interest Payable)

210s—Employee Payroll Related Payables
- 211 Employee Income Tax Payable
- 212 Social Security Tax Payable
- 213 Medicare Tax Payable
- 215 City Earnings Tax Payable
- 216 Health Insurance Premiums Payable
- 217 Credit Union Payable
- 218 Savings Bond Deductions Payable
- 219 Wages Payable

220s—Employer Payroll Related Payables
- 221 FUTA Tax Payable
- 222 SUTA Tax Payable
- 223 Workers' Compensation Insurance Payable

230s—Sales Tax
- 231 Sales Tax Payable

240s—Deferred Revenues and Current Portion of Long-Term Debt
- 241 Unearned Subscription Revenue (Also Unearned Ticket Revenue, Unearned Repair Fees)
- 242 Current Portion of Mortgage Payable

250s—Long-Term Liabilities
- 251 Mortgage Payable
- 252 Bonds Payable
- 252.1 Discount on Bonds Payable
- 253 Premium on Bonds Payable

Owner's Equity (300–399)

311 Jessica Jane, Capital
312 Jessica Jane, Drawing
313 Income Summary
321 Common Stock
321.1 Common Treasury Stock
322 Paid in Capital in Excess of Par/Stated Value—Common Stock
323 Preferred Stock
323.1 Preferred Treasury Stock
323.2 Discount on Preferred Stock
324 Paid in Capital in Excess of Par/Stated Value—Preferred Stock
327 Common Stock Subscribed
328 Preferred Stock Subscribed
329 Paid in Capital from Sale of Treasury Stock
331 Retained Earnings
332 Retained Earnings Appropriated for…
333 Cash Dividends
334 Stock Dividends

Revenues (400–499)

400s—Operating Revenues

401 Delivery Fees
401 Appraisal Fees
401 Medical Fees
401 Service Fees
401 Repair Fees
401 Sales
401.1 Sales Returns and Allowances
401.2 Sales Discounts
402 Boarding and Grooming Revenue
403 Subscriptions Revenue (if main line of business)

410s—Other Revenues

411 Interest Revenue
412 Rent Revenue
413 Subscriptions Revenue (if not main line of business)
414 Sinking Fund Earnings
415 Uncollectible Accounts Recovered
416 Gain on Sale/Exchange of Equipment
417 Gain on Bonds Redeemed

Operating Expenses (500–599)

500s—Cost of Goods Sold

501 Purchases
501.1 Purchases Returns and Allowances
501.2 Purchases Discounts
502 Freight-In
504 Overhead
505 Cost of Goods Sold

510s—Selling Expenses

511 Wages Expense (Also Wages and Salaries Expense)
512 Advertising Expense
513 Bank Credit Card Expense
514 Store Supplies Expense
515 Travel and Entertainment Expense
516 Cash Short and Over
519 Depreciation Expense—Store Equipment and Fixtures

520s–40s—General and Administrative Expenses

521 Rent Expense
522 Office Salaries Expense
523 Office Supplies Expense (Also Medical)
524 Other Supplies: Food Supplies Expense (Also Medical)
525 Telephone Expense
526 Transportation/Automobile Expense (Also Laboratory, Travel)
527 Collection Expense
528 Inventory Short and Over
529 Loss on Write Down of Inventory
530 Payroll Taxes Expense
531 Workers' Compensation Insurance Expense
532 Bad Debt Expense
533 Electricity Expense, Utilities Expense
534 Charitable Contributions Expense
535 Insurance Expense
536 Postage Expense
537 Repair Expense
538 Oil and Gas Expense (Also Automobile Expense)
540 Depreciation Expense—Building
541 Depreciation Expense—Equipment (Also Tennis Facilities, Delivery Equipment, Office Equipment, Furniture)
542 Depreciation Expense—Other Equipment (Medical Equipment, Exercise Equipment, Computer Equipment)
543 Depletion Expense
544 Patent Amortization
545 Amortization of Organization Costs
549 Miscellaneous Expense

550s—Other Expenses

551 Interest Expense (Also Bond Interest Expense)
552 Loss on Discarded Equipment
553 Loss on Sale/Exchange of Equipment
554 Loss on Bonds Redeemed
555 Income Tax Expense